MW01411831

*WON BY THE DIVINE EAGLE:*
*MYSTICAL UNION IN*
*HOMILIES, RETREATS, AIDS, & COUNSELS*

CHARLES ANANG

Cover art: *Nozze mistiche di Santa Caterina*
*(The Mystical Marriage of St. Catherine)*
Alessandro Franchi-Gaetano Marinelli, 1896
Home of Benincasa Family in Siena
@ Siena
Cover design by Mary Ellen Douglas

Copyright © 2022 Charles Anang
All rights reserved.
ISBN: 9798762251143
Printed in Canada

To the Holy Angels

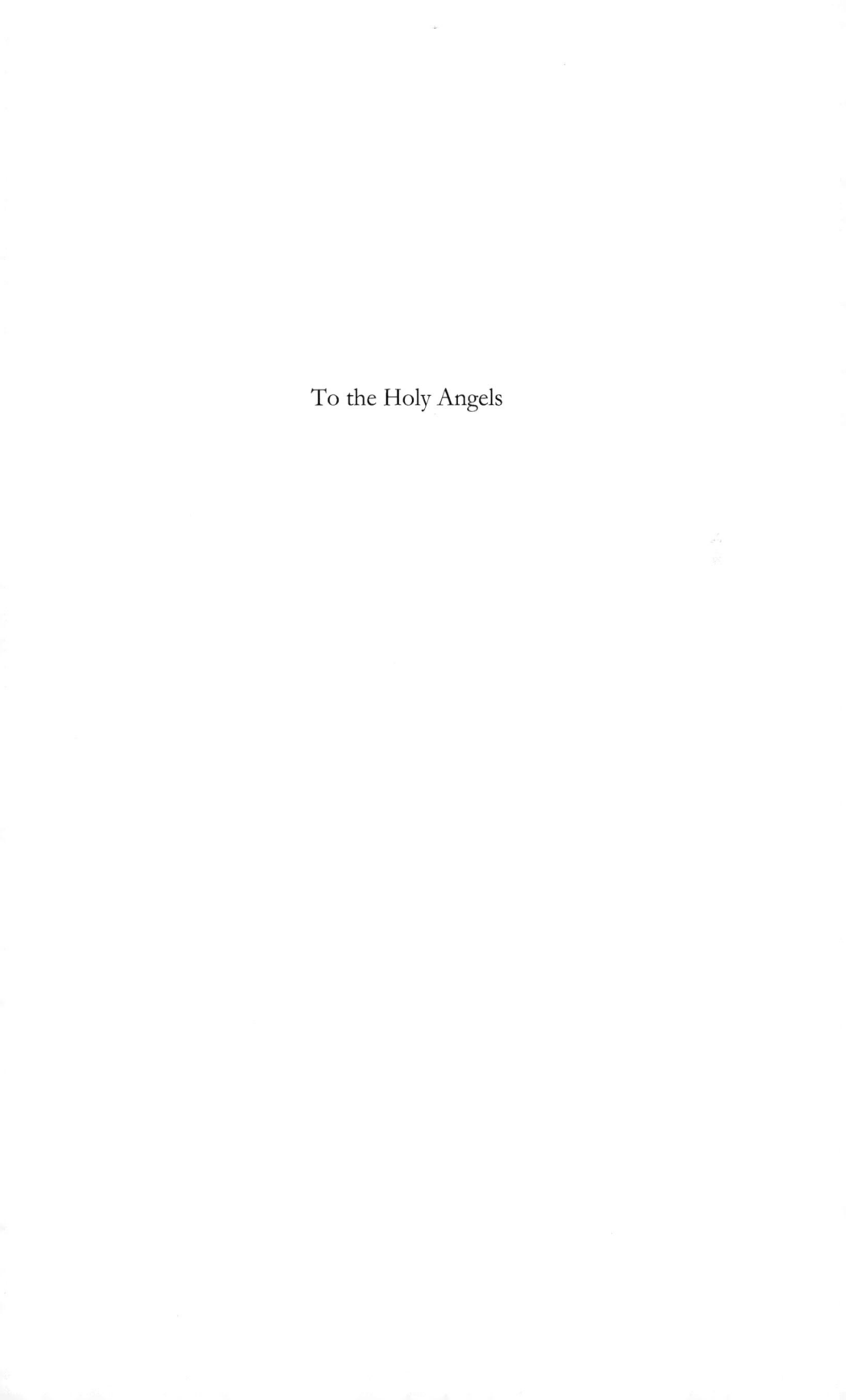

*Nihil Obstat*          Rev. Charles Nahm

                     *Censor Deputatus*

                     24 March 2022

*Imprimatur*          Thomas Cardinal Collins

                     Archbishop of Toronto

                     24 March 2022

# CONTENTS

| | | |
|---|---|---|
| | Preface & Acknowledgments | vii |
| | Detailed Outline | ix |

### I. HOMILIES: APEX ((MYSTICAL UNION)

| | | |
|---|---|---|
| 1 | Filiation: Summit is the Cross, but Heart is Divine Filiation | 1 |
| 2 | Three Levels of Discipleship: Servant, Friend, Spouse | 4 |
| 3 | Wedding Homily: Human Love is Prelude to Divine Marriage | 8 |
| 4 | Wedding Banquet: Openness of Heart for Divine Love | 11 |
| 5 | The Call of Matthew is our Call: "Come, Follow Me" | 15 |
| 6 | Palm Sunday: Jesus' Spousal Vow at Calvary (von Balthasar) | 18 |
| 7 | Exaltation of the Cross: Preaching Christ Crucified | 21 |
| 8 | Beatitudes: Portrait of Christ and Summit of Christian Life | 24 |
| 9 | Expropriation: Total Gift of Self | 29 |
| 10 | Feast of John Paul II: His Secret was the Marian Principle | 37 |
| 11 | Mediation: Being Formed in the Father's Womb by Mentors | 42 |
| 12 | Father's Love: Obtaining all as the Father's Child | 47 |

### II. RETREATS: STRUCTURE (ASCENT)

| | | |
|---|---|---|
| 1 | Retreat 1: Towards Mystical Incarnation and Marriage (5 Conf.) | 53 |
| 2 | Retreat 2: Mystical Incarnation as Lived by St. Joseph (4 Themes) | 111 |
| 3 | Retreat 3: Ecclesial Preparations for Mystical Transformation (6 Conf.) | 122 |

| | | |
|---|---|---|
| 1 | **III. AIDS: BUILDING BLOCKS** | |
| 2 | Eucharist: Calvary as Heart of Liturgy and Christian Life | 195 |
| 3 | Confession: Fruitfulness of Frequent Confession | 202 |
| 4 | Sacrament of the Sick: Mirroring Christ's Extensive Healing | 211 |
| 5 | Ascetical Mansions: Foundation Stones for Holiness | 212 |
| 6 | Ascetical Mansions: Begging Divine Mercy for the World (Faustina) | 222 |
| 7 | Ascetical Mansions: Method of Mental Prayer (St. A. de Liguori) | 223 |
| 8 | Mystical Mansions: Abandonment Synthesized (J.-P. de Caussade) | 231 |
| 9 | Mystical Mansions: Texts by Saints & Model of Bl. D. Bélanger | 238 |
| 10 | Spiritual Warfare: Discernment of Three Spirits | 247 |
| 11 | Spiritual Warfare: Jesus' 25 Rules to St. Faustina | 253 |
| 12 | Spiritual Warfare: An Exorcist's Counsels for Everyday Life | 258 |
| | Spirit's Gift: Lay Charisms as a New Springtime in the Church | 266 |

<u>2 Aids for Renewals</u>

| | | |
|---|---|---|
| 1 | Life of Grace: Infused Virtues & Gifts with Actual Grace | 269 |
| 2 | Priesthood Renewal: Jesus' Appeal in *In Sinu Jesu* | 281 |

## IV. COUNSELS: TOOLS

1    Counsel 1. Intellectual: Satisfied with Rote-Formula Learning    297
2    Counsel 2. Human Growth: Woman with Human Weakness    303
3    Counsel 3. Present: Seminarian Anxiously Anticipating the Future    305
4    Counsel 4. Spiritual Direction: Key Elements (R. Garrigou-Lagrange)    309
5    Counsel 5. Spiritual Direction & Confession: Digressions    314
6    Counsel 6. Conscience: "Whether Sin is an Infinite Offense?"    324
7    Counsel 7. Unity: Disquiet about the Holy Father    328
8    Counsel 8. Occult: Couple whose Son is Reading Occult Works    331
9    Counsel 9. Divine Joy: Jesus' Three Dispositions during Trials    335
10    Counsel 10. Sacrifice: Offering Christ with His Mysteries    337
11    Counsel 11. Chastity: Seminarian's Desire to Protect Celibate Vows    339
12    Counsel 12: Struggles: Overcoming all through Jesus in our Midst    344

**CONCLUSION**    345

*Preface & Acknowledgements*

The lay Catholic who encouraged me to self-publish (first four books) also recommended that I collect my homilies, retreat conferences, and counsels (responses to spiritual or pastoral questions) for a fifth book. Believing that there was not substantial material for this, I had not seriously considered this project. But in September 2021 a strong interior impulse moved me to do so, upon which I immediately acted.

But desiring to ascertain, as with the earlier works, that this was the will of God, I sought the confirmation by, and blessing of, a superior, who told me that finding the unifying idea would be my validation. In the fourth book, *Mystical Incarnation*, the unifying idea was primarily becoming Christ, and secondarily mystical marriage. This fifth book, *Won by the Divine Eagle*, dwells primarily on mystical marriage, and secondarily on mystical incarnation. Thus both books treat the two heights of mystical incarnation and marriage but with different primary emphases (linked by a *perichoresis* or mutual interpenetration). Thus, we must understand that "mystical union" with Christ has two dimensions, becoming both His Body (mystical incarnation) and His Bride, understanding that we become His Body by the spousal marriage of becoming His Bride, "two become one flesh." The spousal element creates the union, to become "Christ Himself."

Second, while this book has new material, it also largely applies what was presented in the first four books to Christian life. Thus, this book can be compared to the *Youcat* (youth catechism), an aid to better understand the *Catechism of the Catholic Church*; or to God giving four different Gospels: three concrete Synoptic with one mystical Johannine. The rationale for this practical synthesis is that lay people have shared how the "hands-on" insights relating to their everyday life were the most helpful. One deacon reading my fourth book noted that the practical, concrete portions were helpful to him. Since *much of this book liberally drew from the four books* as a practical synthesis for everyday living but directed towards mystical union, its subtitle could well be: *Four Books Applied to Christian Life in Brief*. One young priest noted the use of real examples as helpful as was reading the spiritual direction correspondence by Columba Marmion. These illustrations of struggles, as in Jesus' life and saints' lives, greatly aid us.

This book's style or format of multiple entries comprise: (i) a collection of homilies (like those published by H. U. von Balthasar and J. Ratzinger); (ii) three sets of retreat talks; (iii) a compilation of aids that are like building blocks for the spiritual life; and (iv) an assortment of counsels, responses to questions (that reflect Dom Marmion's multiple spiritual direction letters).

A third quality of this book is that it is set within the economy of: (i) the sacraments (e.g., Mass, Confession, Baptism, Marriage); and (ii) against the horizon of grace, such as the indwelling of the Trinity (uncreated grace) and incorporation to Christ, through sanctifying grace (created grace), from which arise the cortege of infused virtues and gifts and actual grace.

To find a way to unify the book's four parts, we might consider the analogy to a house:
>   Homilies: Apex (Mystical Union)
>   Retreats: Structure (Ascent)
>   Aids: Building Blocks
>   Counsels: Tools

In this building analogy, the Homilies constitute the apex that directly treats of our destiny of mystical union; the Retreat Talks outline the overall structure of this edifice; the Aids are like building blocks for this edifice; and the Counsels are like tools. The Aids and Counsels are more practical.

*Sources*

While this book draws from the author's earlier works, it is primarily a personal collection of homilies, retreats, aids, and counsels given. There are external sources incorporated that are deemed helpful: A. Miklósházy, H. U. von Balthasar, J. Ratzinger, R. Garrigou-Lagrange, J. Escrivá, J. Coverdale, C. Lubich, L. Giussani, J. Carrón, A. Liguori, G. Chevrot, C. Journet, J. Philippe, Conchita, R. Cantalamessa, F. Fernandez, S. Rossetti, *In Sinu Jesu*, *Living with Christ*, among others. Scripture texts are taken from the RSV Bible translation and Office of Reading quotes mainly from universalis.com.

*Acknowledgments*

I thank Linda Beairsto for her encouragement to write this book. I am indebted to my directors and friends, especially T. De Manche and Fr. J. Fleming, and E. Lopez, who have followed this manuscript with their prayers and support. I draw attention to three groups. First, I am grateful to the archdiocese of Toronto for its imprimatur (Cardinal Collins and Fr. Ed Curtis) and to its theological censor, Fr. Charles Nahm, for his kind work. Second, we wish to thank those who have given permission to reprint material or to share their experiences. I wish to thank Katheryn Trainor for her competent work of editing this manuscript and Mary Ellen Douglas for the beautiful cover design. I had doubts about the value of this work and acted only because I felt it was the will and work of the Spirit, attempted "because of the confidence I have in the Lord, confidence that he will help me to say something, on account of the *great need* of many people…"[1]

---

[1] St. John of the Cross, Prologue to *The Ascent of Mount Carmel* 3, quoted in Iain Matthew, *The Impact of God: Soundings from St. John of the Cross* (London: Hodder and Staughton, 1995).

*Outline*

**De Caussade's Surrender Lived out in St. Thérèse's Oblation of Love**

This book's main title, *Won by the Divine Eagle*, was first inspired by Jean-Pierre de Caussade's *Abandonment to Divine Providence*: "Let us soar like an eagle above these clouds, with our eyes fixed on the sun and its rays, which are our duties." But the actual title is drawn from St. Thérèse, who uses this same language of "sun" and "eagle" of de Caussade. We will frequently look to Thérèse, partly because she represents a universal path.

> I look upon myself as a weak little bird, with only a light down covering. I am not an eagle, but I have an eagle's eyes and heart. In spite of my extreme littleness I still dare to gaze upon the Divine Sun, the Sun of Love, and my heart feels within it all the aspirations of an Eagle. (*Story of a Soul*, Manuscript B, 198)

Many strive for holiness through various acts of prayer, mortification, and sacrifice, but do not realize that the Upper Mansions require only one thing: abandonment to God in love. Holiness is thus a pure heart, that lives total surrender to God by fixing our eyes on Him, allowing Him sovereignty. It is to be captured like St. Thérèse by the divine Eagle, by divine Love:

> All this implies that Thérèse identifies her personal love with the love which burns in the heart of the Church and, ultimately, with the Love who is *God Himself*, the living, transforming fire of eternity. There is only one thing for Thérèse to do; to offer herself as a holocaust to this Love, to let herself be won and carried off by the "eternal Eagle," to fly "on the wings of the divine Eagle to the *eternal furnace* in the bosom of the blessed Trinity".... Every instant of life becomes weighted with eternity.... The soul is able to love and save other souls by bringing the eternal love within it to fruition.... Finally, life, the fruitful dream, is united and made eternal by awaiting the "return of the bridegroom"... on that tomorrow, "the day of eternal nuptials"... and even more by the passionate desire to see at last, unveiled forever, that hidden countenance, that Holy Face which is always hidden here below. (Jean Mouroux on St. Thérèse)[2]

"There is only one thing for Thérèse to do; to offer herself as a holocaust to this Love, to let herself be won and carried off by the 'eternal Eagle,' to fly 'on the wings of the divine Eagle to the eternal furnace in the bosom of the blessed Trinity.'" Possessed by divine Love, St. Thérèse is now "able to love and save other souls by bringing the eternal love within it to fruition," to bring eternity into time for the salvation of the world.

---

[2] Jean Mouroux, "Eternity and the Triune God," *Communio* 18:1 (Spring 1991): 132.

Where *Mystical Incarnation* develops primarily mystical incarnation, this fifth volume develops primarily spousal love with Christ, the divine Eagle, but practically through a collection of homilies, retreat conferences, aids, and counsels. The two dimensions represent Paul's images of the Church as His Body and Bride. This distinction from, and complementarity with, the *Mystical Incarnation* volume only followed after the collection of this material. That is, the inspiration to collect the material came first; the overall unifying theme was discerned after. A background on grace and the all-important sacraments has also been incorporated.

This manuscript ends up following the path of de Caussade's *Abandonment*, living divine love in the sacrament of the present moment, especially in its two influences: (i) the pure love in God's will of St. Francis de Sales; and (ii) the spousal love of St. John of the Cross lived out in his greatest disciple, St. Thérèse, for the salvation of all souls. Ultimately, this book is about Christ. We seek to summarize the theology of the spousal relationship to Christ through the Spirit, the Personal Love within the Trinity.

## Spousal Dimension of Grace through the Holy Spirit

> **1. Personal Union with the Holy Spirit**: According to Peter Lombard and others (e.g., Matthias Scheeben), there is a personal union between the Holy Spirit and the individual soul. In other words, the **Holy Spirit dwells** in men and in the Church not just through His effects but really and personally. It is the "Spirit which God implanted in man" (Jas 4:5).
>
> **2. Bride of God: The indwelling Spirit is the Ground for a Bridal Relationship** that we have with the Lord. This has been already present in the Old Testament covenant-theology: Israel is *Yahweh's bride:* "…your husband is your maker… God has called you a bride still young… with tender affection I bring you home again… my love shall be immovable and never fail…" (Isa 54:4-10; 50; Hos 1-3; Jer 2:2; 3; Ezek 16; Canticle of Canticles). Yahweh enters into a **marriage-covenant** with Israel: (Ex 24:8; Hos 24:25). This is the New Covenant (Jer 31:31; 32:37; Ez 16:60ff.; 34:25-31; 37:25-28; cf. Mk 14:14; Mt 26:28; Lk 22:20; 1 Cor 11:25).
>
> **3. In the New Testament, Jesus is the Bridegroom** (Mt 9:15; Jn 3:29; cf. also the *parables of wedding*: Mt 22:2; Lk 14:16; Mt 25:1). For Paul, this is *the great mystery of marriage between Christ and His Church* (Eph 5:25-27). *The Apocalypse celebrates the wedding-feast of the Lamb*, while the New Jerusalem comes down out of heaven like a *bride* adorned for her husband (Apoc 19:7f.; 21:2).[3]

---

[3] Attila Mikloshazy, "Justification and Sanctification," Grace and Glory: SAT 2431HS (Lecture, Toronto School of Theology at the University of Toronto, 1978).

## Christological Dimensions of Grace

When we are spousally united to Christ, then occurs the mystical Incarnation or substitution of Christ. The following gives something of the intimacy with Christ. It comprises incorporation in and imitation of Christ, becoming "sons in the one Son."

**1. Putting on Christ** (*endusasthe*): "You have all put on Christ as a garment" (Gal 3:27). "Let Christ Jesus Himself be the armour that you wear" (Rom 12:14). "Put on the new nature of God's creation" (Eph 4:24; Col 3:10). Clothing means similarity of form which expresses the essence: "They should be conformed (σύμμορφος) to the likeness of His Son" (Rom 8:29; Gal 4:19). Clothing also means similarity in power, effected by the Holy Spirit. Paul simply states this as a fact: you have put on Christ, which however is also an imperative, imposing an obligation to "put on Christ!" (Rom 6:2-12). Grace is both "Gabe und Aufgabe," gift and task.

**2. Imitation of Christ** (Cross): Grace is a call, a challenge to follow Christ by imitating Him in *carrying the cross*. "No man is worthy of me who does not take up his cross and walk in my footsteps" (Mt 10:38; Lk 14:27). "If anyone wishes to be a follower of mine, he must leave self behind; day after day he must take up his cross, and come with me" (Lk 9:23; Mt 16:24; Mk 8:34). This is not just a pious thought, but a Christian obligation: "God forbid that I should boast of anything but the cross of our Lord Jesus Christ, through which the world is crucified to me and I to the world!... I bear the marks of Jesus branded on my body" (Gal 6:14-17; 5:24).

**3. Incorporation in Christ**: The Christian is a person who is "in Jesus Christ." The expression *"living in Christ"* occurs in Paul about 126 times, often with the "syn" preposition. This union is indicated in the image of the vine and branches: "He who dwells in me, as I dwell in Him, bears much fruit" (Jn 15:1-8; 17:23-26). "The life I now live is not my life, but the life which Christ lives in me... who loved me and gave Himself up for me" (Gal 2:20).

**4. *Filii in Filio*** ("children in the one Son"): Christ is the only Son, the firstborn of many brothers and sisters (Jn 1:14; 3:16; Rom 8:29). Living in Christ therefore means being *"children of the heavenly Father."* Christ sent us the Holy Spirit, in Him we have the Spirit and can call God "our Father," *Abba* (Rom 8:15; Gal 4:6; cf. also the Lord's Prayer and the Beatitudes). We are called to be perfect as our heavenly Father is perfect, especially challenging us to love our enemies as well. This is possible only while being in life-communion with Christ.

## Participation in the Trinitarian Life of God

This leads to participation in the Trinitarian life of God, with profound dimensions: divine filiation to the Father, participation in the Trinitarian communion, divinization, friendship with God, and actually participating in the attributes of God (e.g., loving with God's love).

> **1. Relationship with the Father**: The relationship with Christ (and the Spirit) always leads us to the Father. "I will acknowledge you before my Father…" (Mt 10:32). "Seeing me, you see Him who sent me" (Jn 12:44). "The word you hear… is the word of the Father who sent me" (Jn 14:24). "The Father loves you Himself, because you have loved me…" (Jn 16:27). "I am in the Father and You are in me…" (Jn 17:22). Finally: "Anyone who loves me will heed what I say; then my Father will love him, and we will come to Him and make our dwelling with Him…" (Jn 14:23).
>
> **2. Communion with the Divine Nature**: "We come to share in the very being of God" (*theias koinónoi physeós*) (2 Pet 1:4). Grace not only relates us to each of the three Divine Persons, but brings us in communion with the Trinitarian divine life; we participate in the communicable properties of God.
>
> **3. Divinization**: The idea is based on Christ's words: "My Father and I are one" (Jn 10:30), and "Is it not written in your own Law, 'I said: you are gods?'" (cf. Ps 82:6). "Those are called gods to whom the word of God was delivered - and Scripture cannot be set aside" (Jn 10:34f.). On this basis Origen claimed that "God became man so that man may become god." Clement of Alexandria speaks about "becoming like God"(*homoiósis tó theó*), "assuming the form of God" (*theoeidés*), or "divinization" (*theiósis*). Gregory Nazianzen speaks similarly. The Oriental Church considers grace simply as divinization.
>
> **4. Friendship with God**: Friendship means common spiritual values, goods, ideals; it creates trust, faith, reliance. Jesus calls: "You are my friends…" (Jn 15:14). And Paul says: "You are no longer aliens in a foreign land, but fellow-citizens with God's people, members of God's household" (Eph 2:19).
>
> **5. Participation in God's Attributes** (*energeias*): According to the Palamites, grace is participation in God's uncreated, communicable attributes: goodness, mercy, wisdom, fidelity, etc. "Yes, I am coming soon, and bringing my recompense with me…" (Apoc 22:12). Or as Paul expresses it: "The grace of our Lord Jesus Christ, the love of God, and the fellowship of the Holy Spirit be with you all!" (2 Cor 13:13).[4]

---

[4] Ibid.

*Synthesized in Von Balthasar's Marian Principle within a Theodrama of Love*
All this can be synthesized in Hans Urs von Balthasar's Marian Principle (elaborated on by Brendan Leahy and was summarized in *Mystical Incarnation*, Ch. 10). It is captured in the mystical experience he had in a thirty-day retreat at the age of 18: "'You do not have to choose anything, you have been called! You will not serve, you will be taken into service. You do not have to make plans of any sort, you are only a pebble in a mosaic prepared long before.' All that I had to do was simply to leave everything behind and follow, without making any plans, without desires or particular intuitions. I had only to remain there to see how I could be useful." This reflects the Son's disposition of His "yes" to the Father.

In contradistinction to the Petrine Principle (hierarchy, institution) that represents God the Father, the Marian Principle (baptismal holiness) reflects the Son before the Father. Mary as the archetypal Church; hers is the charism of charisms, spirituality of all spiritualities, found in the saints and new ecclesial charisms that God sends ("regenerative energies of the Church," "bombs of the presence of the Spirit").

The Trinity forms the background to the Marian Principle. Mary lives the Trinitarian communion: as the perfect daughter of the Father, perfect mother to Christ, and perfect spouse of the Spirit. She is the "helper" (new Eve) of the new Adam (Christ) who mirrors the Son's relationship to the Father. She is thus the vessel of holiness who receives the all-holy One, the *summum* of love, to be poured out into the darkness of creation; and the spouse who gives the "yes" of humanity (makes a covenant in the name of humanity). She is the model of the Theodrama of love between God and man: her spousal relationship is the "highest parable" for expressing God's encounter with humanity; the woman is a symbol of allowing oneself to be taken up by God, with a participation in Christ's death and Resurrection (to be shattered in order to be healed); the Church becomes Christ's Body-Bride. Each becoming Christ, mission (redemption of the world) is key in von Balthasar's thought: the shape of the Church is persons in a Christ-like and Marian self-surrender, living Christ as Mary did.

Part I comprises homilies that point to possession by divine love, e.g., Three 3 Levels of Discipleship: Servant, Friend, Spouse; Human Love Leads to Divine Marriage; Filiation is the Heart, Cross is the Summit.

Part II, comprising retreat talks that outline: (1) the structure of the overall edifice (leading to mystical incarnation and marriage); (2) the mystical incarnation lived out by St. Joseph; ecclesial preparations for evangelization of the world (e.g., Spirit's renewed Pentecost, rising above today's culture of the human, our identity as God's children).

Part III comprises aids to, or pillars for, this path to divine love. They are drawn from external sources as well as the author's own material. Three resources for Church renewal have been added: life of grace, theology, and priesthood.

Part IV comprises counsels that aid in this path to divine love from the author's responses to queries (e.g., trap of rote-formula, children delving into the occult, difficulty with the pope).

*Note on Selection of Material and Decision to Include some External Sources*
A note of clarification should be added here, as the reader will encounter some external material among "Aids" and "Counsels." A decision was made to include a few key texts from external sources that we believe can be very fruitful for Christians to read, some especially for our time. They include the 25 rules of Jesus to St. Faustina on spiritual warfare; an exorcist's helpful teaching on everyday deliverance and healing; an online summary of the mystical insights of Blessed Dina Bélanger; and the author's short summary of Reginald Garrigou-Lagrange's discernment of the three spirits. It was felt that these additions can contribute in key ways to our spiritual growth and education.

In addition, we have selected material for three areas of renewal: the priesthood and the life of grace. While most of the book's material is addressed to all Christians, including priests and religious, we felt that the addition of a work based on private revelation, *In Sinu Jesu*, which the visionary presents as interlocutions from Jesus. The text chosen reflect significant and specific calls for reform, a program for renewal in the priesthood. Added was a summary of Reginald Garrigou-Lagrange's teaching on grace, which powers our spiritual growth. We had hoped to include Marc Cardinal Ouellet's Conference on John Henry Newman's call for reform in theology (for which he had kindly granted permission), but the anticipated book length had already been already exceeded.

Please note that this book's materials have been collected from various homilies, talks, aids, and counsels given *over years*, and the reader consequently will likely encounter some *duplication* within the book, not to mention reiteration of themes given in earlier books, though in a more concrete or pastoral form. To assist readers, here are the four titles: *New Christ: Divine Filiation*; *New Christ: Priestly Configuration*; *Mystical Incarnation: You are my Son, the Beloved*; and *New Evangelization: Starting Anew from Christ*.

# PART I

# HOMILIES: APEX (MYSTICAL UNION)

I am a lowly creature but I am still his [God's] servant, and I hope that he will choose to wake me from slumber. I hope that he will **set me on fire with the flame of his divine love, the flame that burns above the stars**, so that I am filled with desire for his love and his fire burns always within me!...

Beloved Saviour, show yourself to us who beg a glimpse of you. Let us know you, let us love you, let us love only you, let us desire you alone, let us spend our days and nights meditating on you alone, let us always be thinking of you. Fill us with love of you, let us love you with all the love that is your right as our God. Let that love fill us and possess us, let it overwhelm our senses until we can love nothing but you, for you are eternal. Give us that love that all the waters of the sea, the earth, the sky cannot extinguish: as it is written, *love that no flood can quench, no torrents drown*. What is said in the Song of Songs can become true in us (at least in part) if you, our Lord Jesus Christ, give us that grace. To you be glory for ever and ever. Amen.[5] (St. Columban, Abbot)

---

[5] *Instructions from St. Columban*, Abbot, OOR, Tuesday 28th Week of Ordinary Time, https://universalis.com/readings.htm.

## I. HOMILIES: APEX (MYSTICAL UNION)

1. Filiation: Summit is the Cross, but Heart is Divine Filiation
2. Three Levels of Discipleship: Servant, Friend, Spouse
3. Wedding Homily: Human Love is Prelude to Divine Marriage
4. Wedding Banquet: Openness of Heart for Divine Love
5. The Call of Matthew is our Call: "Come, Follow Me"
6. Palm Sunday: Jesus' Spousal Vow at Calvary (von Balthasar)
7. Exaltation of the Cross: Preaching Christ Crucified
8. Beatitudes: Portrait of Christ and Summit of Christian Life
9. Expropriation: Total Gift of Self
10. Feast of John Paul II: His Secret was the Marian Principle
11. Mediation: Being Formed in the Father's Womb by Mentors
12. Father's Love: Obtaining all as the Father's Child

These homilies in large part focus ultimately on spiritual marriage to, or transforming union with, God. Since this is the ultimate goal in the plan of predestination in Christ willed by the Father, all aspects of our daily Christian life should aim at it. Whether it describes three levels of discipleship of Christ or human love, they all lead to the spiritual marriage with and mystical incarnation of Christ, implicitly or explicitly. For this publication, to some of the homilies have been added background material. Since these homilies were composed over the years, there is, as to be expected, some repetition.

# HOMILY 1

**Filiation: Summit is the Cross, but Heart is Divine Filiation**
(Friday 25th Week of Ordinary Time, Year II, Sept. 24, 2021)

**Background: Heart of Holiness is Filiation**

Bishop Fulton Sheen offered a remarkable insight into today's Gospel in which Jesus asked, "Who do people say that I am?" He explained that Peter's response, "You are the Christ, the Son of the Living God," is only the first half of who Christ is; the second half was completed by Jesus in His next words that He would be crucified and put to death. While meditating on this Gospel, one naturally assumes that Sheen's insight into Christ's cross is the summit of who Jesus is, since the Paschal mystery is indeed the summit of His life, as it is the apex of the liturgical year and of the portrait of Christ in the Beatitudes, "Blessed are those who are persecuted…" This apex, we note, applies also to the ministerial priest, with Sheen repeating tradition that the priest is both "priest and victim."

But in meditating further on this Gospel text, a deeper insight came that, while the summit of Christ's life is the cross, the heart of Christ is in the first half of the definition in Peter's words: that He is the Son of the Father. This is confirmed by the Father's own words, twice revealing from heaven, at the river Jordan and on the Mount of Transfiguration, "You are my Son, the Beloved." To illustrate and deepen this distinction between the cross and Christ's sonship, let us look to St. Thérèse, since her spirituality is one of spiritual childhood (linking it with Christ's sonship) and since Pope Pius X called her "the greatest saint of modern times." There are three elements to this link of St. Thérèse to Christ: littleness, filiation, and the cross.

**1. The Greatest is the Child**

First, Jesus Himself revealed to the apostles that the greatest on earth is the child. For Jesus Himself was not just the Father's Son, He was His "little" Son. Jesus allowed the Father to have sovereignty over His entire life and to lead Him by the hand each day (von Balthasar).

After her sister, Sr. Marie of the Sacred Heart, found out that Thérèse was having desires for martyrdom and said to her, "Do you think that I can one day love Jesus as much as you do?", Thérèse immediately discounted these desires as peripheral and explained that spiritual life is not about asceticism and climbing higher (adult), but about descending to be a child in the Father's arms. She explained that her secret was that she never grew up but remained little, which obliged the Heavenly Father to do everything for His little child. This meant that all her virtues and talents belonged to God and she borrowed them as she needed them. More deeply, she acknowledged that, when she dies, being a child who is incapable of doing anything for God, she would have nothing to offer Him, and would rely solely on the mercy of the Father. To live this concretely, she counselled her sister, "Stay away from everything that shines." In our fallen human state, we are more likely to be tempted to make a big fuss about our gifts and personality and to rely on ourselves, and not rely on God like a needy child. We find this predilection commonplace in the Church.

## 2. The Father's True Child Seeks only His Will

Second, the little child seeks only to please the Father. Jesus did not seek to do charitable works or ministry; He sought only to please the Father. For Jesus, everything was the Father's will: at the age of 12, "Mother, do you not know that I must be about my Father's work"; during His ministry, "My food is to do my Father's will"; in Gethsemane, "Let not my will but yours be done."

St. Thérèse, like her spiritual mother, St. Teresa of Jesus, once she knew the Holy Spirit wanted something, rushed to do it. Like Jesus, she quickly acted on any inspiration of the Holy Spirit. Inspired by the Spirit, she made an Oblation of Love, and, after receiving permission from her superior, she offered her life to God that she perceived, when she saw blood issuing from her mouth (from lungs), was accepted by Jesus. While she understood that it was "a great grace to die in the springtime of her life," she sought neither a short life nor a long time. For her, the key is neither desires for martyrdom nor offering her life, but being docile in the Father's hands. To illustrate this point further, we look to her spiritual Carmelite sister, St. Elizabeth of the Trinity, who shared with her director that she had desires to suffer. He counselled her to not limit herself to that, but to allow God to do whatever He wanted in her. This would converge with Mother Teresa's "Give God permission." This is the highest spirituality.

To explain this further, let us employ a philosophical distinction. The "formal aspects" of things are the source or form, the "material aspects" are the specifications or expressions of that form. Clearly, the form is the foundation of the "matter," like the soul of the body. The form of faith is surrender to Christ, the matter are the doctrines and precepts of the Church's teaching. Martha was focused on the matter, "you worry about so many things, only one thing is necessary." All she had to do was to choose the form, which is sitting at Christ's feet, and allow that to determine what the matter of discipleship from the priority given to Jesus entails. Cardinal van Thuan, a supremely talented and dynamic archbishop, was chafing in prison because he wanted to shepherd his flock in Saigon following the Viet Cong invasion, and Jesus took him to task: "Do you want God or the works of God?" What mattered was not his shepherding his flock, nor even being in prison or in exile, but whatever was God's will (the form). All of these "material" or specific details are secondary; it is God and God's will that mattered, and this was the only rule by which Jesus lived as the Father's Son. We feel good about ourselves when we are able to do missionary work, help the poor, visit inmates in prisons, and protect the unborn. But all this is secondary; only and first God's will!

## 3. Yet Filiation to the Father Leads to Ascending the Cross with Jesus

Third, all along, we have been arguing that the heart of Jesus was not the cross but His abandonment as a little Son in His sonship. The paradox is that the very one who lives filial surrender is the one that God stretches on the cross the most. We find confirmation of this in St. Jane Frances de Chantal's teaching of a new martyrdom, the martyrdom of love. She explained to her Sisters that this martyrdom of love was at least as great as martyrdom by blood, but that it is granted only to "great-souled" people who hold nothing back. God would sever these noble people from all that is dear to them, receiving the greatest crosses. So the sonship or filiation is linked to the cross, as St. Escrivá discovered after his mystical experience of filiation: that to be a son of God (from Baptism) is to, like Christ, go on the cross with Him. But again, the key is not the cross; the key is sonship (filiation), the greatest gift the Son obtained for us on Calvary, a share of His own Sonship of the Father, to be His beloved children. And it is this sonship or daughtership that will lead us to offer redemptive suffering for God's children, who in turn become our children too. St. Escrivá, stationed in Rome, was perhaps much more fruitful than his spiritual children in their missionary apostolate, with his deep filial heart and apostolate of prayer and suffering helping to carry the Church on his shoulders. Greatness comprises the abandonment of the child, of Jesus Christ.

<u>Synthesis</u>
When we die, the most wonderful words that we can hear addressed to us from the Father will be those of filiation, "You are my child, the Beloved, in whom I am well pleased." Or, "You are like my Son (Jesus), the apple of my eye, who all through His life sought only to please me."

# HOMILY 2

## Three Levels of Discipleship: Servant, Friend, Spouse
Sunday 28th OT Year 2, October 10, 2021

In today's Gospel in which Jesus asks the rich man to sell all his possessions and to "come, follow me," Jesus appears to be bringing up the theme of discipleship. For he used these same words, "Come, follow me," in the call of the apostles ("following of Christ," *sequela Christi*). Now there appears to be degrees or levels of following Jesus. We should not be surprised as we find different levels in all human growth. We might consider the first Reading on acquiring Wisdom as representing the highest level, since the greatest wisdom is to choose God above all created things: "Therefore I prayed, and understanding was given me; I called upon God, and the spirit of wisdom came to me…. All good things came to me along with her, and in her hands uncounted wealth." (Wisd 7:7-14). The point of this homily is that our hearts desire the spousal love, divine union.

We can look to the paradigm of the apostles, for there we seem to find three levels of discipleship of servant, friend, spouse. These three levels are analogous to the three degrees in other homilies. We might even assign these three levels to three periods: (1) the apostles' first call, (2) evangelization after Pentecost, and (3) martyrdom. We find the first level reflected in Peter's question in the Gospel, "Look, we have left everything and followed you" (self-interest of the servant). Then we find the distinction between the first two levels made by Jesus at the Last Supper:

> No longer do I call you *servants,* for the servant does not know what his master is doing; but I have called you *friends,* for all that I have heard from my Father I have made known to you. (Jn 15:15)

### 1. Material Detachment: Servants of Jesus

Jesus' discipleship is radical, calling the young man to sell everything, to radical poverty. This is continued in the pattern of the Holy Spirit's inspiration in new ecclesial foundations to this level of material detachment, as we find in the communities of St. Ignatius (radical vs. mitigated poverty), Madonna House (begging, one shower a week), and the Franciscan Friars of the Renewal. This is the level of the servants of Christ, like the apostles who have left everything, a physical detachment. We find today's Psalm reading twice referring to God having mercy on His "servants." We note, however, that there is something new here in the New Testament, as the Old Testament finds God's blessings rather in temporal blessings received.

## 2. Detachment of the Heart: Friends of Jesus

Beyond the level of material detachment, there appears to be the level of detachment of the heart, the "friends" of Jesus. While the apostles have left family and everything, there appeared to be attachments of the heart, expressed by Peter's words, "Look, we have left everything and followed you" (Mt 19:27). Peter was still at the level of rewards, not yet arrived at that of pure love. It is reflected also in their arguing of who was the greatest of the apostles, and the mother of James and John asking Jesus that her sons be allowed to sit at His right and left in heaven. This happens to priests and religious as well. We can leave everything (family, professions) as the apostles did and still have attachments of the heart. Jesus points to this attachment as being unworthy of his divine friendship: "He who loves father or mother more than me is not worthy of me; and he who loves son or daughter more than me is not worthy of me…" (Mt 10:37-39). The second Reading today refers to how God reads our hearts. St. John of the Cross writes:

> Love consists not in feeling great things but in having great detachment and in suffering for the Beloved. The soul that is attached to anything, however much good there may be in it, will not arrive at the liberty of Divine union. For whether it be a strong wire rope or a slender and delicate thread that holds the bird, it matters not, if it really holds it fast; for until the cord be broken, the bird cannot fly. (St. John of the Cross)

This text suggests that Christ's disciples, lay or consecrated, may have left everything behind and live poverty but still have their hearts attached to their families and not yet love Jesus above all with detachment. This may seem unnatural at the human level, as with the practice of the Missionaries of the Poor in Jamaica who only get to visit their families once every ten years. A second attachment is to seek to be popular and loved, represented by the apostles seeking to be the greatest. A third attachment is to have our own plans instead of allowing God to choose for us (e.g., ministry to the poor), not to live abandonment of letting go control. Today's Office of Readings (OOR) describes how Yahweh, speaking through the prophet Haggai, remonstrates with the Hebrew people returned from exile for thinking about themselves and not about God, the ultimate attachment:

> Because while my House lies in ruins you are busy with your own, each one of you. That is why the sky has withheld the rain and the earth withheld its yield. I have called down drought on land and hills, on wheat, on new wine, on oil and on all the produce of the ground, on man and beast and all their labours. (Haggai 1)

## 3. Total Gift of Heart: Spouses of Jesus

But we can argue that there is a third level of lovers or spouses of Christ, represented by John, the "beloved disciple." They find Christ within, as St. John of the Cross taught:

> What more do you want, O soul! And what else do you search for outside, when within yourself you possess your riches, delights, satisfactions, fullness and kingdom — your Beloved whom you desire and seek? Be joyful and gladdened in your interior recollection with Him, for you have Him so close to you. Desire Him there, adore Him there. Do not go in pursuit of Him outside yourself. You will only become distracted and wearied thereby, and you shall not find Him, or enjoy Him more securely, or sooner, or more intimately than by seeking Him within you.[1]

## Illustration of Three Stages in Sr. Clare Crockett
*Conversion and First Stage*:
She recalled in her personal testimony that when she arrived in Spain she was "very superficial and a wild child." But that began to change when she took part in a Good Friday adoration of the cross in Spain, kissing the feet of Jesus.

> I do not know how to explain exactly what happened. I did not see the choirs of angels or a white dove come down from the ceiling and descend on me, but I had the certainty that the Lord was on the Cross, for me. And along with that conviction, I felt a great sorrow, similar to what I had experienced when I was little and prayed the Stations of the Cross. When I returned to my pew, I already had imprinted in me something that was not there before. I had to do something for Him Who had given his life for me.

This was the first stage. Unlike the young man in the Gospel, she immediately left her family and acting career in Ireland at the age of 18 to join a religious community in Spain. It was the start of a long journey of conversion and healing that led to her taking her first vows in 2006.

*Second Stage*
We sense a second stage already present when she was asked by a student if she was concerned about her family, some of whom had abandoned the faith. She replied that she allows God to take care of them and she focused on bringing others to Christ. She was living Jesus' teaching, "He who loves father and mother more than me is not worthy of me..."
*Third Stage*

---

[1] St. John of the Cross, *Spiritual Canticle*, in *The Collected Works of St. John of the Cross*, trans. K. Kavanaugh & O. Rodriguez (Washington, DC: ICS Publications, 1979), 1:8.

Now we see glimmers of a third stage in her spousal language:

> "Her deepest desire was to have an undivided heart for God and for Him to totally transform her into Himself," said Sr. Kristen. "She knew she could not achieve this on her own and she constantly begged His help, 'Grant me an undivided heart. *Do not let anything ever enter in between Your heart and mine*'".... "And right before going to Ecuador she wrote, 'My heart is Yours, my mind is Yours, my thoughts are Yours. Ask me for anything. Nothing matters now, since nothing I have is mine! Possess me, Jesus,'" Sr. Kristen recalled.

This total gift of the third stage may also be manifested by the "blank cheque" she gave God every day (allowing God to do whatever He wanted with her), and especially by her words mere hours before her death after other sisters expressed fear of being killed: "Why should I be afraid of death, if I'm going to go with the One I have longed to be with my whole life." This may be the crown of her life.[2] The pure in heart longs increasingly for this union.

## Spiritual Marriage of St. Catherine of Siena

Spiritual marriage is illustrated especially in a mystical episode in St. Catherine of Siena's life. St. Catherine was given a vision of a spiritual marriage with Christ, during which He gave her a mystical ring that humans could not see. This spiritual marriage has been depicted by many famous artists and one of two such depictions from her family home in Siena was selected for the cover image of this book. Near the end of her life, she was given to understand that she would no longer see spiritual director, Raymond of Capua, the only one who had some understanding of her spiritual life. She understood that, for union with God, every single attachment must be broken. For God is infinite love and infinite purity, and what He wants most from us is not intensity or fervor but the **purity** of the love of our hearts, which can lead to an early death or martyrdom. She has become the co-patron of Italy and Europe. The final stage is the summit of intimacy but also of power. "Those whose hearts are pure are temples of the Holy Spirit" (St. Lucy). We find the detachment of all three levels also illustrated uniquely in the different stages of detachment of Abraham, beginning with leaving family and home, and leading to finally sacrificing his own son, Isaac. Through this detachment for total love of God, God has made Abraham the father of all who have faith in God.

---

[2] The material for Sr. Clare's life was drawn from "Sister Clare and Companions," accessed November 6, 2021, https://www.sisterclare.com/en/her-life/biography?id=7536. Highly recommended is the documentary on her life, "All or Nothing: Sr. Clare Crockett," https://www.youtube.com/watch?v=-0LKZm2BqZo.

# HOMILY 3

## Wedding Homily: Human Love is Prelude to Divine Marriage
Genesis 1.26-28, 31a, Psalm 33, 1 Corinthians 12.31-13.8

**Preface**

In this wedding homily, we wish to highlight the heart of human life, namely, love, which is what the readings you have chosen for your wedding are all about: Genesis text of Adam and Eve's union and Paul's famous "without love…" in Corinthians. Our popular music typically dwells upon that which most attracts our hearts, and it is love that dominates. Its beauty can be captured in a love song like "The Wedding" below, in which the singer envisions her wedding day.

> You by my side, that's how I see us
> I close my eyes, and I can see us
> We're on our way to say I do
> My secret dreams have all come true
>
> I see the church, I see the people
> Your folks and mine happy and smiling
> And I can hear sweet voices singing
> Ave Maria
>
> Oh my love, my love
> Can this really be?
> That some day you'll walk
> Down the aisle with me
>
> Let it be, make it be
> That I'm the one for you
> I'll be yours, all yours
> Now and forever
>
> I see us now, your hand in my hand
> This is the hour, this is the moment
> And I can hear sweet voices singing
> Ave Maria
> Ave Maria
> Ave Maria[1]

---

[1] Joaquin Prieto, "The Wedding," 1964. Lyrics drawn from Songlyrics.com, accessed October 27, 2021, http://www.songlyrics.com/julie-rogers/the-wedding-lyrics/. These song lyrics are being used under, so to speak, "Research and Academic" purposes.

## 1. Man is Made for Love and to Love

God blesses human love and takes delight in it. Adam and Eve were created in the image and likeness of God. Since His essence is love, we are created for love, to receive and to offer love; this is the heart of human life. In his inaugural encyclical, *Redemptoris hominis* (n. 10), John Paul II wrote that:

> Man cannot live without love. He remains a being that is incomprehensible for himself, his life is senseless, if love is not revealed to him, if he does not encounter love, if he does not experience it and make it his own, if he does not participate intimately in it.

John Paul II's "Theology of the Body" also proclaims this truth. But this truth of love as the core of human reality is already borne out from human experience. One illustration of this is from the practice of the Apache people at marriage. One novelist explains that they did not have a word for marriage, but the couple simply say to one another one word, *Varlebena*, which means "forever" (L'Amour, *Hondo*). Within the Catholic Church, we see the beautiful love between the famous Catholic philosopher, Jacques Maritain, and his wife, Raïssa. They had fallen in love at the Sorbonne University in Paris and married, and when he had to take leave for some period of time (e.g., Rome as France's Church ambassador), he would write love notes that she would open each day of his absence.

*Love Requires Continued Self-Giving*
After years of marriage, the romance will not be felt as strongly (with care of the children, work). But what matters is not your feelings but your heart, the "forever" core. And you have to continue to grow in this love because you cannot stand still on the slope of life; you will slide backwards, especially given your natural differences and life's challenges. This was captured in the first *Spiderman* Marvel movie, in which Dr. Octavius and his wife described how they met and fell in love at university, with the latter explaining to the young Peter Parker, "But it takes work." The work entails especially: (i) *understanding* as the greatest charity: coming out of yourself to put yourself in your spouse's shoes; and (ii) *affection*: e.g., squeezing the other's shoulders when he or she is going through a hard time, listening. Yet, Mary Healy warns us of a temptation (sliding) in our times: "a new and destructive possibility emerges: sexuality can be distorted into a means of self-gratification rather than self-gift; love can be twisted into lust.... The human heart now also inclines toward disordered desires for money, possessions, food, drink, comfort, entertainment, admiration, success, popularity, prestige, and power" ("The Good News of Biblical Sexual Morality," *Inside the Vatican* [ITV], December 2018: 25-26).

## 2. A Great Love has an Eternal Quality (von Balthasar)

Your desire to give yourself totally corresponds to von Balthasar's insight that a great love can never be content with an act of love performed only for the present moment. Love wants to abandon itself, to surrender itself, to entrust itself, to commit itself to love. As a pledge of love, it wants to lay its freedom once and for all at the feet of love. As soon as love is truly awakened, the moment of time is transformed for it into a form of eternity. Even erotic egoism cannot forebear swearing "eternal fidelity" and, for a fleeting moment, finding pleasure in actually believing in this eternity. How much more, then, does true love want to outlast time, and for this purpose, to rid itself of its most dangerous enemy, its own freedom of choice. Hence, every true love has the inner form of a vow.[2]

We find this first lived by Jesus. He made His perpetual "yes" or vow at the cross, the New Adam expressing his love for His Bride, the New Eve or the Church or each soul. He is the latter-day Romeo, who expresses his love in a divine melody under the balcony of Juliet, waiting breathlessly for her "yes" of reciprocal love. This is the true heart of human history, and the greatest tragedy is "unrequited love," where this infinite Love is not reciprocated, when divine love does not find hearts to fill (Dina Bélanger).

## 3. Human Marriage is Preparation for Divine Marriage

Blaise Pascal teaches, "The heart has its reasons which reason knows nothing of… We know the truth not only by the reason, but by the heart."
St. John of the Cross teaches that God the Father made us to be spouses of Christ: "My Son, I wish to give you a bride who will love you." Because God made us for this spiritual marriage with Christ, there is a wound, a deep yearning, within us that leads us to desire union with the Beloved (Christ). But He in turn leads us to the Father's love: "He [Christ] would take her tenderly in his arms and there give her his love; and when they were thus one, he would lift her to the Father where God's very joy would be her joy" (*Poetry, 9: Romances, stanza 5, Prologue of John regarding the Trinity*). The glory and intimacy of this divine marriage has been vividly painted on the canvas of the works of St. Teresa of Jesus (*Interior Castle*) and St. John of the Cross (*The Spiritual Canticle* and *Living Flame of Love*), and synthesized in other works, such as Thomas Dubay's *Fire Within* and Luis Martinez's *The Sanctifier*. St. Teresa of Jesus teaches that we will be willing to give up everything once we have experienced it: "Lord, how you afflict your lovers! But everything is small in comparison to what you give them afterwards."

---

[2] Hans Urs von Balthasar, *The Christian State of Life* (San Francisco: Ignatius Press, 1983), 39.

# HOMILY 4

## Wedding Banquet: Openness of Heart to Divine Love
(28th Sunday in Ordinary Time, Year A)

Today's Gospel parable on the Wedding Banquet depicts a king who punishes the citizens who had killed his servants' sent to invite them to his son's wedding banquet. He then sends yet other servants to invite everyone, among whom one shows up without the wedding garment and was cast into Hades. One commentary illuminates who these wedding figures represent in salvation history. In this parable, the king is God the Father who prepared a wedding banquet for His Son. The servants sent to invite people represented the prophets, many of whom were killed. The razing of their city were the two forced exiles of the Jews or the future destruction of Jerusalem in 70 AD. The servants sent out to invite everyone are the apostles, sent out to the Gentiles after the refusal by the Jews. St. Gregory the Great affirms that **the wedding is Christ's marriage to the Church (and to each elect soul)** and that the wedding garment is **charity**.[1] We find over and over again that Christians are satisfied with being good and doing good, but do not follow the deep longings of the heart of St. Augustine: "Late have I loved you, O Beauty ever ancient and new." Thus the heart of spiritual life is not perfection or doing good, but union, and specifically the spiritual marriage of each predestined soul to Christ.

*Pharisees and Priestly Class Closed their Hearts to Christ's Call*
Spiritual life revolves around the heart. That this parable is directed toward the Pharisees' closedness of heart is clear from the context, from the two parables that immediately preceded (two sons, one of whom obeyed; and vineyard owner whose son was killed by those leasing the vineyard), and by the awareness of the chief priests and Pharisees that Jesus was speaking about them and their subsequent plotting to kill him. Jesus is thus highlighting their lack of openness of heart. Their fundamental problem was that their hearts, as Jesus had variously pointed out, were closed and that they resisted the Holy Spirit. As we see with John Henry Newman, all spiritual life flows from the work of the Holy Spirit in our hearts, and thus the spiritual life depends on the openness of the heart, where we meet God and make our choices for or against God. Our sins are secondary to the openness of heart, given that it was with the sinners, prostitutes, and tax collectors that Jesus associated, to the chagrin of the Pharisees.

---

[1] We can't recall the Commentary source, but it may have been George Leo Haydock's *Comprehensive Catholic Commentary*, on the wedding parable treated on the nineteenth Sunday after Pentecost.

## 1. First Step: Heart Closed by Self-Justification Needs Christ's Gaze

Since the heart is central to our relationship with God, this raises the question of what causes it to close. Francis Fernandez, in the context of Jesus' weeping over Jerusalem, which would be razed to the ground, because of their hardness of heart, describes how He had tried everything:

> Every means had been tried, including miracles, actions and words, sometimes in a tone of severity, and other times with leniency.... This is the deep mystery of human freedom which always retains that sad possibility of rejecting the grace of God. *Free man, subject yourself to a voluntary servitude, so that Jesus won't have to say of you what He is said to have told Saint Teresa about others: "Teresa, I was willing. But men were not.*[2]

As Paul pointed out, they were guilty of self-justification ("Pharisaism"), satisfied with themselves because of their many external religious acts. We all need Christ's justification after Adam's sin, having become enemies of God. But now with sanctifying grace restored after Baptism, we still often do not correspond to the Spirit's calls. Unless we weep over our sins, as Paul did after his persecution of Christians (1 Cor 15:9), our hearts remain closed in self-satisfaction, lacking the tears of repentance that melt and open hearts. Julián Carrón, successor to Luigi Giussani, captures this well.

> Jesus did not allow Himself to be trapped in a legalistic attitude; He allowed Himself to be struck by the wounds of the people and showed another way of conceiving of things... His gaze introduced an absolutely new way of relating to people, to their fragility and their need: the Sabbath was made for man, not man for the Sabbath.... He did not come for the healthy, the just, those who already knew, but for the sick, the sinners, those who suffered from their weakness and helplessness. It is crucial for each of us: the day we are no longer aware of our infirmity and wretchedness, we will no longer realize the grace of having Someone who can heal our wounds. We will no longer need Christ. (*Where is God?*, 18).

Carrón goes more deeply into Jesus' gaze. Only Jesus can pierce to the depths of the heart of the Samaritan woman, not blind to her five "husbands," but seeing her thirst. "In all His mysterious nature, Jesus sees the thirst for fullness even when it is buried under a heap of sins.... Deep down, everything we do, including any of our sins, is an attempt to respond to the thirst that constitutes us.... Jesus introduces a different gaze on the human person and reveals that we have a structural relationship with something Other..." It is "a gaze that welcomes, forgives, and regenerates, enabling people to journey to reach the ideal" (ibid, 19-20, 25).

---

[2] Francis Fernandez, *In Conversation with God*, vol. two (NY: Scepter Press, 1993), 250-251.

## 2. Second Step: Open our Hearts to Make Return to Christ's Love

Let us return to the key criterion of openness of heart. For us sinners, it is the openness that flows from contrition like Peter's: "Peter took an hour to fall; but in an instant he rights himself and sets about raising himself higher than he was before his fall" (G. Chevrot, *Simon Peter*). Many are unaware of this power of contrition to raise us to a deeper relationship with Christ: "'Peter is united to our Lord in an instant, and much closer than he had ever been before, because of his sorrow for his denials. Out of his denials is born a faithfulness that will take him even to martyrdom" (*In Conversation*, v. 2, 258). But we must go beyond Peter's contrition to John's sublime mystical union. The wedding banquet in the parable prefigures that depicted in John's Book of Revelation in eternity (Rev 19:7-10), an image of the marriage of Jesus to the Church and each soul (in the Seventh Mansions). Thus, all spiritual life is not about perfection or about doing good, but *about union with Christ*; and then, in Christ, becoming children of the Father. In becoming one with Him, Christ desires to give us His own heart, that is, the Holy Spirit, so that we can love Him and His children with *His own love*. Then, the spousal love, which begins with the love of Jesus, also leads to the love of Christ's children (what good wife and mother does not love her children?). Let us examine both loves, which derive from self-forgetfulness.

First, we highlight Christ's love and thirst for our love. After descending to become man, dying for us, and then releasing the treasure in His heart, the Holy Spirit, who is the Gift from which all other gifts in the Church flow, Christ could say to each one of us, "Is there anything that I can do for you that I have not already done?" Yet, what we typically do is be constantly concerned about what Jesus can give to or do for us (family, work, health woes), and are wrapped up in our daily family life, work life, interests, and even our work for Him; but give little thought to Jesus' desire for our love. His words on the cross, "I thirst," express not primarily the desire for our salvation but the desire for our love, the desire to possess our hearts, as lovers do. Thus the greatest tragedy of all human history is not sin or the evils flowing from it but **unrequited love** ("For God so loved the world that he sent us His Son, that whoever believes in him should not perish but have eternal life," Jn 3:16). There is a lack of reciprocation: the bride (each soul) has failed to love the Bridegroom, who has given His life for her.

Second, when we possess Jesus' own heart, when the Holy Spirit possesses that heart, then we cannot rest while His children all over the world are suffering their Calvaries. We get so wrapped up with family and work that we forget that we live in the First World (finest health care system, health insurance, best universities, peace and democracy, freedom to practice our faith, wealth for food, clothing, multiple cars and computers, international travelling, etc.), and forget the 50 plus millions in refugee camps, those living in countries with oppressive or corrupt governments or great poverty, etc. But above all, Jesus weeps for those who will reject His call, as He did for Judas at the Last Supper, and thus are condemned for all eternity.

## 3. Third Step: Love of God's Children (Wedding Garment)

Now we can understand Jesus' reference of the wedding garment being charity. Charity is not primarily about feel-good compassion or philanthropy, which is good but rather limited, and can be superficial. Charity is our being a successor to the prophets and apostles represented in today's parable, to do the one thing that ultimately matters: to go out into the byways and call everyone to the wedding banquet. There are degrees of charity. The movie, "10,000 BC," has a scene that captures three degrees of love. In a scene around a campfire, a young man was sharing with the chief his shame of his father's (former chief) abandonment of their primitive tribe in a time of need and hunger. The chief finally revealed to the young man the truth about his father. Knowing the tribe's dire situation in regard to food, his father had set out to find other means of feeding the tribe, but he did not tell others so that they would not follow him, as the tribe needed, so to speak, every hand on deck. Then the chief pointed out the greatness of his father by describing three circles that each person can draw. The first circle is of the one who faithfully looks after his or her own family. A second and wider circle is of the one who, moving beyond family, looks after the tribe. But the largest circle is of the one who circumscribes an entire nation, and this was his father, who sacrificed himself for his people. Thus, if we love Jesus with a spousal love, then, like St. Thérèse of Lisieux, we will want to leave heaven to work on earth to bring all to Him, and not stop until the angel says that time is no more.

Summarizing what we have said, God has created us for marriage with His Son. But, as a man cannot force a woman to marry him, Jesus cannot force us to enter spiritual marriage with Him. We have to give our "yes," and we do so by opening our hearts to allow the Holy Spirit, the Living Flame of Love, to possess us to accomplish a divine marriage in the Seventh Mansions. But our hearts remain closed until we recognize our sinfulness and how we have wounded His spousal heart (repentant love) and weep over our neglect; and they also remain closed until we learn self-forgetfulness and seek the one thing necessary: to love Him in return and to love Him in His children. All Christian life is a love story between Christ and each soul; everything else are like props in this drama of love (see von Balthasar's "Theodrama").

# HOMILY 5

## The Call of Matthew is our Call: "Come, Follow Me"
(Sat. of First Week of Ordinary Time, Year I, has overlap with last homily)

The famous Renaissance painter, Caravaggio, has famously depicted three stages of Matthew's life. We would like to propose his triptych of Matthew (call, inspiration, martyrdom) as the story of salvation history, and that St. Matthew's call is our call too. A priest post-graduate classmate from Portugal shared his rather unique ordination holy card, of Caravaggio's "Call of Matthew." As is well known, Caravaggio employs light and darkness to highlight the themes of his paintings. In this famous painting housed in St. Louis of the French church in Rome, Jesus, with Peter beside him, is standing at the doorway of the tax office, and light streams from Christ into the room. The light falls upon figures sitting at a table. As grace interiorly streaming from Jesus' heart strikes Matthew's heart, he looks at Jesus, pointing to himself, as if asking, "are you calling me?" We see how the open heart of Matthew responds, immediately leaving everything behind. In striking contrast, most at the table were still mesmerized by the coins on it, and did not allow the light to strike their hearts.

### 1. Human History is Story of God's Knocking on our Hearts

Herein we find **the story of all human history**. Jesus reveals it in Rev 3:20: "Behold, I stand at the door and knock; if anyone hears my voice and opens the door, I will come to him and eat with him, and he with me." It is captured also by the title of one of St. Josemaría Escrivá's books, *Christ is Passing By*. Jesus knocks on each heart, which is the deepest part of our being, where we meet and decide for or against God. We see a fine example in the conversion of St. Augustine, who, after he entered the depths of his heart, was ravished: "Late have I loved you, O Beauty so ancient, so new."

Unlike the apostles, there were those who closed their hearts, as with the priestly class and the Pharisees, whom Jesus condemned (we will develop this in Homily 12). We find this in Jesus' own people in Nazareth who, after he chastised them for lack of faith, tried to throw him off a cliff, and there followed one of the saddest expressions in the New Testament: "But passing through their midst, *he went away*." Thus heaven and hell are decided ultimately, not by sin, but by the openness of our hearts. The greatest light must have come especially from the cross: some derided or disregarded Jesus, some beat their breast, some turned to him (e.g., good thief, centurion). The touching responses in the movie "Ben Hur" of Judah and his mother to the crucified Christ manifested deep openness of heart.

*Repentance*

If Christ's call to each human heart is the story of human history, what is it then that causes our hearts to open or close (Homily 4)? We find a clue in today's Gospel, in which the Pharisees accused Jesus of eating with sinners. Andrea Tornielli and Julián Carrón goes more deeply. Christians today can act with the Pharisees' "presumptuous closed-mindedness" by sitting in the teacher's chair (to know everything), not allowing ourselves to be wounded.

> Letting ourselves be wounded means we allow ourselves to be challenged, and realize we do not know everything. It means we have not already judged everything, and that we are not always in the teacher's chair. It seems to be that often this attitude is missing among certain Christians, too. (Tornielli, *Where is God?*, 17)

> People can always harden their hearts, close in on themselves, not allow themselves to be touched by reality, whether it be through the sound of a flute [Jesus on Pharisees: "we played the flute for you"] or through Jesus.... Anyone can have this attitude, Christians included, anyone who thinks, like the scholars of the Law and the Pharisees, that they already know everything. This is the position that Jesus reproves the most in the gospel. It is very interesting to see how He reacts when faced with such presumptuous closed-mindedness. (Julián Carrón, ibid)

This living as if we know everything and not allowing ourselves to be touched or wounded leads to closedmindedness. Both the Baptist and Jesus began with the same words, "Repent, for the kingdom of God is at hand" (Mt 3:2; Mt 4:17). Peter showed his lack of self-knowledge of his sinfulness when he professed to Jesus, "Though they all fall away because of you, I will never fall away" (Mt 26:33). Scripture records that, after he denied Jesus three times, he wept bitterly (*flevit amare*). Reminding him of his failure with the three-fold, "Simon Peter, do love me?," Jesus is now able to use him.

## 2. Inward Turn to Dialogue with Trinity Dwelling in Soul's Center

We have looked only at the first step of opening our hearts to Christ who is knocking on our door, that requires repentance, the weeping over our sins. But we can complete this by delineating all three steps, corresponding to the three panels of Caravaggio's triptych of Matthew, the other two being the "inspiration of Matthew" and his martyrdom. His inspiration here refers to his writing of the Gospel of Matthew, which, as a sacred writer, requires such a profound interior union with God that it is God who writes in and through him, and his Gospel becomes the word of God. This union with a sacred writer reaches its height in the union that Paul attained: "It is no longer I who live, but Christ who lives in me" (Gal 2:20).

We see how St. Augustine discovered that, to find God, he had to go within his soul, *"ad interior, ad superior,"* and he became known as the "doctor of interiority." Christians, as the Pharisees did, generally find their identity in all the external fidelity to duty and good works. Like St. Augustine before his conversion, we are so caught up in the world of sense that we do not perceive a divine world within, of the indwelling of the Trinity from Baptism. To St. Teresa of Jesus it was revealed that the soul is like a crystal globe, in which center God dwells and from which His Light radiates, and that the Christian life is an interior journey toward this center, to meet God. The greatest world is not the cosmos or our daily life but within our souls.

## 3. Imbued with Jesus' Heart to Co-Redeem the World

The encounter with Christ leads us further. After the first two steps of opening our hearts through repentance and then encountering Christ within so that He possesses our hearts, the third panel of Matthew is that, possessed by the Holy Spirit, he goes on the cross like His Master. This constitutes the triptych of Matthew: call, writing of Gospel, and martyrdom. Matthew's Gospel, intercession, and martyrdom have brought many to Christ, beginning with the dinner he set up for his fellow tax collectors. The author has always had a special attraction to Matthew's Gospel. The goal of the first two steps (opening of the heart in encountering Christ and of allowing the Holy Spirit to possess it interiorly) has this endpoint: to co-redeem the world with Christ. For Matthew's Gospel ends with the separation of the sheep and goats, that we will be judged by the criterion of love. Christianity is not primarily about compassion or even social justice; it is above all about winning souls from the devil and for Christ. Let us turn to the example of St. Thérèse for true courage in following Christ's path, which comes at the cost of spiritual battle:

> The time I have spent in working for the novices has been *a time of war*, of struggle. I labored for God. He worked for me, and my soul never advanced more rapidly than at that time. *I did not seek to be loved.* I merely sought to do my duty and to please the good Lord without desiring that my efforts should bear fruit. We must serve our Lord; sow what is good around us without worrying about its growth. For us the labors; for Jesus, success! *We must never fear the battle when the good of our neighbour is involved. We must reprove others at the cost of our personal tranquility* and we must do this much less in order to open the eyes of our subjects, than to serve God. He will take care of the results.[1] (emphasis added)

---

[1] François Jamart, *Complete Spiritual Doctrine of St. Thérèse of Lisieux* (New York: Alba House, 1961), 285-287 (Chapter 6).

# HOMILY 6

## Palm Sunday: Jesus' Spousal Vow at Calvary (von Balthasar)
(Homily for Palm Sunday 2016, see *Mystical Incarnation*)

### 1. Synthesis of Nicholas Healy's Article on von Balthasar's Vow

The following is simply a synthesis of Nicholas Healy's article on von Balthasar's image of every true love as having the inner form of a vow (introduced earlier). This can serve as a theology of marriage for couples.

> One can never be content with an act of love performed for the present moment only. **Love wants to abandon itself, to surrender itself, to entrust itself, to commit itself to love.** As a pledge of love, it wants to lay its freedom once and for all at the feet of love. As soon as love is truly awakened, **the moment of time is transformed for it into a form of eternity**. Even erotic egoism cannot forebear swearing "eternal fidelity" and, for a fleeting moment, finding pleasure in actually believing in this eternity. How much more, then, does true love want to outlast time and, for this purpose, to rid itself of its most dangerous enemy, its own freedom of choice. Hence every true love has *the inner form of a vow*. [*die innere Form des Gelöbnisses*]: It binds itself to the beloved and does so out of motives and in the spirit of love.[1]

Much of von Balthasar's *The Christian State of Life* is an attempt to unfold this claim for the evangelical vows (poverty, chastity, obedience) as a form of Christian life, that this vow applies equally to marital spousal love. What interests us is the relation between the historical life of an individual and the concrete "moment" of exchanging vows. The first thing to be noted is the *totality*: there is no aspect of a person's being that is not gathered up and included in the gift, "I am my beloved's and my beloved is mine" (Song of Songs 6:3). The gift must be both irrevocable and total. Following Ignatius, von Balthasar sees the early stages of human existence as preparation for the momentous occasion of divine election and the consequent choice to enter a vowed state of life (consecrated or married). Everything is preparation for the self-surrender, one that can only be compared to death. For example, for marriage, all of the past experiences and memories are now understood in their true significance, one's past is the soil that will make possible a new and fruitful form of life in communion with the other.

---

[1] Hans Urs von Balthasar, *The Christian State of Life*, 38–39; quoted in Nicholas J. Healy, "Inclusion in Christ: Background to a Christian Doctrine of Providence," *Communio* 29, no. 3 (2002): 483. The author takes the liberty of summarizing his thought without Dr. Healy's permission to introduce his thought to Catholic faithful.

At the same time, the moment of self-surrender is the creation of a new form of life. In other words, the "death to self" involved in the exchange of vows is life-giving. To claim a new form of life is created is another way of saying that one's future is also included within the self-surrender of a vow. It is a commitment that embraces whatever happens— whatever illnesses or blessings may come, will now unfold within the relationship of communion that is constituted by the vows. This includes, above all, the greatest gift, presupposing an openness to the future gift of children, who will be the very incarnation of newness and surprise. Romano Guardini avers that "in the experience of a great love, all that happens becomes an event inside that love." In the form of a vow, a great love is able to include all that has happened and all that will happen. Every event, especially those that call forth new forms of self-surrender, is simultaneously an unveiling of the depths of what has already been given in the form of a vow. In short, what is given to another in this once-for-all gift is precisely a life.

## 2. Christ Made a Spousal Vow (Yes) with Everyone at Calvary

We are overwhelmed to discover that Jesus made a spousal vow of love at the cross. We can speak mystically of the relation between God and the world as a **spousal relationship**. The marriage between God and the world is consummated, in an initial answer, with Jesus' own affirmation at the end of His mission, "*consummatum est*" ("It is finished," Jn 19:30). The difficulty is that Christ is given a mission that comprehends the whole of world history; He has to "return" to the Father with all of creation. Applying von Balthasar's fruitful conception of a total self-surrender that takes the form of a vow, we can say that Christ's mission is in fact consummated at the hour of His death, but in the form of a promise or vow, a covenant of new life in communion with Him (lived out through the Spirit in the Church).

The key is Jesus' gift of the Holy Spirit and the Church. This vow is now lived out through the Holy Spirit and the Church (symbolized by blood and water) given as the fruit of Jesus' death on Calvary. Taken together, the Spirit and the Church are the form and fruit of the God-creature marriage covenant in its *historical unfolding*. Everything that happens in the *future* life of the spouses will be the unveiling of the hidden depths of what has *already* been given in the once-for-all exchange of vows (Calvary). The newness of the Holy Spirit and His mission of guiding the Church into "all truth" (Jn 16:13) is simultaneously an unveiling of the true depths of Jesus' self-surrender as a revelation of the Father's love, self-surrender that comprehends the past, present, and future. The Holy Spirit is both the "gift" and "fruit" of the mutual love between Father and Son, and the ultimate gift that is bestowed as the "fruit" of Jesus' life-giving death.

## 3. Two Examples of the Yes to Christ's Spousal Vow

Thus, the sublime vision that von Balthasar depicts is that salvation history is a marriage between the Son of God and each human heart. The Bridegroom "proposes" and gives His "I do" in pouring Himself out for His Bride on Calvary, while giving birth to her as a New Adam to a New Eve, the Church. His love is irrevocable. Human history is a romance, a wooing by the Son of each heart. Now He requires the "I do" of our total self-gift, as in marriage. St. Teresa of Jesus illustrates that Jesus' total surrender calls for our total surrender:

> To love is to surrender one's self without reserve. This means to surrender one's will in such a way to the divine will, however crucifying it may be, that one finds joy in suffering when this is pleasing to the Beloved; and this intense love is a call for God's presence. The soul enraptured by God tends spontaneously to possess God. The ideal of perfect self-donation corresponds quite naturally in her doctrine with the desire for mystical union. God must then be generous to the generous soul…. The soul's total gift calls for the total gift of God.[2]

St. Teresa Benedicta of the Cross teaches the power of surrender: "Whoever surrenders unconditionally to the Lord will be chosen by him as an instrument for building his kingdom." Adrienne von Speyr, who radiates the same spirit of "receptivity" and "expropriation," teaches how to live this total availability as a "witness" to Christ:

> But apart from these there is the little company of those who are marked out by God to give a special, qualified testimony…. The witness singled out by God, on the contrary, received a distinct and personal task direct from God. Part of this mission consists, in fact, in leading the life of an *exceptional witness*. That means placing one's whole personal life at the service of one's existence as a witness. *The witness binds himself before God to sacrifice himself whole and entire to his mission. He binds himself to do so even before hearing what his mission is.* Nor will he ever get to know the content of his mission fully and completely. He will have to listen and attend to it *afresh every day*. The content may change suddenly from top to bottom; it may change direction at any moment and may even turn into its contrary. While carrying out his mission, its real content will be concealed from the exception, and it will certainly not be something he can view as a whole. He must always be ready for everything. There is no resting in such a mission, for it springs directly from the very source of God's life.[3] (emphasis added)

---

[2] Gabriel of St. Mary Magdalen, "Carmes," in *Dictionnnaire de Spiritualité*, col. 197.
[3] Adrienne von Speyr, *John: The Word Becomes Flesh: Meditations on John 1-5*, vol. 1 (San Francisco: Ignatius, 1994), 70-71.

# HOMILY 7

## Exaltation of the Cross: Preaching Christ Crucified
(Exaltation of the Cross, September 14, 2019)

> "Jews demand signs and Greeks look for wisdom, but we preach Christ crucified: a stumbling block to Jews and foolishness to Gentiles" (1 Cor 1: 23). "For, as I have often told you before and now tell you again even with tears, many live as enemies of the cross of Christ.... Their mind is set on earthly things." (Phil 3:18-19)

**A. The Divine Power of the Cross**: "When I am lifted up, I will draw all things to myself" (touched upon in earlier homilies).

Since the sin of Adam and Eve, there is a new law: "Through death to the Resurrection," that was first lived by Jesus. We point to many examples in the Church that vindicate this principle. It was lived by His apostles, who were martyred (living martyrdom for John). The principle is that "the blood of martyrs becomes the seed of Christianity." St. Paul's power of conversion lay in his sufferings: "I will show him how much he has to suffer for me," which included many scourgings, being stoned, shipwrecked twice, etc. The early Church was a Church of martyrdom (first centuries). It was the same for St. John Vianney. When a neighbouring parish pastor, marvelling at the transformation in St. Vianney's parish, lamented, "Why do my parishioners not live like this?," the latter answered, "Have you added fasts, vigils, sleeping on the floor, castigation of your body?" He rose early in the morning, often after attacks by the devil, and spent hours before the tabernacle. Cardinal O'Connor, making a retreat at Auschwitz, was inspired to start a congregation of religious Sisters to protect life. He understood that protesting and fighting legally against abortion was not sufficient; that expiation was needed, Sisters leaving everything behind and living a penitential life of prayer and sacrifice. John Paul II's great influence lay in his sacrifice: losing his entire family at 21, suffering under two totalitarian regimes, etc. When he saw how much he gained from Parkinson's disease: he called this cross the "Gospel of Blood." St. Rose of Lima was taught by Jesus about the secret of the cross as divine love expressed in action:

> Our Lord and Saviour lifted up his voice and said with incomparable majesty: "Let all men know that grace comes after tribulation. Let them know that without the burden of afflictions it is impossible to reach the height of grace. Let them know that the gifts of grace increase as the struggles increase. Let men take care not to stray and be deceived. This is the only true stairway to paradise, and without the cross they can find no road to climb to heaven."

When I heard these words, a strong force came upon me and seemed to place me in the middle of a street, so that I might say in a loud voice to people of every age, sex and status: "Hear, O people; hear, O nations. I am warning you about the commandment of Christ by using words that came from his own lips: We cannot obtain grace unless we suffer afflictions. We must heap trouble upon trouble to attain a deep participation in the divine nature, the glory of the sons of God and perfect happiness of soul." (OOR for her feast day)

## B. Today's Propensity: Seeking Christ without the Cross (F. Sheen)

If the cross is the power of human history, then to depart from the cross signals not her death knell but the rise of decadence within the Church.

### 1. Pendulum Swinging between Holiness and Lukewarmness
Bishop Attila Miklósházy used an image to capture history's dynamic: that the Church is like a pendulum, swinging back and forth between holiness and lukewarmness. We have seen periods of decadence that were a catalyst for the Reformation and the cause of confusion and exodus from the Church after Vatican II. Bishop Fulton Sheen had clear insights into our times. He said that faith is like a fire, and that the West had the teachings, the light, but Russia, that has suffered, had the heat.

### 2. The Church in Decadence
Fulton Sheen noted of the postconciliar Church: "They want Christ but not on the cross." Cardinal Ratzinger too discerned that at Vatican II we began to talk more about ourselves than of God, so that the postconciliar Church became all about self. We have heard the mantras: "We are a resurrection people," "We are the Church." The Church saw over 62,000 priests leave the priesthood, vocations plummet, and church attendance decline. Congregations distancing themselves from the Church, sacrifice, and prayer seem to lack the power to evangelize and to attract vocations, and older congregations in the main are dying out.

## C. Returning Self-Sacrifice for Love of Christ in Six Areas

### 1. Seeking to Do God's Will and not Merely to Do Good
What is holiness? It is simply doing God's will. Jesus Himself was all about doing the Father's will. Yet most Christians are not even aware of God's will, let alone knowing how to discern God's will.

### 2. Preaching by Witness
Do we take the shortcut of trying to convert people by our preaching instead of our life, which should be a sermon. Jesus said to Dina Bélanger, "My

priests should be other Christs. Many among them possess eloquence and human learning but they lack the fundamental science, holiness." Do we rely primarily on our personality (charm), knowledge, and giving big talks? De Chardin said of his times that "we have ceased to be contagious."

### 3. Avoiding Postconciliar Culture of Niceness, Community, and Busyness
While being full of affection, saints love enough to preach the truth, for which they are attacked. And they don't seem to have much time for the social life, as we find in Fr. Marie-Joseph Lagrange, founder of the École Biblique in Jerusalem. When the Spirit possesses a soul, she cannot rest.

### 4. Self-Forgetfulness to Direct our Concern to Others
St. John Chrysostom taught: "This is the rule of most perfect Christianity, its most exact definition, its highest point, namely, the seeking of the common good.... for nothing can so make a person an imitator of Christ as *your concern for others*. Although you fast, although you sleep on the floor, even though, I dare to say, you kill yourself, if you are not attentive to your neighbour, you have done very little; you are very far from being an image of Christ" (*Commentary on the First Epistle to the Corinthians*).

### 5. Living the Mass (Calvary) as Apex of Christian Life
(a) Is Mass a mystical Calvary for us, imitating souls like Carlo Acutis, who was drawn to daily Mass and spent time before the Blessed Sacrament. "With all the strength of my soul I urge you to approach the Communion table as often as you can. Feed on this bread of angels whence you will draw all the energy you need to fight inner battles" (Pier Giorgio Frassati). (b) Will we choose a Gospel of blood, as did St. John Vianney, who spent some 15 hours in the confessional each day (80,000 penitents per year)?

> One day St. Thomas Aquinas went to visit St. Bonaventure. St. Thomas was amazed at the wonderful learning and knowledge of St. Bonaventure and asked him: "From what book have you learned your Theology?" St. Bonaventure looked at the Crucifix saying: "This is the fountain from where I get all my knowledge and from which I teach, Christ Crucified!"

### 6. Cleaving to the Three Great Loves
Fulton Sheen perceived that, when the faith in the Church is weak, two consequences follow: the Church is attacked from within (when she is strong, she is attacked from outside); and that three great realities are neglected: love of the Church, Eucharist, and Mary. We should do an examination of conscience on these three loves. "I know your deeds, that you are neither cold nor hot. I wish you were either one or the other! So, because you are lukewarm—neither hot nor cold—I am about to spit you out of my mouth" (to the Church of Laodicea, Rev 3:15-16).

# HOMILY 8

## Beatitudes: Portrait of Christ and Summit of Christian Life
(Wed. 10th Week of Ordinary Time, Sept. 13, 2017; see *Mystical Incarnation*)

The Beatitudes are a portrait of Christ, revealing His divine dispositions, and is thereby our highest perfection on earth. Our hearts should long to climb and attain these summits of divine perfection.

### 1. The Four Beatitudes were Lived by Jesus

In today's Gospel (below), Luke gives only four Beatitudes. To the four Beatitudes, by antithesis, Christ opposes as many states of misery and unhappiness. The second four are simply the reverse images of the first four (Beatitudes), but put forth as "woes," hearkening to the woes of the prophets of the Old Testament (Commentary of Cornelius à Lapide).

> And he lifted up his eyes on his disciples, and said:
> "Blessed are you poor, for yours is the kingdom of God.
> Blessed are you that hunger now, for you shall be satisfied.
> Blessed are you that weep now, for you shall laugh.
> Blessed are you when men hate you, and when they exclude you and revile you, and cast out your name as evil, on account of the Son of man! Rejoice in that day, and leap for joy, for behold, your reward is great in heaven; for so their fathers did to the prophets.
>
> But woe to you that are rich, for you have received your consolation.
> Woe to you that are full now, for you shall hunger.
> Woe to you that laugh now, for you shall mourn and weep.
> Woe to you, when all men speak well of you, for so their fathers did to the false prophets." (Lk 6:20-26)

St. Ambrose gives the reason why Luke has reduced the number to four. He was content that they should correspond to the cardinal virtues.[1]

> The *poor* exhibit temperance as they shun the vain and excessive pleasures of the world. The *hungry* display justice as they share the plight of the lowly and give to those who have little. Those who *weep* exercise prudence as they lament the vanity of temporal things and look to what is eternal. Those *hated* by men exercise fortitude because they persevere when persecuted for their faith (CCC 1805–9). (*Ignatius Study Bible*, s.v. Lk 6:20)

---

[1] Cornelius à Lapide, *The Great Commentary of Cornelius À Lapide: S. Luke's Gospel*, trans. Thomas W. Mossman, Fourth Edition, vol. 4 (Edinburgh: John Grant, 1908), 181.

This is a beautiful program for Christian life. Another commentator points out the four things that these four Beatitudes condemn:

> Our Lord here condemns four things: avarice and attachment to the things of the world; excessive care of the body, gluttony; empty-headed joy and general self-indulgence; flattery and disordered desire for human glory—four very common vices which a Christian needs to be on guard against. (*Navarre Bible*, volume on Luke, 97)

In sum, these four Beatitudes are what **Jesus lived**: poverty, thirst for our salvation, weeping over sins (Jerusalem), and despising human glory.

## 2. Eighth Beatitude is the Apex (Sharing Christ's Cross)

The last Beatitude describes the blessedness of those who are consumed by suffering for God's children. To the degree a Christian participates in the cross of Christ, to that degree he will influence others. Our Lady told St. Bernadette, "I do not promise you happiness in this world but in the next." Whenever we sense greatness and great influence in a saintly person, as in John Henry Newman, we can look to see if there is the presence of the cross in their lives, the convincing and sure mark of holiness.

Msgr. Piero Galeone, a protégé of Padre Pio, was asked by a seminarian: "Why is it that you are always smiling but Padre Pio was always so serious." His response was that "Fathers carry a bigger load than the sons" (paraphrased). Spiritual parents carry their children. The cross can be said to be John Paul II's source of greatness: his entire family died by the time he was 21 years old (mother early on, his only brother at 17, his father at 21), he endured two totalitarian regimes (with friends killed), but early on was already thinking of the world's needs (e.g., his concern for couples in his Theology of the Body; counselling a priest friend to write a thesis because of the need).

Acceding to the request of St. Augustine's Seminary, Bishop Attila Mikloshazy shared something of his saintly life: his father killed and died in his arms, arrested twice, was at a hospital when they brought in the victims and wounded after the Budapest uprising was crushed by tanks, his multiple surgeries, being appointed bishop of the diaspora Hungarians all over the world, choosing to be in exile rather than returning to his native Hungary after the iron curtain fell, unable to sleep at night during his last years, lacking visits from the many he helped. He had taught the author: "*Ama nesciri et pro nihilo reputari*" ("Love to be unknown and to be considered as nothing"); and to serve an assignment out of obedience and choose to remain there serving quietly and unrecognized for twenty or thirty years.

## 3. Test of the Beatitudes is Whether our House is Built on Rock

We can test whether we follow the path of the Beatitudes, that is, of Christ, by looking at our foundation through Jesus' parable about a house built on rock and on sand. The houses look the same, yet are vastly different. One is almost exclusively horizontal, the other is primarily vertical.

*House Built on Sand: the Superficially Horizontal Soul*
Fr. Thomas Dubay describes the modern-day inclination to the merely human. No small percentage of current "spiritual direction" is pop psychology: feeling comfortable with one's person and lifestyle; liberation from oppression; raising one's consciousness; ridding guilt feelings; getting along in a group; managing difficult relationships, etc. These directors were not proposing the radical Gospel as lived by Jesus.[2]

This approach has caused much devastation in the postconciliar Church, (see Ratzinger, Sheen). Because everything had become horizontalized, with a low sky, then everything personal and human becomes inflated and blown up: chatting, warm personality, wit, eloquence, culture, congratulating and complimenting each other. The Spirit, Jesus told St. Faustina, does not rest on a talkative soul, and her *Diary* also teaches that He does not come to us if we are superficial. Notice the remarkable transformation when one encounters God intimately in one's depths? When Augustine discovered God in the depths of his soul, he experienced **the infinite abyss of God's majesty and love**, and now he "thirsts" and "pants" for Him. "If the Lord does not build the house, in vain do its builders labour" (Ps 127:1).

*Building on Rock by Meditating Frequently on our Lord's Passion*
The saints, like St. Bonaventure, understood that looking upon the One we have pierced (Jn 19:37) brings graces to follow His path of self-immolation.

> The wound in his side is the consolation of those who are sad, the fortress for those suffering temptation, and the refuge for sinners. It is the gate by which people enter into the heart of Jesus and become sanctified. It is the mountain cleft where the badgers take refuge (see Ps 104:18), and to which those who have "wings like a dove" fly for "shelter from the raging wind and tempest".... it is the "beautiful Gate" to the real Temple of God where salvation and mercy can always be found (see Acts 3:2). "I am the gate; whoever enters through me will be saved" (Jn 10:9); God's friends have the key to that gate, the gate leading to the "cellar" in which one is inebriated with the wine of his love (see Sg 2:4). (*The Sacred Passion*, 207).

---

[2] Thomas Dubay, *Seeking Spiritual Direction: How to Grow the Divine Life Within* (Ann Arbor, MI: Servant Publications, 1993), 106.

## Synthesis: Do we Live by the Beatitudes to Consume Ourselves?

It is not enough to want to avoid being bad priests, religious, or Catholics (e.g., avoiding careerism, falling for money or fame, personal comfort, etc.). All baptized must also desire to attain the heights of sanctity, of the Beatitudes. We see a world of difference in the apostles *before and after Pentecost*. After Pentecost, they learned to forget themselves and to consume themselves for Christ's flock. Jesus remains eternally grateful to the apostles who carried the world on their shoulders. We are to be like the apostles, forgetful of self, and possessed by the Holy Spirit.

The Beatitudes were lived out perfectly by John the Baptist. Jesus' deep sorrow, affection, and gratitude are reflected in His poignant words: "Why then did you go out? To see a prophet? Yes, I tell you, and more than a prophet..." (Mt 11:9). Jesus teaches us to be moved by John's life. We see three levels of his greatness, of "the greatest born of woman." First, he lived a hidden, ascetic life in the desert and proclaimed the Messiah's coming. Even greater was that he proclaimed that he was merely a "voice," and disappears ("he must increase, I must decrease"), until he is arrested and decapitated because of petty jealousy (Herodias) and human respect (Herod) in a dungeon. His greatness here is that he is a will-o'-wisp that disappears; all focus is on His Master. But the apex is his sheer devotion: from the time he announced Christ in his mother's womb, through the silence of the desert, to his hidden death, he lived only for Christ. Jesus revealed to St. Bridget that he was one of three saints who touched His heart the most.

Let us turn to the example of the Beatitudes in Jeanne Jugan, the foundress of the Little Sisters of the Poor. What Pope John Paul II wrote for religious in *Vita consacrata* applies aptly to her: that souls who allow themselves to be seized by the love of Christ cannot help but abandon everything to follow Him. Jugan was expelled as foundress and superior general, and allowed to work in the kitchen of the motherhouse where the young nuns did not know who she was. But the subsequent generations of these nuns seeking divine help bypassed the wonderful mausoleum built for the second superior general (who was instrumental in ousting Jugan) to go to Mother Jeanne's nondescript grave to pray. The website of her congregation, Little Sisters of the Poor, offers a brief but beautiful portrait:

> ... Barely out of her teens, Jeanne felt the call of divine love. Preparing to leave home, she told her mother "God wants me for himself. He is keeping me for a work which is not yet founded." Jeanne took the road less traveled, setting out to work among the poor and forsaken in a local hospital.
> Many years went by before Jeanne discovered her vocation. Finally, one cold winter night she met Jesus Christ in the person of an elderly, blind and

infirm woman who had no one to care for her. Jeanne carried the woman home, climbed up the stairs to her small apartment and placed her in her own bed. From then on, Jeanne would sleep in the attic.

God led more poor old people to her doorstep. Generous young women came to help. Like Jeanne, they wanted to make a difference. Like her, they believed that "the poor are Our Lord." A religious community was born! There were so many old people in need of a home, so many souls hungry for love! The work rapidly spread across France and beyond.[3]

*It is the Cross that is the Brandmark of the Disciples of Christ*

We are talking about being formed according to the Gospel. It is about being possessed by the Holy Spirit, which causes dramatic changes in lifestyle, one that is incoherent or illogical to most people. When we die, Jesus will hold the Beatitudes as the standard: Blessed are you poor, hungry, who weep, when men hate and revile you, for yours is the kingdom of God.

We can clothe ourselves with acts of human charity. But St. Teresa of Jesus teaches that the friends of Christ go further to carry his brandmark (cross) out of love for Him. These are reflected in two of St. Faustina's sayings: "My good Jesus, I have only you"; "We were grafted into the Cross." In this life, we sacrifice our happiness to save God's children; it is the time for labour. We see a different countenance in all those who have learned to carry others. When we look at the face of Mother Teresa, we see one who carries much suffering and is barely able to smile. We meet Pope John Paul II, and we find a great depth and gravity in his countenance. They both carried the world on their shoulders.

The funeral oration by the hermit William Flete for St. Catherine of Siena, who consumed herself for Christ and souls, reveals her sacrifice:

> William Flete left his wood at Lecceto and went to Siena to preach the funeral sermon for Siena's greatest daughter at Saint Dominic's. "It is with hymns of joy, not with tears, that we should celebrate the death of Catherine," he began. Then he broke down and cried. After some time he continued, "Simon of Cyrene carried the Cross of our Lord for a little while; Catherine of Siena tried to carry it throughout her whole life…"[4]

---

[3] "Saint Jeanne Jugan: Her Story," Little Sisters of the Poor, accessed October 27, 2021, https://littlesistersofthepoor.org/saint-jeanne-jugan/her-story/.
[4] Louis de Wohl, *Lay Siege to Heaven* (San Francisco: Ignatius Press, 1960), 358-359.

# HOMILY 9

## Expropriation: Total Gift of Self
(27th Sunday of Ordinary Time 2015, see *Mystical Incarnation*)

### A. The Common Problem of Self-Interest

Dom Marmion, from his experience of guiding consecrated souls, became convinced of this truth: "the great cause of their troubles is that most of them think too much of themselves, and too little of Jesus and souls." Let us use a concrete example of how a spiritual director sought to lead a seminarian directee progressively to higher self-gift. When a new seminarian expressed his desire to overcome his penchant for speaking ill of others, to acquire "prudence of speech," the director pointed to a hierarchy of goods.
(i) The director asked which level he desired: basic prudence of speech (habit) to give others "understanding" from a benevolent heart, or the universal heart of Jesus that cried, "Father, forgive them for they know not what they do." The seminarian chose to seek Jesus' own heart.

(ii) The director then took this a step further with two fundamental options: "You can have two fundamental approaches to seminary formation: 90% focus on your spiritual growth and 10% on the world's needs; or 90% on the world's needs (oppressive governments, war and rape, famine, abortion, souls in Purgatory, addictions and suicide, etc.) and 10% on himself (growth in charity, chastity, zeal, etc.). He chose to focus on the world's needs.

(iii) In a third step, the director pointed out that the two choices above presupposed that he had to learn to forget himself and his issues and focus primarily on the world. Applied concretely, he can choose to be primarily focused on his divorced father's recent civil marriage, the issues with his mother and his pastor, and his spiritual growth, making them the 90% of his life. Or, when he reviews his day with God in his daily Examen Prayer, does he choose to avoid constant self-introspection about how he is doing in the spiritual life and obsessive concerns about personal or family issues? Does he choose to be like the slave who forgets his interests to think only of the Master's interests? There are two opposing cities in Augustine's *City of God*: city of God and of self.

### B. Learning to Make a Total Gift of Self

Our hearts are created to live the total pouring out of self of the Trinitarian Persons, that is expressed in marriage in the unconditional yes of couples at their wedding. For our hearts find fulfillment, not in receiving, but in making a total gift of self. In an interview with Zenit.org, Fr. Urteaga spoke about self-giving, saying "yes," within the charism of Opus Dei. He mentions that, along with Ignacio Echevarría, he was the last to whom the founder spoke directly about giving themselves to God.

> I find people very soft. But at the same time there are plenty of people doing plenty of positive things. The sort of "Yes" we're talking about is made up of daily sacrifice and self-surrender, and sometimes that demands great generosity. But it's worthwhile. In the evening, when you examine your conscience on what you've done that day, you can have a great sense of achievement. All those "Yeses" add up to a lot.[1] (J. Escrivá)

We find that this counsel of total gift of self was also given by St. Escrivá to a saintly Opus Dei member during her first visit to him, Blessed Guadalupe Ortiz de Landázuri. The generosity from saying "yes" all day is worthwhile and adds up to much at the end of day. Ultimately, to test to see if we are sanctifying work, we can look to the three goals of St. Escrivá: "we must sanctify work, sanctify ourselves in our work, and sanctify others through our work." St. Ignatius of Loyola, who sought to conquer the world for Christ, has this well-known prayer for generosity:

> O my God, teach me to be generous,
> teach me to serve you as I should,
> to give without counting the cost,
> to fight without fear of being wounded,
> to work without seeking rest,
> to labour without expecting any reward,
> but the knowledge that I am doing your most holy will.

For concrete resolutions, let us now draw from the mystical transformation in St. Augustine as described by Fr. Agostino Trapé in this area. Progress requires at least two qualities of love: being limitless and selfless (*St. Augustine: Man, Pastor, Mystic*, 302-306).

## 1. The First Mark of True Love is to Love without Limit

"If you want to be what you are not as yet, you must always be dissatisfied with what you are… be ever increasing, ever journeying, ever advancing." He who created you wants your entire being. "No measure is set for the love of God; the only measure here is *to love without measure*. We need not worry about loving him too much, we need only fear of loving him too little." He or she who stops growing becomes stunted.

---

[1] "A Lifelong Yes," St. Josemaría Escrivá, Founder of Opus Dei, December 4, 2002, http://www.josemariaescriva.info/article/a-lifelong-yes.

## 2. The Second Mark of True Love is Selflessness

If love is not selfless, it is not love. "What is not loved for its own sake is not loved." Augustine formulated this principle early in his life and always remained faithful to it. He distinguishes between two fears: servile fear, which is fear of punishment, a fear that has to do with justice and fear of loss; and chaste fear, "a fear that lasts forever; love does not remove or dismiss it but rather embraces it and clings close to it as a companion.... Chaste fear keeps us close to him; it does not disturb but strengthens us. An adulteress fears that her husband may come; a chaste wife fears his leaving her." We must love God without seeking reward. God Himself will be our reward, we shall see Him as He is. A man does not love his wife for her dowry nor a woman for what her husband can do for her.

Alvaro del Portillo, successor of St. Escrivá, gives witness to the selflessness of "disappearing" and offering oneself in sacrifice when evangelizing in a new country (this message was addressed to members in Cameroon).

> My children, you are just beginning. You are the seed sown by the Lord and you need to disappear so that in this land many souls in love with God may sprout.... Will there be difficulties? Inevitably. God always blesses with the Cross. But together with personal or collective difficulties, we will have the grace of God to overcome them and to shout with joy, "Lord, here I am because you have called me!"[2]

What is even more striking is his spirit of self-forgetfulness, here, shortly before his death, counselling the prelature's members to be always thinking of and serving others with a family concern:

> May you love each other more each day. Do not become tired of serving each other. May you lay down your lives for each other to the point of acquiring a psychological predisposition of thinking always about others. What do they need? What are they interested in? What do they like? We cannot allow the family warmth of our homes to growth cold even in the smallest degree.[3]

The International Theological Commission points to the need of total sacrifice in self-giving in the ministerial priesthood (which applies also to all baptized): to assimilate Christ's expropriation, His "being-for-others":

> On the one hand, there are an office and objective power based on an objective "*configuratio Christo Sacerdoti*" [configuration to Christ the Priest]; on the other hand, an order... requiring as close an assimilation as possible

---

[2] John F. Coverdale, Saxum: *The Life of Alvaro del Portillo* (New York: Scepter, 2014), 160.
[3] Ibid., 162.

to Christ's attitude in giving his life out of love. All priestly spirituality is governed by this postulate inherent in the ministry and made possible by the grace of the Lord.... *He shares in the "expropriation" of the Son of God, which gives him his being-for-others.* By expanding this fundamental idea, we can discover the elements of a priestly spirituality.[4]

## C. It is the Humbled Heart that Opens itself to Love

A seminary rector once shared his being edified by a seminarian deacon, seeing the 180-degree about-turn from being self-absorbed to a remarkable general openness of heart, docility to the rector's suggestions, and generosity in giving of himself. He began to change after being corrected by his spiritual director in his first year. But we often find "good" seminarians with good hearts and intentions, having common weaknesses, but happy merely with being faithful (e.g., to prayer, fidelity to study, etc.), but not an expropriation of themselves to give themselves totally to Christ (deep conversion). They tend towards mediocrity: satisfied with being good Christians, focused on their duties, but never approaching total self-gift.

We might argue, based on the lives of the saints, that it is openness of the heart that primarily determines our spiritual progress. As Christians, we tend to rely on the sense of our goodness and accomplishments, which tend to leave us lukewarm. But it is **the humbled, corrected, and even humiliated soul** who is likely to have her heart opened and softened to allow the entry of the Holy Spirit. We can compare the two hearts to a wine bottle and a large cistern open to rainfall: the bottle captures little water because of the restricted opening, but the cistern collects enough water to be piped into the house. The soul with an open heart from being humbled can receive deeply of the Spirit, as happened with a priest with an addiction and earlier promiscuous lifestyle who has become an exemplary religious.

This insight is confirmed from Fr. Thomas Dubay's experience about the degrees of receptivity he found in the context of spiritual direction:

> But in Fr. Dubay's experience, he finds that everyone assumes that they love and want truth, but "the evidence is *overwhelming that most really love their preferences and pleasures, and their own agenda.*"[5] This should give us all pause for self-examination. We should ask ourselves: "Do I want truth, all of it? Do I want holiness, or will I settle for a refined mediocrity? Do I covertly have my own agenda, rather than the Lord's?"[6] The great danger is that the

---

[4] International Theological Commission, *International Theological Commission: Texts and Documents, 1969-1985* (San Francisco: Ignatius Press, 1989), 81.
[5] Ibid., 128.
[6] Ibid., 89-90.

directee may end up directing himself: "One should honestly ask oneself: am I really seeking spiritual direction? Or am I merely looking for a soul-friend or a sympathetic ear, a sounding board— someone who is likely to affirm me or to agree with my own views?"[7] There are degrees of receptivity, and "saints are disposed for maximal effort from spiritual direction, just as they benefit thoroughly from the Church's proclamation of doctrine and morality."[8] With such a receptivity, many humble people can make great progress: "I find in my experience that these open and receptive ones, these humble and docile ones, do make steady and often remarkable progress. God loves the humble and he gives them rapid growth."[9]

## Illustration: Three Examples of Total Gift of Self

If the Holy Spirit finds that we don't cooperate with them, He will give them to someone else (St. Teresa of Jesus). Spiritual growth is not determined by strong sentimentality nor moral perfection, but by our openness of heart, above all to experience Christ's love. Pope Benedict XVI said at Msgr. Luigi Giussani's funeral homily (founder of Communion and Liberation movement): "He understood that Christianity is not an intellectual system, a packet of dogmas, a moralism; Christianity is rather an encounter, a love story; it is an event" (Milan, Feb. 24, 2005). Morals and doctrine only then grow out of this relationship. We find this in the examples of St. Dominic Savio, Chiara Corbella Petrillo, and Benedict XVI.

### *1. Example of Holiness of Youth in St. Dominic Savio*

Even before he died at the tender age of fifteen, St. Dominic Savio learned this lesson from his teacher and mentor, St. John Bosco. When coming to the Oratory for the first time, he went directly to see Don Bosco, and upon entering the ante-room that led to the latter's room, Dominic saw a sign over the door of that first room that read, "Da mihi animas, cetera tolle." St. John Bosco came in and, seeing Dominic looking at the sign, was anxious that he understand it, as it was his life's programme chosen at Ordination. The text was a saying of St. Francis de Sales and is translated, "Give me souls, take away the rest [everything else]." It emphasized that saving souls was everything for St. John Bosco, for which he was willing to lose everything and suffer poverty, persecution, and loss of reputation. Dominic did not fully understand the words, but a great desire burned in his heart, "This is what I want, this is what I want!" With time, his life began to mirror that motto with a great zeal for souls. (*Priestly Configuration*, 74)

---

[7] Ibid.
[8] Ibid., 90.
[9] Ibid., 91 (summarized in Charles Anang, *New Christ: Priestly Configuration*, 77-78).

## 2. Example of Christian Marriage in Chiara Corbella Petrillo

*The following writeup is found on the Sophia Institute Press website of a remarkable young wife and mother, whose story has been published by Sophia Institute Press, "Chiara Corbella Petrillo: A Witness to Joy." We note two additional points not mentioned here: the couple met at Medjugorje, and Chiara was drawn to the Franciscan charism and had a Franciscan spiritual director at Assisi ("Chiara" = Clare, "Francesco" (her son) = Francis).*

Chiara Petrillo was seated in a wheelchair looking lovingly toward Jesus in the tabernacle. Her husband, Enrico, found the courage to ask her a question that he had been holding back. Thinking of Jesus's phrase, "my yoke is sweet and my burden is light," he asked: "Is this yoke, this cross, really sweet, as Jesus said?" A smile came across Chiara's face. She turned to her husband and said in a weak voice: "Yes, Enrico, it is very sweet."

At 28 years old, Chiara passed away, her body ravaged by cancer. The emotional, physical, and spiritual trials of this young Italian mother are not uncommon. It was her joyful and loving response to each that led one cardinal to call her "a saint for our times."

Chiara entrusted her first baby to the blessed Virgin, but felt as though this child was not hers to keep. Soon, it was revealed her daughter had life-threatening abnormalities. Despite universal pressure to abort, Chiara gave birth to a beautiful girl who died within the hour. A year later, the death of her second child came even more quickly. Yet God was preparing their hearts for more—more sorrow and more grace. While pregnant a third time, Chiara developed a malignant tumor. She refused to jeopardize the life of her unborn son by undergoing treatments during the pregnancy. Chiara waited until after Francesco was safely born, and then began the most intense treatments of radiation and chemotherapy, but it was soon clear that the cancer was terminal.

Almost immediately after giving birth to Francesco, Chiara's tumor became terminal and caused her to lose the use of her right eye. Her body was tested, and so was her soul as she suffered through terrible dark nights. She said "yes" to everything God sent her way, becoming a true child of God. And as her days on earth came to an end, Enrico looked down on his wife and said, "If she is going to be with Someone who loves her more than I, why should I be upset?" Each saint has a special charisma, a particular facet of God that is reflected through her. Chiara's was to be a witness to joy in the face of great adversity, the kind which makes love overflow despite the sorrow from loss and death.[10]

---

[10] Charlotte Fasi, "Chiara Corbella Petrillo: *A Witness to Joy*," Sophia Institute Press, accessed December 1, 2021, https://www.sophiainstitute.com/products/item/Chiara-Corbella-Petrillo. We presume permission, as we hope by reprinting this writeup to encourage readers to look at her biography.

For more background, an excerpt of CNA is offered here, especially with remarks by the authors of Chiara's biography, that give a wider sense of her example for Christian life.

> Troisi and Paccini believe that Chiara's legacy is still living on because she gave witness to the truth that "love exists." Neither she nor Enrico were afraid of love, marriage, or of committing themselves to their family.
>
> According to the authors, the young couple showed how "the purpose of our life is to love... to be married is a wonderful thing, an adventure that opens you up to Heaven in the home."
>
> Chiara and Enrico's remarkable story is "a story of salvation in which God shows himself as a faithful God: they trust in Him and are not disappointed," they stated. However, they were quick to note that Chiara was not "an extraordinary young woman, in a way that makes her different from us." Rather, she struggled with many human fears and anxieties, especially with thoughts of pain, vomiting, and purgatory.
>
> "She had the same questions that we have, the same objections and struggles, the same fears," Troisi and Paccini noted, saying what made her different was her "capacity to cast everything on the Father, to welcome the grace needed for whatever step she had to make."
>
> With Chiara, the ordinary always became the extraordinary. Troisi and Paccini have fond memories of everyday life with the Petrillos, when a conversation about cooking chicken would end in talking about heaven. "We would share simple things like dinner, chatting, games on the rug with little Francesco... always very simple, without masks," they remembered. "But when we were together, there was no difficulty in believing that eternal life was here and now!"
>
> Chiara has been called "a saint for our times." Although her death was only five years ago, her legacy lives on and has inspired others around the world to be the same witness to joy. "Today, this joy is visible in those that lived alongside her: even if they miss her, they experience a mysterious and profound joy," Troisi and Paccini stated.
>
> "We cannot insist enough on the fact that Chiara did what she did, not trusting in her own strength, but trusting in the grace and the consolation of God... She never doubted God's faithfulness to His promise of happiness for her story."[1]

---

[1] "'A saint for our times' – the inspiring story of Chiara Corbella Petrillo," CNA, accessed December 1, 2021, https://www.catholicnewsagency.com/news/33057/a-saint-for-our-times---the-inspiring-story-of-chiara-corbella-petrillo. Again, permission is presumed.

### 3. Example of "A Theological Light" in Pope Benedict XVI

*Inside the Vatican* (March-April 2022 issue) has published a reflection on the life and influence of Joseph Ratzinger, whom the author considers to be "a light to the world" (title of one of his books). Here are three key insights.

*Theological Light*: Tracey Rowland teaches that he is a serene light that guides us in this time of confusion: "In the midst of so much chaos I often tell young students to 'keep calm and read Ratzinger.'" They will then be able to find their theological bearing (ibid. 18). Scott Hahn related that, during his arduous search that led to the Catholic faith, Ratzinger's works provided much clarity and light.

*Family as Interpretative Key*: Andrea Gagliarducci makes a perspicacious discernment that it is "family" that is a key to interpreting Benedict XVI. It begins with his close and enduring bonds with his biological family, his continued meetings with past students (creating a theological family), his familial connection with people who knew him (e.g., apartment in Rome, vacation site), the inclusion of everyone in the Congregation of the Doctrine of the Faith to be part of decisions (everyone had to be family), his genteelness and respect of freedom with those who erred (e.g., theologians; bishops amid Ireland's 2010 abuse scandal): "Benedict XVI looks beyond people's errors; he looks at people and the personal growth of each one. He holds everyone responsible.... Benedict XVI could not understand the plots and intrigue in the Vatican because there could be no such intrigue in a family. There are rivalries and disagreements, but there is also love and reciprocity." This model may well be a warm, family living out of the spirituality of communion called for by John Paul II. (Ibid., 22-23)

*Christianity is about an Encounter with a Person (Christ)*: Paschal M. Corby pinpoints love as the heart of Benedict XVI's pontificate, expressed in *Deus caritas est*, that begins thus: "*We have come to believe in God's love*.... Being Christian is not the result of an ethical choice or a lofty idea, but the encounter with an event, a Person, which gives life a new horizon and a decisive direction" (DCE 1). The encounter with Christ reveals the truth of our being and further awakens our capacity for transcendence: "Immortal life does not consist in an extension of the experiences of this life, but in a personal communion of love with God in Jesus Christ." Regarding the horizontalism addressed later, he teaches that "it is not laws of matter and of evolution that have the final say, but reason, will, love— a Person" (*Spe salvi* 5). He links hope to love, that eternal life "would be like plunging into the ocean of infinite love" (*Spe salvi* 12). He counsels that technology and organization will not resolve our problems; divine love will (Ibid., 16-17)

# HOMILY 10

## Feast of John Paul II: His Secret was the Marian Principle
(Feast day of John Paul II, 2021, see *Mystical Incarnation; New Evangelization*)

Accolades were not slow in coming after Pope John Paul II died: many dignitaries attended his funeral, some called him "John Paul the Great" (as with St. Leo and St. Gregory), and there was a chant, "*santo subito*" (a cry that he be canonized immediately). These accolades no doubt arose from his many accomplishments, such as his noted role in helping bring down the Iron Curtain. Yet his greatness may derive from an inner spring that, if one probes more deeply, has to do with his Marian Profile or Principle. We rely on Brendan Leahy's doctoral thesis on von Balthasar's Marian Profile.

### 1. The Secret of John Paul II was his Marian Profile

John Paul II's Marian Profile goes beyond his well-documented devotion: that he was greatly influenced by de Montfort's *True Devotion to Mary*, was consecrated to her, with his papal motto, *Totus Tuus*, drawn from de Montfort's work. It is captured rather by a startling statement he made: "We notice with joy **the emergence of the Marian profile of the Church that summarizes the deepest contexts of the conciliar renewal.**" Given that he saw his mission as pope as simply to implement the teachings of Vatican II and to bring the Church into the Third Millennium, this statement has enormous import. To put it simply, it has to do with von Balthasar's Marian Profile, in contradistinction to the Petrine Profile, the background of which can be found in the Trinity. The Marian Profile is simply the feminine or receiving dimension of the Son before the Father, who initiates and gives (masculine). That this Marian Profile is the secret of John Paul II was seconded by a close friend, Chiara Lubich (foundress of the Focolare movement). She notes that his motto *Totus Tuus* is a code by which he lived and that explained his Marian personality, his greatness, his human sensitivity, which elevates him, and makes him truly a genuine "servant of the servants of God."

The Spirit today points to this path. Brendan Leahy captures the vital importance of the Marian Profile, key to the renewal of Vatican II.

> Already before the Second Vatican Council… von Balthasar contended that a renewed Mariology was preparing the way for a future theology of the Church. He felt that new bases were being provided for a modern ecclesial consciousness, and this especially for the laity. In short, he wrote of a new *sentire Ecclesiae* [being Church] which was emerging, and it was

Marian. And so he could write that **Mary as model, ideal, and essence of the Church** is assuming a particular importance in today's ecclesial era.[1]

The key to understanding the Marian Principle is the mystical experience granted to von Balthasar at the age of 18. In this, God called him not to go into service or have plans, but to expropriate himself and leave himself available for God to take him up and use him. It reminds us of Mother Teresa's being "a pencil in God's hands." But we ask whether the Church today has not constantly gone in the opposite direction of this availability and expropriation, whether this is the cause of her crises?

*Trinity in Mary*
So powerful is Mary that we find the Trinitarian life manifest in her. For von Balthasar, the Trinity chose from eternity to involve Mary in the plan of redemption, and she cooperated by living the Trinity. At the Anunciation most especially, we see the revelation of the three Persons of the Trinity: the Father asking for Mary's cooperation, the Holy Spirit incarnating the Son; the Trinitarian inversion of the Son to the Spirit; and finally the Holy Spirit becoming "quasi-incarnate" in Mary. And so in her life, Mary lives the Son's same interior "yes" to the Father, her eyes only on Him and not on the many events taking place in the world, up to the end, when at Calvary she becomes "forsaken" with the "Forsaken One."

*Male, Functionalist Church*
Von Balthasar diagnoses the cause of the Church's ills today: we have become a "masculine, functionalistic" Church, that focuses on doing and not being (Christ). She now focuses on meetings, congresses, buildings, busyness. It is the perennial problem: our Lord telling Cardinal van Thuan to distinguish between God and the works of God; the diagnosis by Dom Chautard (in *Soul of the Apostolate*) in the French Church of the "heresy of good works"; or the discovery by Derek Prince, a well-known evangelical author, that we perennially rely on ourselves instead of on God, e.g., putting programs before the leading of the Holy Spirit. The trap is to live by the Petrine principle, which is God's role. The heart of the Church and Baptism is not the doing of Peter, of governing and dispensing grace through the sacraments, but the receiving of grace as with Mary; not the "doing" of Peter but the "being" of Mary. Peter, who gives grace through the sacraments, has to himself receive grace, to become Marian. John Paul II himself sees the Marian Profile as preceding the Petrine Profile. Christian baptismal holiness is first and foremost, and comes before the question of hierarchy or organization. In

---

[1] Brendan Leahy, *The Marian Principle in the Ecclesiology of Hans Urs von Balthasar* (New York: New City Press, 2000), 16-17.

heaven, what matters is not whether one is a priest or a religious but the degree of union with God. Thus there are three levels of devotion to Mary: prayer to her, imitating her, and what this Marian Principle is about, living Mary, **becoming Mary**. This happened mystically to Chiara Lubich and her companions. After feeling a deep desire to consecrate herself and her group to Mary, she requested this of Jesus after receiving Holy Communion and was granted a special transformation.

> That was not simply an act of devotion. Jesus had really transformed those young women— already fused into a single "Soul" — into another little Mary. Indeed, this group, the Soul, became aware of having "the immaculatized flesh" that contained Mary (*Living City*, March 2020, 18).

Von Balthasar highlights the tragedy arising from sidelining Mariology— for the Church's reform goes through living Mary's form:

> Without Mariology, Christianity threatens imperceptibly to become inhuman. The Church becomes *functionalistic, soulless, a hectic enterprise* without any point of rest, estranged from its true nature by the planners. And because, in this world, all that we have is one ideology replacing another, everything becomes polemical, bitter, humourless, and ultimately boring, and people in their masses run away from such a Church.[2]

## 2. The Church is to Live her Marian Form to Become Christ

In synthesis, *Mary mirrors the Son* ("Jesus and Mary are indissolubly linked") *and is the form of the Church* ("the Church is Marian in her essence"). This Marian or feminine profile of the Son overturns our whole approach in the Church, as presented in an article by Cardinal Ouellet, "Witnesses of Love": a commentary on John Paul II's discernment that the greatest challenge of the Third Millennium was to cultivate a spirituality of communion. The section titles of Cardinal Ouellet's article may represent the constituent pillars of a spirituality of communion: (i) Trinitarian origin; (ii) resulting ecclesial communion; (iii) love as prior to both contemplation and action; (iv) receptivity as a condition for communion; (v) the priority of "person"; (vi) the Eucharist accomplishing communion; and (vii) the call to become witnesses of love. These titles can provide the fundamental framework for a program of a spirituality of communion in the Church, a Marian path.

*Renewal Entails the Marian Dimension in Every Aspect of the Church*
Second, beyond the daily living of Mary, the Marian Profile has to do with the whole way and all dimensions of the Church. The Marian Profile has to

---

[2] Ibid.

do, not with Marian devotions, but with a living of the feminine or receiving of Jesus: holiness as goal, Church renewal through saints and ecclesial charisms, Mary representing baptismal holiness, theology with mysticism, ecumenism through Marian-Petrine profiles, etc. Here are two examples. (i) With regard to *theology*, after a lecture on the Trinity, we typically return to our rooms and process the Trinitarian processions in our minds. Padre Pio, in contrast, returning to his cell, would fall on his knees and become ravished by the ineffable Trinitarian furnace of love; his theology became a dialogue between the Bridegroom (Christ) and soul, and was a "kneeling theology," not a head trip. (ii) Regarding *evangelization*, we get caught up with an analysis of the world's and the Church's issues and seek to come up with techniques and programs of evangelization, such as focusing on the efficacious tool of rhetoric in St. Augustine. But the real key to St. Augustine's efficacy is holiness and the infused knowledge flowing from it applied to rhetoric. St. Thomas Aquinas' secret is not Aristotle but also his holiness and infused knowledge applied to the framework of Aristotle. This is the Marian core.

For von Balthasar, neither Church documents (like the new 2016 *Ratio Fundamentalis* for seminary formation), nor the Magisterium, nor the theologians, convert the Church. It was St. Francis of Assisi, the beggar, the one most like Christ, who was told: "Francis, go and rebuild my church which, as you see, is falling down." This is the Marian dimension of holiness that von Balthasar speaks of, where there is a "breath-taking adventure," "explosive or regenerative energies" and the founders and others, who have a special mission from God, proceed "*like lightning from heaven and light up some unique point of God's will for the Church*" (as we see with St. Francis, St. Dominic, St. Ignatius, and in today's ecclesial charisms).

## 3. From the Marian Soul the Spirit Overflows to the World

One can say that the Marian Principle revolves around the Holy Spirit. The secret of Jesus on earth was the Holy Spirit, who possessed Him, and of whom He became a vessel at His Baptism to be pierced on Calvary to release the Holy Spirit. The secret of Mary is, as St. Gabriel the archangel revealed to her, that she was "full of grace." But grace is primarily uncreated grace, who is the Holy Spirit. What we have been created to become are *theophoroi*, "God-bearers," God's "heavens" on earth. Thus, our hearts are like vessels, and saints are those who are filled with the Holy Spirit, until He overflows from them to the world. What most in the Church attempt to do is acquire a little of the Holy Spirit and then go around trying to evangelize. What our people need is not the priest or his personality or his human gifts, but the Holy Spirit overflowing from his soul. Our people need God!
*Key is to be Filled with the Holy Spirit*

All this is to say that we have to allow the Holy Spirit to dominate once more as He did in the Acts of the Apostles. The secret of the first Christian martyr, Stephen, was that he was "full of the Holy Spirit" through which his vision pierces to the heavens: "But he, full of the Holy Spirit, gazed into heaven and saw the glory of God, and Jesus standing at the right hand of God" (Acts 7:54). The apostles were transformed at Pentecost when they were filled with the Holy Spirit. We perceive the vast role of the Spirit in the Acts of the Apostles, e.g., His taking charge, moving the apostles around like chess pieces: "Set apart for me Barnabas and Saul [Paul] for the work to which I have called them" (Acts 13:2); guiding them to choose Judas's replacement: "Lord, who knowest the hearts of all men, show which one of these two thou hast chosen to take the place in this ministry and apostleship from which Judas turned aside, to go to his own place" (Acts 1:24-25). The Holy Spirit must reign in the Church, He is the Gift Jesus died to give and is the answer to all the problems in the Church.

*Emptiness to Allow Entry of Holy Spirit*
What is needed from us? The wrong direction is to be thinking primarily of techniques and programs of evangelization (good, but secondary). The reliance on our human gifts is the one thing that hinders the entry of the Holy Spirit. What He seeks is the emptiness of Mary ("for He has looked with favour on the *lowliness* of his servant"). When He finds this emptiness (lowliness), He fills us with Himself, and overflows from us into the world. Our people want and need God. It is this emptiness that allows the *summum* of love to be poured from the Trinity into Mary, and through her into the world (von Balthasar). It is the first pillar that our Lord taught St. Catherine of Siena, self-knowledge, "My daughter, you are she who is not, I am he who is," the deep sense of her nothingness. It is the secret of St. John the Baptist ("He must increase, but I must decrease," Jn 3:30) and the hidden Holy Family, from whom grace (Holy Spirit) was issued into the world.

*The Spirit is the Still-Unknown Secret of Renewal in the Church*
The opposite is what Jesus complained of to Blessed Dina Bélanger, that "my priests are learned and eloquent, but they lack the fundamental discipline: holiness," that is, they lacked the Holy Spirit. Our people do not need the warm personality, knowledge, and human gifts of "Father John." The episode is recounted of a priest doing a doctorate on psychology, and, while visiting Madonna House, waxed effusively and interminably about it, to which the foundress, Catherine Doherty, twice slammed the table and cried out, "Give them God!" (our people need God first). As God needed a "void" to create the universe (Gen 1), He needs a void in us to re-create Christ. But the facilitator is Mary, the path is Marian through the Spirit.

# HOMILY 11

## Mediation: Being Formed in the Father's Womb by Mentors
(Sunday December 1, 2019; see *Mystical Incarnation*)

A popular saying teaches, "It is not about the destination, but about the journey." For Christianity, it is primarily about the destination (heaven); yet how we live our journey will determine our destination. Today's Advent Mass readings (e.g., the Psalms, Isaiah) are all about living our journey so as to prepare for Christ's coming at Christmas and especially at the eschaton. St. Charles Borromeo in today's Office of Readings (OOR) focuses more on the goal: that Jesus is born in Bethlehem so that our hearts become mangers, new Bethlehems, for Jesus. He teaches us how to allow Christ to come spiritually into our hearts. This is what St. John the Baptist means in today's Gospel when he says, "Prepare the way of the Lord," so that "all flesh will see the salvation of God," even during the journey now.

> Prepare the way of the Lord, make straight his paths.
> Every valley shall be filled; and every mountain and hill shall be brought low; and the crooked shall be made straight; and the rough ways plain;
> And all flesh shall see the salvation of God. (St. John the Baptist in Mt 3)

Our experience is that growing up and finding our vocation in today's world can be very difficult. As youths, we may get caught up in the party scene or confused by what our peers, teachers, and media affirm, including on moral issues. It can be hard to know what to do with our lives. As the question goes, "So how is that working out for you?" Our conscience, good work ethic or family upbringing can assist, but it can still feel as if we are trying to climb out of a dark hole. When the light of Christ shines (e.g., from Scripture, lives of saints, personal conversion), our world becomes new and looks different. But it is especially living saintly mentors who can become our rock, and when we cling to them, they help us to break out, like a caterpillar becomes a butterfly. One American seminarian found in the Franciscan Friars of the Renewal a home and lifeline.

### 1. The Father's Paternity is Re-presented in an Economy of Mentors

Holy souls see that the Father's love accompanies us through His **mentors**. We see that the Father prepared directly the way for Jesus, who was led every step of the way, even to Egypt and back, waiting in Nazareth till the word came to him. His point of reference was the Father: "I have shown you many good works from the Father; for which of these do you stone me?" (Jn 10:32). John's life too was providentially arranged, right up to his martyrdom. Their path can be likened to being formed in a womb, of being mentored or fathered *directly* by God. Even after Jesus' death, as we see in the Acts of the Apostles, it was the Spirit directing the Church.

But both Jesus and John initiated a new path for us, becoming mentors to their disciples or apostles, becoming extensions of the Father. We see that this has been the perennial pattern of the Church, beginning with the Desert Fathers. We find disciples with many recognizable great figures, like St. Catherine of Siena, St. Philip Neri, St. Ignatius of Loyola, St. John of the Cross, St. Francis de Sales, and Blessed Columba Marmion.

This mediation path was preached by a parish priest in a homily that inspired a parishioner to seek a spiritual director (shared with author).

> Our life is too short to put it to the test, to experiment with it.... There is no second chance. We have to decide who to follow and who to trust... I follow people who have this path already behind them— Paul the Apostle, Augustine of Hippo, Francis of Assisi, Teresa of Calcutta. I follow them....
> The discussion of today's Gospel teaches first that in life we cannot go down this path by ourselves, we need a guide.
> The second thing is that on this path we need wisdom to choose a good guide.
> And the third thing is that during the latter part of our journey, it will be essential to be faithful to the guide we have chosen. Why does a faithful person, following the saints, not have to worry about making a mistake? It is because they followed Christ, and He was their guide. (priest homilist unknown)

This parish priest has given an incisive summary of the three key points: to find a guide, to choose a holy guide, and to be faithful to the Spirit's instructions through him. We will review later the wrong approach of a visiting religious priest professor on sabbatical struggling immensely in the spiritual life. His main problem was that he was *flying solo, unguided, doing his own thing*: had late retiring (3 am) and rising times (11 am), and was very erratic in his prayer life. He chose to bypass a city where there was a renowned center for the theologian he chose to specialize in for his doctorate. This unguided religious priest did not have strong formative influences, and chose two theologians who were brilliant but had difficulties in obedience or orthodoxy (supporters claim that they laid the foundation for dissent against Church teaching). The author suggested that he should look to theologians who are also *saints*, as three priests in this diocese did who began in the seminary to study Newman, or John Paul II who was formed by the spirituality of, and wrote a doctoral thesis on, St. John of the Cross.

## 2. Not Walking Alone: Being Formed by the Father's Spiritual Guides

Cardinal Arinze shared that, when Pope John Paul II's representative pushed him to choose whether he wanted to go to Rome to work in a Roman dicastery or remain in Nigeria, he refused to choose, because he sought not his will but only God's will— and this would be indicated by John Paul II's decision. A priest from St. Augustine's Seminary asked to obtain a doctorate also chose to be guided: sent to Rome by his bishop, told to live with brother priests at the Canadian College, and the Gregorian University was recommended as the strongest for systematic theology. Following these counsels, he also listened to his spiritual director in studying Aquinas for his first thesis, and when he switched to the Church Fathers for his doctorate with permission, he heeded the advice of both his archbishop and thesis director to not specialize in St. Augustine because of time constraints. In each step, this priest was guided.

One is led above all by a spiritual director. John Paul II explains why spiritual direction, which takes much time, is so vital— because each person is destined for Trinitarian communion. Jesus Himself taught St. Faustina: "Your spiritual director and I are one. He is the veil behind which I am hiding. His words are my words." Reginald Garrigou-Lagrange makes an analogy to climbing a mountain: "Everyone knows that a guide is needed in order to climb a mountain without difficulty. The same thing happens when it is a matter of a spiritual climb… and even more so in that one must avoid pitfalls set by the devil, who dearly wants to bring us down."[1]

The principle is to *not walk alone*: "Woe to him who is alone when he falls and has not another to lift him up" (Eccles 4:10). We want to avoid the path of a Ronin, a Japanese mercenary for hire, who were looked down upon in that culture. In our life, do we go solo or seek counsel regarding deciding whether to get married, discerning a consecrated vocation or what to do this summer, deciding upon a great theologian mentor or new year resolutions. It is the critical economy of mediation.

*Theological Mentors*
We find an outstanding example of being theologically mentored in the life of Pope Benedict XVI. He had many formative influences in his life, formed as it were, within the tradition or womb of the Church. He was formed by the early liturgies of the Church, influenced spiritually by St. Benedict and Luigi Giussani and theologically by saintly theologians and key professors,

---

[1] Reginald Garrigou-Lagrange, *The Three Ages of the Interior Life: Prelude of Eternal Life*, vol. 1 (Rockford, IL: Tan, 1947).

and wrote theses on Augustine and Bonaventure. Besides the theological influence of Newman, he wrote this of von Balthasar and de Lubac: "Never again have I found anyone with such a comprehensive theological and humanistic education as Balthasar and de Lubac, and I cannot even begin to say how much I owed to my encounter with them."[2]

## 3. We Choose to Live as the Father's Child or as a Free Agent (Ronin)

What is the worst thing in the spiritual life: it is to **walk alone**. Robert Hugh Benson teaches that heretics are usually ones who have received some special insights in the Illuminative Stage of the interior journey. But they then turn inwards, relying on their own spiritual interior lights, and this often led to schism from the Church. St. Francis of Assisi went to the Pope for approval of his spiritual charism. Cardinal Ratzinger stayed in Rome at the request of Pope John Paul II, and after his retirement, lived in Rome virtually as a monk because he believes it is the will of God. More generally, saints place themselves within wombs: St. Thérèse of Lisieux was formed especially by St. John of the Cross, after which she can be creative and further develop his teaching, because she has stood on the shoulders of a giant. St. Augustine's Seminary has been blessed to have Bishop Miklósházy for over 20 years. His presence with his influence may mirror that of the presence and influence of the saintly priest, Fr. Walter Ciszek (author of "*With God in Russia*") after his return from Russia. We follow the wisdom of the song, "You never walk alone." We can choose to have spiritual fathers and be sons and daughters (mediation), or be spiritual Ronins.

We can add here the tremendous influence of a fatherly figure like Luigi Giussani (e.g., he influenced Fr. Aldo Trento). Giussani himself had been guided, reading all of J. H. Newman's works. The national coordinator of Communion and Liberation, John Zucchi (translated *The Religious Sense* into English), described how Giussani taught him not to be concerned about apostolate so much as to first have the experience of the exceptional presence of Christ, through which Christ would do all (see a fine introduction to CL in *Communion and Liberation: A Movement in the Church*):

> I kept asking Fr. Giussani whether I should try going to the chaplaincy or visiting diocesan offices to "recruit" people for the community (I had no idea!), and I thought these were great ideas. He would always respond, "if it's important for you, for your life, by all means [do so]." In other words, he did not care about my starting a community as an activity; he wanted me to live a Christian experience, as Christ would bring that community about and not my activism. (from personal email, permission granted)

---

[2] Tracey Rowland, "The Newman of our Era," *Inside the Vatican*, March-April 2022, 18.

## Appendix: Overview of the Sacramental Economy

A sacrament is defined as "an outward sign of an inward grace," a "mystery" of divine-human structure by which we encounter God. As a divine spouse, God desires to pour His grace out to unite us to Himself. Unlike angels, man has a body through which the soul encounters the world, and thus God chooses to meet him according to his structure through the body. The highest meeting is through God's Son becoming a man, with a divine-human ("sacramental") structure. Those who met Jesus met God, received His grace, and were united to God through His humanity as a "conjoined instrument." Thus, Jesus as a visible sacrament is like Jacob's ladder (by which the angels ascended and descended) for powerful encounters with God. This mediation structure of encounter with God is what we call the sacramental economy (contrary to Luther's vision of God meeting us directly in our hearts without mediation— like a stork bringing babies from heaven rather than through procreation by parents).

(1) The sacramental economy is built upon Christ, the "primordial sacrament" of the Father, the milieu of God's acceptance and man's response, through whom we have redemption. (2) Giving birth to the Church from His side on the cross as High Priest (or as the mystical body of Christ the Head), the Church in turn becomes a "universal sacrament of salvation." As Christ's continued presence in the world, the Church in a visible way is a sign of the Father's new covenant (interiorly and exteriorly) and of His unconditional love, the meeting place with Him, that is infallibly efficacious (she acts *ex opere operato*). (3) The Church's highest action is through the seven sacraments, that make present Christ's past mysteries, which are also celebrated in the heavenly liturgy. Conformed to the seven sacraments, (4) each person is to become a "sacrament" of Christ or Christ Himself, renewing Christ in the world, as we see powerfully in the saints.

Thus, in this sacramental (divine-human) economy, God the Father is present to the world in His risen Son's presence, Christ is present to the world in His Mystical Body, encounters us in His sacraments, dwells in us through the indwelling Spirit, who makes us "sacraments" of Christ to the degree we allow Him to invade us. For we are to become "another Christ, Christ Himself," a mystical incarnation, continuing His presence. God chooses to engage the entire family (e.g., a child is formed by the wider family, teachers, priests), but only in this life until we are transformed into Christ. As it were, God floods the world to make many "sacraments" for encounter with Him: Christ, Church, seven sacraments, Scripture-Tradition-Magisterium, angels, saints, parents, teachers, priests, shrines, etc. We have Christ "in our midst," *Emmanuel*, in many presences (*Sacrosanctum concilium* n. 7) : "I am with you always, to the close of the age" (Mt 28:20).

# HOMILY 12

## Father's Love: Obtaining all as the Father's Child
(Saturday of 32nd Week of Ordinary Time, Year II)

Today's Gospel reading preaches Jesus' counsel to persevere, using the example of the persistent woman obtaining her request from the unjust judge. An initial reading of the Gospel might suggest merely that we have to persevere in our petitions to God. But when we set it within the teaching of the whole Gospel and of our mystical Tradition, we find that this very confidence constitutes the *core* of our relation to God. For we have the greatest gift of divine filiation to the Father through Baptism in the power of the Holy Spirit of sonship and our response to this unconditional love of the Father is to, as it were, sit on His lap, allowing Him to prepare everything, and accept whatever He allows to happen in His providence.

### 1. "Perfect Confidence" is the Heart of the Spiritual Life

The centrality of today's Gospel teaching strikes us when we remember the example of Christ: how He allowed the Father to prepare everything till His ministry (e.g., mother's immaculate conception, His divine conception and birth in Bethlehem, fleeing to Egypt and returning, etc.); how He waited for the Father to send the help of angels in the desert and in Gethsemane; how the Father provided all during His ministry; and especially in throwing Himself into the Father's arms in the dreadful darkness of Calvary, "Into your hands, I commend my spirit." We find Jesus' teaching on this confidence sprinkled throughout the Gospels (e.g., the Sermon on the Mount's teaching us not to worry about what we are to eat or wear, as the Father knows all our needs). Perhaps the greatest teaching of this confidence flows from our sharing of His sonship through our Baptism; that we have God as Father, who never fails His child, as it was with Jesus.

We can go further to the profound insight of the saints. To summarize their trust, we might turn to the beautiful prayer of St. Claude de la Colombière of "Perfect Confidence."

> Let others seek happiness in their wealth, in their talents; let them trust in *the purity of their lives, the severity of their mortifications, in the number of their good works, the fervor of their prayers; as for me, O my God, in my very confidence lies all my hope.* "For You, O Lord, singularly have settled me in hope." This confidence can never be in vain. "No one has hoped in the Lord and has been confounded." I am assured, therefore, of my eternal happiness, for I firmly hope in it and all my hope is in You. "In You, O Lord, have I hoped; let me never be confounded."

This is a remarkable insight into the heart of spiritual life. It is synthesized in the motto inscribed at the bottom of the Divine Mercy image, "Jesus, I trust in you." All good comes from this trust in Jesus; and, conversely, what wounds Jesus the most, as revealed to St. Faustina, is the lack of trust in His love for us. We can imitate the daring of St. Angela Merici in her apostolate: "Do something, get moving, risk new things, stick with it, get on your knees, then be ready for big surprises." Similarly, St. Teresa Benedicta of the Cross taught: "Just take everything exactly as it is, put it in God's hands, and leave it with him. Then you will be able to rest in him— really rest." For it is to God's weak but reliant child that all is given. This path turns our human common sense upside-down. For our Pelagian tendencies incline towards our own striving, acquisition, and conquest, reflecting of the Ascetical Mansions, but not the Mystical Mansions that require surrender.

## 2. St. Thérèse's Confidence in God the Father's Care

*Being a Child before God*
This truth is wonderfully elaborated and illustrated in the spiritual childhood of St. Thérèse of Lisieux. She has a rather unique path and unique logic that goes against our grain and our natural instinct. With divine intuition, she realized that, if she grew up, God the Father would no longer look after everything for her, just as parents allow their children to look after themselves once they are grown up. Using this logic, she resolved to always remain little, so that the Father would have to do everything for her. Let us illustrate with specific examples of a path at which most of us would balk. Where most attribute their human gifts to themselves, she saw that all talents belong to God, and she would borrow them and after use return them to God; where most become proud of their human accomplishments, she warned her sister, "stay away from everything that shines" (as St. Claude de la Colombière taught that, when we are praising each other, we are stealing from the glory that belongs to God); where most are Pelagian in seeking to earn our salvation and God's favour, she said that, at death, she would be too small to merit anything and would just rely on the Father's love and mercy. Her path was simply Jesus' own path, who experienced the Father's unconditional love, "You are my Son, the Beloved," and who relied on divine Providence for everything: food, clothing (Calvary revealed that His only possession was one garment), daily inspirations, even the coin from the fish's mouth to pay a tax. He taught us what He Himself lived, for the Father knows all that we need.

*God's Child through Baptism*
At the heart of all this is not the being "little" of a child, but specifically about being God's little "beloved *son or daughter*." What cherished child does not

know that the love of his parents is unconditional, and how much greater must this awareness be regarding the Father's love. Let us illustrate this with an example a spiritual director once gave the author. During a very turbulent stage on a flight in which it appeared that the plane was in imminent danger, a man, struck by the calm and composure of a boy sitting beside him, asked, "Are you not afraid?" The boy replied, "No. My daddy is the pilot." Sisters of the very sick St. Thérèse approached her to express concern. She replied simply that God the Father knew what was best.

## 3. Living Confidence in the Father's Paternity

Many Christians beset by troubles, like when their grownup children no longer practice the faith, or even worse, have entered into unsafe or immoral areas, like occult dabbling or homosexual relationships, may look to our Lady but yet remain deeply and constantly troubled, weighed down in their thoughts by these heavy concerns. What this path of "perfect confidence" teaches is that our Lady now takes over. She loves our dear ones with a much greater love than parents' love, for she is their Mother in the order of grace. St. Teresa of Jesus lived by this saying: "Let nothing disturb you, let nothing frighten you. All things are passing. Patience obtains all things. He who has God has everything— God alone suffices." She also said that "You pay God a compliment by asking great things of him." Jesus taught St. Faustina that what we get is a function of what we hope for: the more we hope for, the more we get. Paul condemned the opposite direction of the self-justification of the Pharisees, so preoccupied with external norms. Jesus, in contrast, replied, "Why do you call me good. Only God is good." In the Sermon on the Mount, He taught us how to be a child, for our Father is truly and ontologically our Father through Baptism. The great Trinitarian bonds and graces we receive begin with the bestowal of Baptism:

> I ask you now to pay close attention, for I want to return to that fountain of life and contemplate its healing waters at their source. The Father of immortality sent his immortal Son and Word into the world; he came to us men to cleanse us with water and the Spirit [Baptism]. To give us a new birth that would make our bodies and souls immortal, he breathed into us the spirit of life and armed us with incorruptibility. Now if we become immortal, we shall also be divine; and if we become divine after rebirth in baptism through water and the Holy Spirit, we shall also be coheirs with Christ after the resurrection of the dead.
> Therefore, in a herald's voice I cry: Let peoples of every nation come and receive the immortality that flows from baptism. This is the water that is linked to the Spirit, the water that irrigates Paradise, makes the earth fertile, gives growth to plants, and brings forth living creatures. In short, this is the water by which a man receives new birth and life, the water in which even

Christ was baptized, the water into which the Holy Spirit descended in the form of a dove. (St. Hippolytus, OOR, Jan. 4)

## Appendix: Baptism's Ineffable Dimensions

We see the beauty of divine filiation when we consider the profound dimensions of Baptism ("Sacramental Theology" notes of A. Miklósházy).[1]

- *Theological dimension* reveals that God shares His divine life and makes us His children. He enters into a covenant and irrevocably commits Himself to us, never withdrawing His love for us.

- *Christological dimension* describes how we are engrafted into Christ, so that He can live His life in us. We are assimilated, configured to Him, in order to fulfill our primary vocation of bringing everything in unity in Him (recapitulation of Eph 1). We become members of His Body, "*filii in Filio*" [sons in Son], enabled to offer our life in, with, and through Him to the Father.

- *Pneumatological dimension* depicts the marvellous work of the Holy Spirit. Through Baptism, we become the temple of the Holy Spirit, because He is dwelling in our hearts. The Holy Spirit makes us God's children, configures us to Christ, and unites us in "koinonia" (κοινωνια, communion) within the Church. The Spirit teaches us to pray, to worship, and to live our "spiritual" life.

- *Ecclesial dimension*: Through Baptism, the Church acquires new members, grows, and is built up into the Body of Christ. Our baptismal faith is primarily the faith response of the Church as a community addressed by God's gracious call. Baptism is the basis for the missionary activity of the Church (AGD 7), for the apostolate of the laity (AA 3), and for Christian education (GE 2).

- *Anthropological dimension*: Baptism snatches us away from the power of evil by remitting our sins. It gives us the principle of new and divine life. This life of faith, hope, and love arises from our baptismal grace and should characterize our journey toward God, to Whom we committed ourselves through our baptismal vows. Baptism, which requires by its nature our personal sanctification, consecrated us to permanent holiness.

- *Eschatological dimension*: Baptism marks us forever with an indelible seal and admits us into the kingdom of God, which is already here but not yet complete. But we have the pledge of our future redemption and salvation when we become the heirs of heaven. Meanwhile we are obliged to work for the realization of the kingdom here on earth.

---

[1] A. Miklósházy, "Sacraments of Initiation," Sacramental Theology II: SAT 2432HS (lecture, Toronto School of Theology at the University of Toronto, Toronto, Ontario, 1978).

# PART II

# RETREATS: STRUCTURE (ASCENT)

O abyss! O eternal Godhead! O deep sea! What more could you have given me than the gift of your very self? You are a fire always burning but never consuming; you are a fire consuming in your heat all the soul's selfish love; you are a fire lifting all chill and giving light. In your light you have made me know your truth: You are that light beyond all light who gives the mind's eye supernatural light in such fullness and perfection that you bring clarity even to the light of faith. In that faith I see that my soul has life, and in that light receives you who are Light....
Truly this light is a sea, for it nourishes the soul in you, peaceful sea, eternal Trinity. Its water is not sluggish; so the soul is not afraid because she knows the truth. It distills, revealing hidden things, so that here, where the most abundant light of your faith abounds, the soul has, as it were, a guarantee of what she believes. This water is a mirror in which you, eternal Trinity, grant me knowledge; for when I look into this mirror, holding it in the hand of love, it shows me myself, as your creation, in you, and you in me through the union you have brought about of the Godhead with our humanity.[1] (St. Catherine of Siena)

---

[1] St. Catherine of Siena, *The Dialogue, The Classics of Western Spirituality* Series, Suzanne Noffke, trans. (Toronto: Paulist Press, 1980), n. 177, 365.

## II. RETREATS (ASCENT)

1. Retreat 1: Towards Mystical Incarnation and Marriage (5 Conf.)
2. Retreat 2: Mystical Incarnation as Lived by St. Joseph (4 Themes)
3. Retreat 3: Ecclesial Preparations for Mystical Transformation (6 Conf.)

Within Church: Path to Mystical Union/Incarnation
Retreat 1 attempts to outline the **entire edifice** for the spiritual life: from St. Catherine of Siena's two pillars of (1) self-knowledge and (2) looking to Jesus' love, (3) through being led by the Holy Spirit, and finally (4) living the cross that leads to (5) Trinitarian communion of love. This edifice for mystical union allows us to see the end goal, to present first our destiny so as to explain the journey in the other two retreats.

Model of St. Joseph
Retreat 2 illustrates this edifice as **concretely lived out** by St. Joseph, especially through his filial abandonment.

World: Christ's Recapitulation to Bring the World to the Father
Retreat 3 turns to elements to prepare the terrain for this edifice: (1) the outpouring of the Holy Spirit; (2) rising above the contemporary horizontalism to find God; (3) the Church having the right to evangelize to make this possible; (4) but this requires a reform within the Church through the Marian Profile; and also (5) to recover the Church as communion, our true identity as beloved children of God (Baptism); (6) all can be summarized in a panorama of how Christ's grace spreads universally into history and the world.

*Note regarding Retreat 1 Conferences*
These talks arose from the seminary rector asking the author to give five talks to the seminarians in September 2021. Rather than composing entirely new themes, the author decided to synthesize the recently published "Mystical Incarnation," as well as material from the earlier three books. Thus these five talks of Retreat 1 draw significantly and liberally from these four works.

# RETREAT 1
# 5 CONFERENCES

Table of Contents

Retreat 1 attempts to draw out an outline of the major elements of the spiritual journey for mystical union and incarnation, given here in five steps. The first two steps employ the two pillars of St. Catherine of Siena of self-knowledge of our poverty before God (foundation) and of fixing our eyes on Jesus' love and holy will (apex). The third step outlines the path from this foundation to the apex as taught in the vein of St. Teresa of Jesus and St. John of the Cross, highlighting especially the surrender needed for holiness. The fourth and fifth steps represent the two summits: on earth of pain and in heaven of love.

While drawing from all four earlier books, Retreat 1 conferences constitute especially a practical synthesis of *Mystical Incarnation*. The first three Talks end up drawing out the physiognomy of Christ, the last two depict the interior dispositions of Christ that match the new altar emblem at St. Augustine's Seminary (Sacred Heart with fire of love and with thorns).

<u>Physiognomy of Christ</u>
1. First Pillar of St. Catherine of Siena: self-knowledge, the secret of weakness (e.g., St. Paul) that allows God to act.
2. Second Pillar of St. Catherine: our eyes on Jesus through the Sacrament of the Present Moment (J.-P. de Caussade).
3. From "our living in God" to "God living in us": Jesus obeying the Father's will.

<u>Summits of Cross and Love</u>
4. Cross: Pain is the highest reality on earth, to co-redeem the world. Being consumed with zeal gives the desire to suffer.
5. Love: Love is the highest reality in heaven. Being consumed with love makes one seek union.

# Retreat 1: Towards Mystical Incarnation and Marriage

## Conference 1
## The First Pillar of St. Catherine of Siena

### I. The Foundation of Self-Knowledge (St. Catherine of Siena)

The doctrine of St. Catherine of Siena was chosen for this spiritual edifice because of her significant impact on the Church, both ecclesially and spiritually, and because of her insights as a doctor of the Church. St. Catherine is probably best known as the one who helped restore the papacy from Avignon to Rome in the 14th century. But, along with St. Teresa of Avila, St. Thérèse, and St. Hildegard of Bingen, she stands out as one of only four female doctors of the Church, despite her having written only one work, *The Dialogue of Providence* (which consists mainly of God speaking to her in a dialogue), though there are also some extant letters. So powerful was her saintliness, dominant persona, and teaching that many sought her guidance and some became her spiritual children or disciples, in person or by correspondence. Spiritual writers generally acknowledge that self-knowledge, the first pillar, is the foundation of the entire spiritual life *New Christ: Divine Filiation* synthesizes St. Catherine of Siena's two foundation pillars of the entire spiritual life for everyone and of this talk: (A) knowledge of my poverty or nothingness before God; and (B) fixing our sight on Jesus, "Think of me and I will think of you." This conference focuses primarily on her first pillar or foundation of the entire spiritual life: self-knowledge.

### A. "You are she who is not; whereas I am He who is"

St. Catherine reveals that it was Christ Himself who taught her these two pillars in private revelation. The first teaching concerned knowledge of self, "self-knowledge." During the three years of her personal formation by our Lord, Catherine's experience of God evolved based upon what Christ taught her about the foundational relation between creatures and Creator, or, more specifically, knowledge of herself and knowledge of God. It was presented in the following profound statement:

> Do you know, daughter, who you are, and who I am? If you know these two things, you will be blessed. You are she who is not; whereas I am He who is. Have this knowledge in your soul and the Enemy will never deceive you and you will escape all his wiles; you will never disobey my commandments and will acquire all grace, truth and light.[1]

---

[1] Blessed Raymond of Capua, *The Life of St. Catherine of Siena* (Rockford, Illinois: Tan, repr. 2003), 79. A fine narrative-style biography is Louis de Wohl's *Lay Siege to Heaven* (San Francisco: Ignatius Press, 1991).

"You are she who is not; whereas I am He who is." Here we see a reiteration and perhaps even a deepening of the great revelation to Moses, when he asked, "Who should I say is sending me?" And Yahweh revealed who He was in that lofty and dense statement, a statement full of awe, "I am who I am" (Ex 3:14). God is being or existence itself, possessing all the attributes of being, including beauty, truth, and justice.

Igino Giordani's (co-founder of the Focolare charism) biography elaborates upon the depth of this revelation: "Catherine's ascent to God is all in this truth: all her enlightenment came from this discovery; her teaching and the secret of her power in dealing with souls proceeded from this idea…"[2]

> With that lesson Catherine became fundamentally learned: she was founded upon a rock; there were no more shadows. *I, nothing; God All. I, nonbeing; God, Being*….
> For Catherine this was a discovery so memorable that from then on, she explained it to everyone who would listen… The discovery enabled the girl from Fontebranda to remove the barricade of egoism which always impedes progress….
> This humiliating of herself, this weeping, this annihilation of herself in the conviction of her nothingness, all served to purify Catherine's soul of every shadow, to make it a limpid crystal, an absolute void through which the light of God passed unhindered.
> …. The answer [to her greatness despite her simplicity] is evident: she succeeded in being no longer herself, so that Christ might live in her; because becoming completely humble, she was, like Mary, a handmaid of the Lord, a void which the spirit of God made full of grace. And this divine grace made her godlike.[3]

## Delineating Several Foundational Elements

It is helpful to delineate its foundational elements. First, all her enlightenment and power and secret proceeded from this truth, and with it, she was now "founded upon a rock," she could not be misled. Second, this truth could be synthesized thus: "*I, nothing; God All. I, nonbeing; God, Being.*" This knowledge enabled her to detach herself from the world of nonbeing, realizing its transience and contingency, establishing her nothingness before and her dependence on God. Third, in this knowledge of her nothingness, she sought annihilation of self, to open herself to be filled with God's being, which made her "godlike." These three dimensions reveal the tremendous power of this truth of self-knowledge that God revealed to her. This first foundation stone constitutes the absolute foundation of all Christian life, establishing at the outset the primordial relationship between God the Creator and his creatures.

---

[2] Igino Giordani, *St. Catherine of Siena* (Boston, MA: Daughters of St. Paul, 1980), 35.
[3] Ibid., 36-37.

Once this objective relationship is correctly established, the subjective intimacy with the Creator can develop.

Second, we must make a critical distinction, to avoid an erroneous sense of self-knowledge. This knowledge of our poverty is not a certain offhand putting myself down, "Oh, I am such a miserable sinner." It is not about my existing at a very low grade in the order of reality, being nothing special. What is being spoken of here is an ontological poverty in relation to God. There is an utterly infinite chasm that separates the creature from the Creator, who is existence itself, who has brought all into existence by His Word. The Scholastic philosophy of St. Thomas Aquinas, drawing from the teachings of Aristotle, captures this reality by teaching that God is *"esse subsistens,"* "subsistent being," being itself, and all creatures receive and participate in the being of God.

Third, the importance of this overarching self-knowledge cannot be overemphasized. This first truth of knowledge of our nothingness before— and dependence on— God is reflected strongly in the very self-abasement in Christ and His Mother in Scripture. Though He is God, as Philippians 2:6-8 reveals, the Son descends in self-abasement at the Incarnation and even more deeply in ascending to the cross. God seeks to descend in order to identify Himself with us and to save us. As the Church Fathers teach, "God has become man so that man can become God."

This truth is revealed as the foundation of our Lady's greatness, inspired by the Holy Spirit in the *Magnificat*: "for he has regarded the low estate of his handmaiden" (Lk 1:48). It is found also in the inversion of all reality in the rest of the *Magnificat:* to cast down the mighty and to lift up the lowly; and in the whole orientation of the Beatitudes, "Blessed are the poor in spirit… blessed are the meek." The entire mystical tradition follows this path, as exemplified by St. Thérèse's teaching that holiness is not about growing bigger but rather about becoming smaller. Its efficacy also lies in its effect on the devil: "The most powerful weapon to conquer the devil is humility. For, as he does not know at all how to employ it, neither does he know how to defend himself from it" (St. Vincent de Paul). This may explain why the devil fears our Lady the most— because of the depths of her humility.

## B. Explaining the Power of Self-Knowledge

### 1. Self-knowledge (Innate Poverty) Allows the Spirit to Invade our Souls

This teaching goes against our common human logic. We have to rise to the level of faith. How important is self-knowledge, the knowledge of my innate poverty and sinfulness? It allows the invasion by the Holy Spirit:

> God asks for nothing better than to fill us with himself and his graces, but he sees that we are so full of pride and self-satisfaction that it prevents him from communicating himself to us. For if souls are not founded upon true humility and self-contempt, we are incapable of receiving God's gifts, because our self-love would devour them. So, God is obliged to leave us in our poverty, darkness, and sterility to make us realize our nothingness. This is how necessary the virtue of humility is. (Catherine de Bar, *Adorer et adhérer*, 113)

The trap is to think we are good, which reflects the Ascetical Mansions.

> Yet, most Christians seem to rely on human gifts, and not be led by the Spirit for mystical transformation, which requires the poverty or emptiness of St. John Vianney: "God gave me the great mercy of not putting anything in me that I can rely on: *no talent, no knowledge, no wisdom, no strength, no virtue*"; and of St. Thérèse: "We experience such *great peace when we depend upon no one but God*."[4] St. Teresa of Jesus teaches that most do not go and stay beyond the Fourth Mansions. (*Myst. Incarnation*. p. 334)

Cardinal Ratzinger teaches that what is required for union with God and others is "the true loss of oneself," of our ego (Dietrich von Hildebrand). Meister Eckhart affirms that to become one with Christ means to lose "oneself," to cease to regard one's own ego as an absolute. Becoming incorporated in the Son is not just a sacramental process but also an ethical process. We have to become Christ. What separates the Christian from Christ is his own individuality, the assertion of his ego. The measure of his "being in Christ" is the extent to which he has destroyed his own ego. To become one with Christ means to lose "oneself," to cease to regard one's ego as an absolute, to become one in brotherhood with all those in Christ.[5] This "renunciation of our ego" was also taught by Chiara Lubich: "Without loving beyond all measure, without losing our own judgment, without losing our own will and our own desires, we will never be one!" (*Jesus in our Midst*, 30, 61). We are to be imbued with only the Spirit's or Jesus' mind.

St. Escrivá offers an illuminating lesson of his total human incapacity and the path forward. Given a mission to bring the faith to society worldwide, he once experienced great discouragement in a visit to business London as he sensed its materialism and secularism. He cried to the Lord, "I can't do this"; to which the Lord replied, "*You can't, but I can.*" From such experiences, he developed a plan for evangelization through dependence: "Prayer, expiation, and in the very last place, action."

---

[4] John-Marie Vianney, *Pensées* presented by Bernard Nodet, Arège, 260; Yellow Notebook, August 6, 4. Both quoted in Fr. J. Philippe, *Priestly Fatherhood: Treasure in Earthen Vessels*, 86.

[5] J. Ratzinger, *The Meaning of Christian Brotherhood* (San Francisco: Ignatius Press, 1993), 54-55.

## 2. Illustrations Confirming that a Sense of Sinfulness Melts Hearts

Hans Urs von Balthasar validates this thesis through a remarkable insight: "This ability to be poor is the human person's deepest wealth":

> This ability to be poor is the human person's deepest wealth: this is revealed by the Christ-event, in which the essence of being became visible for the very first time: as glory. In giving up his Son, God the Father has opened up this possibility for all. But the Spirit of God is sent to change this possibility in us into reality. He shows the world that the poverty of the Son, who sought only the glory of the Father and let himself be robbed of everything in utter obedience, was the most exact expression of the absolute fullness, which does not consist of "having," but of "being= giving." It is in giving that one is and has. (*Glory of the Lord*, vol. VII, 391)

(a) **Pope Francis**: When asked in an interview, "Who is Jorge Bergoglio," after a deep pause, the pope replied, "I am a sinner." Bergoglio had a profound experience of God's mercy when going to Confession at the age of 17 on the feast day of St. Matthew, and he subsequently chose Venerable Bede's words in the Office of Readings of St. Matthew's feast day for his episcopal and papal motto: "Looking upon him with mercy, he called him."

> The pope stares at me in silence. I ask him if this is a question that I am allowed to ask.... He nods that it is, and he tells me: "I do not know what the most fitting description might be.... I am a sinner. This is the most accurate definition. It is not a figure of speech, a literary genre. I am a sinner".... "Yes, the best summary, the one that comes more from the inside and I feel most true is this: 'I am a sinner whom the Lord has looked upon.'" And he repeats: "I am one who is looked upon by the Lord. I always felt my motto, *Miserando atque Eligendo* [By Having Mercy and by Choosing Him], was very true for me." (Antonio Spadaro, "Interview with Pope Francis," quoted on p. 54 in *Mystical Incarnation*)

(b) **St. Escrivá and Bl. del Portillo**: For his epitaph, St. Escrivá had suggested, "Josemaría Escrivá de Balaguer y Albas. A Sinner. Pray for him." For years he had signed himself, "Josemaría, the sinner," and had viewed himself like the donkey that brought Jesus to Jerusalem. Alvaro del Portillo lived this humility of his founder. Preaching at the electoral congress Mass, he said: "God's grace penetrates like a ray of light in a humble soul where it shimmers. Pride, on the other hand, cuts the ray of light and leaves the soul in darkness." When elected as successor, he told the electors that they had chosen him "because you knew that I had spent more time than anyone else at our Father's side, and you were looking for continuity. You have not voted for Alvaro del Portillo but rather have elected our Father."[6]

---

[6] John F. Coverdale, *Saxum*, 141-143.

## *3. God Chooses to use Failures*

St. André Bessette teaches that "It is with the smallest of brushes that the artist paints the best paintings." But St. Bessette and St. Vianney were failures in health or academics, but successes in grace. Here we are referring to failures to correspond to God's grace. For example, the priest who always felt like a "screw-up" failed during formation and by leading the poor to love him instead of Christ. His transformation took place after becoming angry during a second thirty-day retreat, after which he was able to no longer seek to earn God's love (to redeem his failings) but to simply allow it to flow through him in his misery to others. The seminarians hearing this talk were enthralled and were basically asking, "how can we attain this transformation for our own priesthood?" When one deacon asked how he could preach given his weakness and feeling like a hypocrite, the priest replied, "We are all hypocrites. The main thing is to know that we are hypocrites." It is the hypocrite or "screwup" that draws down God's graces. He is apt to share his weaknesses: "Speak to them of the great mercy of God. Sometimes people are helped by your telling your own lamentable past" (St. F. Xavier). The paradox in Christian life is that God uses failures, humiliations, and even sin, to conquer the world; saints are basically "divine failures." When the author of *In Sinu Jesu* asked the Lord why he went through so many trials, Jesus explained that these prepared him to make him God's *instrument* (March 28, 2014).

> "Why, beloved Jesus, were there so many false starts in my life? So many attempts to reach Thee that turned to bitterness, or delusion, or failure?" "These were all an attempt to escape from the pain and inner confusion that had been inflicted upon you as a child? I *allowed* all of these things to befall you; I allowed you to make mistakes and to knock at the wrong doors, because, by this, I was preparing you to accept My plan for you. I humbled you so as to make of you an instrument for My use."[7]

Alice von Hildebrand shared something of her own "happy failure," the shameful treatment she faced for many years, but that has given rise to much influence, including conversions of students.

> My first question: Why name your book "Memoirs of a Happy Failure"? "Because it conveys an important message," she answered. Failure, even radical failure, is a justified term because she was "shamefully treated at Hunter: lowest salary in the department, for years… no medical coverage, never knowing whether I would have a job the next semester… given the most exhausting schedule." Yet, despite it all, she had immense success with her students and earned their affection and admiration.

---

[7] A Benedictine monk, *In Sinu Jesu: When Heart Speaks to Heart— The Journal of a Priest at Prayer* (Kettering, OH: Angelico Press, 2016), 242.

The response of her colleagues? "Jealousy, edging on hatred…(they) could only explain my success by claiming that all I was doing was (preaching) Catholicism." She describes, among other things, ridicule at faculty meetings, injustice, meanness, sending spies into the classroom, and telling new appointees to warn students not to take her classes. Upon finally receiving tenure, she was told, "that you received tenure is nothing short of a miracle."

Yet, there was a great joy seeing some of her students convert. Therefore her career could still be called "happy because many of my students – truth hungry – were fed… then a *coup de théâtre* [spectacular turn of events]: (I was) evaluated by students as the best professor competing against close to 800 professors. All things are possible with God!"[8]

This was offered to a priest who asked how he could concretely live out being a "divine failure." But we do not seek out these "failures," but accept them if offered by God, which would be a sign of His predilection.

| Humanly Blessed | Divinely Blessed (Saints) |
|---|---|
| Strong friendships | Lose friendships |
| Esteemed by everyone | Not recognized, misunderstood |
| Travel widely | Unable to travel |
| Robust health | Sickly constitution |
| Acquire intellectual prowess | Struggle academically |
| Attachment to knowledge | Reading guided by Spirit only |
| Go from success to success | Ride waves of failures, conflicts |
| Growing up like most people | Family life is full of struggles |

### 4. Humiliating Trials Prepare us to Become God's Instruments

Many people have undergone heavy trials, and the memories of these tend to remain and hover in the background. A late archbishop once shared privately both his long-standing stomach issues as well as how at nights in bed he had doubts about decisions made. J.-P. de Caussade confirms that this is the path through which our Lord prepares His apostles: "We cannot be settled in the state of pure love until we have experienced **a lot of setbacks and many humiliations**" (*Abandonment*, Ch. IV, n. 2). We find them in saintly people, such as in the life of Ratzinger (Nazi government, failure of Habilitation thesis, branded as "panzer cardinal," attacks at Regensburg, etc.). St. John Vianney, in the midst of persecutions by brother priests, astounds by signing a petition asking for his ouster from the parish.

> The persecutions of some of his brother priests provided him with the opportunity of climbing another rung of the ladder of humility. He

---

[8] Claire Dwyer, "Alice von Hildebrand: 'A Happy Failure,'" spiritualdirection.com, accessed January 28, 2022, https://spiritualdirection.com/author/claire-dwyer. Permission granted to reprint this text on March 30, 2022.

countersigned and himself sent to the bishop's house a letter of denunciation which chance had caused to fall into his hands. "Now they have my signature," he observed, "so there will be no lack of material to lead to a conviction."[9]

We see the beautiful example of the humility and living martyrdom of St. Bernadette, whose profound "failure" with its transformation is likely the true, secret "miracle" of Lourdes.

> She was a very humble person. Once someone asked her to say a few words for the edification of the novices. She answered smiling: "I don't know anything! No one can take anything good from a stone." The Mother Superior asked her if she were not proud to be chosen as a confidante of Our Lady. She answered: "What idea do you have of me? The Holy Virgin only chose me because I was the most ignorant. If she could have found someone else more ignorant, she would have chosen her." The continuous suffering and vomiting of blood she experienced slowly weakened Bernadette. Her physical appearance became pitiable. Once a postulant came to see her so that she might know the seer. As the saint passed by, a companion pointed her out and said with scorn: "Bernadette? It's just this!" (Bernadette, c'est ça!)[10]

## C. Our Misery can be a Void to Draw down God's Mercy

### *1. Contemplation (Holy Spirit) Gives Self-Knowledge for Transformation*

St. John of the Cross teaches that, at the second or Illuminative stage, there is the beginning of "contemplation," a secret, peaceful, loving inflow of the Spirit. This Living Flame of Love, like the fire that first purifies a log of its impurities, reveals our hidden, repressed weaknesses to heal them. It is what St. Thérèse experienced in her dark night before death, when God revealed her humanity, allowing her to be convicted of her poverty and littleness, a great grace. Then the soul, like the log that becomes one with the flame after being purified, is consumed by this Living Flame and is transformed into Christ. This wounding happens not only within the soul or at prayer, but through many external trials (e.g., sickness, conflictual relationships, temptations, etc.), God acting thus intermittently in life to consume us in His divine flame.[11] Self-knowledge is a prerequisite for this transformation.

> If we could, with a single interior glance, see all the goodness and mercy that exists in God's designs for each one of us, even in what we call

---

[9] François Trochu, *The Curé d'Ars* (Westminster, Mary: New Press, 1960), Ch. 13, 275-276.
[10] Plinio Corrêa de Oliveira, "St. Bernadette Soubirous, Saint of April 16," *Tradition in Action*, Dec. 19, 2021, https://www.traditioninaction.org/SOD/j068sdBernadette4-16.htm.
[11] Daniel Chowning, "Created for Love: A Retreat on St. John of the Cross " (Retreat to St. Augustine's Seminary, Toronto, Ont., April 22, 2022).

disgraces, pains and afflictions, our happiness would consist in throwing ourselves into the arms of the divine will, with the abandon of a young child that throws himself into the arms of his mother. (St. Marie of the Incarnation)

## 2. What Matters most is not Overcoming Sinfulness but our Malleability

"It is not sinners, but the wicked who should despair; it is not the magnitude of one's crime, but contempt of God that dashed one's hopes" (St. Peter Damian). What matters is not our sinfulness, but our softness of heart. It may help us to read Attila Miklósházy's theological excerpt on sin.

### Nature of Sin

Sin is <u>personal misdeed against God</u>. The creature wants to be God (Gen 3:5), does not want to serve God ("*Non serviam*," Jer 2:20). He is ungrateful towards God, his Lord and Father, he is disloyal and mutinous (Deut 32:20): "What do you possess that was not given to you? If then you really received it all as a gift, why take the credit to yourself?" (1 Cor 4:7). The sinner rebels against the order of creation, and also against the order of salvation: "What more should I have done for you?" (cf. Lamentation on Good Friday).

Sin is <u>rebellion of man against God</u>, which manifests itself in his behavior regarding God's law and commandments, against the natural law and covenant law.

Sin is <u>perversion of the human heart</u>. The human heart is supposed to recognize God and His commandments:

> God gave men tongues and eyes and ears, the power of choice and a mind for thinking. He filled them with discernment, and showed them good and evil. He kept watch over their hearts, to display to them the majesty of His works. They shall praise His holy name, proclaiming the grandeur of His works. (Sir 17:6-10)

But man through sin perverted his heart: he wants to know the universality of good and bad like God, he disobeyed God's commandment by doing his own thing, he wanted to follow his own law (autonomy!). And so it came to be that "sin dwells in man" (Rom 7:17-20). This is aversion from God and conversion to creatures (Augustine). Instead of living according to the Spirit, man lives according to the flesh (*kata sarka*: Rom 7:25; 8:11; Gal 5:16-26). This produces a whole <u>catalogue of sins</u>: fornication, impurity, indecency, idolatry, sorcery, quarrels, a contentious temper, envy, fits of rage, selfish ambitions, dissensions, party intrigues, jealousies, drinking bouts, orgies (Gal 5:19-21); shameful passions, unnatural intercourse, homosexual behavior, injustice, mischief, rapacity, malice, murder, rivalry, treachery, malevolence, whispering, scandal-mongering, insolence, arrogance, boasting, hating God, no loyalty, no conscience, no fidelity, no pity, unnatural affection (Rom 1:24-32); lust, foul cravings, ruthless greed, idolatry, anger, passion, cursing, filthy talk, lying (Col 3:5-11).

Guilt (= *culpa*) is a reality that man brings upon himself through his sin, but he cannot free himself from it. He can only beg God for forgiveness, to take away the guilt (cf. "Who can forgive sins but God alone", Lk 5:21; Jn 5:14; Is 43:25; 55:7). The true meaning of sin becomes visible in the sacrifice of Christ, whose blood was poured out "for the forgiveness of sins" (Mt 26:28). To the mystery of iniquity therefore corresponds the scandal and foolishness of the Cross (1 Cor 1:23). The mystery lies in the absolute distance between the Creator and creature, and in the love of God for His creature, which can lead even the sinful creature to his final destiny, albeit through conversion, forgiveness and the Cross of Christ.

## Effects of Sin

a) - Guilt and Punishment: Sin makes one guilty before God and draws punishment with it (Mt 3:7; Jn 3:36; Rom 2:5; 9:22; Eph 2:3). The judgment of God about sin wants to restore the disturbed order even at the price of the blood of His Son (cf. Is 63:3; Ap.14:19f.; 19:15). Thus even the fire of Purgatory and of Hell is the expression of God's justice and love (Mt 18:21-34).

b) - Destruction of Grace: Sin destroys grace, either by turning away from the source of light (Bonaventure), or by destroying the natural conditions in man for supernatural grace (Thomas Aquinas). Together with grace, all previous merits are also destroyed (mortified, can be revivified). The supernatural virtue of love is lost; faith and hope, however, remain, though they are weakened (DS 1544).

c) - Bad Conscience: Sin produces a bad conscience or bad heart, pangs of conscience (cf. 1 Sam 24:6; 2 Sam 24:10), fear, anxiety, and deep inner turmoil. The sinner is more apt to follow the way of flesh (Gal 5:16-26; Rom 7:14-18), the concupiscence becomes overpowering (Rom 7:7f.), and one becomes a slave to sin and to Satan (Rom 6:15-23; Gal 4:9-10). This creates constant inner conflicts. In addition, sin darkens the soul, and causes mental blindness and the obduration (hardening) of the heart.

d) - Social Effect: Sin is doing something wrong in the objective realm, which is wrong even if one does not know it (cf. Lev 5:17). But sin has also a social effect: the individual sins not only for himself but also for his family, tribe, people, and even for his posterity (Lev 4:3; 2 Sam 21:1; Is 14:21; Ex 20:5; 34:7). This is due to the solidarity in the history of salvation.

e) - Disturbance in Nature: Sin produces disturbance in the world of nature: these appear in the form of punishments, or "visitations of God," which are aimed for inducing conversion (cf. Joseph's punishment of brothers, Gen 42:21ff.); David's punishment with respect to Bathsheba and Uriah (2 Sam 12:1-13). Jesus weeps over Jerusalem's destruction: "If only you had known the way that leads to peace... but you did not recognize God's moment when it came" (Lk 19:41-44).[12]

---

[12] Attila Mikloshazy, "Hamartiology," Creation Anthropology, Sin: SAT 2321F (Lecture, Toronto School of Theology, Toronto, Ontario, 1978).

# Retreat 1: Towards Mystical Incarnation and Marriage
## Conference 2
## Second Pillar: Eyes on Jesus through the Present Moment

### I. Meeting Christ in the Sacrament of the Present Moment

**A. The Secret of God's Will**

*1. The Second Pillar of St. Catherine of Siena and God's Will*
Having established the first pillar of St. Catherine of Siena, the self-knowledge of our innate poverty, we turn to her second pillar: "Think of me and I will think of you." The moment we think of God, He thinks of us. More deeply, when we keep our eyes on Him, He both looks after all our concerns but, more importantly, He obtains the opening to substitute himself for us (Dina Bélanger), to act and take over in us: "It is no longer I who live, but Christ who lives in me" (Gal 2:20). St. Peter Claver affirms this truth: "Seek God in all things and we shall find God by our side."

St. Teresa of Jesus teaches that "Perfection... does not consist in ecstasy. True union with God consists in the union of our will with his."[1] St. Alphonsus de Liguori, a devotee of St. Teresa, gave a striking example of the importance of doing God's will. He recalled a monk with a reputation for sanctity being questioned by his abbot about what he did differently: "He answered that there was little or nothing special that he did beyond making a great deal of willing only what God willed, and that God had given him the grace of abandoning his will totally to the will of God." When pushed about whether he felt any resentment about the recent raid that plundered their granaries and cattle, he replied: "'No, Father,' came the reply. 'On the contrary, I returned thanks to God — as is my custom in such circumstances— fully persuaded that God does all things, or permits all that happens, for his glory and for our greater good; thus, I am always at peace, no matter what happens.' Seeing such uniformity with the will of God, the abbot no longer wondered why the monk worked so many miracles."[2] But it is the experience of "I will think of you" that comes first.

*2. Everything Begins with Encountering the Love of Christ*
Our sanctification begins with encountering Christ. Andrea Tornielli insightfully explains a key insight of the future Pope Paul VI: "that the

---
[1] St. Teresa of Jesus, quoted in Alphonsus de Liguori, *Alphonsus de Liguori: Selected Writings*, Classics of Western Spirituality, Book 93 (New York: Paulist, 1999), 178.
[2] Caesarius: *Dial. distin.* 10: cap. 9, quoted in Alphonsus de Liguori, *Uniformity with God's Will* (Rockford, IL: TAN, 2008), 9-10.

Christian does not look at the world as an 'abyss of perdition' but as 'a field ripe for the harvest.' The world remains the world, as described in the Book of Revelation. What changes is the *positive gaze* of the Christian." Julián Carrón explains that Montini, appointed as archbishop of Milan, found that sectors had become impervious to the faith. Yet his attitude was not one of condemnation but "a gaze full of compassion, tenderness, fondness." It was the gaze of the Good Shepherd, "being moved with pity for them, for they were like sheep without a shepherd." He makes a profound affirmation:

> God became flesh so that we could experience and "see" His mercy, His infinite love for us, His moved emotion in the face of our nothingness. When the Invisible became visible through the birth of Jesus— a baby, who then grew, who walked the roads of Galilee— we were able to see One who was deeply moved by the pain of a widowed mother at the funeral of her only son at Nain. That woman felt herself looked at in a way that has no equal. Jesus, with a tenderness beyond compare, in a way that is inconceivable for us, told her, "Woman, don't cry!" and then He restored her living son to her, but first He told her, in a rush of emotion, 'Don't cry!'"[3]

But Julián Carrón explains that this gaze of love and mercy cannot be just a memory of the past written in the Gospels, but a "present presence," through the lived experience of meeting Christ in Christians today. We recounted in *Mystical Incarnation* a correction from God to a priest, who had been sick for a long period and not recovering, and who was interiorly rebelling. He received a tender "word" of love (like the widow above) from the Father passed on to him through a charismatic religious community:

> Each day you must renew your union with me [Father], with the Holy Trinity, guided by your Mother, who bears you like her child. She defends you in temptation and teaches you how to respond as a faithful servant: "I am the handmaid of the Lord, may it be done according to your will." This word must be what guides you in every moment. You are not seeking to do your will but mine, which is perfect and full of graces.
> Remember always that I love you, I have showed you my love, and will show it to you always. Be confident in Me, because I listen to all your prayers, I listen to the desires of your heart on behalf of my Church and of souls. May my joy be always in your heart because my kingdom dwells in you for ever! A word of the Lord to his child called to holiness.

St. John Bosco taught, "I did not become a priest to look after my health." He lived his motto, "Lord, give me souls, take away the rest," consuming

---

[3] Julián Carrón, *Where is God?: Christian Faith in the Time of Great Uncertainty* (Montréal & Kingston: McGill-Queens University Press, 2020), 13, 14.

himself for souls. This is God's mission for us. A remarkable Italian Capuchin friar, Gino Alberati, now 80 years old, has served the Indigenous people in 80 poor communities in the Amazon by boat for 50 years. Their need is great: poverty, alcoholism and suicides among youth. His linking of Christ, love, and present moment is edifying, and he has touched many:

> When I came to Brazil, it did not matter to me who I was— because the other was Christ. It did not matter [what happened] in the past, nor what I was going to do in the future, since the important thing to do was to live day by day, and in the present moment. After all, that is the only way we can love concretely. Also, in the hard times, I saw the crucified Christ.[4]

## B. J.-P. de Caussade's Sacrament of the Present Moment (Ch. 2, no. 7)

### 1. The Secret of Meeting God in each Present Moment

Jean-Pierre de Caussade's *Abandonment to Divine Providence* is an inspired and brilliant road map that pinpoints the heart of holiness. It is the secret of ancient times when there were no spiritual directors or systems of spirituality, but simply conformity with the will of God as it manifested itself in daily life. De Caussade teaches how to find God's will that comes in the hidden "disguises" of each present moment. As Mary saw the Son of God in the baby in a cave and in the battered body of Christ, so today we must see that Christ comes to us now in the poverty of humdrum events, especially in the midst of trials. With eyes of faith, we should see Him offering Himself to us in each present moment as He offers Himself in the Blessed Sacrament: "What a festival and never-ending feast is ours!"

> And how true it is that every painful trial, all we have to do, and every impulse of the spirit give us God exactly as he comes to us in the mystery of the Blessed Sacrament. Nothing is more certain. For both reason and faith tell us that God's love is present in every creature and in every event... His love wishes to unite itself with us through all that the world contains, all that he had created, ordained, and allowed.... So, **every moment of our lives can be a kind of communion with his love**, a communion which can produce in our souls **fruits similar to those we receive with the body and blood of the Son of God**.... What a festival and never-ending feast is ours! God ceaselessly gives himself and is received with no pomp and circumstance, but hidden beneath all that is weak and foolish and worthless.... From these castoffs he creates miracles of love and gives himself to us as often as we believe we have found him there.[5]

---

[4] Rodrigo Arantes, "A Boat Made of Generosity Glides through the Heart of the Amazon like a Prayer," *Aid to the Church in Need*, 2021 issue, 2.

[5] Jean-Pierre de Caussade, *Abandonment to Divine Providence* (Toronto: Doubleday, 1975), 48.

## 2. De Caussade's Insightful Depiction of Two Levels of Spiritual Life

He depicts two levels. At the initial level, *"those who live in God"* do all the usual exercises to draw closer to God, such as faithful prayer, adoration, Mass and Confession, spiritual direction, retreats, etc. But *"those in whom God lives,"* who have already developed fidelity in living in God, have moved to the next level. While faithful to these duties or norms, they are not focused on the spiritual exercises but on God's leading in each present moment, for God's presence and holy will lie in it. *These are the ones who have given themselves totally to God and in whom God rules by their abandonment.* These latter have untold power of influence, from them grace flows to the world:

> Those who live in God perform countless good works for his glory, but those in whom God lives are often flung into a corner like a useless bit of broken pottery [image also used by St. Thérèse, but as a ball]. There they lie, forsaken by everyone, but yet enjoying God's very real and active love and knowing they have to do nothing but stay in his hands and be used as he wishes. Often, they have no idea how they will be used, but he knows. The world thinks them useless and it seems as if they are.
>
> Yet it is quite certain that by various means and through hidden channels they pour out spiritual help on people who are often quite unaware of it and of whom they themselves never think. *For those who have surrendered themselves completely to God, all they are and do has power. Their lives are sermons. They are apostles. God gives a special force to all they say and do,* even to their silence, their tranquility, and their detachment, which, quite unknown to them, *profoundly influences other people.*[6] (emphasis added)

Herein lies the power of Nazareth. Our Lady lived the abandonment of being led from moment to moment by the Holy Spirit, as His spouse and in whom He is "quasi-incarnate." While faithful to her duties as wife and mother, Mary was "simple": her eyes were always on God and on fulfilling His will in each moment.

The abandoned soul, like Mary, is thus possessed by the Spirit, and becomes a mystical incarnation of Christ such that He lives again: "The life of each saint is the life of Jesus Christ."[7] Our life too can be a saintly history if we know how to *meet God and His holy will* in each present moment: "God's love calls us to move beyond fear. We ask God for the courage to abandon ourselves unreservedly, so that we might be molded by God's grace, even as we cannot see where that path may lead us" (St. Ignatius L.). We need not fear: "The Holy Spirit leads us like a mother. He leads his child by the hand as a sighted person leads a blind person" (St. J. Vianney).

---

[6] Ibid., 60.
[7] Ibid., 84.

*Illustration of Two Levels in Fr. Robert Dodaro*
We can perhaps discern these two levels in Fr. Robert Dodaro, a highly regarded Augustinian scholar (permission granted Nov 7, 2021). Before his debilitating sickness, he was president of the Patristic Institute in Rome, guided a community of over 50 people, and was involved in various ecclesial works (Roman Congregations, symposia, meetings with important figures), one of the shining lights in Rome. With a breakdown in burnout, he left all this behind to go to Mary Lake shrine, no longer in the spotlight nor consulted, and now has to turn to intensive medical help. He may no longer have the familiar landmarks or duties and may remain in spiritual darkness. For such, even books and directors do not bring significant understanding, one has to depend on God in each moment. One can argue that this second stage represents a dark night that gives greater power.

### 3. Elements of the Sacrament of the Present Moment
*Holy Spirit Writes a New Gospel in our Hearts*
As the Word of God wrote divine Scripture, so now He writes a new history on hearts: each heart becomes the paper, the sufferings and actions are the ink, and the incomprehensible back of the tapestry we see now will be revealed as *a divine masterpiece in heaven* (p. 43).

> We are now living in a time of faith. The Holy Spirit writes no more gospels except in our hearts. All we do from moment to moment is live this new gospel of the Holy Spirit. We, if we are holy, are the paper; our sufferings and our actions are the ink. The workings of the Holy Spirit are his pen, and with it he writes a living gospel; but it will never be read until that last day of glory when it leaves the printing press of this life. And what a splendid book it will be— the book the Holy Spirit is still writing! The book is on press and never a day passes when type is not set, ink applied and pages pulled…. We shall be able to read it only in heaven.

*Eyes on God during Human Storms*
Like the holy family at Nazareth, the abandoned soul remains hidden (even their activity seems worthless). The greatness of Jesus and Mary was not perceived by the townspeople of Nazareth ("Is this not Jesus, the son of Joseph?", Jn 6:42). The greatness of abandoned souls often remains hidden to them, and they go through interior turmoil, often seeing others as making far greater progress. While Jesus as God knew divine glory, he was being "destroyed" in His humanity. During His Passion, "the hearts of Jesus and Mary, in that darkest of nights, let the violence of the storm break over them."[8] What is striking is that they are not marked by external luminosity: by great heroism or generous exercises of austerity or charity.

---
[8] Ibid., 94.

> There is nothing more distressing for a soul that wants to do only the will of God and yet cannot feel certain that it loves him.... Perfection is presented to it contrary to all its preconceived ideas, to all that it feels and to all that it has learned. It now comes to the soul in the form of all the afflictions sent by providence... This seems very far from all the sublime and extraordinary glory of holiness. A veiled and hidden God gives himself and his grace in a strange, unknown manner, for the soul feels too weak to bear its crosses, distaste for its duties, and is attracted only to very ordinary spiritual exercises. The image of sanctity which it has reproaches this soul for its own mean and despicable nature.... Yet through this loss the soul gains everything.[9]

*Spirit Playing Violin*
The abandoned soul's whole treasure is God: "God strips them of everything except their innocence so that they have nothing but him alone."[10] This state, as with Jesus and Mary, is the highest perfection: "Nevertheless, to obey this apparent disorder is to have reached the summit of virtue, and it is one we do not reach without long years of effort. This virtue is pure, unadulterated virtue. It is, quite simply, **perfection**."[11] It is the perfection of a musical genius like Mozart, who obeys but does not allow musical rules to fetter him, and "writes without constraint and his impromptu pieces are very rightly thought to be masterpieces." And the abandoned soul, after long cooperating with grace, "gradually falls into the habit of acting always by an instinctive following of God's wishes."[12]

> God still speaks as He spoke to our Fathers, when there were neither spiritual directors nor set methods.... Then they saw that each moment brings with it a duty to be faithfully fulfilled. That was enough for spiritual perfection. On that duty their whole attention was fixed at each successive moment like the hand of a clock that marks the hours.[13]

A Third-Order lay woman struggled with coping with her husband who has returned after years of work abroad, but is sick, complains, and does nothing. She searches far and wide for peace of heart: online retreats, novenas, a priest's counsel that prayer is the secret, praying from the heart. But finally the author had to rein her in, reminding her of his several counsels that the one thing necessary was abandonment to the will of God (not devotions,

---

[9] Ibid., 92-93.
[10] Ibid., 89.
[11] Ibid., 105.
[12] Ibid.
[13] Jean-Pierre de Caussade, *Abandonment to Divine Providence*, I, 1, quoted in a modern translation (author uses Image Books version), Fr. Brian Mullady, "A Matter of Abandonment to Divine Providence," accessed June 29, 2015, http://www.cloisteredlife.com/2011/08/reflection-on-the-contemplative-life-2/.

etc.), that each present moment gives us God. *Trying to understand God's design hinders this*, we simply give ourselves to it blindly. She was flying off everywhere, not finding God's counsel right in front of her.

## C. Father's Providence is Backdrop to Living in the Present Moment

### *1. Overall Panorama Reveals God's Immense Providence*
Let us present the overall panorama to help understand that we depend on God for our existence, action, and redemption. In the material world, God is involved intimately with everything. Everything that exists is created by Him, all is held in existence in each moment: He arranges the orbit of the stars and the arrangement of the galaxies, the tides of the sea, all animal, sea, and plant life; if there is evolution, it falls within His governance; every action we do has to be accompanied by His collaboration (*concursus divinus*). As St. Augustine taught, God is closer to us than we are to ourselves, as He holds together each atom and molecule. As Jesus taught, God knows the number of tendrils of our hair and every sparrow that falls. Every cell is vastly complex, and He will not allow the earth to come to disaster (exception is the Flood), despite what movies like *The Day after Tomorrow* depict (though we can despoil it). If we are to assume, as scientists suggest, that evolution is taking place, we might include evolution as a fifth creative activity guided by God. Most importantly, He has established Himself as the inner sanctuary of our conscience, and has built a dwelling place for Himself in our hearts.

Greater yet are two realities that increase the depth of this chasm that separates us from God. First, the tragedy of sin moves us beyond that original state of nothingness, as it were, from this state of being "nothing" to the negative portion of the scale— we have now become enemies of God. Second, remembering that God does not need us, as Scripture attests, while yet enemies of God, He proceeded to redeem us by sacrificing His own Son. *God's immense, universal, and comprehensive providence is the foundation of the "Sacrament of the Present Moment."*

### *2. God has a Providential Plan for each Person*
There is a similar governance called providence, through which God as Father directs all to our salvation. We see this providence expressed in salvation history in the Old Testament typology. God uses not only prophecies, but also events, like the Exodus, and people, like Abel and Moses, to prefigure Jesus and His redemption. God can use even the evil of the Jewish authorities to kill Jesus to bring about our redemption. Within our free will, God's hands encompass all human history, such that each person has a personal destiny, as each has a personal guardian angel.

As for Jesus, the Father has a **personal plan** for each of us that is unique to us, and He has arranged everything in each present moment as a Father would for a little child. And within the Father's providence, Jesus Himself simply allowed the Father to provide everything with filial confidence— this is the path of the "Son" of God, and not of the "worker" for God. Jesus' focus is to please the Father and, with great trust that pleases the Father, allows the Father to lead and provide for Him in each moment. God's plans for us will lead us to holiness; but the degree of holiness depends not on doing great things for God but simply the degree of submitting to God's plan and providence. We have to see this vast economy in which the Father's hands encompass everything, as a father (or mother) who holds his child in his arms and protects him and gives him everything that he needs (home, love, teaching, example, food, education, clothing, etc.). All the child has to do is allow the Father to do everything and to love Him back in return. His eyes are on the Father's providence.

Pope John Paul II, in an address after St. Escrivá's canonization, said that "For each of us the Lord has a plan, to each he entrusts a mission." Then he goes on to speak of the Father's providential care of His children:

> The Lord gave him [St. Escrivá] a profound understanding of the gift of our divine sonship. He taught him to contemplate the tender face of a Father in the God who speaks to us through the most varied events of life. A Father who loves us, who follows us step by step, who protects us, understands us and awaits from each of us a response of love. The consideration of this fatherly presence which accompanies the Christian everywhere gives him steadfast confidence; he must trust in the heavenly Father at every moment. He should never feel lonely or frightened. When the Cross is present, he should not see it as a punishment, but *a mission* entrusted by the Lord himself. The Christian is necessarily *optimistic*, because he knows he is *a son of God in Christ*.[14] (emphasis added)

### II. *The Foundational Logic of the Power of Abandonment*

### A. Explaining the Secret of Dependence

*1. Surrender is what the Son lives in Relation to the Father in Heaven.* The Father pours Himself out eternally into the Son. Being the perfect Son, He is the perfect yes to the Father, receiving all from the Father and pouring Himself back in love to the Father. This is surrender, receptivity, transparency.

---

[14] "Address of John Paul II in Praise of St. Josemaría Escrivá, Founder of Opus Dei," Vatican.va, accessed Dec. 30, 2021, https://www.vatican.va/content/john-paul-ii/en/speeches/2002/october/documents/hf_jp-ii_spe_20021007_opus-dei.html.

*2. Surrender is the Secret of Jesus and Mary.* Jesus did not plan, He allowed the Father to plan everything and He received everything from moment to moment from the Father through the Holy Spirit. This is evident in Jesus' life: the Father arranged everything for His birth and protection from Herod, sojourn in Egypt, the beginning of His ministry with His Baptism and 40 days in the desert, and during His ministry, Jesus did not have money or food but the Father provided, partly through women benefactors. The Father provided food at the end of Jesus' 40 days in the desert, He provided an angel to strengthen Him at Gethsemane; He revealed which apostles to choose; He provided Him strength and rest to pray at night; the Father furnished Jesus with wisdom to confound His enemies. Being an instrument gives great power, as seen in C. Lubich's founding of Focolare.

> Yes, because the pen does not know what the author wants to write... So, when God takes a person in his hands to produce a particular work within the Church, that person does not know what he or she will have to do. They are merely the tool, the instrument... When this life started in Trento, I had no plan, no program. The idea of this Movement was in the mind of God, the project was in heaven. That's how it was in the beginning, and that's how it has been over all the years the Movement has developed. (Michel Pochet, *Stars and Tears*, New City Press)

A text from Jean-Pierre de Caussade's *Abandonment to Divine Providence* reveals God's secret plan of the "illogical" path of this dependence:

> Yet a vastly great number of souls in this state have their virtue known only to God. Their condition sets them free from nearly every external obligation, and they are not suitable for worldly affairs or for anything demanding thought or steady application. They seem quite useless, weak in mind and body, with no creative power and lacking in all emotion. They involve themselves in nothing, they plan nothing, they foresee nothing and set their hearts on nothing.... God strips them of everything except their innocence so that they have nothing but him alone.... They are the laughingstock of everybody. The more closely they are observed, the more they are disliked. No one knows what to make of them. Yet there is an indefinable something which seems to testify in their favor... (p. 89)
> They are spiritually and mentally troubled, and their everyday lives are full of disappointments. They are often unwell and need many attentions and comforts, the very opposite of the austere poverty so much admired in the saints. In them we can see no burning zeal, no achievement of great enterprises, no overwhelming charity and no heroic austerity. Though united to God by faith and love, they find nothing but confusion within themselves. What makes them still more self-contemptuous is that when they compare themselves with those who pass for saints, they find no difficulty in their spiritual lives in submitting to rules and methods and show nothing out of the way in their characters or actions. They are overwhelmed

with shame. Their sorrow and misery at this are responsible for their sighs and tears. We must remember that Jesus was both God and man. As man he was destroyed, but as God all glory was his. These souls have no part of his glory, but they feel all the annihilating anguish of what seems to be their wretched state. Everyone values them about as much as Herod and his court esteemed Jesus. As far as their senses and mind are concerned, these poor souls are disgusted. Nothing pleases them. They crave for something completely different, but every road which leads to the sanctity they long for is blocked. They must live on this bitter bread of anguish and exist under unrelenting pressure, for they have a conception of sanctity which never ceases to torment them. Their will hungers for it, but they cannot attain it. Why is this? Surely it is to mortify them spiritually so that they can find no pleasure or satisfaction in anything, but must give all their affection to God. He deliberately leads them along this path so that he alone can delight them. (pp. 90-91)

Perfection is presented to it contrary to all its preconceived ideas, to all that it feels and to all that it has learned. It now comes to the soul in the form of all the afflictions sent by providence, in the duties of the present moment, in various desires which have no good about them beyond the fact that they do not lead to sin. This seems very far from all the sublime and extraordinary glory of holiness. A veiled and hidden God gives himself and his grace in a strange, unknown manner, for the soul feels too weak to bear its crosses, distaste for its duties, and is attracted only to very ordinary spiritual exercises....

In this condition the soul feels as if it were lost without any guide. It no longer has the support of those spiritual meditations which used to strengthen and enlighten it, and it no longer feels the workings of grace. Yet through this loss the souls gain everything. The same grace, adopting, as it were, a different form, gives back to the soul, by the simplicity of its hidden promptings, a hundred times more than it took away. (pp. 92-93)

## B. "For when I am Weak, then I am Strong" (2 Cor 12:10)

### *1. Failure Opens us to God's Acting in us*
*The Path of Failure is Accessible to Everyone: Model is Jesus' Kenosis in Phil 2:6*
We can develop this further. Jean-Pierre de Caussade says that God not only formed patriarchs and great saints in the past (e.g., Moses, St. John the Baptist, St. Anthony of Egypt), but God's sanctifying continues and forms new saints in each age as great as in previous ages. What is required is surrender or obedience to His will in each present moment; and God once more pours forth new graces to form anew great saints.

There is another hidden and more common path that our feelings instinctively reject and that is *failure*. Consider the failure of Brother André Bessette. Because of poor education and poor health from a birth issue, he had difficulty finding work and also being accepted by Congregations, and had to resort to going to the U.S. to find work. On his return, he was finally accepted by the Holy Cross Congregation at the recommendation of his pastor, but was going to be let go until a bishop intervened on his behalf, and, even then, he was only allowed to be a lay brother as porter all his life. Consider the similar failures of St. John Vianney: expelled from the seminary because of poor academics, allowed to be ordained by special exemption, looked down upon by diocesan clergy, and some parishioners seeking from his bishop his removal from the parish, passing around a petition. Consider Fr. Solanus Casey, who was not allowed to preach or hear Confessions because of his poor academics. Consider St. Bernadette who was considered useless by her superior because she often landed in the infirmary because of long-term illness, and St. Faustina, in whose file it was noted by the interviewing Sister that she would never amount to anything much. Consider Jeanne Jugan, who was thrown out as foundress and superior general, and allowed to beg for alms and worked in the kitchen of the motherhouse, where Sisters did not know who she was. We keep in mind that this failure is a work of the Spirit; it is He who is leading us along.

This is the great secret of St. Paul, who was given a thorn in the flesh, a devil to attack him, to keep him humble, which thorn St. Francis de Sales, a doctor of the Church, held were temptations against chastity. The great lesson learned by this prince of the Church was: "When I am weak, then I am strong" (2 Cor 12:10). This admission came from Paul, a supremely gifted Jewish rabbi, though his erring ways may derive from the influence of a Pelagian Judaism of his time. Blessed too are we if we look into the past and see a long history of failure. Failure can be the apex of our spiritual life, as it was with St. Catherine of Siena near death and being overwhelmed by attacks from evil spirits who tried to convince her that her life was a failure (e.g., papacy), as it was for John Henry Newman. This "failure" was the mark of Jesus: "He was humbled in the womb of the Virgin, needy in the manger of the sheep, and homeless on the wood of the Cross. Nothing so humbles the proud sinner as the humility of Jesus Christ's humanity" (St. Anthony of Padua). We find this failure also in Abraham Lincoln.

> I knew of a man who was defeated by just about everything. He failed in business back in 1831. He was defeated for the legislature in 1832, failed in business again in 1833, was elected to the legislature in 1834. His sweetheart died in 1835. He had a nervous breakdown in 1836, was defeated for speaker in 1838, defeated for land officer in 1843, defeated for Congress in 1843, elected to Congress in 1846, defeated for re-election in 1848, defeated for the Senate in 1855, defeated for vice-president in 1856, and defeated for the Senate in 1858. This man didn't quit either. He was elected president in 1860. His name was Abraham Lincoln. (L'Amour, *Treasure Mountain*, Ch. 16, p. 129)

*The Failure of Others Toward Me (e.g., Judas' betrayal, Jerusalem's "Crucify him")*
Along with our own personal failings and failures, there is another type, the failure of others towards us: the failure of friends and friendships, the failure of a failed relationship with our bishop or superior, failure of understanding by others (fidelity to the Church's teaching leading to not being understood, following the path of the saints to being considered extreme and not being human; new charisms from the Spirit enduring opposition in the Church).

## 2. Dependence in the Path of St. Thérèse

Our Lord's way of divine wisdom for abandoned souls appears to entail taking things away so that we depend on him from moment to moment, to not be concerned about what might happen. St. Thérèse taught that God does not give food for the next few days but only for today. All we need will be given today, including inspirations and promptings, and we have to learn to stop thinking about what we will need in the future (e.g., pandemic, sickness, job loss) and trust that He will provide everything.

God governs every present moment and pours out Himself and His graces. A very devout priest, affiliating himself to a new lay movement, went to Paris so that he could spend time with the founder. He studied St. Thomas and sought out outstanding books. This self-chosen search for growth is praiseworthy, but de Caussade points to the higher level of abandonment, with surrender as the apex. Here, we do not feed ourselves through *rivulets* when we can have the very source, an ocean of grace being poured out in *every present moment*, and all we have to do is open our mouths. In doing so, God would make us a force to help many, like St. Thérèse who received so much infused wisdom, yet only mainly dwelt deeply on *The Imitation of Christ* and St. John of the Cross' writings— it is about depth, not breadth, and more so about what allowing the Holy Spirit to lead and guide. We find a touching example of this in Alvaro del Portillo who, because of his reserved personality, hesitated but then agreed to follow St. Escrivá's giving annual Easter talks to the Work's members' annual visit to Rome: "I won't do the work. It will be the Holy Spirit who works in souls." The warm results led him to say to them: "The important thing is not what I can say but what the Holy Spirit makes each one of you hear in the depths of your heart. The Sanctifier acts if we let him, and with his action transforms our souls." He went on to make many international trips with tremendous fruits.[15]

More deeply, St. Thérèse was led by inspirations, not by her own desires. She offered her life as an oblation to make up for the love that Jesus was not receiving. But we note that she obtained permission from her superior and confessor first, and she realized only when she spat blood out that Jesus

---

[15] John F. Coverdale, *Saxum*, 179.

accepted the sacrifice of her life, and rejoiced, because "to die in the springtime of her life was a great grace." Yet, the key is not her sacrifice but her abandonment: she desired neither a long life nor a short life. In other words, she was totally abandoned to God's will. But in this abandonment, she was moved by the Spirit to make this oblation, but only did so when she received permission of God's representative (her superior). After being moved to compose this oblation of love, with Céline, she used it only after approval by Mother Agnes, who gave permission because of her wisdom.

We see another example of how St. Thérèse was led from moment to moment in daily life. At one time, many in France were flocking in droves to Lourdes, for it had become a sensation and phenomenon. She quietly said to herself, "we don't need this" (pilgrimages should be encouraged but we can meet God powerfully in the daily, mundane life). Many can put primary focus on making a big pilgrimage or retreat, but disregard the primary path of sanctification of the small things of daily life. She understood that she was able to find God in the littleness of each present moment. And she understood deeply that she must not go into the past or the future, for God would provide everything she needed in the present.

## 3. Dependence Lives the Spousal Embrace of the Eternal Now
Saintly souls, like de Caussade and Piccarreta, learn to live the eternal now.

> John Beevers points out that de Caussade insists, over and over again, that we must live from minute to minute. The past is past, the future is yet to be.... We must realize that there is nothing at all which happens unless willed by God, and our all-important duty is to co-operate with that will. Every act, every thought of every second, is significant.... They [mystics] want God as he is; we want God as we imagine him to be. (J.-P. de Caussade, *Abandonment*, 20-21).
> For this contemplative soul [Piccarreta] there is no past, present, or future: everything is **an eternal now**. She reproduces the scenes of the Passion with as strong an impression as if they were actually present to her sight. In an excess of compassion and love for her Beloved, she kisses his eyes, Face, mouth, hands, feet, and Heart, asking Him to return her kisses with a confidence never before known save in a very few enamored souls. She is the **spouse of the Canticle of Canticles**, exclaiming: "Let Him kiss me with the kisses of his mouth."[16] (emphasis added)

---

[16] Luisa Piccarreta, *The Hours of the Passion of our Lord Jesus Christ* (Messina: St. Annibale Maria Di Francia, 1924), xi-xiii.

# Retreat 1: Towards Mystical Incarnation and Marriage
## Conference 3
## The Crisis of Saints

**Preface: Recovery of the Universal Call to Become Saints**

We begin by reiterating the profound truth that all without exception, by virtue of Baptism, are called to holiness. The neglect to establish this goal may be the root of all Church crises. In *Mystical Incarnation*, we described how Fr. Juan González Arintero fought in his time against the then-current traditional position of many Jesuits and Carmelites that taught there were two types of holiness: ascetical (with only acquired contemplation) for the majority; and mystical for the privileged few. Arintero argued strongly that all baptized are called to mystical contemplation.[1] His position was confirmed in *Lumen gentium*'s "universal call to holiness" (LG 40-41). St. Escrivá, of whom Pope Pius XII said, "He is a true saint, a man sent by God for our times," identifies today's crises as "crises of saints":

> A secret, an open secret: these world crises are crises of saints. God wants a handful of men "of his own" in every human activity. And then… *"pax Christi in regno Christi* — the peace of Christ in the kingdom of Christ." (*The Way* n. 301)

Pope Benedict XVI too affirms that, in our times, the world does not respond to moral appeals or Christian values, but to holiness.

> The courageous and integral appeal to principles is essential and indispensable; yet simply proclaiming the message does not penetrate to the depths of people's hearts, it does not touch their freedom, it does not change their lives. What attracts is, above all, the encounter with believing persons who, through their faith, draw others to the grace of Christ by bearing witness to him…. One could say, "the Church has need of these great currents, movements and witnesses of holiness… but there are none!"[2]

It is reliance on human gifts that prevents possession by the Spirit, who purifies, elevates, and transforms us into Christ. We reaffirm that **it is saints who renew and reform the Church**. We fail if we don't become saints, because the grace of Baptism is like the mustard seed that is to become a big tree that shelters many.

---

[1] Benedict M. Ashley, *The Dominicans* (Eugene, OR: Wipf & Stock, 2009), 225-227.
[2] Pope Benedict XVI, Fatima, Address to the Bishops of Portugal, 13 May 2010.

## I. The Bottleneck that is Reliance on the Human Spirit
*(drawing from "New Evangelization: Starting Anew from Christ")*

### A. Becoming Stuck at the Human Mansions

Discernment reveals the cause of today's crisis of saints: the Church relies primarily in the mediocrity of self-reliance, on the human spirit. Augustine taught: "Sin is believing the lie that you are self-created, self-dependent and self-sustained." We get stuck in the first stage, the Ascetical Mansions.

> Why is progress rare? What impedes it? Many simply lack the inspiration. But there is something worse than holding back out of humility: it is the *self-sufficiency* of those who persuade themselves that they do not have to give more than "edifying action"... This, in a word, is the mentality of upstarts, sterile because it is lacking in humility, the seed of all progress. Thus the Third Mansions, if badly understood, can become *a rut in which one gets bogged down in the mud of "self."*[3] (Sr. Madeleine of St. Joseph)

#### *1. Excessive Reliance on Human Gifts*
We typically make the 10% of our puny human efforts, the Ascetical (human) Mansions, dominant. Chiara Lubich, who teaches that mutual love, which presupposes our dying to self, brings Christ's presence: "dangers flee and obstacles vanish... He conquers everything, because he is love!" (p. 26)

> Brothers, God has given us an ideal that will be the salvation of the world.... Go ahead! Not with our own strength, meagre and weak as it is, but with the omnipotence of unity.... And don't be afraid to surrender everything to unity. Without loving beyond all measure, without losing our own judgment, without losing our own will and our own desires, we will never be one! (*Jesus in our Midst*, 30)

#### *2. Proclivity to Feel-Good Sentimentality (Romanticism?)*
One can characterize the past few centuries in terms of development of faculties: imagination (1600s), reason (1700s), sentiment (1800s, Romanticism), with a change to "subjectivity" in the 1900s (e.g., humanism, existentialism). Are our times characterized by both the "sentimentality" of eighteenth-century Romanticism and twentieth-century "subjectivity"?

> In reaction to the Enlightenment, it [Romanticism] exalted nature as a creative force and the chaotic maelstrom of *sentimentality*. In the book, *Genius of Christianity*, François-René de Chateaubriand demonstrated the beauty of Christianity, which he saw not as a barbaric cult, but as a more poetic and human religion. (Stefano De Fiores, *Maria Madre di Gesù*)

---

[3] Sr. Madeleine of St. Joseph, *Within the Castle with St. Teresa* (Lafayette Carmel), 76.

The culture we seek to evangelize might be embodied by a world-famous musician featured in a national newspaper. It was full of warm human sentiment but lacked the "close encounter" with the All-Holy One. St. John of the Cross teaches: "Love consists not in feeling great things but in having great detachment and in suffering for the Beloved." Chiara Lubich teaches us that love is not a love-in, but a supernatural love that sees Christ in the other, which moves out to love all Jesus' forsaken ones in the world.[4]

### 3. Reliance on Numbers and not Holiness
Third, as Georges Chevrot pointed out, God conquers with a few, but who are saints. He chose Israel, and not powerful Egypt or Rome; only twelve apostles and mainly fishermen at that. St. Philip Neri once said, "Give me ten detached men and I will conquer the world." Give him ten of St. Leo and Gregory the Great, St. Benedict, St. Bernard, St. Francis, St. Dominic, etc., and then we will see the ensuing transformation of nations. During the exorcism of a possessed woman, the devil howled at St. John Vianney, "If there were three like you on earth, my kingdom would be destroyed. You have taken more than 80,000 souls from me."[5]

### 4. Reliance on Fixing Others and not Conquest of Self
Fourth, God's logic of using only a key few derives from the immense power of saints— **"victor sui, dominus mundi"** ("the one who conquers herself conquers the world"). There is a trap of seeking to convert the world by much preaching and evangelization, without a mystical incarnation to become another Christ in the world. Luigi Giussani delves more incisively by critiquing the 1968 youth protests that sought to create a "hegemony," to fix society according to their own thinking ("what melancholy!," he exclaimed). Human plans and thinking without relying on God and His timeline will ultimately fail. What matters is first having an encounter with Christ, from which flows all initiatives: "Giussani already realized in the 1950s that the Church would be unable to attract people except through the beauty of a life shaped by the encounter with Christ."[6]

## B. Immolating our Personality to Allow God to Live in Us

### 1. Jesus Immolated His Human Personality to the Divine Word
There is in the Church **an inertia**, a clinging to human inclinations, a lack of desire to "change," or a fear of leaving the familiar and comfortable way of life, and thus not ascending the Mystical Mansions. Let us establish a key

---

[4] Chiara Lubich, *Jesus in our Midst: Source of Joy and Light* (NY: New City Press, 2019), 88.
[5] George W. Rutler, *Saint John Vianney: The Curé D'Ars Today* (San Francisco: Ignatius Press, 1988), 174-175.
[6] Julián Carrón, *Where is God?*, 99-100.

principle using two examples. First, St. Francis de Sales teaches a profound truth: living purely at the human level inhibits the kindling with divine fire: "The Israelites had no manna until the bread they brought out of Egypt was exhausted. Similarly, God's favours are rarely granted to those who cling to their earthly tastes and desires."[7] When we hold on to the human self-reliance of Egypt, we will not receive heaven's manna (God's graces).

A second example is Abraham, for whose fidelity God made his descendants in faith as numerous as the stars in the heavens and the sand on the seashore (Gen 22:17). Like the Israelites leaving Egypt behind, Abraham had to leave his family and homeland to go into the wilderness without looking back, and finally to sacrifice his only son, Isaac. Unlike Abraham, we do not wish to make the sacrifice of *leaving behind* our comfortable human spirit (our homeland) and of *killing* our human propensities of self-reliance (our Isaacs), to being led by the divine Spirit through the Dark Nights to the upper Mansions (Canaan). Von Speyr calls us to cleanse our own temples (souls) from our profane "business" (affairs):

> And again: do not allow your contemplation to be wholly swallowed up by action; keep a sacred space in your life and do not immerse yourself in your activity to such a degree that everything becomes profane and your temple a market hall where the Father's voice is drowned by all the turmoil.[8] (emphasis added)

We can combat self-reliance by the foundational "distrust of self." Dom Scupoli's *The Spiritual Combat* lists it as the first of the four pillars of spiritual life, that God "looks upon it [self-reliance] with **horror**."[9] Dom Marmion employs a striking insight: Christ immolated His personality to the Word:

> The Sacred Humanity *had no human personality* (it is that *human* personality that is the object of our self-love and all its consequences, sensitiveness, susceptibility, etc.; *we must immolate it to the Divine Spouse*, the Word, and thus all such barriers are broken down). And this Sacred Humanity gave itself to the Divine Spouse, the Word, without *any barrier*. This is your example. If you could *dash every child born of self-love* against the Rock, Christ, your union would be perfect.[10] (emphasis added)

---

[7] Jean-Pierre Camus, *The Spirit of St. François de Sales* (New York: Harper & Brothers, 1952), 157.
[8] Adrienne von Speyr, *John: The Word Becomes Flesh*, vol. 1 (San Francisco: Ignatius Press, 1994), 175-176.
[9] Lorenzo Scupoli, *The Spiritual Combat* and *A Treatise on Peace of Soul* (Charlotte, NC: St. Benedict Press, Tan Books, 2010), 9.
[10] Columba Marmion, *Union with God: Letters of Spiritual Direction by Blessed Columba Marmion* (Bethesda, MD: Zacchaeus Pr., 1957), 34. This recalls the teaching of Jean-Jacques Olier.

## 2. "God Living in Us" Leads to Mystical Union

Jean-Pierre de Caussade teaches that there are two dimensions of "living in God" and "God living in us." Our perennial temptation is to live the first, relying on our energies (programs, techniques, preaching). The interview by Andrea Tornielli of Julián Carrón captures the problem of Prometheism:

> *At times is there the risk of forgetting the primacy of grace that acts in us, and of believing instead that salvation is the fruit of our capacity, our goodness, our faithfulness and coherence?*
> The risk is enormous and continual, because in the common mentality the ideal is the human person who produces himself. The temptation of Prometheus is always at hand. The human person is so great, has such powerful aspiration, an ability to dream and to desire that is so beyond any measure that in a certain sense this temptation is unavoidable. But let's ask ourselves, is Prometheism the appropriate road for reaching the fullness that the human person desires? The Tower of Babel is an emblem of the outcome of the human attempt to build something to resolve the situation with our own energies. (*Where is God?*, 141)

This discussion of the perennial temptation to Prometheism, more commonly described as Pelagianism, was preceded by an extremely vital insight: that the Christian is changed primarily, not by his will, but by the Eucharist: "The Eucharist is for us, for all of us, precisely because we are weak and need His grace moment by moment" (ibid). This demonstrates the radical need for God's grace, and more deeply, for "God living in us."

## 3. Like "Blu" the Macaw, We Walk but don't Learn to Fly

We find an analogy to "our living in God" in the animated movie, *Rio*, in which a Macaw hatchling (later named "Blu") was captured in the wilds of Brazil, transported to the US, where it was accidentally dropped from a truck, found by a girl, Linda, and grew up with her. As it grew up, it knew how to do many human things, but had never learned to fly, for which it was belittled by other birds. In contrast, an eagle chick that learns to fly becomes a feared predator, a silent assassin, with incredible sight, silence, and speed, along with fearful talons, and the inattentive rabbit does not stand a chance. The eagle chick who has only learned to walk is nothing compared to its hunter mother, who soars majestically in the heights. "The one in whom God lives" in the Mystical Mansions soars in the heights on the currents of the Spirit, the *ruah*, and has his eyes on the Sun, on God. He sees spiritual insights that most do not, his very words and actions become sermons, he has influence on others whom he has not met. He represents saintly souls like St. Charles Borromeo, St. Martin de Porres, Bl. Catherine of St. Augustine, and St. Elizabeth Seton. Chiara Lubich, Focolare foundress, exerts in ecumenical and inter-faith endeavours exponentially far greater influence because of her sanctity.

Thérèse's novices believed that she could read their hearts, but the truth was rather that in each moment God Himself was guiding her and speaking through her.

### 4. New Lay Movements Reveal the Spirit's Path of Renewal for our Times

The dioceses and parishes constitute the fundamental structure of the Church, but they seem to reach mainly the converted, are preaching to the choir. A key problem is that society has changed, and the Church is no longer reaching the masses. The lay movements, as with past charisms, appear to be the Spirit's gift to address the specific and root problems of our time. Luigi Giussani, founder of Communion and Liberation, is among those who received the discernment to diagnose and address this challenge. For example, he was able to perceive the "collapse of the self-evident":

> "It is no longer history, or doctrine, or tradition, or a discourse that will move men and women today. Christian tradition and philosophy, Christian tradition and discourse have created and continue to create 'Christianness,' but not Christianity." The current landscape shows that "Christendom no longer exists" and the content of Christianity no longer serves as a widely held point of reference. This is at the heart of the pressing questions that pervade the Christian world: what is the current state of Christianity? How can it be convincing for men and women today? And what does it mean to Christians in the midst of the "epochal change"? Fr. Giussani's proposal centers around the conception of Christianity as a real, historical event that is not confined to the past, but is contemporary in our lives; it continues today. (*Communion and Liberation: A Movement in the Church*, 5-6)

Msgr. Giussani points out that the truth of Christianity lies not in the past but in the today through people meeting Christ in us, asking, "why are you so joyful?" Peter, seeing Andrew being transformed by meeting Jesus, was led by him to Jesus. Christianity was credible for Andrew and John because they "experienced in their encounter with Jesus an unpresented correspondence to the needs of their hearts." They had no doubts, for they experienced the tangible change in their hearts. We can lead others to Christ if they see the transformation of these two apostles in us. (*Where is God?*, 75)

## II. Jesus' Love of the Father Lived in Obedience to His Will

### A. Sanctity Summed up in Obeying the Father's Will

(1) The heart of holiness is Jesus' obedience to the Father. His secret was not His divinity, as He did not use His divine powers as man; otherwise, he would not, as Scripture teaches, be a "man like us in all things but sin." His secret was simply the Spirit, whom He received twice: at His Incarnation and at His

Baptism. He obeyed the Father through the Spirit: in going to His Baptism and into the desert, beginning His ministry, speaking with authority, choosing the apostles, being led to Calvary. Von Balthasar notes that Jesus let go of sovereignty of His own existence, so as to become a reflection of His Father through docility to His Father's Spirit. Lay people ought to consult the Spirit: "Should I marry this person," "should I move to New York for work," "what resolution should I make," "should I ask this priest to be my spiritual director," "what project should I take on?"

This Christian, like Jesus, focuses on obedience. Our Lady was virtuous in rushing to help her cousin Elizabeth. But the primary thing is not her charitable act; what mattered was whether the Holy Spirit wanted her to go. If He did not wish her to go, she should not have gone— it's all about obedience. For Christian life *is not about doing good but God's will*. St. Teresa of Jesus wrote: "I often thought my constitution would never endure the work I had to do, (but) the Lord said to me: 'Daughter, *obedience gives strength*.'" On the flip side, St. Faustina wrote: "Satan can even clothe himself in a cloak of humility, but he does not know how to wear the cloak of obedience" (*Diary*, n. 939).

(2) Fr. Raniero Cantalamessa offers us a remarkable model of how to allow God to guide every decision we make, even in daily things. He says that "there is nothing mystical or extraordinary in this; it is open to all those who are baptized. It consists in presenting the questions to God."

> I may decide by myself to make or not make a journey, to do a job, to make a visit, to buy something.... But if love of obedience to God grows in me, I will first ask him [God] by the simple means of prayer that is at everyone's disposal, whether it is his will that I make that journey, do that job, pay that visit, buy that object, and then I will act or not. But whatever the decision, it will be an act of obedience to God and no longer a free initiative of mine. It is clear that I normally hear no voice in my short prayer and I shall not be told explicitly what to do.... I have submitted the question to God. I have emptied myself of my own will. I have renounced deciding for myself and I have given God the chance to intervene in my life, if he so wishes.... Just as a faithful servant never takes an order from an outsider without saying: "I must first ask my master," so the true servant of God undertakes nothing without saying to himself: "I must first pray a little to know what my Lord wants of me!" The will of God thus penetrates one's existence more and more, making it more precious and rendering it a "living sacrifice, holy and acceptable to God"...[11]

---

[11] Raniero Cantalamessa, *Life in Christ: A Spiritual Commentary on the Letter to the Romans* (Collegeville, MN: Liturgical Press, 1990), 190-191.

## B. But God's Will Begins with Sanctifying the Human Foundation

*Sanctifying the Human Foundation*
Nevertheless, to ascend to the Mystical Mansions, we must first sanctify the human foundation. As noted above, "He who is faithful in a very little is faithful also in much" (Lk 16:10). Of Jesus, Mark wrote, "He has done all things well" (Mk 7:37). If we want to know how to do this concretely, we might look to St. Escrivá, whose spirituality highlights holiness in daily life, and offers a concrete way of sanctifying our work in the little things:

> Let's listen to our Lord: "He who is faithful in a very little is faithful also in much; and he who is dishonest in very little is dishonest also in much." It is as if he were saying to us: "Fight continuously in the apparently unimportant things which are to my mind important; fulfil your duty punctually; smile at whoever needs cheering up, even though there is sorrow in your soul; devote the necessary time to prayer, without haggling; go to the help of anyone who looks for you; practice justice and go beyond it with the grace of charity. (*Christ is Passing By*, 77)

Salvatore Canals, based on St. Escrivá's teachings, employs an image for writing divinely a page each day of our life. At the top of each blank page for each day, he writes, "I will serve," as both a desire and a hope. He then tries to write with "neat, clear hand-writing. That means work, prayer, apostolate— all my day's activity." The following is a beautiful exposition:

> I try to pay a lot of attention to punctuation— which is the practice of keeping presence of God. These pauses— commas, or semi-colons or colons— represent the silence of my soul and the aspirations I try to use to give meaning and supernatural outlook to everything I write.
> I particularly like the full stops, because after every full stop I begin, in a way, to write again. They are a kind of indication that I am correcting my intention, saying to our Lord that I am going to start writing again: I'm going to start again with the right intention to serving him and dedicating my life to him, moment by moment, minute by minute.
> I am also careful about dotting my "i's" and crossing my "t's"— the little mortifications which give my life and my work a truly Christian meaning. When I fail to dot an "i" or cross a "t" it means that I didn't accept in a Christian way the mortification which our Lord was sending me, which he had lovingly prepared for me and wanted me to recognize and receive with pleasure.... It hurts me to see that there is hardly a single page that does not have some sign of my awkwardness and clumsiness. But I quickly console myself and recover my serenity by remembering that I am just a little child who hasn't yet learned to write properly, and has to use a ruled sheet under the page to help him write straight, and needs a teacher to guide

his hand to make sure he does not write nonsense: what a good Teacher God our Lord is; what infinite patience he has with me![12]

## C. Highest Obedience to God's Will is through His Representatives

The first inspiration that the Holy Spirit gives is to obedience. The devil does not fear asceticism; he fears obedience and mortification. St. Philip Neri teaches that obedience is the shortcut to heaven, and took the shortcut of constantly consulting his director. Francis de Sales and M.M. Philipon highlight the great importance of following the spiritual director's counsels:

> Go to your confessor; open your heart to him, reveal to him all the recesses of your soul, and accept the advice that he gives you with the utmost humility and simplicity. **God has infinite love for obedience. He often makes profitable the counsels we take from others**, especially those who are the *guides of our souls*, when otherwise there might appear to be *little show of success*. Thus, he made the waters of the Jordan beneficial to Naaman, after Elisha without any sign of human reason had ordered Naaman to use them.[13]
>
> Quite the contrary. The saints have always been anxious to obey their superiors, convinced that **obedience is a royal highway, the surest and quickest way to the greatest holiness**. The Holy Spirit himself inspires such filial submission to the lawful representative of Christ's Church: "He who hears you hears me, and he who rejects you rejects me" (Luke 10:16) [M. M. Philipon, *The Gifts of the Holy Spirit*].[14]

Fr. Jacques Philippe also teaches that this act of obedience pleases God, even if it may sometimes apparently slow down the acting on what He himself is asking.

> God prefers prudence and submission on our part to undue precipitation. Without that obedience, by contrast, it is very probable that we will soon become the plaything of the devil... [who] will lose no time in deceiving us and leading us little by little to do things that no longer have anything to do with the will of God. In case of doubt on what line of conduct to follow, it is normally best to open our hearts to one or more than one person and to *follow their advice* (unless there is a decisive reason for acting otherwise) rather than spend a *long time reflecting and weighing* things up personally, which might cause us to go around in *circles* and increase our confusion rather than diminishing it. (J. Philippe, *School*, 62)

---

[12] Salvatore Canals, *Jesus as Friend* (New York: Scepter Publishers, 1986), 64-65.
[13] Francis de Sales, *Introduction to the Devout Life* (Toronto: Image Books, 1989), 264.
[14] Francis Fernandez, *In Conversation with God*, vol. Two, 558-559.

Regarding Covid-19 vaccinations, the author shares his personal discernment, but does not claim to be a moral theologian nor understand how God works in the consciences of others. But God led him to receive vaccinations in four ways: (i) a sister who said, "we don't have a choice," presumably indicating that she felt it a duty to protect her family by getting vaccinated; (ii) the overwhelmingly clear judgment of the leading epidemiologists; (iii) a priest, a former surgeon, who had consulted experts, and explained that Pfizer-BioNTech and Moderna produced mRNA vaccines that do not employ abortion derived cell lines (though testing did), that teach cells to produce proteins that would trigger an immune response. And he believed that (iv) both the Vatican and the Canadian Conference of Catholic Bishops, after medical and theological consultation, were correct in their approval, yet felt that those who still had concerns about the abortion lines factor could at least use the mRNA vaccines. Here we are not entering into the areas of conscience rights, opposition to mandatory vaccination, and the moral duty to petition for the development of ethical alternatives.

We must preserve each person's right to follow his conscience. Yet, we affirm that, converging with and beyond conscience, there is a higher guide, the indwelling Spirit given at Baptism (St. Ignatius). And God's guidance is given in a privileged way through obedience to His representatives, those given to guide us. Rather than agonizing over conscience only, given that mRNA vaccines do not use aborted fetus cell lines, the author simply follows God's representatives. Barring medical exceptions, the way of spiritual childhood is not to filter decisions through our own ideas, but to submit our God-given will to His representatives (Aid 10). A discernment done through *obedience* typically comes *effortlessly*; when not, it is arduous. When God acts in us, things become effortless (e.g., Fr. Cantalamessa). St. Kolbe underscores this path to great holiness through obedience to God's representatives. He explained that, as long as superiors don't prescribe moral wrongs, we can never go wrong if we obey them, even when they err. For him, along with being led by our Lady, obedience is everything.

Henri de Lubac teaches that the man of God will not spend much time at the human level but will have confidence in his superiors and make it his business to see their point of view from the inside, and see in them Christ Himself. He can never forget that the man's salvation was accomplished by an act of total self-abandonment (cross). He must maintain a certain distrust with regard to his own judgment, that even with the best of intentions he can still grossly deceive himself; he must first and foremost be a submissive member, quick and docile in response to the direction of the Head.[15]

---

[15] Henri de Lubac, *The Splendor of the Church* (San Francisco: Ignatius Press, 2006), 257-267.

## Retreat 1: Towards Mystical Incarnation and Marriage

### Conference 4
### Christ's Universal Love Leads to the Cross

### I. *"They Think too much of Self and not enough about Jesus and Souls"*

Dom Columba Marmion teaches that our greatest problem is self-interest and that intercession for the Church and souls takes us out of ourselves:

> We become so to speak one with Him, *when we take upon us, with Him, all the sorrows, sighings, the sufferings of Holy Church and intercede in the name of all*, full of confidence in His infinite merits…. My dear child, I am speaking to you in this way because the more I see of religious, both men and women, the more I am convinced that the great cause of their troubles is that **most of them think too much of themselves, and too little of Jesus and souls**. If they could once and for all go out of themselves and consecrate their whole life to Jesus and souls, their hearts would become wide as the ocean; they themselves would fly upon the path of perfection…[1] (emphasis added)

St. Vincent de Paul, the great saint of the poor, understood the gift of divine openness of heart to the suffering of others: "We should keep our hearts open to the suffering of other people, and pray continually that God may grant us the spirit of compassion which is truly the spirit of God." A faculty priest once pointed out to seminarians their privileged state within a seminary of the First World. They have professors with doctorates, Cardinals and bishops to give talks and retreats, spiritual direction every two weeks, plentiful meals, an extensive library, two gyms and two kitchen lounges, and much more. But he reminded them that Jesus' heart of love is bleeding for his children in great need: millions of unborn killed each year, genocides (e.g., Armenia), human trafficking, child soldiers and children with Aids in Africa, famine in Sudan, the volatile Middle East, Third World prisoners, lepers, addicts, etc. But that which surpasses all is damnation, for hell never ends! One possessed man shared with Msgr. Rosetti a vision of hell: "Fire engulfed all of the bodies of the souls, the smell of rotting flesh and melting skin was atrocious; it made me want to throw up."[2] The loss of God is overwhelmingly the greatest tragedy, but the devil's presence is horrifying: "As soon as they died, the demons were ready to take their souls and carry them off to hell, there to pay their debts in full," for all eternity (*Sacred Passion*, 189). Salvation of souls is our dominant priority.

---

[1] Columba Marmion, *Union with God*, 130-131.
[2] Stephen Rossetti, *Diary of an American Exorcist* (Manchester, NH: Sophia I. Pr., 2021), 205.

## A. Two Examples of Self-Interest

This example is presented anonymously. A priest's family friend and his wife liked to meet him periodically. What he discovered after numerous meetings was that this friend inevitably brought the subject of conversation around to his siblings, sharing how frustrated he was and how he was at wits' end about what to do with them. After their mother had died, as the eldest, he felt it was his responsibility to help hold them together as a family. He became instead the source of contention, two even distancing themselves from him. After years of listening to his preoccupation, the priest received an insight, that, given that his friend was no longer practicing his Catholic faith and no longer focusing on the Church's needs, everything personal began to take on an inordinate importance; hence his obsession with his relationship with his siblings. The antidote was to expand his world once more, especially to bring God again into his life, perhaps through being mindful of eternity and God's future judgment, and to break open his tunnel-vision to think of families in the world with great troubles. We might perhaps see this as *narcissism*. For those serving God, there can be the specific danger of *lukewarmness,* that Francis Fernandez describes as involving "carelessness, lack of interest, laziness and disinclination in fulfilling our duties," here quoting St. Escrivá:

> You are lukewarm if you carry out lazily and reluctantly those things that have to do with our Lord; if deliberately or "shrewdly" you look for some way of cutting down your duties; *if you think only of yourself and of your comfort*; if your conversations are idle and vain; if you do not abhor venial sin; if you act from human motives. (*The Way* n. 331, emphasis added)[3]

In the person of Judas, we see how self-interest can lead to resistance and a heart conquered by evil. Scripture reveals that he was a thief, stealing from the common purse. He murmured at Mary's largesse and at Jesus's teaching that they must consume His body and blood:

> As he more and more got into this habit [of stealing], he little by little came to hate Jesus, who was teaching love of poverty and condemning greed. He so hardened his heart that he came to blame the Lord for his own uneasiness and discomfort, and to criticize everything the Lord did, instead of acknowledging that he himself was the one at fault. It got to the point where, finally, he stopped believing in the Lord; he regarded his teachings as fabrications and deception, and his miracles as sorcery; and he harmed the others with his words and bad example.[4]

---

[3] Francis Fernandez, *In Conversation with God*, vol. 1 (New York: Scepter, 1988), 100.
[4] Luis de la Palma, *The Sacred Passion* (New York: Scepter Publs., 2004), 15.

## B. Only God can Heal our Deep Egoism through the Dark Nights

We cannot overcome egoism and self-interest except through God's divine healing in the Dark Nights. St. John of the Cross teaches that we are called to become God through participation (divinization), by which we are more and more transformed into Trinitarian life, into life in Christ, to radiate the Christ's love in our world. But because we are broken, arising from original and personal sins, we need to be healed through the passive (God is active) process of purification, the Dark Nights. We cooperate through living the theological virtues of faith, hope, and love (received at Baptism). Faith purifies and communicates God, who transcends our reason and concepts of God. The key for John is that faith latches on to Christ; we focus on and imitate Jesus, who is the Way, the Truth, and the Life: "no one comes to the Father but through Me" (Jn 14:6). Thus, those who seek visions are not only guilty of foolish behaviour but of taking their eyes off Christ. Walking with Christ His path of the cross through the garment of faith, we are tested by internal and external trials of life. God conveys Himself primarily through the trials in life; it is the principle of "through death to resurrection." St. John believes that many people do not grow because they refuse the crosses God allows.[5] "The most beautiful act of faith is the one made in darkness, in sacrificing and with extreme effort" (Padre Pio).

## C. The "Form of a Slave" (Phil 2:6) to Shoulder World's Sins

Saints follow Christ's taking the form of a slave to take upon Himself the world's sins as if they were His own. But we cannot fathom the depth of His self-abasement because it is equal to His love, and we cannot penetrate the depths of His love that flows from His seeing the infinite offense against the Father and taking upon Himself the sins of humanity. It pained Him deeply to see that some would choose eternal damnation. Here is a profound insight into His identification with all suffering for love of Him:

> The Lord made all this pain [all past sufferings in history endured for love of Him] his own, and he suffered it. If, when his followers were later being persecuted by Saul, he said to him, "Why are you persecuting me?" (Acts 9:4), he must in the same way have been injured by the stones with which the deacon Stephen was killed, and burned by the fire that burned Saint Lawrence, and afflicted by all the tribulations of his saints. He knew them all, and understood better than anyone else this pain, and accepted it, and offered it to his eternal Father in his prayer. The suffering of his Mystical Body [members of Church] was the suffering of his own body.[6]

---

[5] Daniel Chowning, "Created for Love: A Retreat on St. John of the Cross."
[6] Luis de la Palma, *The Sacred Passion*, 44 (cf. 42-43).

This was a trait of the great Jesuit and theologian, Jean Daniélou, known for making no distinction between his sins and the sins of the world. Such saintly souls typically have little time for themselves; for self-concern, self-introspection, and for social life.

> Jesus, I have come to know that you do not want me to distinguish my sins from the other sins of the world, but to enter more deeply into your heart and consider myself responsible for the sins of those persons whom you may wish: those of Alain, of anyone else as it may please you. You make me feel, Jesus, that I must descend even lower, take with me the sins of others, accept as a result all the punishments that these may draw down upon me from your justice, and in a particular way the disdain of the persons for whom I will offer myself. To accept, or rather to long for dishonor, even in the eyes of those whom I love. To accept the great abasements, of which I am not worthy, in order to be ready at least to accept the small ones. Then, Jesus, my charity will resemble that with which you have loved me.[7]

This becoming one with the world's sins appears to be the work of possession by the Spirit, reflected in the spirit of Georges Chevrot:

> The collective sins of a society which tolerates public immorality and the misery of the slums are in part his [Christian's] sin, since he is one of the members of that society. He cannot stop the sins, which he abhors, from being committed. He must live and suffer in this continual tension.
> In this terrible contradiction, we Christians, like the Lamb of God, bear "the sins of the world," and by this laceration of our consciences and our hearts we continue the sufferings of the Saviour, who was crucified for the redemption of men. It is our vocation to suffer this torture, to endure the solitude of the Cross in the midst of the multitude, to be shrouded in the shadows of Golgotha and to have only the bitterness of our failures to quench our thirst for justice. (*The Eight Beatitudes*, 145)

As noted by Fr. Arintero, it is possession by the Spirit in transformation into Christ in the Unitive Mansions that brings about this transformation.

> All its [the soul's] aims have been changed and have become so divine that no self-interest is left in the soul. All its interest now lies in **the glory of God, the prosperity of the Church, and the welfare of souls**. It pays no heed to its own interests for it has placed them in the hands of the sweet Master, and He is charged to care for the soul and see that it is not bothered by these interests while engaged in His divine service.[8]

---

[7] Matthew Schmitz, "Despising Jean Daniélou," *First Things*, accessed Dec. 19, 2021, https://www.firstthings.com/web-exclusives/2015/03/despising-jean-danielou.
[8] John G. Arintero, *The Mystical Evolution* (Rockford, IL: Tan Publns., 1978), vol. 2, 172.

## II. Participating in Christ's Victimhood

Before continuing, we first clarify that suffering at the human level is a great mystery, and constitutes perhaps the greatest scandal to acceptance of a Christian God who is love. Yet Christ chose to use the cross to redeem the world, and now uses our crosses to co-redeem the world. Ratzinger calls for the elect to become the reject. While the Christian is called to evangelization and charity, his highest task is to suffer vicariously as the Master did ("The Son of Man… to give His life as a ransom for many," Mk 10:45): "When all other ways fail, there will always remain the royal way of vicarious suffering by the side of the Lord. It is in its defeat that the Church constantly achieves its highest victory, and stands nearest to Christ."[9] In the face of much opposition, Alice von Hildebrand with faith could say: "God has woven a beautiful nest out of the 'twigs' of my life… reassuring us of the providence of God in everything and His tender love for even the little sparrows whom He delights in using" (Claire Dwyer, "A Happy Failure").

### A. Explaining the "Stumbling Block" of the Cross (1 Cor 1:23)

#### 1. The Apostolate of Prayer and Sacrifice
The greatest model of victimhood, of prayer and sacrifice, is our Lady.

> There was awakened [at the Last Supper] in the Blessed Virgin a great and ever more ardent love. By light from the Holy Spirit she understood well the majesty of God, the wickedness of human beings, and the bitterness of the pain that her Son would endure for them. She "reflected on these things in her heart" (Lk 2:51) and realized the immensity of God's love and of the benefit that God was bestowing on us all. And in her humility she responded to that knowledge with a profound gratitude to him and a burning love for the world that he "so loved that he gave his only Son" (Jn 3:16). Stirred by God's generosity, she too desired to be wholly and entirely dedicated to the salvation of sinners…. At seeing her Son standing, the Blessed Virgin withdrew to await by herself for their last embrace, that final farewell which would cost her such effort…. The tears flowed down our Lady's cheeks. Her heart was pierced [broken] with pain by constant effort to obey and love what God disposed. But her love was great; for she was able to offer up her Son, whom she loved so much, for the glory of God and the salvation of human beings.[10]

Fulton Sheen saw instead that some in the postconciliar period wanted Christ but not the cross; a facsimile of Christianity, a reversal of the Spirit's path of love in leading Jesus to the cross and the early Church through persecution.

---

[9] Joseph Ratzinger, *The Meaning of Christian Brotherhood*, 84.
[10] Luis de la Palma *The Sacred Passion*, 30-32.

Each soul, possessed by Jesus' universal heart, must permit the Holy Spirit to stretch it to accept being led to the cross. The *Unitive stages*, beginning in the Fifth Mansions, spur souls towards a life of reparation and even desires for martyrdom for sinners, to the conformation to Christ crucified found in saints. We find this paradigm lived out in the living martyrdom of St. Paul of the Cross. We highlight his secret of fruitfulness: "Eventually they [like Paul] bear a perfect resemblance to Christ crucified and are the means of saving many souls. It is this apostolate of suffering and prayer which is the hidden source of the fruitfulness of the apostolate of preaching and instructing— a fact well known to God and the Angels."[11]

This pattern abounds in the lives of saints, who all live victimhood. Here is a description of St. Thérèse's silent martyrdom. For Thérèse, suffering was the price for souls: "Yes, suffering opened wide its arms to me and I threw myself into them with love... Jesus made me understand that it was through suffering that He wanted to give me souls."[12] She said, "My whole strength lies in **prayer and sacrifice**, these are my invincible arms; they can move hearts far better than words, I know it by experience." We wish to acknowledge a marvelous Russian saint, Princess Elizabeth Feodorovna, who converted from Protestantism to Orthodoxy. When her beloved fiancé died before their wedding, out of duty she married his brother, and forgave his killer. She gave up her wealth, and became a nun devoted to the poor. Lenin ordered her arrest and death. In danger, she had refused to escape Russia. Known for her charity, her husband had called her "the guardian angel of Russia," and one biography was titled, "Little Mother of Russia."

## 2. Mother Teresa Explains Need of the Cross for Apostolic Fruitfulness

We find in Mother Teresa an identification with India's poor in poverty and darkness in her 50 years of a dark night of the soul (1946-1997). One fruit is the light brought to the world, fulfilling Jesus' call, "Come, be my light."

> She was called to share in a distinct way in the mystery of the Cross, to become one with Christ in His Passion and one with the poor she served. Through this sharing she was led to a deep awareness of the "painful thirst" in the Heart of Jesus for the poorest of the poor. The darkness she experienced and described in her letters, in which the strength and beauty of her soul shines forth, was a terrible and unrelenting torment. In the lives of the saints, it is almost without parallel; only the experience of St. Paul of the Cross is comparable in length.[13]

---

[11] Reginald Garrigou-Lagrange, *The Priest in Union with Christ* (Rockford, IL: Tan Books, 2002), 225-226.
[12] St. Thérèse, quoted in ibid., 150.
[13] Brian Kolodiejchuk, *Come Be My Light* (Toronto, ON: Image-Doubleday, 2007), 335.

The key to this is the desire to share in Christ's painful "thirst," a spirituality of quenching Christ's thirst on the cross, so central that, in each chapel of all Missionary of Charity houses in the world, the words of Jesus, "I thirst," are found below the crucifix. Mother Teresa also came to know the power of this suffering for the work of her Sisters. The people they served were in darkness and at the cross: "The same great crowd—they were covered in darkness. Yet I could see them. Our Lord on the Cross. Our Lady at a little distance from the Cross— and myself as a little child in front of her."[14] In the following revealing text, she taught her Sisters that, as Jesus identified with us in our darkness, they too would have to identify, to be one, with the darkness of the people they served:

> My dear children— without our suffering, our work would just be *social work*, very good and helpful, but it would not be the work of *Jesus Christ, not part of the redemption*— Jesus wanted to help us by sharing our life, our loneliness, our agony and death. All that He has taken upon Himself, and has carried it in the darkest night. Only by being **one with us** He has redeemed us. We are allowed to do the same: all the desolation of the poor people, not only their material poverty, but their spiritual destitution must be redeemed, and we must have our share in it.— Pray thus when you find it hard— "I wish to live in this world which is so far from God, which has turned so much from the light of Jesus, to help them—to take upon me something of their suffering."—Yes, my dear children—let us share the sufferings—of our poor—for only by being one with them—we can redeem them, that is, *bringing God into their lives and bringing them to God*.[15] (emphasis added)

This became a joy for Mother Teresa. She marvelled at God's love for the poor in India, and she longed to identify with Christ in His passion for India.[16] Here we find the apex of spiritual life that mirrors Christ's passion. St. Francis of Assisi also knew great joy in being wedded to Lady Poverty, in His ineffable union with God, in His hope, and in suffering out of love:

> "This [perfect happiness] does not consist in giving good example, in performing miracles, in knowing... the Scriptures; it does not consist in converting all unbelievers to the Father of Christ, but *in suffering all things with patience and with happiness, thinking of the pains of the blessed Christ*, which he had to suffer for love of us."[17]

---

[14] Ibid., 99.
[15] Ibid., 220.
[16] For deeper insight into Mother Teresa's darkness, see Carol Zaleski, "The Dark Night of Mother Teresa," *First Things* (May 2003). Carol Zaleski is a professor of religion at Smith College in Northampton, Massachusetts.
[17] Luis Martinez, *The Sanctifier* (Boston, MA: Pauline Books & Media, 2003), 223-230.

### 3. St. Jane Frances de Chantal's Alternative "Martyrdom of Love"

St. Jane Frances de Chantal describes a martyrdom of love that is at least as great as the martyrdom by blood, which is the martyrdom of great confessors, like St. Jerome and St. Augustine. When asked to elaborate on this love, she explained that in this martyrdom God severs these souls from all that is dear to them (as He did with her, e.g., death of her husband and a few children). But this, she revealed, is only granted to those who give themselves totally in abandonment and hold nothing back, great-souled persons (OOR for her feast day). For those who do not, God, not wishing to lose them, allows them to follow their own limited and more tepid path.

### 4. We are to be Taken out of Self for God and His Flock

The height of sanctity is the cross: "[Christ] may be leading me out to a cross. If so, I can have no hesitation about following Him! I must follow Him closely, so that… I shall be near Him, my good Shepherd, Who will help me to carry it, for He still bears His Cross in each one of His children" (St. K. Drexel). St. Augustine, in his *Commentary on John* on Jesus' three-fold questioning of Peter to lead him to "feed" His flock, warns shepherds against treating Christ's flock as their own, loving themselves and not Christ (OOR for St. Nicholas' feast day). Pastoral ministry, especially at the parish, can be a two-edged sword. We are to seek to do all only for Christ and souls by interiorly choosing not to seek thanks, appreciation, or esteem. God granted Francis de Sales a special gift at his episcopal ordination of a mystical experience by which he was taken out of himself for his people:

> When I was consecrated Bishop, God took me away from myself, that He might take me to Himself, and then He gave me to the people. That is to say, He converted me from what I had been *for myself* to what I should be *for them*, and thus may it come to pass that being taken away from ourselves, we may be converted to Him by the sovereign perfection of His most holy love.[18]

## B. The Saints Live the Path of Victimhood for the Universal Church

Luis Martinez explains that Christian victimhood must be understood against the fifth Beatitude, "Blessed are the merciful." Where it can be *merely human and even egoistic to love only those dear to us, we are to love or pity those who are weak, for mercy is infinite and takes on the troubles of our enemies*. It is the overflowing ocean of the infinite God that descends "to the abyss of all miseries in order to fill it with the opulence of his plenitude." Ascending the ladder of the Beatitudes

---

[18] St. Francis de Sales, taken from *The Depositions of St. Jeanne de Chantal in the Cause of the Canonisation of St. François de Sales*, pp. 78-79, quoted in Jean-Pierre Camus, *The Spirit of St. François de Sales*, 248-249, footnote 10.

through the Spirit's gifts, it breaks the bonds of the narrow human moulds and *throws itself into action*. Through two gifts of the Holy Spirit, the light of counsel that contemplates misfortune as Christ did and the strength of fortitude, along with the infused virtues, the soul sweats the blood of Gethsemane and becomes a victim on Calvary. Through the Spirit, mercy is a divine flame, that cannot be satiated, that seeks to carry the burden of and enfold the miseries of all.[19] John Paul II teaches: "Prayer joined to sacrifice constitutes the most powerful force in human history."

***1. St. Catherine Desired the Church's Wounds be Visited on Her Body***
Thomas McDermott, O.P., writes of St. Catherine of Siena's Christ-like intercession and reparation (e.g., stigmata, a pope turned against her):

> Catherine's love for the Church was certainly not confined to the sanctuary. Her long journeys to Avignon, Florence, and Rome and her letters to virtually all the leaders of Europe attest to the practicality of her love. About two years before her death, the Lord commanded her to "wash the face of my Bride, holy Church" with her prayers, sweat, and tears. Every day she would drag her frail body to St. Peter's Basilica, where she would pray for hours on behalf of the Church. Her final act of self-offering to God occurred in another mystical experience exactly three months before her death, in which she cries out to God: "What can I do, inestimable Fire?" He answers: "Offer your life once more, and never let yourself rest. This was the task I set you, and now set you again, you and all who follow you." Catherine replies: "O eternal God, receive the sacrifice of my life into this mystical body of holy Church. I have nothing to give except what you have given me, so take my heart and squeeze it out over the face of the Bride." Catherine recounts that God then removed her heart (which, in a previous vision years earlier, he had mystically exchanged with his own) and squeezed out every drop of blood over the face of the Church, washing it clean of all impurity.[20]

***2. Victimhood in Cardinals Joseph Ratzinger and George Pell***
Joseph Ratzinger, labelled as "God's Rottweiler," as severe and doctrinaire, lived this victimhood, willing to preach truth no matter the consequences:

> Both before and after his election as pope, Joseph Ratzinger bore the slings and arrows that were hurled at him by many within and outside the Church. Members of the secular and ecclesial liberal elite media were, and still are, relentless in their criticism and in the characterization of him as an

---

[19] Luis Martinez, *The Sanctifier*, 321-326.
[20] Thomas McDermott, "St. Catherine of Siena and Leaving the Church," *The Catholic World Report*, accessed Nov. 10, 2021,
https://www.catholicworldreport.com/2021/04/29/catherine-of-siena-and-leaving-the-church/.

unyielding rigid conservative.... Benedict, as a person, as an academic, as an archbishop, as Pope, and now in his retirement, is a light in the darkness of our present world. His light will continue to shine even when he has passed from this world into his heavenly reward.[21]

This iron with compassion is evident also in George Pell, one of the senior Cardinals in the Church. After being under a cloud of suspicion for sexual abuse for about six years, was found guilty, imprisoned for over a year, and then finally and unanimously freed of charges by the supreme court (*Prison Journal* 1-3). Benedict XVI and Pell lived the divine level of the dark nights, where they follow the Master's path of persecution and public humiliation.

### *3. The Opposition to the Holy Spirit's Charisms in the Church's History*
Francisca J. del Valle, in *About the Holy Spirit*, reveals that the Spirit taught her that, when a person resolutely decides to become a saint, Satan himself enters the fray, as a saint causes untold damage to his "kingdom." The Church has witnessed virulent reactions to the Spirits' charisms, e.g., the resistance from the secular clergy to the Franciscan and Dominican Orders, and later, the opposition that St. Ignatius and St. Teresa of Jesus endured for their foundations. John Paul II once asked Mother Teresa, "Why does the press always talk well about Mother Teresa, but not about Opus Dei or me?" After Paul VI, subsequently endorsed by John Paul I and John Paul II, suggested the ecclesial status of a personal prelature as conforming to the "secular" charism of Opus Dei, virulent opposition surfaced: documents were twice stolen from a Vatican Congregation, with phrases taken out of context, and a report/pamphlet sent to newspaper and bishops that portrayed the Work as seeking to escape bishops' control to become a "parallel Church"; after approval, false calumnies were circulated in the media; and "inaccurate expressions" appeared in the Bull that would have undermined its nature. Through it all, A. del Portillo remained calm, turning to our Lady, having only the glory of God and service to the Church as his motivation, asking for prayers for the perpetrators as "benefactors."[22]

## C. Two Victim Souls

### *1. Sr. Carmelina Tarantino*
Many in the Church are at this point still unfamiliar with Sr. Carmelina Tarantino, called by Jesus to be a victim soul. There are indications that Jesus appeared to her periodically and asked her to make expiation for the sins of the world. It was to this humble bed at Riverdale Hospital that many Italian immigrants flocked for counsel and prayers.

---

[21] T.G. Weinandy, "I Appreciate His Quiet Humility," *Inside the Vatican*, Mar.-Apr. 2022, 15.
[22] John F. Coverdale, Saxum, 197, 200-211.

On July 4, 1964, 27-year-old Carmelina Tarantino was brought to Toronto from Naples, Italy, by her brothers and sister who were worried about her health. Canadian doctors suspected she had a rare type of cancer. They amputated her left leg, parts of her right leg and she had a mastectomy. Her hospital blanket was canopied over her body to avoid the blanket becoming stained by her bloodied bandages, which had to be changed every few hours as her wounds refused to heal. Doctors said she had only months to live, but she endured for 24 years, bedridden in Room 306 West at Riverdale Hospital (now Bridgeport Health).

In conversation one day, she mentioned to Piccinini how she had wanted to become a religious sister since the age of 10 or 11.... On Nov. 26, 1977, 40-year-old Sr. Carmelina was professed in her hospital room as the first Passionist Sister in Toronto....

As her spiritual director and close confidant, Piccinini visited every week. He watched her receive morphine shots every six hours, suffer constant fevers and endure frequent blood transfusions because her wounds would not heal. She kept a journal.[23]

## 2. Adrienne von Speyr ("Servant of God" as of this writing)

Adrienne von Speyr was a medical doctor who became a collaborator of Hans Urs von Balthasar, her spiritual director. She is the greatest mystical theologian of the twentieth century, dictated some 60 books to von Balthasar, and they founded the lay institute Community of St. John. She wrote profoundly about Jesus' suffering and suffered with Him.

Von Balthasar wrote that shortly after her conversion, "a veritable cataract of mystical graces poured over Adrienne in a seemingly chaotic storm that whirled her in all directions at once. Graces in prayer above all: she was transported beyond all vocal prayer or self-directed meditation upon in order to be set down somewhere after an indeterminate time with new understanding, new love and new resolutions." This included "an increasingly open and intimate association with Mary..." Driving home one night shortly after her conversion, she saw a great light in front of the car and she heard a voice say... "You shall live in heaven and on earth." This was "the key to all that was to follow" in her life. The years following 1940 were filled with much physical pain (including a heart attack, diabetes, and severe arthritis and, eventually blindness), mystical experiences (including the stigmata), and a close relationship with Fr. von Balthasar, who became her spiritual director and confidant and with whom she helped found a secular institute, the Community of St John. She began to dictate works to Balthasar, including her interpretations of several books of Scripture (the Johannine writings, some of Paul, the Catholic Epistles, the Apocalypse, and parts of the Old Testament). Balthasar wrote,

---

[23] Jean Ko Din, "The Case for Sr. Carmelina's Sainthood," *The Catholic Register*, accessed Dec. 19, 2021, https://www.catholicregister.org/item/29216-the-case-for-sr-carmelina-s-sainthood.

"She seldom dictated for more than half an hour per day. During vacations she would occasionally dictate for two or three hours, but this was rare." The result was some sixty books dictated between 1940 and 1953. "Her spiritual productivity knew no limits," wrote Balthasar, "we could just as well have two or three times as many texts of hers today."

By 1954 Adrienne was so ill that she had to discontinue her medical practice. She spent hours each day in prayer, knitting clothing for the poor, and reading Bernanos and Mauriac, among other French authors. From her mid-fifties on, she was so ill that physicians wondered how she could remain alive. In 1964 she went blind; her last months were filled with "continuous, merciless torture," said Balthasar, "which she bore with great equanimity, always concerned about the others and constantly apologetic about causing me so much trouble." She died on September 17, 1967, the feast of St. Hildegard, also a mystic and a physician.[24]

## Synthesis

We synthesize the paradigm of the apostles: they encountered Jesus; followed Him ("Come, follow me"); conformed themselves to Him (becoming Christ); and co-redeemed the world, especially through martyrdom. The path to God entails both self-knowledge of our spiritual poverty and abandonment to the Spirit. But the apex of this path of love is ascending the cross to co-redeem the world: "My sole merit lies in Christ's wounds" (St. Gabriel of our Lady of Sorrows). That the world's evils seem to be ascendant can overwhelm us. We can draw hope from Jesus' reassurance to Julian of Norwich. When she felt that all would have been well had we not sinned and wondered why God had not prevented sin, Jesus responded: "Sin is necessary but all shall be well, and all shall be well, and all manner of things shall be well."[25] She learned that "God loved us before He made us; and His love has never diminished and never shall." All this gives hope for the world.

Regarding the Church, Jesus consolingly revealed to St. Catherine about "the persecution of the Church is now undergoing and of the renewal and exaltation that is to come. He told me that what is happening now is permitted in order to make the Church once more what she should be."[26] The cross has lasting power: "Our Saviour's Passion raises men and women from the depths, lifts them up from the earth and sets them in the heights" (St. Maximus of Turin).

---

[24] "Adrienne von Speyr," *Ignatius Press,* accessed Jan. 8, 2022, http://www.ignatiusinsight.com/authors/adrienne_von_speyr.asp.
[25] Julian of Norwich, *Showing of Love,* ed. Julia B. Holloway (The Liturgical Press), Ch. 27.
[26] Thomas McDermott, "St. Catherine of Siena and Leaving the Church," 112.

## Retreat 1: Towards Mystical Incarnation and Marriage
### Conference 5
### Endgame: Mystical Incarnation and Trinitarian Communion

### *Background: Sacred Heart Apparitions*

This retreat thus leads to the two greatest realities: the cross of pain on earth (fourth talk) and the dove of eternal love in heaven, treated here in this fifth talk. Both realities are portrayed in the Sacred Heart apparitions to St. Margaret Mary Alacoque at Paray-le-Monial in France in the 17th century. We find in Jesus' lament to her two main elements: His profession of love for us; and His lament that we do not reciprocate with our love. These two elements can be said to constitute the core of salvation history, a Theodrama of love between God and creature. God seems to intensify His call for love with deeper revelations of His love (e.g., Sacred Heart, Divine Mercy, mystics).

> Behold this Heart which has so loved men that It spared nothing, even going so far as to exhaust and consume Itself, to prove to them Its love. And in return I receive from the greater part of men nothing but ingratitude, by the contempt, irreverence, sacrileges and coldness with which they treat Me in this Sacrament of Love. (Sacred Heart apparitions)

The ensuing mystical marriage ("two become one flesh") accomplishes our mystical incarnation, for each to become "another Christ, Christ Himself." Thus, the goal of Christ's Incarnation is to accomplish a mystical incarnation or a substitution of Christ. Christ lives again in our humanity as an extension of Himself and glorifies the Father and recapitulates humanity. But our "being in Christ" is attained to the extent to which we have destroyed our own ego (p. 57), to become one in with all those in Christ (D. von Hildebrand). C. Lubich points to our need to become "nothing."

> The Father generates the Son out of love. Going completely out of himself, so to speak, he makes himself, in a certain sense, "non-being" out of love and for this very reason he is Father. The Son, in turn, as an echo of the Father, returns to the Father out of love, making himself, too, in a certain sense, "non-being" out of love and for this very reason he is Son. The Holy Spirit who is the mutual love between the Father and the Son, their bond of unity, also makes himself, in a certain sense, "non-being" out of love—that "non-being" and "emptiness of love" in which the Father and Son meet and are one. And for this very reason he is Holy Spirit.[1]

### *I. God's Love for Us*

---

[1] Chiara Lubich, "The Spirituality of Unity and Trinitarian Life," New Humanity Review n. 9, *livingcitymagazine.com*.

## A. Jansenism and God's Response

### *1. God Desires that we Experience Deeply His Love for us*
A Missionary of Charity Sister, addressing residents in a youth detention center, asked: "How many of you believe that God loves you?" When not one person put up his hand, she pleaded with them: "Remember that the devil is a liar, and the greatest lie he tries to foist on you is that God does not love you." The Christian faith forcefully proclaims God's love as the heart of history (as just seen in the Sacred Heart apparitions). In this vein, Jesus revealed to Faustina that that which wounds His heart most is a lack of trust, that we "do not understand the greatness of My Mercy."

> A greater wound to the Heart of the Lord (which He often spoke about in His dialogues with Saint Maria Faustina) is *our lack of trust in His unfathomable Divine Mercy*. St. Faustina told her fellow religious, Sister Justine, that "When a soul fears getting close to the Lord Jesus after a fall, then it wounds the Sacred Heart of Jesus horribly, for the lack of trust hurts Him more than the most terrible sins."
> 
> "My Heart is sorrowful because even chosen souls do not understand the greatness of My mercy. Their relationship with Me is, in certain ways, imbued with mistrust. Oh, how much that wounds My Heart! Remember My Passion, and if you do not believe My words, at least believe My wounds." (*Diary* n. 379, emphasis added)

Since experiencing Jesus' love, St. Faustina wrote that she has no fear and could abandon herself totally into Him. Saints deeply understand this truth.

> Love casts out fear. Since I came to love God with my whole being and with all the strength of my heart, **fear has left me**.... I have placed my trust in God and fear nothing. I have given myself over to His holy will; let Him do with me as He wishes, and I will still love Him (St. Faustina's *Diary* 589).
> Our sins are nothing but a grain of sand alongside the great mountain of God's mercy. (St. John Vianney)
> It is not because I have been preserved from mortal sin that I lift up my heart to God in trust and love. I feel that even had I on my conscience every crime one could commit, I should lose nothing of my confidence: my heart broken with sorrow, I would throw myself into the Arms of my Saviour. I know that He loves the Prodigal Son, I have heard His words to St. Mary Magdalen, to the woman taken in adultery, and to the woman of Samaria. No one could frighten me, for I know what to believe concerning His Mercy and His Love. And I know that *all that multitude of sins would disappear in an instant, even as a drop of water cast into a flaming furnace.* (St. Thérèse, *Story of a Soul*)

## 2. Jansenism

Jansenism is a modern-day rigorism ("Beware of trying to accomplish anything by force," St. Angela Merici), a pernicious heresy that presents God as a harsh judge. God combatted this through revelations (e.g., Sacred Heart, Divine Mercy) and saints, like St. John Vianney:

> Some years he heard over 70,000 confessions, spending up to 17 hours a day in the confessional. He had shed the Jansenistic influences in his spirituality and while he remained fiercely ascetic, *he became an ever more passionate witness of God's infinite mercy*: "Our sins are like grains of sand beside the great mountain of the mercies of the Good God."
>
> He himself described priesthood as "love of the Heart of Christ." No doubt he would have agreed with Thomas Merton's description of the Holy Trinity: *"Mercy within Mercy within Mercy."* The secret of his sanctity and of the fruitfulness of his ministry lay in the fact that John Vianney depended on God for everything. "We are but beggars before God." His pastoral life was nourished by deep prayer: "Prayer is the inner bath of love into which the soul plunges itself". He lived the mysteries of the faith he celebrated in the sacraments, especially the Eucharist.[2]

## B. Experience of God's Love as Mercy on Sinners

Francis Fernandez, in a meditation on Advent, expresses deeply how God's central attribute is mercy.

> Each page of the Gospel is an example of the divine mercy. We should meditate on the life of Jesus because Jesus is a summary and compendium of the story of divine mercy..... Many other scenes of the Gospel also made a deep impact on us, such as his forgiveness of the woman taken in adultery, the parables— the prodigal son, the lost sheep, the pardoned debtor— and the raising to life of the widow at Nain.... Jesus did not perform His miracle out of justice, but out of compassion, because his heart was moved by the spectacle of human suffering.... The mercy of God is the essence of the whole mystery of salvation, the reason for all his saving acts.
>
> God is mercy. And this divine attribute is like the engine supplying the power that energizes the life-story of every human being. When the apostles wanted to sum up God's revelation, his mercy always appeared to them to be the essence of an eternal and gratuitous plan springing from God's generosity.... What a joy to be able to say to God, with St. Augustine: *All*

---

[2] "A radically humble priest who overcame formidable obstacles," *The Irish Times*, accessed Dec. 19, 2021, https://www.irishtimes.com/opinion/a-radically-humble-priest-who-overcame-formidable-obstacles-1.717037.

*my hope lies solely in your great mercy.* Solely in that, Lord. On your mercy rests all my hope. Not on my merits, but on your mercy.[3]

The love of God for sinners is represented especially in Paul, the feared persecutor of Christians (arrested many and even cast votes for their deaths), who encountered Christ "who loved me and gave himself for me."

> The most important thing of all to him, however, was that he knew himself to be loved by Christ. Enjoying this love, he considered himself happier than anyone else; were he without it, it would be no satisfaction to be the friend of principalities and powers. He preferred to be thus loved and be the least of all, or even to be among the damned, than to be without that love and be among the great and honoured. To be separated from that love was, in his eyes, the greatest and most extraordinary of torments; the pain of that loss would alone have been hell, and endless, unbearable torture.
>
> So too, in being loved by Christ he thought of himself as possessing life, the world, the angels, present and future, the kingdom, the promise and countless blessings. Apart from that love nothing saddened or delighted him; for nothing earthly did he regard as bitter or sweet. (St. Chrysostom, OOR, St. Paul)

## C. Experience of Christ's Spousal Love

Here are several figures in which Christ's spousal love is manifest.

***Fergus Kerr on Spousal Recovery in the Twentieth Century***: His research concluded that there has been a recovery of what is already in the Old Testament (e.g., Hosea, Song of Songs), New Testament, Church Fathers, and St. Bernard, of a spousal element in theology that we find in John Paul II (e.g., Theology of the Body), von Balthasar, Henri de Lubac, and others.

***Nicholas Cabasilas, Blessed Isaac of Stella***
The writings of the Church Fathers and mystics present Christ as the Bridegroom (e.g., in their Commentaries on the Song of Songs).

> ... it is the Bridegroom who has smitten them with this longing [ecstasy of love]. It is he who has sent a ray of his beauty into their eyes. The greatness of the wound already shows the arrow which has struck home, the longing indicates who has inflicted the wound. (cf. Cabasilas, *The Life in Christ*, the Second Book, § 15)
>
> But God has taken a bride. The Almighty has taken the feeble one, the Most High has taken the lowly one – out of a servant he has made a queen. She was behind and beneath him and he raised her to be at his side. From out

---

[3] Francis Fernandez, *In Conversation with God*, vol. 1, n. 83 (pp. 26-27).

of his wounded side she came, and he took her to be his bride. Just as all that the Father has is the Son's, so too what the Son has is the Father's, since they share the same undivided nature. In just the same way the bridegroom gave all that was his to the bride and shared all that she had, making her one with himself and the Father. Hear the Son making his plea to the Father for his bride: *I desire that just as you and I are one, so these should be one with us.* (Blessed Isaac of Stella, Abbot)

**St. Bernard**: St. Bernard stands out because of his mystical writings on God's spousal love. In the Church's mystical tradition, **St. Bernard** counsels *moving from the intellect to the heart* (OOR of his feast day) and disputed with Peter Abelard's dialectical Scholasticism.

**John Paul II**: "What really matters in life is that we are loved by Christ and that we love Him in return. In comparison to Jesus' love, everything else is secondary. And, without the love of Jesus, everything is useless"; "Life with Christ is a wonderful adventure"; "God made us for joy. God is joy, and the joy of living reflects the original joy that God felt in creating us."

**Chiara Lubich**: Chiara was given the charism to see Jesus' presence, not only in the Eucharist, but also in families, streets, work; in any community of those who loved one another as He loved us, thereby making "Jesus present in the midst." They "experienced peace that is 'not of this world' (see Jn 14:27), new ardor, the ability to penetrate the Scriptures and understand the steps they had to take." It is built upon three main Scripture texts. First, these fruits were the fulfillment of "Where two or three are gathered in my name, I am there among them" (Mt 18:20). But the basis for this presence was living the New Commandment, "Just as I have loved you, you also should love one another" (Jn 13:34). Where the Church of her time still had a juridical and institutional image of herself, Chiara proclaimed the fundamental vision of the Church as unity or communion, a recovery of the early Church's image. But what underlie both Jesus in the midst and their unity is *Jesus forsaken*: "My God, my God, why have you forsaken me?" (Mt 27:46; Mk 15:34). We give her concrete steps in living this last pillar.

> Jesus forsaken teaches how to not turn in on ourselves, but rather to project outwards in love for others, having an attitude that involves the death of oneself, the crucifixion of one's ego. It is an act of free and deliberate self-denial, almost cancelling out one-self, and yet it is inspired by love, and so is not negative or destructive. "This total renunciation is important," Chiara said, "and it is necessary also to renounce even our inspirations, even what might be divine in us, like Jesus forsaken did, in order to reach unity, in order to have Jesus in our midst." Jesus forsaken therefore expressed the radical nature of the love required of Christians, to achieve unity, loving one another *as* Jesus loved us.

Christian life is ultimately to love others as Jesus loved us, which requires a "cancelling" of self, renouncing even our inspirations. Chiara thus leads the way in today's call of the Holy Spirit in the Third Millennium to cultivate a Spirituality of Communion, to live the heart of the Trinity. She pinpoints this love as the greatest evangelizing force in the Church.[4]

### D. Experience of the Paternal Love of the Father

There has been a highlighting in our times of divine filiation. The goal is for Christ to lead us to the Father, to hear, "You are my Son, the Beloved."

***St. Josemaría Escrivá***: St. Escrivá was given a profound experience on a streetcar of divine filiation that left him in a mystical trance and only able to utter *"Abba, Father, Abba, Father."*

***St. Marguerite D'Youville***: St. Marguerite too, in the deepest ebb of her life, was given an experience of God as "Eternal Father," which sustained her in her trials (e.g., burning down of hospital, opposition and ridicule).

### E. Experience of God's Love Leads to Trinitarian Communion

***Cardinal Sarah***: He writes profoundly that all Christian life, such as mission and liturgy, is to lead to the experience of God's Trinitarian love.

> The liturgy should put us face to face with God in a personal relationship of intense intimacy. **It should plunge us into the inner life of the Most Blessed Trinity**.[5]

> To be a missionary is not about giving things but **communicating the foundation of Trinitarian life**: the love of the Father, of the Son, and of the Holy Spirit. To be a missionary is to lead people toward a personal experience of the immeasurable love that unites the Father, the Son, and the Holy Spirit so as to allow oneself to be seized at the same time by the ardent furnace of love that manifested itself so sublimely on the Cross. To be a missionary is to help others to become disciples of Jesus, to experience a profound friendship with Jesus, and **to become one and the same being with Jesus**. (*God or Nothing*, 234, emphasis added)

***St. Elizabeth of the Trinity***: To Elizabeth was granted unique insights into God's Trinitarian love. This was expressed in expressions like her loving to sink into the ocean of love of "her Three."

---

[4] Chiara Lubich, *Jesus in our Midst*, 10, 13.
[5] Robert Cardinal Sarah, "The Liturgy 'Plunges us into the Inner Life of the Trinity,'" *Inside the Vatican* (June-July 2019): 33.

## II. Greatest Return of Love is our Mystical Union & Incarnation

God's love calls for a return of love. But the greatest return of love is to become Christ, and eventually the "Whole Christ" (Augustine). There are three steps: spiritual marriage, mystical incarnation, Trinitarian communion.

### A. First Stage is Spiritual Marriage

*Human Life finds Culmination in Spiritual Marriage with Christ*
The Father created us to become spouses of Christ, for spiritual marriage, and thereby to become Christ Himself, that is His Mystical Body. How ineffable an intimacy must Trinitarian communion be ("The Father and I are one") if even human love in the poignant song "Honey" can deeply touch our hearts. In this song, a man deeply pines for his deceased wife: "And honey, I miss you and I'm bein' good, and I'd love to be with you if only I could." He recalls various episodes (of tree she planted), these verses recall the moment the angels came for her.

> One day while I was not at home
> While she was there and all alone, the angels came
> Now all I have is memories of honey
> And I wake up nights and call her name
> Now my life's an empty stage
> Where honey lived and honey played.[6]

*Mass*
Mystical union in this life finds its apex in the Mass. Holy Communion at Mass is already a foretaste of heavenly union. Its intimacy can be compared to the consummation of marriage between husband and wife, which is expressed as "ecstasy," but which is only a limited foretaste and anticipation of heavenly ecstasy.

*God's Masterpiece is Mystical Union with Christ that Allows Him to Relive His Life in us as Co-Redeemers*
The spousal marriage with Christ allows us to become Christ, "Two become one flesh" (Gen 1). That is, being the spouse of Christ allows us to become the Body of Christ seen in Paul (Gal 2:20). It is as if Christ takes up a new humanity in a new but mystical incarnation, so as to relive His life in each of us. Then we too (as was Christ) are sent forth by the Father to co-redeem the world.

---

[6] Bobby Russell, "Honey, I Miss You," 1968. Lyrics drawn from Song Lyrics Today, accessed October 27, 2021, https://songlyricstoday.com/honey-i-miss-you. These song lyrics are being used under, so to speak, "Research and Academic" purposes.

### *Mystical Incarnation in us Depends on the Degree of our Spousal Yes*

St. Elizabeth of the Trinity lived deep relations with the Trinity: "you will know that I am with my Divine Guests. I cannot and ought not to care for anything except to live in intimacy with Them."[7] Tragically, "laden with gifts, He [God] finds no one; the soul has gone out to exterior things":

> Live with Him. Ah! How I wish I could make known to every soul what a source of strength, of peace, and of happiness as well, they would discover, did they only consent to live in this intimacy. But they will not wait. If God does not give Himself to them in a way that they can feel, they leave His sacred presence, and when He comes laden with gifts, He finds no one; *the soul has gone out to exterior things and does not dwell within itself. Recollect yourself from time to time* dear mother, then you will be quite close to your Elizabeth...[8] (emphasis added)

St. Elizabeth of the Trinity discovered that abandonment is greater than desire for suffering: "When she confided her desire of suffering to the reverend Father, he told her not to limit herself to that, but to yield herself in all simplicity to God, leaving Him free to act in any way He chose."[9] Dom Marmion understood this truth profoundly:

> In our activity, we are so inclined to **substitute our natural human activity for God's action**! But when God throws us down, despoils us of *our* activity, He takes entire possession of us and **deifies** all the activity which springs from Him. That is what God is doing for you.... Blosius says that *a soul that gives herself without reserve to God, permitting Him to work in her as He pleases*, does more for God in a few hours, and, for certain souls, in an hour, than others do by their activity *during long years.*[10]

### *Cooperation in Abandonment*

We have to trust, as described by C. S. Lewis, as He is building a home for himself.

> Imagine yourself as a living house. God comes in to rebuild that house. At first, perhaps, you can understand what He is doing. He is getting the drains right and stopping the leaks in the roof and so on: you knew that those jobs needed doing and so you are not surprised. But presently He starts knocking the house about in a way that hurts abominably and does not seem to make sense. What on earth is He up to? The explanation is that He

---

[7] St. Elizabeth of the Trinity, Letter, in B. Zimmerman, *The Praise of Glory: Reminiscences of Sister Elizabeth of the Trinity, a Carmelite Nun of Dijon, 1901-1906* (New York: R. & T. Washbourne, Ltd), 183.
[8] Ibid., 178-179.
[9] Ibid., 204.
[10] Columba Marmion, *Union with God*, 74-75.

is building quite a different house from the one you thought of – throwing out a new wing here, putting on an extra floor there, running up towers, making courtyards. You thought you were going to be made into a decent little cottage but He is building a palace. He intends to come and live in it Himself. (C. S. Lewis, *Mere Christianity*, 205)

The subjective transformation into Christ depends on our yes, on the degree of surrender and abandonment. The saintly archbishop Luis Martinez describes the necessary docility or abandonment to the Spirit:

> The true Director of souls, the intimate Master, the soul of the spiritual life, is the Holy Spirit. As we have already said, without him there is no sanctity. The perfection of a soul is measured by its **docility to the movement of the Spirit, by the promptness and fidelity with which its strings** produce the divine notes of the song of love. A soul is perfectly holy when the Spirit of love has taken **full possession** of it, when the divine Artist finds no resistance or dissonance in the strings of that living lyre [which resembles a small harp], but only celestial strains coming forth from it, limpid, ardent, and delightfully harmonized.[11]

## B. Second Stage is Mystical Incarnation ("Another Christ, Christ Himself")

***Configuration to Christ:*** In Conchita's spiritual ascent, mystical incarnation followed her spiritual betrothals and marriage (see "Conclusion"). But most who read about configuration to Christ (e.g., the priest is to be an "another Christ") think of some vague union with Christ. We do not realize that it refers to what Cardinal Sarah points for all baptized, to become "another Christ, Christ Himself," or Jesus' teaching that priests are called to become "replicas" of Him, all allowing Jesus free rein in us, and so save souls.

> Several of them [priests] are eloquent and learned humanly speaking, but they lack the most basic knowledge; that of holiness.... they do not live in sufficient intimacy with me through self-denial and unalloyed love... How I love them!... I call them to be *other Christs. To be replicas of me*: that is their vocation. How I love them! And there are many who love me so little... *The Evil One is more afraid of a single soul in whom I can act freely than a whole army of tepid, indifferent souls* in whom my action is paralysed, because in the former I act with power, while I have no choice but to abandon the latter to their weakness. If all consecrated souls **refused me nothing, if they always allowed me to act freely in them, all other souls would be saved**.[12] (emphasis added)

---

[11] Luis Martinez, *The Sanctifier*, 21.
[12] Blessed Dina Bélanger, *The Autobiography of Dina Bélanger* (Québec City: Les Religieuses de Jésus-Marie, 1997), 294-295, 302.

We can add here the valuable insight of St. John Eudes, who goes further to explain that Christ's mysteries have to be re-lived and completed in us.

> This is the plan by which the Son of God completes and fulfils in us all the various stages and mysteries. He desires us to perfect the mystery of **his incarnation and birth by forming himself in us and being reborn in our souls** through the blessed sacraments of baptism and the eucharist. He fulfils his hidden life in us, hidden with him in God. He intends to perfect the mysteries of his passion, death and resurrection, by causing us to suffer, die and rise again with him and in him. Finally, he wishes to fulfil in us the state of his glorious and immortal life, when he will cause us to live a glorious, eternal life with him and in him in heaven. (OOR, Friday 33rd Week of OT, Year II, emphasis added)

***Configuration to Christ Requires the Spirit in the Mystical Mansions:*** There is a one-time objective configuration to Christ at Baptism, but that is only a seed that needs to grow into a tree that shelters many. But fidelity to prayer and the evangelical virtues in these states only conform us at the foundation level of the Ascetical Mansions. The main configuration is the subjective configuration that is only attained through the Spirit in the upper Mansions that brings about a spiritual marriage and mystical incarnation. The latter corresponds to Christ's birth in us. Sheen teaches: "There are two births of Christ: one unto the world at Bethlehem; the other in the soul."

***Blessed Dina Bélanger:*** This mystical union with Christ is illustrated by the "Substitution of Christ" that Blessed Dina Bélanger experienced: "Jesus and I are no longer two, we are one. It is Jesus alone." There was an annihilation of the fallen ego of Dina, and it is now Christ who lives and loves in her. The consequence is that she lives from the heart of Jesus and re-lives His mysteries.

## C. Final Stage is Trinitarian Communion

### Set Goal: The Father's Love and Trinitarian Communion

But the end goal is to lead us to the Father, to share in His greatest treasure, divine Sonship, to hear the words He heard, "You are my Son, the Beloved." It is accomplished through the Holy Spirit, the Personal Love within the Trinity. "Believe me that I am in the Father and the Father is in me" (Jn 14:11); "As you, Father, are in me and I am in you, may they also be in us" (Jn 17:21). It is also described in another image, "I am the vine, you are the branches" (Jn 15:5): "Father, I desire that those also, whom you have given me, may be with me where I am, to see my glory, which you have given me because you loved me before the foundation of the world."

***Apex: Supremacy of Love***: This supremacy of love is highlighted most in the most mystical of the four Gospel writers, John the beloved disciple: "Beloved, let us love one another, for love is of God" (1 Jn 4:7). But love is not sentimentality. Chiara Lubich, who understood that the Church is to live Trinitarian love, understood the link between unity and the cross.

> "That they may all be one" could mean nothing less than the unity of all humankind. Chiara Lubich lived for unity, but understood that "Unity with God and among human beings could be achieved on one condition: by embracing the cross." Chiara focused on "Jesus Forsaken".... Years later, she would affirm: "Jesus Forsaken won every battle in us, even the most terrible ones.... But it is necessary to be madly in love with him, who is the synthesis of every physical or spiritual suffering, the remedy... for every pain of the soul. (Wikipedia, s.v. "Chiara Lubich")

***Two Greatest Realities: Love and Pain***: Thus, as just noted and as we have said at the beginning, there are two coordinates, the two greatest realities, the cross of pain on earth and the dove of eternal love. St. Elizabeth of the Trinity understood Jesus' need to suffer in her:

> ... the Master has deigned to choose your daughter, your own child, to aid Him in His great work of redemption; that He has signed her with the seal of the cross, and suffers in her as an extension of His Passion. The bride belongs to the Bridegroom; mine has taken me for His own. He wishes me to be a second humanity in which He can suffer still more for His Father's glory and to succour the needs of His Church. The thought consoles me greatly.... I kiss my Master's cross at each fresh pang, saying: "I thank Thee, but I am not worthy of it," remembering that suffering was the comrade of His life, and that I do not deserve that His Father should treat me as He treated His Son.[13]

***Two Sacraments***: We might say that there are two dominant sacraments. The first is the sacrament of the Mass, which is the source and summit of Christian life, that assimilates us to Christ (Augustine's "Become what you eat"). The second sacrament can be said to be the sacrament of the present moment, because it is what is lived in the course of the day subjectively that assimilates us to Christ especially through the Eucharist. The former remains largely dormant if the latter is not lived out in daily life.

***Two Mothers***: We can also say that there are two primary spiritual mothers. The assimilation into Christ is accomplished by two Mothers: the Church, which feeds and guides us, especially in the Eucharist; and our Lady, who, like the sacrament of the present moment, personally forms us during the

---

[13] St. Elizabeth of the Trinity, *The Praise of Glory*, 170.

day. While there are three great loves (Church, Eucharist, Mary), the key to the entire Christian life is really our Lady, for she concretely applies what is given through the Church and she leads to Christ, the Church, and to everything we need: "Our Lady's love is like a stream that has its source in the eternal fountains, quenches the thirst of all, can never be drained, and ever flows back to its source" (St. Marguerite Bourgeoys).

***Two Tools***: We might also say that there are two primary tools: spiritual direction and fraternal correction. [see St. Thérèse's Corrections in *Mystical Incarnation*, 190-192]

***This Path Entails Developing a "Priestly" Soul***: The key is abandonment to Mary and the Holy Spirit in the sacrament of the present moment. Our foundational baptismal priesthood is a call to develop a "priestly" soul who mediates the world to God. Following Nazareth, we co-redeem the world through the small things. We do this by not staying at the human level of our difficulties or even tragedies but accepting by allowing eternity to flow into the world through our everyday tasks. It requires interiority, a unity of life, by which God acts through us as another self. Dina Bélanger understood that, after the "substitution of Christ" ("We are one. It is Jesus alone"), keeping her eyes away from herself and on Jesus allowed Jesus to act in her: "*One single act of love offered by Him to the Father [within her] could save millions of worlds.*"[14]

To this end, Dina teaches that we can influence the world through daily actions that console Jesus. We conquer the world through everyday mundane events, as the Holy Family did at Nazareth. And if God deigns to bless us with the cross, we have the highest apostolate, the *apostolate of suffering*. This aligns with what we have seen in de Caussade: "the events of each moment are stamped with the will of God... we find all this is necessary in each present moment."

> Jesus is seeking souls to console him. His Eucharistic Heart is suffering. O! How it is suffering…! He desires souls that are totally abandoned to his love: sensitive souls that **not only refuse him nothing, but seize eagerly upon every opportunity to give him pleasure**, who anticipate his desires and surround him with attentions, small in themselves yet very great because of the love that prompts them: souls that offer him all those trifles that his goodness scatters through each moment of an entire day, those thousands of trivia that, fragrant with **pure love**, are like a brilliant bouquet of a thousand immaculate roses. (*Abandonment to Divine Providence*, 252-253)

---

[14] Blessed Dina Bélanger, *The Autobiography of Dina Bélanger*, 161.

> # Retreat 2: The Model of St. Joseph
> ## Mystical Incarnation as Lived by St. Joseph (4 Themes)

> If discouragement overwhelms you, think of the faith of St. Joseph; if anxiety has its grip on you, think of the hope of St. Joseph; if exasperation or hatred seized you, think of the love of St. Joseph, who was the first man to set eyes on the human face of God in the person of the infant conceived by the Holy Spirit in the womb of the Virgin Mary. Let us praise and thank Christ for having drawn so close to us, and for giving us Joseph as an example and model of love. (Benedict XVI, 19 March 2009)

This retreat attempts to see how the four main themes in *Mystical Incarnation* were lived out by Joseph. The Father forms each of us in Joseph, who was formed according to the physiognomy of Jesus in these four main marks. Since Scripture is modest about Joseph, we will draw from mystical insights.
> A. God's Calls Impel "Blank Slates" to Follow His Will
> B. Pure Love: Self-Forgetfulness for Love of God
> C. Royal Road of Holy Cross: Entails God's Pruning the Tree
> D. Abandonment: Daily Life

## A. God's Calls Impel "Blank Slates" to Follow His Will

### *1. Consulting the Holy Spirit who Speaks Continually*
The author was gladdened when for the first time he encountered the insight, when reading Fr. Jacques Philippe's *In the School of the Holy Spirit*, that, beyond doing the duties of our state of life, we are called to the higher level of listening to the inspirations of the Holy Spirit, which itself is completed by the summit of "surrender." During all the years of seminary formation and most of the years of priesthood, he had never been explicitly taught that there was a higher level beyond avoiding sin and being generous in one's faith life and ministry. He provides a vista of the concrete ways by which God calls us; it presupposes that God is always speaking to us.

> These calls come to us in many ways. Sometimes they come through experiences or by the example of others who touch us, sometimes from desires that arise in our hearts or requests from people who are close to us, often from Holy Scripture. They originate from God, who gives us life, never ceases to watch over us, and wants tenderly to lead and constantly intervene for each of his children in a way that is discreet, often imperceptible, yet efficacious. Although many are, unfortunately, unaware of this presence and action of God, they reveal themselves to those who know how to place themselves in the attitude of listening and availability.[1]

---

[1] Jacques Philippe, *Called to Life* (New York: Scepter Publishers, 2008), 2-3.

## 2. Receptivity of Padre Pio as a Blank Slate

The interior disposition of St. Pio of Pietrelcina is salutary. Reading his letters of correspondence with his spiritual directors is very uplifting (*Padre Pio of Pietrelcina: Letters, vol. 1, Correspondence with his Spiritual Directors 1910-1922*). Here is a Franciscan friar, widely acclaimed for his sanctity, with many "angel saint" qualities (crowds queuing at his confessional at San Giovanni Rotondo, stigmata, reading of hearts, bilocation, attacks by the devil, etc.), who likely surpassed his directors in sanctity, and yet acted like a little, dependent child before them. He clearly understood that he could not guide himself. But what is staggeringly edifying is his pure obedience as if he was obeying Christ Himself in the director. He went before his spiritual director like a little child, a blank slate ready to be formed.

Many are unaware that, already as a religious brother in formation, Padre Pio already had a motto of deep obedience, that he would immediately obey any superior, no matter his spiritual state or office. When he received with great sorrow the news that the pope, misinformed, had shut down his ministry, his superior reminded him of his motto of obedience. Some who have spiritual directors go merely as spiritual "directees"; Padre Pio went as a spiritual "son," which was St. Joseph's disposition before the Father.

## 3. Blank Slates are Led to Do God's Will

As St. Teresa of Jesus teaches, *all union with God in the higher Mansions lies simply in conformity to God's will*. In contrast, we can serve God, not being led by the divine Spirit of sonship to do the Father's will, but with the human spirit by following our own will. As mentioned earlier in this book, Hans Urs von Balthasar's mystical experience of abandonment and availability in the Black Forest in Bavaria was also the secret of Jesus, who gave up sovereignty of His whole existence and lived the expropriation of following the demanding rule of the Holy Spirit. St. Joseph too must have given up sovereignty of his whole life.

Joseph had been given a mission, the greatest after that of Mary. He may have had human plans, but, as is evident in the Gospel, would have given them up to follow the lead of the Holy Spirit. He accepted everything as coming from God: setting out for Bethlehem, the deaths of the Forty Innocents, leaving for Egypt, waiting patiently for instructions for their return, moving to Nazareth because Herod was still alive, etc. He must have been constantly available to God's calls, abandoning his plans, focusing on Mary, Jesus, and his carpentry trade. We can tell that St. Joseph was following the Holy Spirit, because the fruits of the Spirit are manifest: "You will know them by their fruits" (Mt 7:16). One can argue that the "fruits of the Holy Spirit" enumerated in Scripture are also those found in St. Joseph, the "just" man:

e.g., love, joy, peace, patience, gentleness, chastity, etc. We sense that it is perhaps St. Francis de Sales who specially mirrors Joseph in his hidden and natural way of Nazareth. For example, Francis, rather than focusing on doing harsh penances, chose the constant availability to those who sought him (even at meals or if he had vested for Mass). It appears that many Christians have not been taught about docility to the Spirit.

## 4. Two Examples of Self-Will (Opposite of Blank Slate)

The opposite of God's will is self-will (see St. Augustine's description in his *City of God* of the two cities of God and self). Here are two concrete examples. A priest scholar was asked by his superiors to do evangelization, but so preoccupied and obsessed was he with Scripture that they found they could not use him for the mission they had in mind. He was exceptional in his praiseworthy recovery of Scripture, but did not go beyond this foundation. Most telling was that his obsession with Scripture was such that his retreats rarely dwelt upon his founder's sublime spirituality and he was primarily promoting Scripture in Confession and Direction. Scott Hahn expressed that, as a Presbyterian, he had the "menu" (Scripture) but Catholics had the "meal" (Mass). Vatican II's *Sacrosanctum concilium* teaches that the liturgy is the "source and summit of Christian life." Scripture should lead especially to the two sacraments of Mass and Confession.

The second example is of another priest scholar visiting on sabbatical (mentioned earlier) who approached the author for spiritual direction. As a young man, he already displayed looseness, imprudently becoming involved with an Eastern non-Christian spirituality, and believing he had become infested by spirits by contact with them, became so obsessed about it, that he sought deliverance from various groups far and wide. At the spiritual level, the visiting priest was found to lack any structure or rule of life. He would go to bed around 3 am and get up around 11 am; and he was not faithful to prayer and, when he did pray, he would spend over an hour on his daily Examen (too much self-introspection). Even the priest's decision making was erratic. Wanting to study a brilliant theologian, he chose not to go to a city with a world-famous centre and went instead to another country for a less substantial reason. He exhibited much looseness and *self-will* also in theology, specializing in two theologians who laid the foundations for dissent against *Humanae vitae*. The actions of this priest suggest that his whole approach reflected a lack of order. St. Escrivá taught that one cannot attain sanctity without order as foundation. A plan of life was recommended to him, with fixed times for spiritual norms to build a stable foundation that allows him to be attentive to the voice of the Spirit within. In general, he had to first learn basic common sense, and then to be guided through others as the Holy Spirit's special instruments.

## B. Pure Love: Self-Forgetfulness for Love of God

> The true spirit of faith leads a man to look off from self to God, to think nothing of his own wishes, his present habits, his importance or dignity, his rights, his opinions, but to say, "I put myself into Thy hands, O Lord; make Thou me what Thou wilt; I forget myself; I divorce myself from myself; I am dead to myself; I will follow Thee."[2] (John Henry Newman)

### 1. "It is not all about you!" ("Dr. Strange" Movie)

Let us illustrate the truth of self-forgetfulness with a recent science fiction movie *Dr. Strange*, based on the Marvel comic book character, presents a supremely gifted, world-famous surgeon who had a debilitating car accident. After trying every medical means available to heal his hands to allow him to continue doing surgery, he turned to the Eastern arts after meeting a healed man severely injured beyond medical expertise. From the very first, while he was being trained by the "Ancient One" herself, he was told to forget everything he learned, as the human learning counted for little before these (so-called) "mystical arts." She pointed out that the success of his great skills and knowledge that derived from his fear of failing was in reality holding him back from true greatness. He needed to let go and be formed by this higher art. Dr. Stephen Strange came to see the poverty of his medical skills in contrast to the "mystical" mastery of the Ancient One.

Even more, he came to see the depths of his egoism and self-serving (as his love interest, Dr. Christine Palmer once noted, "Stephen, everything is about you"). As the Ancient One was dying, she shared with him the great lesson in life— "Stephen, it is not all about you." The Ancient One told Dr. Strange of the ultimate choice he would have to make in life: to use these "mystical" arts he mastered to heal his own hands (as the injured man had chosen to do) or to redirect them instead to help humanity in great cosmic danger. Dr. Strange, according to the movie's plot, came to accept his damaged hands and set aside his personal plans so as to serve the world by protecting it from dark, powerful enemies of that "mystical" world.

### 2. Not Seeking Self in Inward Turning to "Community"

Cardinal Ratzinger warned us about a crisis of God after Vatican II, another turn to self. He recalled a venerable German bishop theologian encouraging the German bishops as they prepared for Vatican II to talk about God, not about themselves, and his concern proved to be prescient. Many began to speak about "we the Church." Instead of focusing on God, they focused on themselves. An example of this is that the liturgy became about

---

[2] Cf. "The Testimony of Conscience" in *Parochial and Plain Sermons*, V, 17 (Longmans, Green and Co., 1907), 242.

"community," a dialogue between the priest as entertainer or leader and the congregation, instead of the entire community directing themselves to God in adoration. They neglected the transcendent, i.e., adoration, which misdirection is a form of self-worship. St. Francis de Sales taught that, if we are thinking of ourselves praying, then we are not praying. For true prayer is to be absorbed in God. We are doing something wrong when we are primarily focused on community and not adoring God.

Here is a concrete illustration. A priest taking summer courses at a Catholic university happened to be walking by when the university chapel Mass was concluded, and was shocked to see that many had stood up right in the middle of the chapel to chat. They had forgotten that they had just participated in the all-holy Mass (no adoration and thanksgiving) and that the Lord was still present sacramentally in their bodies as well as in the tabernacle, surrounded by angels— everything became turned in on self. After Vatican II, there was much talk about love, compassion, and community, and everything became touchy-feely, lacking the iron of sacrifice to convert souls. When we look at the first disciples of St. Ignatius who must have had some sense of community, we find that their hearts were not turned in on themselves but outwards towards conquering the world for Christ; they possessed Christ's concern for the salvation of souls.

### *3. No Time for Self*
Because of his enormous influence, the FBI made a file on Fulton Sheen, and one of the things noted was that he had no social life. John Henry Newman too had no social life, and became a great scholar who would be able to help many. Both led intense intellectual lives. When God uses us powerfully, we don't have much time for social things. We become like Br. Lawrence of the Resurrection, Bl. Marie (Acarie) of the Incarnation, St. Francis Xavier, St. Maximilian Kolbe, and St. Pio, who were constantly sought out and who had to choose between social engagements and salvation of souls. Priests, having given up spouses and a family, also give up all this constant search for the social life to serve the flock. This earthly life, as the saints have noted, is not the time for rest but for work. We will rest in eternity, and then we will have the social of an eternal banquet.

### *4. Not Seeking Praise nor Giving Flattery*
We mentioned "*Ama nesciri et pro nihilo reputari*" ("Love to be unknown and to be considered as nothing"), a saying from the *Imitation of Christ* shared with the author by his saintly seminary spiritual director, Attila Miklósházy. This is the deeper path of self-forgetfulness, after the example of St. Joseph and the Holy Family. Let us consider ways in which we fail to live this path.

There is a temptation today to be constantly praising each other. Consider the speeches we hear at Ordination and wedding receptions, and especially at eulogies. When we continually praise ourselves and others, we are robbing God of the glory that belongs to Him, for all our evil comes from ourselves and all good comes from God (e.g., every good thought comes from God). To illustrate, a religious priest once asked a diocesan priest why his diocese was putting the transitional deacons at the Ordinandi dinner on pedestals when they had not yet laboured for the Lord. One might choose to follow the edifying example of the author's first pastor, who did not tell parishioners about his 50th anniversary of priestly ordination but had but a homecooked meal for classmates in a small room over the parish garage. He also recommended that priests celebrate their own significant priestly anniversaries (e.g., 25th, 40th, 50th) without fanfare.

St. Francis de Sales once corrected his dear friend and protégé, Bishop Jean-Pierre Camus, after he fulsomely and lavishly praised in a homily the Sisters of the Visitation that St. Francis had co-founded, telling him that this flattery leads to pride and vainglory. When he preached to them a second time soon after in which he exhorted the Sisters to the arduous road of holiness, St. Francis praised him. Padre Pio too replied to a woman who exuberantly exclaimed that he was a great saint: "God sees stains in the angels. What must he see in me? I am surprised that this Franciscan habit does not run away from me being so unworthy to wear it" (paraphrased). In contrast to the higher Mansions, the lower Mansions involve much running around, doing good things, and seeking applause and respect. The latter is more about congeniality and not about deep charity. The few hidden mentions of Joseph and Mary in the Gospels suggest that they intentionally "hid" themselves so that all light would shine on their Son. The Holy Family lived such hidden lives that the townspeople of Nazareth did not realize that they were the greatest saints of God nor perceived Jesus' identity, "Is this not the carpenter's son" (Mt 13:55).

## C. Royal Road of Holy Cross: Entails God's Pruning the Tree

The higher Mansions are the level of the child of God (not servant or worker). Their divine pedagogy, contrary to the human instinct, goes through the cross: "Unless a grain of wheat falls into the earth and dies…" (Jn 12:24). It entails going through the Dark Nights, that often jar and shock us, and may turn our comfortable world upside down. This higher level entails undergoing the cross in the path of St. Joseph, which does not comprise great asceticism or martyrdom. It is rather the path of abandonment to God's will of a Sr. Clare Crockett, who accepted everything sent her way, including sleeplessness, migraines, exhaustion, and finally death from an earthquake.

This too was the formation of St. Joseph as a child of God, who ascends to the higher Mansions by abandonment.

## *1. Pruning the Tree*

God's constant calls to St. Joseph include His correction or discipline. Here, the *Imitation of Christ* reveals to us that God visits His elect in a "double fashion" of temptation and consolation:

> The Voice of Christ. I taught the prophets from the beginning, and even to this day I continue to speak to all men, but many are deaf and obstinate in response.... I am accustomed to visit my elect in a double fashion, that is, with temptation and with consolation. And I read to them two lessons each day: one to rebuke them for their faults; the other to exhort them to increase their virtue. He who possesses my words yet spurns them earns his own judgment on the last day. (*Imitation* Bk 3, Ch 3)

We find this truth validated in Scripture: "Every branch in me that does not bear fruit he takes away, and every branch that does bear fruit he prunes, that it may bear more fruit" (John 15:2). Here are a few contemporary examples that affirm this truth. In a talk, Scott Hahn said that, if his teenage son was hanging around gang members, he would correct and even ground him, even if his son were to respond with resentment and a cold shoulder. Because Dr. Hahn loved his son, he would do anything to protect him from destroying his future life. Dr. Hahn also taught that, if God did not care about us, He would let us do whatever we wanted; but that, because He loves us, He corrects us: "For the Lord disciplines him whom he loves, and chastises every son whom he receives" (Heb 12:6). St. Joseph's many challenges reveal God's pruning him (e.g., Bethlehem, Egypt, early death).

God's correction includes formation or education through the cross. We find in the life of Sr. Briege McKenna such a formation: death of her mother at age of 13, entrance into Poor Clares at 14, her superior in London trying to break her spirit, attacks by a superior general, condemnation by one of the Church's highest prelates, the opposition to her fidelity to Christ's Church in the turbulent postconciliar era, as well as her crosses (debilitating rheumatoid arthritis, face condition that required major brain surgery, Jesus' request to begin ministry of healing against her inclinations, constant missionary travels).

*The Imitation of Christ* teaches that the disciple of Christ, experiencing the great benefits and the knowledge that they please God this way, chooses tribulations. We can apply this especially to St. Joseph. They realize it comes from Christ's grace "that human nature can choose and even love that which by nature they hate and reject":

> It is not the tendency of human beings to bear the cross and to love it, to chastise the body and to subdue it, to flee honors and to put up with reproaches, to despise themselves and to wish others to despise them, to bear all opposition and losses and not to desire any prosperity in this world. (*Imitation of Christ*, Bk 2, Ch 12, n 9)

## *2. Overcoming Resistance to Change*

There are many different ways in which we resist change. Here are a few examples. A seminarian can go to spiritual direction and always be lamenting the state of the Church, while he ends up at ordination without having corrected his own many personal defects. St. Joseph readily obeyed the angel's instructions and accepted all that God allowed in His providence. The ideal way to change is through the little things. Here is what Francis Fernandez wrote on "Ways to practice humility":

> Among the ways of attaining humility is, in the first place, ardently to desire it, to value it and to ask God for it. Then our aim should be to foster docility in resolutely carrying out the advice received in spiritual direction, to receive fraternal correction joyfully and thankfully, to accept humiliation in silence for love of God, to obey quickly and wholeheartedly and, above all, to strive to attain this precious virtue through the exercise of charity in continual details of cheerful service to others. Jesus is the supreme example of humility… "I am among you as one who serves." (*In Conversation with God*, vol. 1, 27.3)

## *3. Gaining Self-Knowledge*

There may be a deeper underlying cause for such resistance to change— a lack of self-knowledge of our identity as sinners. To use a Gospel illustration, let us contrast the example of the sinful woman at Simon's house to that of the Pharisees. Simon, lacking faith, expressed an inner doubt: "If this man were a prophet, he would have known who and what sort of woman this is who is touching him, for she is a sinner" (Lk 7:39). But Jesus noted Simon's lack of love compared to that of the woman, pointing to the "fruits" or evidence of her love:

> Do you see this woman? I entered your house, you gave me no water for my feet, but she has wet my feet with her tears and wiped them with her hair. You gave me no kiss, but from the time I came in she has not ceased to kiss my feet. You did not anoint my head with oil, but she has anointed my feet with ointment. Therefore I tell you, her sins, which are many, are forgiven, for she loved much; but he who is forgiven little, loves little. (Luke 7:44-47)

The onlookers too did not know their sin. Simon and his friends were "respected" members of their society and clearly had a high opinion of themselves, as evidenced by their condescending thoughts about the woman. They were at the level of duty and fulfilling the Law; the woman lived at the level of the heart, which was clearly manifested by her contrition and love, expressed by her tears, affectionate kissing, anointing with an ointment, and wiping Jesus' feet with her hair. We note that many saints have identified this woman with St. Mary Magdalene, whose greatest attribute or mark was her love of the person of Jesus. Duty characterizes the Ascetical Mansions, love the Mystical Mansions.

Similarly, the difference between the Pharisees who persecuted Jesus and Paul is that the former did not know they were sinners, the latter came to deeply understand his sin. We are all sinners, but only some know we are sinners. What belongs to us is sin, all the good we do derives from grace. A very deep example of self-knowledge is found in St. Philip Neri's saying to Jesus: "Lord, beware of Philip, for he will betray you." St. Joseph's meekness and docility to the Spirit reflect deep self-knowledge.

**D. Abandonment: Daily Life**

*1. God Bears the Child*
The saints, such as St. Agnes, St. Agatha, and St. Bridget, who have experienced God's personal love for them, are all drawn to abandon or surrender themselves totally to God, deeply understanding that God, as Father, would provide all. Such was especially St. Thérèse's understanding, that, as long as she remained little like an infant, the Father would provide everything, and that she would not have anything to give at her death but would rely on His Fatherly mercy. She lived, as it were, on the Father's lap.

This too must have been the experience of St. Joseph, and his trust would have been vindicated after having undergone a number of periods of testing: marrying Mary pregnant with child, leaving for Bethlehem when she was close to giving birth, not finding a place at the inn, having to flee to Egypt across the desert, not having the financial means to relocate in a foreign city, awaiting word to return to Israel, and perhaps his faith that this child was indeed the Son of God. A priest recalls a religious Sister, a vicar in her Congregation, expressing that she often experienced doubts about God's providence in difficult moments, but marvelled how, in reviewing of her day and life in her Examen Prayers, she came to see how He always came through for her.

We see also how God provided during the poverty of the Holy Family. The Church has regarded the House of Loreto as the home of the Holy Family. Tradition suggests that it had been transported to that region of Eastern Italy in the province of Ancona either by crusaders or preternaturally by angels. Many saints have visited this shrine, including St. Louis de France and St. Thérèse, and it has been noted that Chiara Lubich received the confirmation of her Focolare charism there. This home of the Holy Family was very poor, consisting of one room and likely sparsely furnished (it recalls the one-room former prison in which St. Bernadette's family lived in Lourdes after the bankruptcy of her father's mill). If they were indeed poor, then they would have had little means when they travelled to Bethlehem and even less so in fleeing to Egypt: no home, clothing, or furnishings, and then having to seek work. Jesus must have learned poverty from Mary and Joseph. He had only one tunic, walked everywhere, and carried no money.

St. Francis de Sales teaches that attachment to the human level prevents us from ascending to the divine level. Now we know, on the one hand, for our human well-being, that we should strive to eat healthy diets, get regular exercise, and be competent in daily human affairs or commerce. Yet, St. Joseph, being possessed by the Holy Spirit, while fulfilling the duties of his state of life at the human level, would have put primary emphasis on listening to the Holy Spirit and God's will. As our Lord taught St. Catherine of Siena, "Think of me and I will think of you." But not only must they have been self-forgetful to focus on God's work, saints like Joseph who have no time for themselves become exponentially more influential in the world. The Church Fathers, like Ambrose and Augustine, were likely too busy as bishops to be thinking about their health, tied up with Church affairs and sought after daily by many people. For God bears His children in His arms. What trust must Joseph have had of the Father's providence!

**2. God's Child does not Focus on Protecting Self but the Needs of Others**
A pastor, out of concern for a recently ordained priest, warned him to not trust his bishop and the chancery officials, that they would end up turning against him, arguing from Jesus' words, "Be innocent as doves, wise as serpents." The young priest, while grateful for the concern of the pastor, felt uneasy about this counsel, that prescribed a worldview that pitted the bishop and chancery against diocesan priests (recalls the class warfare promoted by Communism). Years later, the young priest found the balanced and proper approach in a teaching of St. Francis de Sales. The saint compared the cunning of the serpent to the poison we receive in vaccines, which can only be administered in minute quantities. St. Francis taught that, while human prudence (cunning) is necessary, he did not "like" it, that he much prefers simplicity (the innocence of doves). When someone encouraged St. Francis de Sales to get involved with the politics of the day to help the Church, he vigorously objected, pointing out that he could never be a politician who played two sides, but was one who simply spoke from his heart. Regarding

being "cunning as serpents," he said that it is better to be persecuted than to persecute, to be martyred than to martyr. Where many might fear to follow a course of action because of its likely consequences, he preached the simplicity of following God's principles, allowing whatever followed to happen. Let us look at two examples.

A seminarian shared that he felt jealousy in seeing the popularity of another seminarian. This is a very natural human reaction but one that derives from the human spirit. Fulton Sheen explained that such gifts are "charisms," given to help others, yet they do not make the possessors holy, nor do these gifts make others holy. We should value and use them, but they are so poor compared to the inestimable indwelling of the Trinity, sanctifying grace, and infused virtues of faith, hope, and love. These divine gifts divinize and make us god-like, saints. The director told the seminarian to envy rather the humble seminarian, for the Spirit invades "empty" souls for divinization: "For he has regarded the lower estate of his handmaiden" (Lk 1:48).

Given that he is spiritual father of the Church, Joseph must have been united with the concerns of the world. This was lived by Chiara Lubich.

> We have to love the other person, but not with words or feelings. We have to be concrete in our love and the best way to do this is to "make ourselves one" with them, "live the life of the other" in a certain way, sharing their sufferings and their joys, understanding them, serving and helping them in practical ways. "Making ourselves one" is the attitude that guided the apostle Paul, who wrote that he made himself a Jew with the Jews, Greek with the Greeks, all things to all people (cf. 1 Cor 9:19-22). We must follow his example so that we can establish a sincere, friendly dialogue with everyone. (*Essential Writings*, 332)
> This attitude suggested by Chiara also eliminates any idea of winning the other person over to one's religion or point of view. Instead, it leads people who were strangers to discover that they are all brothers and sisters in the one human family. John Paul II defined the members of the Focolare Movement as "apostles of dialogue." (Wikipedia, "C. Lubich")

The path of the Holy Family appears to be the one that saints as a rule follow. They often don't seem to know worldly things (e.g., computers, diet). Their gaze was fixed on bigger things: the poor, souls, renewal of the Church. St. Joseph was not endowed with many human gifts. He was not a rabbi, nor a great orator nor highly educated nor informed about world affairs, but a carpenter living in a small village. His richness was a deep divine life that cooperated with His Son's salvation of the world. St. Teresa of Jesus taught: "Though you have recourse to many saints as your intercessors, go especially to St. Joseph, for he has great power."

> # Retreat 3: Jesus' Recapitulation of the World
> *Ecclesial Preparations for Mystical Transformation*

Retreat 1: Towards Mystical Incarnation and Espousals (5 Talks) outlines the entire edifice: from St. Catherine of Siena's two pillars of self-knowledge and eyes of Jesus, to being led by the Holy Spirit, and living by love that leads to the cross.

Retreat 2: Mystical Incarnation Lived by St. Joseph (4 Themes) illustrates the edifice as concretely lived out by St. Joseph, especially through his filial abandonment.

Retreat 3: Jesus' Recapitulation of the World
Where Retreat 1 outlined the entire edifice or journey to mystical incarnation and divine espousals, and Retreat 2 illustrates it by the life of St. Joseph, Retreat 3 now **prepares the terrain** for this transformation in the Church in Jesus' recapitulating the world to hand it over to the Father.

1. Holy Spirit: New Pentecost Needed to Renew the Church
2. Horizontalism: Rising above the Human to the Divine
3. Evangelization: The Church's Right and Mission to Evangelize
4. Church Renewal: Marian Profile and Sacraments of Initiation
5. Recovery: Church as Communion, Divine Filiation, & Marriage
6. Horizon of Grace: The Five Existential States of Grace

First, (1) it is the "Great Unknown," the Holy Spirit's Pentecost that powers the evangelization of the Church, the living water that renews human hearts. When we "read the signs of the times," we find two obstacles or oppositions: (2) the contemporary focus on the human to the exclusion of the divine; and (3) the denial of today's culture of the Church's right to evangelize. (4) For this, we need a reform and a renewal in the Church through the Marian Profile and Sacraments of Initiation. (5) But we also have to recover the patristic image of the Church as communion, our true identity as children of God, and marital love as reflecting Christ's spousal love for His Church. To counter today's horizontalism, (6) we summarize Cardinal Journet's beautiful panorama of the five existential states of grace: how grace from the cross pervades most of human history and how the grace by contact within the Church gives rise to the blossoming of divine grace, eminently visible in the saints.

# Retreat 3: Ecclesial Preparations for Mystical Transformation

## Conference 1
## Holy Spirit: New Pentecost Needed to Renew the Church

**Background: "The Great Unknown"**

The early twentieth century saw the publication of a work on the Holy Spirit entitled, *The Great Unknown*. This forgetfulness of the Holy Spirit was noted during the Second Vatican Council when the East reminded the West that we have neglected the Holy Spirit, have shunted Him into the background. But this is shocking in light of the plan of God in which redemption and sanctification are accomplished only through the Holy Spirit. It is true that, after the sin of Adam and Eve, Yahweh immediately promised a child, the Messiah to come, whom Christians understand as the Son of the Father made man, Jesus Christ. Thus the entire Old Testament points to the coming of Jesus, and, specifically, His cross (typology). The Church Fathers synthesized the typology thus: the Old Testament prefigures or prepares for the New Testament, and the New Testament fulfills or illuminates the Old. But what is not understood as clearly is that Jesus came to die so as to give us the Holy Spirit; that is, the Old Testament points to Jesus' coming, and ultimately to His sacrifice to give the Holy Spirit. Another way of expressing this is that the height of Jesus' life, the Paschal mystery, is complete only with the Ascension to the right hand of the Father (where He has power) and with Pentecost, where Jesus gives the great fruit of His sacrifice. For the Holy Spirit is the great "Gift" of heaven, the bond between the Father and the Son, and the dynamism (*dynamis*) from which all the gifts of the Church derive. The Spirit is the great divine Secret.

Let us now synthesize the Holy Spirit's work in three chronological stages: Old Testament, Jesus, Church (treated in *New Christ: Divine Filiation*).

**Old Testament: Prefigurations of Holy Spirit and Pentecost**

St. Augustine teaches that the grace from the cross not only goes forward to embrace all the future (realized eschatology) but also goes backwards, giving grace by anticipation, as a dawn anticipates the coming of the sun. Thus the Holy Spirit is already given in anticipation in the Old Testament: perhaps the Spirit hovering over the waters is the Holy Spirit; but all grace working in the Old Testament is the work of the Holy Spirit, as with the state of original justice of Adam and Eve, the patriarchs, the prophets, etc. But this lesser grace anticipates the fullness of grace given by Christ on the cross, with uncreated grace, the indwelling of the Holy Spirit, which causes the created effect on our souls of sanctifying (habitual) grace, that divinizes us.

Within the Old Testament, we must highlight two key events or figures. First, Luke in the Acts of the Apostles intends for us to see a fulfillment of the Covenant at Sinai in Pentecost. We find elements common to both Sinai and Pentecost: both involve fifty days (after Egypt and Jesus' sacrifice), both involve the giving of a Law, and both accomplish three great results: establishing a Covenant, constituting God's People, and making of them "a kingdom of priests and a holy nation" (Ex 19:4-6). We must add that Luke, as well as Paul, sees the Holy Spirit as the New Law (Rom 8). In the larger picture, we see the parallel between redemption for the Hebrew people in the liberation from Egypt and of the world in the sacrifice on Calvary, both giving a law, which for the latter is the Holy Spirit.

The second anticipation in the Old Testament in relation to the Holy Spirit are the prophecies of Jeremiah and Ezekiel of an interior Law or new heart. They are the first to move from an external Law (Torah) to an interior Law, namely, the Spirit: "A new heart I will give you, and a new spirit I will put within you; and I will take out of your flesh the heart of stone and give you a heart of flesh. And I will put my Spirit within you, and cause you to walk in my statutes and be careful to observe my ordinances" (Ezek 36:26-27).

**New Testament: Holy Spirit in Christ and Released from Christ**
We now proceed to Christ in two steps: Christ's Incarnation and life; and His death. The secret of Jesus is remarkably the Holy Spirit. Contemporary theology (e.g., Walter Kasper, von Balthasar) finds the work of the Incarnation not from the action of the Son, as described by St. Thomas Aquinas (following Phil 2:6), but as the work of the Holy Spirit in the "overshadowing" at the Annunciation in Lk 1:35. This will be critical for the Church, as the goal is to make all Christians "another Christ, Christ Himself," a mystical incarnation, also accomplished by the Holy Spirit.

The Spirit is not merely the secret Agent of the Incarnation. He is also the secret of Jesus' entire life and power. Conchita (Concepción Cabrera de Armida) reveals that the Holy Spirit interiorly formed Jesus: He adorned Him with infused virtues and gifts, He consoled and strengthened Him during distress and abandonment. He loved Jesus and was like a mother to Him, and Jesus returned that love. Thus the secret of Jesus was the Holy Spirit whom He received twice: at His conception to become God-man and at His Baptism. Now the heart of Jesus is His Sonship to the Father: "You are my Son, the Beloved." But it is the Holy Spirit who mediates this Sonship, for He is the Spirit of Sonship (Rom 8:14-16). Thus Jesus lived this Sonship in filial abandonment to the Father, not anticipating the future, but in being from moment to moment led by His hand, so to speak, like a little child ("Whoever humbles himself like this child, he is the greatest in the kingdom of heaven," Mt 18:4). He waited for the word from the Spirit to go to John the Baptist for Baptism, was impelled by the Spirit to go into the desert ("the Spirit drove him into the desert") and then to begin His ministry, and ultimately to go to the cross (Hebrews 9:14: "how much more shall the blood of Christ, who through the eternal Spirit offered himself without blemish to God, purify your conscience…"). And many Christians do not realize that, to be like us in all things but sin, He did not use His divine powers (e.g., the first temptation in the desert was to use His powers to change stone into bread). Rather, all His power (e.g., speaking with authority, forgiving sins, baptizing, miracles of healing and expulsion of demons) was the work of the Spirit in Him. We conclude and once again emphatically affirm, the secret of Jesus is the Spirit, the "Great Unknown."

*Jesus' Giving up His Spirit from the Cross*
Now we come to the release of the Holy Spirit. Jesus came to die; but if He does not release the Holy Spirit, redemption would have been frustrated or thwarted, so to speak. Scripture teaches us that, at His death, Jesus "gave up his spirit." John, as he often does, intends a double meaning: the literal meaning for this phrase is death; but the spiritual meaning is the breathing forth the Holy Spirit, as He did in the proleptic pentecost after His Resurrection, breathing upon the apostles and saying, "Receive, the Holy Spirit." We can also envisage other images of this release of the Spirit: the centurion piercing Jesus' side into His Sacred Heart and releasing the Holy Spirit in the blood and water (the sacraments), giving rise to the Church, or the second Adam giving rise to the second Eve (Church); and the Church Fathers' use of the image of Mary breaking the alabaster jar to release the ointment to parallel the sacrifice of the breaking of Jesus and allowing the perfume (Holy Spirit) to fill the whole house (Church).

**The Church: Holy Spirit is the Gift from which Flows All Gifts**
Everything in the Church, from the beginnings, is the work of the Spirit. It is the work of the Spirit in the Early Church to give us the apostles and first disciples, the great martyrs, the Desert and Church Fathers, and who propels evangelization to the ends of the world. It is the Holy Spirit who has given us Monasticism, the Scholastics, the Doctors of the Church, development of doctrine, the Councils (e.g., Vatican II), Scripture and Tradition. It is He who inspired sacred writers to compose Scriptures and it is He who helps us interpret Scripture. It is He who today gives us hierarchical charism and charismatic charisms (e.g., ecclesial foundations) and continues to raise saints and martyrs and confessors within the Church. Yet He is the "Great Unknown." This was Jesus' lament to Conchita, that we do not have recourse to His great gift of the Spirit: "There exists a hidden treasure, a wealth remaining unexploited and in no way appreciated at its true worth, which is

nevertheless that which is the greatest in heaven and on earth.... It is time that the Holy Spirit reigns... Then the world will change."[1] There are three ages: of the Father before Adam's sin; of Christ, from Adam's sin to Pentecost; and now of the Spirit, of the Church, as is manifest in the Acts, the "Gospel of the Holy Spirit." One foundress teaches that our primary task is to follow Jesus in being led by the Spirit:

> One of the main ministries of the Holy Spirit is to transform us into the very image of God Himself, of Jesus Christ. It's a beautiful mystery that God actually dwells within us and that He can dwell more fully within us each day as we open ourselves in that beautiful surrender to His overshadowing Spirit, to His power. Jesus was always led by the Holy Spirit: led out of Nazareth, led into the desert, led back out of the desert, led into different ministries, led to Calvary, and then led on into Heaven. We, too, must always be led and directed by the Holy Spirit. This is what will make our intercession effective— that the Holy Spirit is leading and teaching us at all times, just as He led and taught Jesus.[2]

Today we find a forgetfulness or neglect of God that reflects Teilhard de Chardin's description of the atheistic times he encounters as having a "low sky," "a sensation of asphyxiation," "the horror of a 'closed world,'" "the dreadful solitude of a humanity that would be unified without God." On returning to Paris in 1945, Teilhard de Chardin reacted very strongly to the pessimistic and atheistic existentialist wave engulfing Europe. Realizing that modern man lacking the Transcendent is "sad," he wished to relieve man of this sadness and tedium. His is an optimism, like that of Aquinas, that flows from saying "yes" to creation with a "certain zest for existence," "a zest for Being."[3] *Without the historical wedded to the Transcendent in the materialist evolutionary view, the option that lies before us is a low sky that suffocates, man needs an outlet to escape "total death"*: "To know that we are not imprisoned. To know that there is an outlet, and air, light, and love, in some measure, on the other side of total death. To know this without delusion or fiction!"[4] Thus man is faced with a choice, to stay within a self-enclosed world or to find the outlet, to choose between "the alternative of the attitude of the Titans and Prometheus, or the attitude of Jacob; the attitude of 'revolt' or 'adoration'; of 'haughty Power' or 'evangelical sanctity'; of 'arrogant autonomy' or 'loving excentration'; of the rejection or acceptance of Omega."[5] This is the world of the horizontalism (author's idiom) of today.

---

[1] Marie-Michel Philipon, ed., *Conchita: A Mother's Spiritual Diary* (New York: Alba House, 1978), 130-131.
[2] Nadine Brown, *Interceding with Jesus* (Omaha, NE: Intercessors of the Lamb, 2000), 38.
[3] Henri de Lubac, *Teilhard Explained* (New York: Paulist Press, 1969), 67-68.
[4] Teilhard de Chardin, *Le goût de vivre* (1955, *Oeuvres*, vol. 7, 246), quoted in ibid., 69.
[5] Henri de Lubac, *Teilhard Explained*, 70.

# Retreat 3: Ecclesial Preparations for Mystical Transformation

## Conference 2
## Horizontalism: Rising above the Human to the Divine

There appears today in our First World society a forgetfulness of God, with a concentration on the horizontal, and glorification of human wealth: bodily beauty (latest fashions, huge cosmetic departments on stores' main floors); turning in on self (e.g., reality TV shows); sports' glory (major league sports); singing/dancing (e.g., "America's Got Talent"); nature (ecology, but without concern for unborn, poor); New Age esoterism and Eastern mysticism. This can be accompanied by a prejudice against Christianity. To investigate the sources of atheism, that claims we have moved beyond God, we might look to de Lubac's penetrating *The Drama of Human Atheism*.

We wished to explore today's culture through a contemporary novelist. It so happened that the author's health condition necessitated enforced "zoning out" through rest with light reading. The genre was secondary (e.g., J. Grisham, T. Clancy). Seeking a story-teller whose characters epitomize today's culture, we found this in Louis L'Amour (107 Western novels, 6 awards). His characters manifest many laudable human qualities and wisdom, but with a horizontal glorification that comes with a heavy price, and the issues are several. First, their exclusion of God leads to a worship of nature and pagan mysticism, of knowledge, wide experiences, skills, warrior spirit, and man. His characters are like "Western" versions of Marvel comic super-heroes. Second, even from a literary perspective, we can easily identify many frustrating inconsistencies in logic in books read. Third, what is disturbing is that one senses a serious prejudice against Christianity. Fourth, we will see that his characters typically reflect the fruits of the evil spirit (e.g., pride, see Aid 8), and he may have entered the occult terrain (Aids 9, 10). We shall examine a cross-section of L'Amour's books because of their representative value of, and dangers for, our culture that is marked by atheism, secularism, relativism, and indifference. We wish to flush and flesh out the specific typologies of today's resistance to Christ.

### A. L'Amour's Characters Epitomize Today's Horizontal Predilection

Henri de Lubac asks if we have maintained the purity of our Christian faith. Have we have fallen into "immanentism," by which God is not denied but is being assimilated, becoming the symbol of man, and "the religion of God made man becomes wholly an anthropology?"[1]

---

[1] Henri de Lubac, *The Splendor of the Church*, 225.

## 1. Idealization (Worship?) of Nature

"When see a beautiful object, a beautiful garden, or a beautiful flower, let us think that there we behold a ray of the infinite beauty of God, who has given existence to that object" (St. A. Liguori). Instead, L'Amour's novels repeatedly hints at the New Age and creation-centered spiritualities that have been the vogue: a one-sided love of creation and a modern esoterism.

> To my way of thinking there was nothing finer than to top out on a lonely ridge and sit in my saddle with the wind bringing the smell of pines up from the valley below and the sun glinting off the snow of distant peaks. There was an urge to drink from all the hidden springs, catch my fish in the lonely creeks, and leave my tracks on all that far, beautiful country. (*Milo Talon*, Ch. 27, page numbers from eBooks)

## 2. Obsession with Knowledge

We find in L'Amour a glorification of knowledge that smacks of idolatry. It has become an obsession, "a fever," with a ransacking for knowledge:

> A fever of discovery lay upon the world; old libraries and bookstalls were ransacked for books; scholars from all countries were welcomed; men delved, experimented, tried new things. Nothing like it had ever happened within the memory of man. (*The Walking Drum*, 179)
> The love of learning was of first importance, the poet and scholar ranked with the general and the statesman. Nor were these latter respected unless they, too, were poets and scholars. (Ibid., 84)

There are several serious issues with this. First, as Fr. Benedict Nivakoff perceived, learning is not enough, citing the example of the chief priests and elders who had Jesus crucified possessing a J.D. or doctorate of law equivalent ("The Limitations of Learning," *Magnificat Advent Companion 2021*). Second, the Bible is to be read mainly because "there is much to be learned of men and their ways" (*To the Far Blue Mountains*, 24). But Scripture teaches: "The fear of the Lord is the beginning of wisdom, and the knowledge of the Holy One is insight" (Prov 9:10), and "The wisdom of this world is folly with God" (1 Cor 3:19). Worse still, indiscriminate learning (e.g., *The Walking Drum*, 87) can lead to imbibing poisons, e.g., communism, condemned in several encyclicals (e.g., *Divini Redmptoris*: "flow with satanic logic"), has led to Stalin "annihilating 60 to 70 million people," with M. Zedong credited with even more (*ITV*, Nov.-Dec. 2021, 29,31).

## 3. Turn to Pagan Spiritualism and the Occult

We are saddened that L'Amour's characters are unable to rise above the human to see the transcendent. They are also begin to develop a reverence for the occult: "ancient ones" (*Californios, Jubal Sackett, Lonesome Gods*). We find serious issues in *The Walking Drum*: druids' magic, death spirit, the nightwashers, *teursts* and *gorics* (evil creatures), werewolves, vampires, entrance to Purgatory of *Youdig* (p. 230).

> We know there are shadows for the shadows of things, as a reflection seen in a mirror of a mirror. We know there are circles within circles and dimensions beyond dimension. Reality is itself a shadow, only an appearance accepted by those whose eyes shun what might lie beyond. We of the Druids know the lore we have withheld and kept for ourselves alone, passed down father to son. What, I wondered, would John of Seville think if he knew that within my skull there reposed the sacred knowledge of the Druids? (*The Walking Drum*, 232; cf. 78)

L'Amour does not understand the dangerous terrain into which he has entered. Deut 18:9-14 unequivocally condemns pagan spiritualism as an "abomination." St. Patrick is described as fighting against wizards, witches, and druids (Aid 10). Exorcists, moreover, have found demons identified with pagan gods (e.g., Baal). When Msgr. Rossetti, an exorcist, was asked about many non-Christian practices (e.g., yoga, Reiki, ancestor worship, Ouija boards, "Charlie Charlie," white witchcraft), he responded: "if you are not calling on the one true God and Jesus, His Son (or the Blessed Virgin Mary, the saints, or St. Michael and the good angels), then there is only one other spiritual option, and that is Satan." He relates how a former Reiki dabbler called upon her deceased faither and received consoling messages through her less dominant hand being moved, until things started getting ugly (they were actually evil spirits), and she had to seek deliverance.[2]

### *4. Disparagement of Christianity*
What is worse is that, particularly in his twelfth-century historical novel of *The Walking Drum* (set in Europe and Middle East), he repeatedly, lavishly praises Islam (superiority of scholarship, libraries, hygiene, culture), with an implicit (and explicit) denigration of Christianity (of Crusades, few books, unwashed). Msgr. Rossetti notes that "One of the strongest signs of Satan's presence is the hatred for the Catholic Church" (*Diary*, 175). L'Amour goes over to the opposite side with an "Arab enthusiasm" (his words, p. 179).

> Again I thought of the ancient beliefs of my people. In Christianity I found much good, but judging by its effect upon the lands in which they were supreme, the Moslem religion seemed the most successful…. There was no doubt that Mohammed was a wise man. Did he not marry a widow owning many camels? Such a man is worth listening to. (*The Walking Drum*, 78; also 29)

---

[2] Stephen Rossetti, *Diary of an American Exorcist*, 39-40; 201.

Snipes, implicit and explicit, reveal L'Amour's slanted view of the Latin Church: "The universal lack of cleanliness, as well as the *overbearing pride and ignorance* of both nobles and *churchmen*, astonished me."(Ibid., 242). Is this sheer arrogance? Does reading much enable a man to judge a work that may be of God, to go where even angels fear to tread? Even the revered Gamaliel warned the Sanhedrin about persecuting the apostles and Christianity: "… but if it is of God, you will not be able to overthrow them. You might even be found opposing God!" (Acts 5:39). And is L'Amour a medieval scholar who is in a position to critically judge the Crusades and slander monks?: "The Crusaders may have had noble motives, but loot was at least a secondary object…" (p. 274); "Warlike monks raided caravans or demanded tribute from villages. Often they fought with the nobles who were no more than *titled brigands* such as Tournemine" (p. 71). Can he even begin to substantiate this latter outlandish claim, while absurdly praising Mathurin's father, a pirate (!), to high heaven? One cannot distort history: a historical novel must conform to the facts of history (e.g., military Orders).

L'Amour goes even further. First, he denigrates the bishop of Paris (editorial note: it should be "archbishop"): the bishop gave away his "'great library,' consisting of just eighteen volumes. At the same time the Caliph al-Hakam, in Cordoba, possessed a library of four hundred thousand volumes" (p. 71). Has L'Amour never heard of the monasteries or the later universities that preserved great libraries? Mathurin goes to the Islamic centers of learning (Cordoba), reads the Koran, making this the acme. Has he never heard of the great universities of Paris, Cologne, Padua, Bologna, Salamanca, Oxford, Cambridge, etc., of which Wikipedia lists 72?

The Islamic scholars like Maimonides and Avicenna are deservedly praised. But does he not know that the greatest philosophers were the Greeks, and the greatest among them were Plato and Aristotle; and that Augustine "baptized" Plato (through Plotinus) and Aquinas "baptized" Aristotle (mediated through Avicenna and Averroes), to bring forth sublime syntheses? "For all their effect on the Western world, the Greek thinkers, except for Aristotle, might never have lived" (*The Walking Drum*, 242). Has he never encountered the incomparable Church Fathers of East and West (Irenaeus, Athanasius, Cappadocian Fathers, Ambrose, Augustine, etc.), or the great Medieval doctors (Anselm, Hugh of St. Victor, Bonaventure), or the great mystics (e.g., St. Teresa of Jesus), and can any "mystical" work Mathurin has read surpass that of the uneducated Catherine of Siena's *The Dialogue*? The ignorance in this ecclesial area is palpable. Reading widely and prodigiously does not make one wise or learned. Is this "overbearing pride" (to use his own words)? Against the background of constant snipes against the Church (e.g., against the Knights of Malta), what gives him away is how he now worships at the altar of Abelard, an innovator of the later pernicious Nominalism that caused so much harm, while condemning the great Bernard: "Here and there in the monasteries scholars such as Peter Abelard were thinking, writing, talking. They were few, and often in trouble, but their number was growing"; "'Nonsense!' I said irritably. 'Bernard was an old fool!'" (*The Walking Drum*, 242, 249, 258, 262, 263, 273, 291). L'Amour's attachment to his human knowledge with a proclivity to pagan spirits recalls Msgr. Rossetti's conclusion after asking, "Are Demons Brilliant or Stupid?": their actions of appearing powerful are "antics of an immature adolescent. Demons have no wisdom; they rejected God. They have much more raw intelligence than we do, but, without wisdom, they are shallow" (*Diary*, 100, 217). Likewise, L'Amour's ignorance of facts and lack of judgment are astounding.

Far surpassing Abelard's human brilliance is the divinely infused knowledge of the saints. St. Catherine of Siena, uneducated, on two occasions successfully fought intellectual battles with three distinguished theologians simultaneously. Compare the fruits. Where Abelard abandoned his religious vows, seduced and had an affair with Heloise, a nun (see correspondence), Bernard was "one of the most commanding Church leaders in the first half of the twelfth century as well as one of the greatest spiritual masters of all times and the most powerful propagator of the Cistercian reform," advisor to ruling powers, and called the "cithara of Mary" (Basil Pennington). Furthermore, Luther and Calvin were influenced by Ockham's Nominalism, with its uncoupling of God and the order of creation, resulting in a progeny of tens of thousands of Protestant denominations (Gerald Korson, catholic.com; S. Duffy, *Dynamics of Grace*). Nominalism goes against fifteen centuries of Catholic thought and an army of God's saints who, possessed by the one Spirit (Eph 4:4-6), conform to the teachings of the "one, holy, Catholic, and apostolic Church," which points to their divine source.

### *5. Glorifying the Warrior Persona*
*Apache Morality Lacks Christ's Teaching on Divine Love*: There is a serious contradiction in L'Amour's take on Apache morality, not allowing anyone to critique their morality. His solidarity with the Indigenous tribes is praiseworthy. But that the Apaches kill their enemies, torture, mutilate, and scalp them, kill women and children, do not strike their children but can strike their wives, is simply their way and just different from our way (*High Lonesome*, 68; *Sackett*, 74-75). Is there no universal law of right and wrong and

of conscience, that teaches us to do good and avoid evil? What kind of discernment is this that fails to see the evil of violence?[3]

*Praising Desert and Fighting Men*: His constant praise of the desert, that it is full of life and makes men strong, manifests an adolescent worldview, and perhaps pantheism. He could do well to consider Elijah, Moses, St. John the Baptist, the Desert Fathers, and St. Charles de Foucauld, who found God in the wilderness. Counter to Christianity's teaching to forgive enemies and turn the other cheek, Mathurin rejoices in killing his mother's murderer: "Now I could go as a warrior goes, with a debt paid, the blood of my mother avenged" (*The Walking Drum*, 232). It really stands out in *Last of the Breed*, in which the main character, Major Joe Makatozi, of mixed blood, glories in his Sioux and Scottish Highland warrior heritage, speaking of their "spirits" walking with him as he fought the enemy:

> The great men of his boyhood days had not been George Washington or Abraham Lincoln, not Jim Thorpe or Babe Ruth, but Red Cloud, Crazy Horse, Gall, and a dozen others. From his grandmother he heard the stories of Indian war parties, of raids against the Arikara, the Kiowa, the Crow, and the Shoshone. Throughout his boyhood he had been enchanted by tales of the great warriors of the Sioux nation, of scalps taken, of coups, of men who would die rather than yield. (*Walking Drum*, p. 52). "My grandfather was a Scotsman, a Highlander. Some of my ancestors fought beside Bonnie Prince Charlie. There were others riding with Crazy Horse when he defeated Custer." (p. 125)

What makes a man like L'Amour glory in the warrior persona with its violence? Christianity teaches the truth that we are led by one of three spirits, and Msgr. Rossetti, from his exorcist experience, notes that "another strong sign of Satan's presence is discord, violence, and death" (*Diary*, 195). If L'Amour admires fighting men, then he should consider those who left armies to fight for God's army, including soldier martyrs (e.g. St. Sebastian, who converted many soldiers), and later St. Martin of Tours and St. Ignatius of Loyola. St. Ignatius, with his discernment of spirits after his conversion, came to perceive how the love of military glory was *superficial* and soulless.

---

[3] We feel compelled to add a note. We believe that, if Louis L'Amour, who had an inner sympathy for aboriginal cultures, had been consulted, the Canadian government would not have adopted systemic policies of colonialization, of a cultural genocide, regarding the natives as savages, and having a plan for "taking the Indian out." The Truth and Reconciliation Commission of Canada has studied and made a report on the issue of residential schools, including Christian churches' involvement. It is very heart-breaking to hear of forcibly removing children from families, some dying at those schools without families knowing, punished if they used their native language or culture. This affected seven generations, with communities without children, and children survivors unable to properly raise their own children, and perhaps turning to alcohol to assuage the traumas.

## 6. Predilection to Grandiosity

We wonder if being shackled to the horizontal leads to grandiosity; where there is no God, man takes His place. When we look up the definition of narcissism, we find: "predilections (prone) to grandiosity." This narcissism seems to characterize L'Amour's characters. Grandiosity is so heavy in *The Walking Drum* that it is "thick like molasses": "He [a big man] spoke with the voice of an oracle and the commanding presence of a god" (p. 202). Everything is about Mathurin's irresistible looks, famous corsair father, acquiring knowledge (e.g., from Avicenna, Koran) and skills of every type, fluency in languages, meeting Maimonides and Averroes, and women with rare beauty. He boasts of knowledge: "'Greek, Latin, Arabic, some Persian, and some Sanskrit,' I said, 'and much of what lies in a woman's heart'" (p. 251). The name dropping continues with a legendary restaurant's patrons: "General Grenville Dodge, President Ulysses S. Grant, Jay Gould, Russell Sage, Baron Rothschild, the Prince de Joinville…"; and a man who knew Walter Scott, Dickens, Disraeli, lived close to J. Knox (*Proving Trail*, Ch. 7). Here is an astonishing example of this grandiosity in yet another book.

> This was the country for a man, a big country to grow in, a country where every man stood on his own feet and the wealth of a new land was his for the taking. Ah, it's a grand feeling to be young and tough, with a heart full of hell, strong muscles, and quick hands! And the feeling that somewhere in the town ahead there's a man who would like to cut you down to size with hands or gun. It was like that, Hattan's Point was, when I swung down from my buckskin. A new town, a new challenge; and if there were those who wished to try my hand, let them come and be damned. (*Silver Canyon*, 1)

St. John of the Cross teaches that we have a "wound," a longing for union with God, which cannot be healed except by union with Him. Clinging to anything but Him are disordered desires (self-gratification, all about me, pleasure principle), which both deprive us of God and "weary, torment, darken, defile, and weaken us." They blind us to His presence, leaving us to live at the level of sensuality, i.e., feelings and appearances (*Ascent*, Ch. 6.1).

## 7. Inclination to Self-Exaltation (Man Becomes God)

What drives a man to such grandiosity (pomposity)? Common human experience suggests that emptiness inside leads to pomposity outside (e.g., Pharisees of Jesus' time). "The things that we love tell us what we are" (St. Thomas). It is possible ultimately that, not adoring the divine, man exalts himself to a divine-like state. Here is a monumental statement in *Lonesome Gods* of man making himself a god: "Man to himself is the All, the sum and the total…. He is to himself the beginning and the end." If this is true, where does that leave God's Son, "the Alpha and the Omega" (Rev 22:13)?

> It is all very well to say that man is only a casual whim in a mindless universe, that he, too, will pass. We understand that, but disregard it, as we must. Man to himself is the All, the sum and the total. However much he may seem a fragment, chance object, a bit of flotsam on the waves of time, he is to himself the beginning and the end. And this is just. This is how it must be for him to survive. (*Lonesome Gods*, 436)

What condemns this modern self-adulation is the worship of God found in the long history of religions. To take one example, Confucianism, which underpinned East Asian culture and remains influential to this day, acknowledges God (*Tian*, *Shang Di*); though later Chinese modernism emptied the reference to God for *Tian* to mean "nature." When the Jesuits wrote to inform Rome that they found in Confucianism a worship of God, they first sent their letter to the emperor who, with ten Chinese scholars, all agreed that this was correct. The emperor, would annually offer state worship at the winter solstice, reciting a prayer that bears remarkable resemblance to the creation account of Genesis 1.[4] Noteworthy is that Confucius considered himself only a transmitter of the values of earlier periods, indicating continuity in worship of God. The compatibility between Confucianism with Christianity is such that a Confucian could comfortably convert to Christianity. Confucius also teaches the presence of a natural law in man that guides him and that everyday life is the arena of religion. H. de Lubac's "Christ and the Buddha" offers light on Buddhism.

## B. Responding to the Fatal Flaws in L'Amour's Characters

In the Christian realm, we find true greatness lies elsewhere: in the hidden contribution of science, the power of prayer and the path of peace, divine wisdom that rises above human wisdom, spiritual childhood before God.

### *1. Presenting True Excellence in the Example of Physicist June Lindsey*

L'Amour's characters are about self-importance (e.g., important places and people), and Chantry being called "scholar" (note the "I, who had…"):

> Looking upon these men, I knew that I, who had attended lectures at the Sorbonne and Heidelberg, who had himself lectured at Cambridge and William and Mary, I who had lunched with President Jefferson, who was a friend to Captain Meriwether Lewis, Henry Dearborn, Dr. William Thornton, Gilbert Stuart, and Count de Volney, had at last come home. These [fighting men] were my people… (*The Ferguson Rifle*, Ch. 7)

---

[4] See James Legge, in Chinese-Heritage, accessed March 18, 2022. https://www.chinese-heritage.com/index.php/賦梅花館清賞-2/東學西漸/item/266-a-london-lecture-on-confucius-by-james-legge.html. The author acknowledges his total ignorance of this area.

Let us offer in contrast true human greatness in a real figure, physicist June Lindsey (died Nov. 2021). Growing up in England when women were initially not allowed to get degrees, she was the first woman to obtain a full scholarship from Cambridge University and obtained a Ph.D. Her research thesis was key to James Watson and Francis Crick discovering the structure of DNA, possibly the greatest scientific discovery in the twentieth century. When Watson read her thesis, he found the basic keys, especially the "hydrogen bond," and within three days with Crick, excitedly worked out the double-helix structure of DNA. Yet she has not been recognized for her enormous contribution and was self-effacing, not seeking recognition.

Ottawa molecular geneticist Alex Mackenzie, who, after a chance meeting with her, Google searched her background and "found that her work had been central to Watson and Crick's epiphany" and called it "seismic in its scale."[5] She married a fellow Ph.D. candidate at the famed Cavendish lab and subsequently moved to Canada. She also firmly believed that a woman could have either a career or a family but not both, and quit her brief career as a top-notch physicist and became a mother of two, notwithstanding her clearly gifted scientific background and contribution. Mackenzie is working for her recognition. L'Amour's characters represent "Jerusalem," the rugged warrior with elite skills and superhuman endurance who comes to be almost universally praised; while June Lindsey perhaps represents Nazareth, serving quietly, unrecognized, though her accomplishments in science far surpass that of the warrior, and who understands what is higher. We honour many Nazareth types, like Sir Nicholas Winton who, with many collaborators, arranged the evacuation of 669 mainly Jewish children from Czechoslovakia on the eve of World War II, and went unnoticed for 50 years.

### 2. *Superiority of Prayer and Peace to "Warrior's Path" (A Novel's Title)*
Let us see the superiority in Scripture of prayer and peace over war and the warrior culture. In the Old Testament, we see it was not the swords of the Israelites but Moses' *prayer* that defeated the Amalekites:

> Third, the power of prayer in the Spirit can be seen in the symbolism of the battle of the Israelites against the Amalekites. While the entire Israelite army was struggling vigorously on the battlefield, Moses was up the mountain with his arms raised in prayer. While the Israelites strove with Amalek, Moses strove with God, and it was Moses who assured the victory of his people (cf. Exod 17:8-16). Amalek, Origen explains, symbolizes the hostile forces barring the way for God's people: the devil, the world, and sin. When the people of God and their pastors pray, they are stronger and repulse

---

[5] Elizabeth Payne, "'Unsung Hero' Laid the Groundwork for DNA Discovery," *National Post*, November 17, 2021, A3.

Amalek; when they do not pray (when Moses got tired and lowered his arms), Amalek is stronger.[6]

A second example from the Old Testament is that of King David, the great warrior who freed the Hebrew people from their enemies and established a kingdom, but who was not allowed to build a temple for Yahweh because he had blood on his hands: "But God said to me, 'You may not build a house for my name, for you are *a warrior and have shed blood*'" (1 Chron 28:3). Thus, *a temple for God would have to be built by a man of peace*, for God's very nature is love and thus peace. Despite the blood on his hands, he was far greater than Solomon: "I have found in David the son of Jesse a man after my heart, *who will do all my will*" (Acts 13:22). Here lies true greatness, reflecting Jesus' own pleasing the Father: "Here are my mother and my brothers! For whoever does the will of my Father in heaven is my brother, and sister, and mother'" (Mt 12:49-50). To see an example of God's predilection for peace, L'Amour can contemplate a woman of unity and dialogue, Chiara Lubich, who was awarded some 66 international awards, and esteemed by many Christians and non-Christians, including religious and world leaders. We might also look to Andrea Riccardi, founder of the Community of Sant'Egidio, known for its promotion of peace and dialogue in conflict regions, and to Brother Roger Schütz, founder of the Taizé ecumenical community, in his call for the reconciliation of Christians.

### *3. It is Lack of Purity of Heart that Causes Failure to Recognize God*
Not only do many today lack belief in a Creator, there appears to be a substitute New Age type of spirituality, seen in Makatozi, who after killing a bear for food and fat to survive, apologized to the bear (p. 90). Likewise, in the movie *Avatar* (a few movie critics discern a Buddhist background), we find apologizing for killing an animal within pantheism, without a divine God: "Pandora... [was] inhabited by the Na'vi, a species of 10-foot tall (3.0 m), blue-skinned, sapient humanoids that live in harmony with nature and worship a mother [tree] goddess named Eyw" (s.v. *Avatar*, Wikipedia). Francis Fernandez's insightful meditation on "Purity of Heart" clearly reveals the cause of our inability to recognize a transcendent God. He points to the Beatitude, "Blessed are the pure of heart, for they shall see God," quoting St. Leo the Great on the Beatitudes.

> "The pure in heart shall see God." It is with good reason that the beatitude of seeing God is promised to the pure in heart. A life that is defiled can never contemplate the splendour of the true Light, because the very same

---

[6] Insight drawn from Raniero Cantalamessa, *The Holy Spirit in the Life of Jesus* (Collegeville, MN: Liturgical Press, 1994), 56. The text above is reprinted from the author's *New Christ: Divine Filiation*, 86.

thing which is the joy of pure souls will be the punishment of those that are defiled. (St. Leo the Great, *Sermon 95*)[7]

Fernandez teaches us that we should especially be able to recognize God at Christmas if our hearts are clean and free, and we will see the results:

> Christmas is a summons to purity of heart. Perhaps many men see nothing wonderful when this feast comes around because they are blind to what is truly important: Their hearts are full of material things, or of filth and misery. *Uncleanness of heart produces insensitivity to the things of God*, and to much that is humanly good as well, including compassion for the unhappiness of other people. *But from a pure heart spring joy, the ability to see the divine, trust in God, sincere repentance, recognition of ourselves and our sins, true humility, and a great love for God and for other people.*[8] (emphasis added)

Our Lord teaches us that if anything causes us to sin, we must pluck out our eye or cut off our hand (figuratively) rather than be damned (Mt 5:29-30); we must remove every obstacle to our God, our Creator and our Destiny.[9]

## 4. No Excuse for not Recognizing God for whom we are Created (Rom 1)

Rom 1 reveals that we have no excuse for not recognizing God through creation if our hearts are open (all cultures have religious cults). We see that the world was created by God for man, and man for God (e.g., Col 1): "The whole earth is a living icon of the face of God" (J. Damascene); "There is no space where God is not; space does not exist apart from him" (Augustine). The question of the existence of God has been investigated by key figures in the modern era, including J. H. Newman, H. de Lubac, H. U. von Balthasar, R. Guardini, J. Ratzinger, L. Giussani, J. Carrón, A. Riccardi, and many others. Msgr. Rosetti, who was in the US Air Force and is a licensed psychologist with a doctorate in psychology, has taught that there is no inherent contradiction between real truths uncovered by a secular science and the beliefs of the Catholic faith.[10] What leaves us without any excuse is the faith of the mother in the Book of Maccabees who encouraged her own seven sons to die rather than apostatize. While watching them being tortured, she mentions specifically that God created the universe from nothing and that for Him alone we should live, even at the cost of our lives. Even the youngest son cried out there will be a reckoning: "But you, who have contrived all sorts of evil against the Hebrews, will certainly not escape the hands of God." (2 Macc 7:20-31).

---

[7] Quoted in Francis Fernandez, *In Conversation with God*, vol. 1, 123.
[8] Ibid., 119.
[9] Ibid., 121.
[10] "Psychology and the Church's Teaching on Homosexuality," *America* 177 (13), 1-23.

> ... Therefore the Creator of the world, who shaped the beginning of the human race and devised the origin of all things, will in his mercy give life and breath back to you again, since you now forget yourselves for the sake of his laws.... I beg you, my child, to look at the heaven and the earth and see everything that is in them, and recognize that God did not make them out of things that existed. And in the same way the human race came into being. Do not fear this butcher, but prove worthy of your brothers. Accept death, so that in God's mercy I may get you back again along with your brothers.

St. John of the Cross speaks of an "awakening" to the presence of God. in us. Theologically, we distinguish (i) His maintaining us in existence, (ii) His presence in our conscience, and (iii) His personal indwelling by grace.

## 5. Creaturehood Enables Acknowledging Christ as Creator & Redeemer

St. Augustine taught that "Sin is believing the lie that you are self-created, self-dependent and self-sustained." What makes it especially evil is that God the Father created us for Trinitarian Communion, gave us the universe, families, homes, and guardian angels, and sent His Son to die to redeem us, pouring out the Holy Spirit in the Church. In the face of not only His creation, for which we owe gratitude, His infinite transcendence, to which we owe worship, but above all His self-emptying love, for which we owe filial devotion, not acknowledging and loving God is criminal beyond belief. Daniel beautifully describes all creation praising the Lord: "Bless the Lord, seas and rivers; sing praise to him and highly exalt him forever" (Dan 3:57-88). Where there is no God, man becomes god. This was the temptation by the devil to eat of the tree of knowledge of good and evil: "You will be like God" (to know all truth without God and thus not need God). The devil, to whom Christian tradition applies "I will not serve," seeks to build a rival kingdom (third temptation of Jesus, Mt 4:9). We forget we are creatures! Self-worship in the face of God's transcendent love is diabolic.

*Gaudium et spes* teaches that it is Christ who is "the key, the centre and the purpose of the whole of man's history."[11] Baldwin of Canterbury explains that Christ, as Word of God, is Creator, Redeemer, and everything, and that His wisdom far surpasses any human wisdom.[12] John furnishes the test to discern between the good spirit and evil spirit of the antichrist: confessing Christ as God (1 Jn 4:1-3). We will all be judged by Christ (Mt 10:32). When we oppose the Church's teaching, we may already be embarked on the road of self-will and dissent: "He who hears you hears me" (Lk 10:16).

---

[11] GS n. 10.
[12] Baldwin of Canterbury, "The Word of God is alive and active," Universalis.com, OOR for October 29, 2021, accessed October 29, 2021, https://universalis.com/readings.htm.

> If one yields ground on any single point of Catholic doctrine, one will later have to yield in another, and again in another, and so on until such surrenders come to be something normal and acceptable. And when one gets used to rejecting dogma bit by bit, the final result will be the repudiation of it altogether. (St. Vincent of Lérins, *Narrations*, 2)

Our Lord led Chiara Lubich along the path of letting go of her love of study (unlike L'Amour's obsession with knowledge and its self-glorification) to find Him who is Truth itself, Christ. Now her infused mystical insights are influencing diverse areas (e.g., politics, social and economic life, education, spiritual life) and are studied by theologians (the Abba School).

> Approximately sixty years ago I stopped studying and actually put my beloved books in the attic. I did this not only because I was devoting myself to the newly emerging Focolare Movement, but above all because, in my thirst for truth, for THE Truth, I realized that while my studies of philosophy, which I so ardently loved, gave me a taste of it, I would never be able to discover the real and complete truth better than in the One who had said of himself: "I am the truth" (Jn 14:6)— Christ. This is why, through a personal and special call from God, I decided to follow Jesus, sure that I would find in him the heights and depths of the full, authentic, indisputable truth.[13]

Beyond truth, those without faith miss out on God's love: "What really matters in life is that we are loved by Christ, and that we love him in return. In comparison to the love of Jesus, everything else is secondary. And without the love of Jesus, everything else is useless" (John Paul II, St. John Neumann's tomb). We see the contrast of L'Amour with his predilection to a warrior persona and rugged individualism to a Vietnamese martyr, who is not a lone-wolf, but has Christ. He has experienced Christ's love.

> I, Paul, in chains for the name of Christ, wish to relate to you the trials besetting me daily, in order that you may be inflamed with love for God and join with me in his praises. The prison here is a true image of everlasting hell: to cruel tortures of every kind – shackles, iron chains, manacles – are added hatred, vengeance, calumnies, obscene speech, quarrels, evil acts, swearing, curses, as well as anguish and grief....
> In the midst of these torments, which usually terrify others, I am, by the grace of God, full of joy and gladness, **because I am not alone – Christ is with me**. Our Master bears the whole weight of the cross, leaving me only the tiniest, last bit. He is not a mere onlooker in my struggle, but a contestant and the victor and champion in the whole battle. Therefore upon his head is placed the crown of victory, and his members also share in his glory. (OOR for Vietnamese Martyrs)

---

[13] Chiara Lubich, "The Spirituality of Unity and Trinitarian Life" (cited earlier).

## C. Critical Evaluation of the Culture Represented by L'Amour

### 1. Two Critics' Overall Negative Assessment of L'Amour's Novels

That L'Amour's characters mirror his own background (*Education of a Wandering Man*) raises questions. One literary critic, Jon Tuska, points to the good: "At his best, he was a master of spectacular action and stories with a vivid, propulsive forward motion"; but that overall he is repetitively formulary, not original nor deeply literary.

> I have no argument that L'Amour's total sales have probably surpassed every other author of Western fiction in the history of the genre…. What I would question is the degree and extent of his effect "upon the American Imagination." His Western fiction is strictly formulary and frequently, although not always, features the ranch romance plot where the hero and the heroine are to marry at the end once the villains have been defeated. Not only is there *nothing really new in the basic structure* of his stories, even L'Amour's social Darwinism, which came to characterize his later fiction, was scarcely original and was never dramatized in other media the way it was in works based on Zane Grey's fiction. (Wikipedia, s.v. "Louis L'Amour")

Another online assessment that we find on *Lonesome Gods* diagnosed "rugged individualism" in his characters, that the worldview is bankrupt (a devastating critique), but that his books are still worthwhile reading.

> Against this the global Catholic Church (or the Orthodox) must say no. Again, I *love* Louis L'Amour westerns, yet the worldview is bankrupt in the end. Christianity is not some rugged individualism anymore than it is statist communism. We must not prefer either. The gods are not lonesome in Louis L'Amour: the backstory is. Still L'Amour can write: read the book.[14] [like the pantheist *Avatar* movie that is entertaining]

### 2. Summary Evaluation of Diverse Elements

Our objective critique of L'Amour follows the path of Jesus' correcting the Pharisees and Paul's chastising the Galatians (Gal 2:11-3:14) to lead people to Christ. First, we praise his marvellous storytelling skills, but perceive in his characters a spiritual adolescence: being wrapped up in endlessly spouting morality, philosophy, and human wisdom, and idealizing creation, heroism, and endurance. It recalls St. Ignatius' glorying in military glory (and human romance), until he came to see its vanity in relation to divine and eternal glory

---

[14] John Mark Reynolds, "The Lonesome Gods (A Problem of the 1950's Generation and Louis L'Amour)," Eidos, accessed October 17, 2021,
https://www.patheos.com/blogs/eidos/2019/06/the-lonesome-gods-a-problem-of-the-1950s-generation-and-louis-lamour/

and love. It utterly lacks the transcendent for which we are made. Reality is not circumscribed by the created or human; to see only the human is to miss the forest for the trees: "There is no space where God is not; space does not exist apart from him" (St. Hilary).

Second, being confined to the horizontal, his characters seem to revel in human accomplishments. To glorify the Indigenous guerilla skills effusively is analogous to praising the Japanese Samurai culture, which in alliance with Nazism, sought to dominate countries. Perhaps God's response to such glorification of the Indigenous (pagan) culture and warrior mentality is the call of Juan Diego, an Indigenous of Mexico:

> What was Juan Diego like? Why did God look upon him? The Book of Sirach, as we have heard, teaches us that God alone "is mighty; he is glorified by the humble".... "God chose what is low and despised in the world ... so that no human being might boast in the presence of God." The Virgin Mary, the handmaid "who glorified the Lord," reveals herself to Juan Diego as the Mother of the true God.... In accepting the Christian message without forgoing his indigenous identity, Juan Diego discovered the profound truth of the new humanity, in which all are called to be children of God. Thus he facilitated the fruitful meeting of two worlds and became the catalyst for the new Mexican identity, closely united to Our Lady of Guadalupe, whose mestizo face expresses her spiritual motherhood which embraces all Mexicans.... Blessed Juan Diego, a good, Christian Indian, whom simple people have always considered a saint! We ask you to accompany the Church on her pilgrimage in Mexico, so that she may be more evangelizing and more missionary each day. (Pope John Paul II's homily at St. Juan Diego's canonization, see OOR for Dec. 9)

In every way, Juan Diego responds to L'Amour's glorification of the warrior and human acclaim. Rather than a great warrior, God calls an Indigenous who "is low and despised in this world"; he serves not his own greatness or lonesome spirits but, with knightly chivalry, a Lady, the Mother of God; he conquers not a few human enemies but, through her, Satan and his fallen angels ("she will crush your head," Gen 3:15)[15]; he attains not human adulation and excellence but sanctity; he is not this shining example of human greatness but one who helps evangelize all of the Americas, and to whom Pope John Paul II entrusted many people in the Americas.

---

[15] The Douay-Rheims has "and she shall crush your head," referring to the woman as crushing, as does the Latin Vulgate, *"ipsa conteret caput tuum."* Pope Pius IX's *Ineffabilis Deus*, the apostolic constitution for the Definition of the Immaculate Conception, clearly states "the most holy virgin, united with him [Christ]... thus crushed his head with her immaculate foot." (M. Giszczak, "Did Mary Crush the Serpent's Head," CatholicBibleStudent).

Third, J. Carrón teaches that we have an objective inner void, which when not satiated, leads us to attenuate it (no desires in one Greek philosophy) or seek the worldly gratification (possibly what L'Amour's characters are doing). When asked by a student how he can be sure that God exists, Carrón explained that he begins with man and not God. We perceive in our hearts a wound, void, or thirst that no happiness on earth can fill; but that most do not descend deeply enough to be in touch with it. A man waking up after months in a coma discovered the wonder of being and of it being a "given" (by God). A woman, finding a vase of flowers, would not be content until she finds out who loves her enough to send the flowers. (*Where is God?*, 28-33). Carrón also uses another pointer: that "the greatest miracle is the existence of the 'I,'" with its irruption when the cosmos became conscious (T. de Chardin?). This "I" is not attributable to the sum of our biological or historical antecedents. He turns to the example of Newman's mystical insight at the age of 15: "he was thunder-struck by the intuition that there were 'two and only two supreme and luminously self-evident beings: myself and my Creator.'" A revelatory conclusion follows: "Accepting the ultimate implication of the existence of the 'I'— admitting that I am 'You-who-make-me,' Fr. Giussani said, with reference to God, to the Mystery who makes all things— is perhaps the most dizzying decision of freedom and demands the use of reason in all its breadth" (ibid, 34-35).

Fourth, because of L'Amour's loose moral standards and negative judgment of Christianity, we highlight what constitutes mortal sin for a Catholic that suggests issues in his own moral stance (A. Miklósházy, "Hamartiology"):
- those who do not accept faith as the practical norm of their lives;
- who systematically refuse to apply the moral categories of good and evil to their actions;
- who abandon the use of means which help Christians to live the life of grace (prayer, sacraments, Church, etc.).

Fifth, what reveals L'Amour's fundamental flaw is an examination of John's "three lusts" (disordered attachments): "The lust of the flesh and the lust of the yes and the pride of life" (1 Jn 2:16). St. Escrivá offers key insights. The lust of the flesh refers to "the disordered tendencies of the senses in general or to the disorder of sensuality in particular," and includes love of comfort and of all that is pleasurable and of taking the easiest path (*Christ is Passing By*, n. 5). His surgical dissection of the other two lusts cuts to the heart of human predilection and diagnoses it as *self-idolatry* (critique of L'Amour):

> St John tells us that the other enemy is the lust of the eyes, a deep-seated avariciousness that leads us to appreciate only what we can touch. Such eyes are *glued to earthly things* and, consequently, they are *blind to supernatural realities*.

We can, then, use this expression of sacred Scripture to indicate that disordered desire for material things, as well as that deformation which views everything around us — other people, the circumstances of our life and of our age — *with just human vision.*

Then the eyes of our soul grow dull. *Reason proclaims itself sufficient to understand everything, without the aid of God.* This is a subtle temptation, which hides behind the power of our intellect, given by our Father God to man so that he might know and love him freely. *Seduced by this temptation, the human mind appoints itself the centre of the universe*, being thrilled with the prospect that "you shall be like gods." So filled with love for itself, *it turns its back on the love of God.*

In this way does our existence fall prey unconditionally to the third enemy: pride of life. It's not merely a question of passing thoughts of vanity or self-love, it's a state of *general conceit*. Let's not deceive ourselves, for this is the *worst of all evils, the root of every false step*. The fight against pride has to be a constant battle, to such an extent that someone once said that pride only disappears twenty-four hours after each of us has died. It is the arrogance of the Pharisee whom God cannot transform because he finds in him the obstacle of *self-sufficiency*.[16] (emphasis added)

## D. Moving Beyond Human Predilection to Divine Glory

Our Lord teaches us to love all, including enemies, but also to correct the sin (e.g., see St. Augustine's phrase, "with love for mankind and hatred of sins," *Letter* 211). The author's assessment of L'Amour's characters is principally about the many they exemplify today in their quest for the horizontal, with the ensuing ennui and lack of fulfillment. But it is not just about its inadequacy; far greater is the matter of justice: "Render to Caesar the things that are Caesar's, and to God the things that are God's" (Mk 12:17). The whole history of Israel involved Yahweh drawing them away from the false gods to worship the one God (movement towards monotheism), expressed profoundly by the Jewish daily prayer, the *Shema*: "Hear O' Israel, the Lord is our God, the Lord is One…" (Deut 6:4). Bishop Miklósházy was fond of the *Shema*, and would say to seminarians, "There is only one God, and you and I are not it."

### *1. The Grandeur of the Divine Vision of Christian Authors*

At the human level, one can find enjoyment and entertainment in L'Amour, and even quote his human wisdom. But his vision is limited to the horizontal: human, creation. He does not see the sacramentality of creation as a mirror of God, a book of divine revelation: "God is an artist and the universe is his creation" (Aquinas). Even as a seminarian, Fr. Giussani "discovered a way to understand 'secular' works of art… as expressive of the religious sense and

---

[16] St. Josemaría Escrivá, *Christ is Passing By* (Manila: Sinag-Tala Publns., 1974), n. 6.

as unconscious prophecies of Christ's incarnation" (see Wikipedia, s.v. "L. Giussani"). For nature does not ultimately fulfill; its beauty comes from the Creator who is Beauty, Love, Light, Glory— Christ. John Paul II proclaimed: "It is Jesus that you seek when you dream of happiness. He is waiting for you when nothing else you find satisfies you." An early pope, St. Clement I, acknowledges this beauty of the universe but even more of the Creator, who creates this beauty and harmony, and ends in praise of Him, "to him be glory and majesty for ever and ever":

> By his [Creator] direction the heavens are in motion, and they are subject to him in peace. Day and night fulfil the course he has established without interfering with each other. The sun, the moon and the choirs of stars revolve in harmony at his command in their appointed paths without deviation. By his will the earth blossoms in the proper seasons and produces abundant food for men and animals and all the living things on it without reluctance and without any violation of what he has arranged.... The seasons, spring, summer, autumn and winter, follow one another in harmony. The quarters from which the winds blow function in due season without the least deviation. And the ever-flowing springs, created for our health as well as our enjoyment, unfailingly offer their breasts to sustain human life. The tiniest of living creatures meet together in harmony and peace. The great Creator and Lord of the universe commanded all these things to be established in peace and harmony, in his goodness to all, and in overflowing measure to us who seek refuge in his mercies through our Lord Jesus Christ; to him be glory and majesty for ever and ever. Amen. (Pope St. Clement I, *Letter to the Corinthians*, OOR for Oct. 24)

## 2. This Divine Path Leads to Glorious Victimhood (vs. Warrior's Success)

For L'Amour, Islam is greater than Christianity because it has conquered many lands by the sword, by blood (*Walking Drum*, 179). His exaltation of the sword is undercut, even obliterated, by religious history's two paths symbolized by Abel and Cain. God blesses Abel's sacrifice, and rejects Cain, the hunter (warrior). Abel was the man of peace whose offering was pleasing to God and who was killed by Cain. Abel represents all the little ones, including the Hebrew people persecuted in Egypt (Cain) but defended by God. We see how God condemns the warrior conquerors (Cain) of Israel and nations, like Nebuchadnezzar (Dan 2), Antiochus (1 Macc 6:1-13), and the Roman Empire (Rev 13:1 links the dragon with Rome, which had 7 hills and 7 kings, and prophesies her fall).

The Church's history is that of Abel, the victim and not the conqueror. In the Early Church, we saw great persecutions, a period rife with heresies, barbarian invasions, and the rise of Islam that conquered by the sword. The Second Millennium witnessed two great schisms (Orthodox in 1054 and Reformation), periods of decadence. The twentieth century was dominated by two world wars, the rise of totalitarian regimes, and modernism; and our era has seen more insidious enemies: indifferentism, secularism, relativism. Jesus prophesied that we will not have peace but the sword: "Do not think that I have come to bring peace on earth; I have not come to bring peace, but a sword" (Mt 10:34; Lk 12:51). We must not long for a "Christendom," for our Lord taught that "where I am, there shall my servant be also" (Lk 12:26). He brings a divine wisdom: "we preach *Christ crucified,* a stumbling block to Jews and folly to Gentiles" (1 Cor 1:23). To strengthen Agnes of Prague to not accept the monetary endowment from a pope, St. Clare of Assisi counselled her to gaze upon the famous San Damiano cross, to contemplate Christ's sufferings, and then to allow Him to strengthen her to imitate His poverty. St. Clare understood that all riches are found in Christ crucified, the secret of the saints.

There is a new plan: "God judged it better to draw good from evil than not to permit evil to exist" (Augustine, *Enchir.* 27; *PL* 40, 245). God's far greater blessings from Adam's "happy fault" derive from His sending Christ: "God bore with man patiently when he fell because he foresaw the victory that would be his through the Word" (Irenaeus, *Adv. Haereses*). T. D. Williams, writing on John Paul II's "new springtime," sees this plan's ethos expressed in the pope's remarkable hope for renewal after evil.

> With *Memory and Identity,* his last published work, John Paul shocked many by his hopeful reading of even the darkest chapters of the twentieth century. Reflecting on the Nazi occupation of Europe and the communist domination that followed, John Paul made some disconcerting assertions. "There was a sense," he wrote, "that this evil was in some way necessary for the world and mankind.... It can happen, in fact, that in certain concrete circumstances, evil is revealed as somehow *useful,* inasmuch as it creates opportunities for good."[17]

Ratzinger too, in reference to "A New Springtime," could incredibly speak of opportunities that open up after failing, sometimes cruel, ideologies:

> *The internal dead-ends and contradictions, as well as the internal falsity of such theories* [Marxism, Freudian psycho-analysis, the ethics of the sociologists] *will emerge. And that is, in fact, already happening to a large extent.* We are experiencing the *demythologization* of many ideologies. For example, the economic explanation of the world that Marx attempted and that at first seemed so logical and so compelling and therefore could exercise such fascination, especially because it was associated with a moral ethics, simply

---

[17] Thomas D. Williams, "The Springtime of John Paul II," *First Things* (Feb. 4, 2009), accessed Dec. 30, 2021, https://www.firstthings.com/web-exclusives/2009/04/the-springtime-of-john-paul-ii.

doesn't correspond to reality. Man is not comprehensively described in these terms. It has become plain that religion is a primordial reality in man. And the same holds in relation to all these other things.[18] (emphasis)

Concretely striking was a Japanese doctor who lost his entire family at Nagasaki and yet praised God for choosing his city as a sacrifice to end the war. He discerned that it was not primarily the heavy clouds that made the American crew shift to Nagasaki and the nuclear bombs to fall above the cathedral: "Is there not a profound relationship between the annihilation of Nagasaki and the end of the war? Was not Nagasaki the chosen victim, the lamb without blemish, slain as a whole burnt offering on an altar of sacrifice, atoning for the sins of all the nations during World War II?"[19]

### 3. Moving Conversion of André Frossard (Atheist Journalist)
Man has been created for divine joy. Our human history and our personal human experience reveal the bankruptcy of merely human fulfillment. The world is but a creature; the world is not God.[20] Those who know only the world's riches have not been ravished from cleaving totally to God in purity of heart, leaving everything behind. May all have the mystical experience of an atheist who became one of the Church's best-known journalists.

> In 1935, twenty-year-old André Frossard was working as an aspiring journalist in Paris. Though he was an atheist, he had nevertheless befriended a practicing Catholic, André Villemin, who tried unsuccessfully to lead him to a belief in God. On June 8, 1935, Villemin invited Frossard to dinner. They drove to the Latin Quarter in an old clapped-out car and stopped in front of a chapel where the Blessed Sacrament was perpetually exposed. Villemin asked Frossard to wait a moment while he attended to some business in the chapel. After waiting a while, the impatient Frossard got out of the car and entered the chapel. Standing at the back, he ran his eye over the people kneeling inside. In vain he sought out his friend. Looking over toward the altar, he turned his attention to the Blessed Sacrament which stood exposed for adoration. He had no idea what it was, for he had never seen a monstrance before. Suddenly, in a manner he could not explain, he felt a mysterious power outside of himself penetrate his heart. The power released him from the spiritual blindness caused by his atheism and enabled him to experience another world, a world more real than the one we perceive with our senses. "At first, the hint of the words 'Spiritual Life' came to me, as if they had been pronounced in a whisper next to me by one who saw what I was as yet unable to see." Upon hearing these words, Frossard felt himself engulfed by a supernatural reality radiating directly from the Holy Sacrament.

---

[18] Joseph Ratzinger, *Salt of the Earth*, in ibid.
[19] Dr. Takashi Nagai, "A Song for Nagasaki," *Inside the Vatican*, Letter #37, 2010.
[20] Attila Miklósházy, "Eschatology," Grace and Glory Lecture.

"What I saw was an indestructible crystal of infinite transparency [from which radiated] a pale-blue light of almost unbearable intensity... It was a world; another world of a radiance and brightness that in one stroke cast our world among the fragile shadows of unfulfilled dreams. From the dark shore upon which I stood, I gazed on this new reality and truth and saw the order of the universe. At its summit was the Self-Evident Nature of God who was both Presence and Person. A moment earlier I had denied Its existence. Christians call this Presence 'Our Father.' I felt all Its tender goodness and sweetness... a sweetness unlike any other, capable of breaking the hardest stone and that which is even harder than stone—the human heart. The irruption of this reality of God was accompanied by a joy which is the exultation of one rescued from death, the joy of a shipwrecked man at the very moment he is plucked from the seas. Only now did I realize how mired in the mud I had been all this time. I was amazed I could have lived and breathed in such a state. At the same time I acquired a new family—the Catholic Church. Her mission was to lead me to where I had to go, for I had a long journey before me.... The Church was a community; and present within her was the One whose name I would never be able to set down in writing without fear of wounding His love, and before whom I had the good fortune of being a forgiven child who wakes up to discover that everything is a gift....

I can still see the twenty-year-old youth I was then. I can remember his stupefaction when, from the recesses of that humble chapel, there suddenly appeared before him a world, another world of unbearable splendor, of tremendous cohesion, whose light both revealed and concealed the presence of God. Just moments earlier, the youth would have sworn God existed only in the human imagination. At the same time, there washed over him a wave of sweetness mingled with a joy of such power as to soften hearts; the memory of it would never fade, even in the worst moments of his life—moments not seldom filled with fear and misery. From then on, he would set himself no other task but that of testifying to that sweetness and that excruciating purity of God, who revealed to him that day, by way of contrast, the kind of mud out of which he had been fashioned.... The light which I saw with my bodily eyes was not the light that shines or causes skin to tan. Rather it was a spiritual light, i.e. a light that enlightens the soul—the searing glow of truth, as it were. It restored, once and for all, the order of things. From the moment I saw it, I could say that only God existed for me; everything else was mere hypothesis.... Again I stress: this was an objective experience, bordering, as it were, on the realm of physics, and I have nothing more of value to convey than this: that beyond the world around us, of which we are particles, there exists a reality infinitely more substantial than the one in which we normally place our trust. It is the ultimate reality, before which there are no longer any questions."[21]

---

[21] André Frossard, *God Exists: I have Met Him* (NY: Herder and Herder, 1971), 21-24.

Retreat 3: Ecclesial Preparations for Mystical Transformation

## Conference 3
## Evangelization: The Church's Right and Mission to Evangelize

We have discovered that the characters of Louis L'Amour's novels may epitomize today's predilection for the horizontal or human level. Worse yet, at least in *The Walking Drum*, there is clearly a personal bias against the Church and Christianity, displaying fruits of the evil spirit. The New Testament authors indicate that a sign of the antichrist is rejection of Christ (does not include those who have not met Christ), the Son of the Father, who has come to redeem us. John, inspired by the Holy Spirit, manifestly teaches: "Who is the liar but he who denies that Jesus is the Christ? This is the antichrist, he who denies the Father and the Son" (1 Jn 2:22). The fruits of the evil spirit include rejection of Christ, disobedience, pride, lack of faith in God, attacks on Christ's Church, etc. As if this were not enough, we find that L'Amour denies the right of the Church to evangelize. Thus we must begin by validating the very existence and the mission of the Church.

### A. The Church as the "Sacrament of Christ"

#### *1. Christ Willed the Foundation of His Church*
The mission of the Church's evangelization of the world presupposes that God willed her foundation. To theologically validate this foundation, we note that *Lumen gentium* affirms that she is "the Church from the Trinity": that the Father planned her establishment (n. 2), the Son came to establish her (n. 3), through the Spirit (n. 4), so that she has become God's kingdom on earth (n. 5). In addition, the International Theological Commission's (ITC) 1985 "Select Questions of Ecclesiology" enumerates 10 implicit steps of Christ for founding the Church and affirms that it is a process intended by Christ. ITC's document on "The Consciousness of Christ" affirms that "Jesus willed the foundation of the Church" (p. 311) and that "Christ was conscious of his saving mission.... the history of Christianity is founded on the intention and the will of Christ to found his Church" (p. 313).

#### *2. Church as Sacrament of Christ, Extension of Christ in Space & Time*
Attila Miklósházy develops the Church as sacrament. Vatican II employs the image of the Church as "sacrament" in the sense of a "mystery" (Eph 3:1-13 uses *mysterion*, translated into Latin as "sacrament," *sacramentum*), drawn from the Church Fathers of Church as a "divine-human" mystery. It is built upon the analogy of the Incarnate Word as God-man, giving birth to the Church from His side on the cross. The key here in regard to L'Amour is that the Church, because her essence is a mystery in the supernatural sense, is an

object of faith that cannot be comprehended through sociological, psychological, or historical methods. Being scandalized by the Church's weakness usually manifests a certain lack of faith. Happy are those who are not scandalized in the kenosis of (emptying by) the Incarnate Lord who continues His abasement in His Church (cf. Mt 11:6). Following the logic of the incarnation in the Church, those who believe in God look for Him in the Body of Christ, see her as an instrument of salvation, and see God in her. Beyond intellectual acceptance, they give their love and affection to, and live, feel, exist, and work with and within, the Church. While partly sociological and historical, her true reality is hidden: "The content of this mystery is: Trinitarian and theological (the work of God), salvation-historical (People of God), Christological (Body of Christ), pneumatological (Spirit-filled), and an eschatological reality (Kingdom of God)." Because of her divine dimension, she cannot be defined but rather described by multiple images (e.g., flock, temple, spouse, mother, etc.). She is an enigma and paradox of seemingly opposing factors:

- visible and invisible
- unity and diversity
- holy and sinful
- divine and human
- immanent and transcendent
- community and society
- Church of law and of love
- organism and organization
- local and universal
- suffering and triumphant[1]

Fulton Sheen also offers penetrating insights. The Church is not a social or moral body but a Mystical Body, the prolongation of the risen Christ: a member would have to be born into her (Baptism); she shares His divine life (Jn 15:5); expands from inside out like a living embryo (Jn 17:21); has only one Body (Jn 10:16); be born on Pentecost, not before or after Pentecost (Jn 16:7); and would be hated by the world (Jn 15:20). In addition, the nucleus was His apostles; she required the divine Spirit to give her life (chemicals cannot become alive until a soul is breathed into it by God); it would be His mystical presence ("Saul, Saul, why do you persecute me?") so that Christ is now living! It has four marks: unity that is centripetal in preserving unity of doctrine and authority; catholicity that is centrifugal in expanding and assimilating all humanity; holiness that keeps it healthy by being free from heresy and schism; and apostolicity, because it took its roots from Christ and not a man separated by centuries from Him, for "all life comes from Life" (cf. "Christ Takes on a New Body," *The Life of Christ*).

## 3. Church Recognizes Christ's Handiwork in the Good in Cultures

The Church's way has always been to take what is good in each culture (e.g., the 1985 Extraordinary Synod of Bishops' Final Report). One exceptional

---

[1] Attila Miklósházy, "The Mystery of the Church," Ecclesiology Lecture.

disseminator of this was Henri de Lubac, especially in his *Catholicism*. He believes that the Spirit is capable of everything, and at this banquet all are welcome. The Church is neither Latin (West) nor Greek (East) but universal. The Church does not discard but keeps that which is good, by studying sympathetically those forms most remote from us and it is in their highest reaches that they must be understood. It is the path of the sympathetic understanding of cultures of Fr. Matteo Ricci in China.

> ... As she is the only ark of salvation, within her immense nave she must give shelter to all varieties of humanity. She is the only banqueting hall, and the dishes she serves are the product of the whole of creation. She is Christ's seamless coat, but she is too— and it is the same thing— Joseph's coat of many colours.... She knows that the various customs hallowed by her "confirm the unanimity of her faith," that this visible catholicity is the normal expression of her inner riches, and her beauty is resplendent in its variety...[2] (theme treated in *New Evangelization*, Ch. 8, 208-215)

### 4. Yet the Church Avoids Syncretism

Yet de Lubac warns that the Church must avoid syncretism (indiscriminate amalgamating of different religions) that becomes a human religion. The Church is not syncretistic any more than it is naïve. Syncretism is artificial, generally the work of rulers or literary men, and *presupposes declining faith*. It is an *insult to the living God*. In the energetic language of the prophets, syncretism is *fornication*: it is *barren* in the spiritual order, and *lowers and vulgarizes* all elements it combines (reflects worldview of L'Amour's characters). While the Church has rejected Gnosticism, a representative of the syncretist system, such uncompromising boldness has not hindered her in carrying out her work that is more clearly manifest every day. *It is equally unfitting to speak of the assimilation of liberalism, of tolerating error, or making the salt of the Gospel savourless.* For if Christianity must be shown with all its exigencies, it must also stand out in all its **purity** and it would be working to obscure the gentle severity of the Gospel:

> And if it is once understood that the work of conversion consists, fundamentally, not in adapting supernatural truth, in bringing it down to human level, but, on the contrary, in adapting man to it, raising him up to the truth that rules and judges him, we must especially beware, as of blasphemy, of confusing ourselves, its servants, with it— ourselves, our tastes, our habits, our prejudices, our passions, our narrow-mindedness and our weaknesses with the divine religion with which we are so little imbued. We must give souls to God, not conquer them for ourselves.[3]

---

[2] Henri de Lubac, *Catholicism: Christ and the Common Destiny of Man* (New York: Sheed & Ward, 1950), 155-156.
[3] Ibid., 159.

The author's spiritual director at the seminary, Bishop Attila Miklósházy, S.J., taught him how to learn from human wisdom and books, e.g., such as books by Dale Carnegie, Stephen Covey, and David Allen. From L'Amour we can learn many things, including his exceptional story-telling. At the same time, we discern objectively *serious flaws* at the higher levels: morality, denigration of Christianity, turn to evil spirits, a very grandiose self-exaltation, and exasperating inconsistencies in the story-telling (e.g., the characters are like puppets to be moved on and off the stage willy-nilly to artificially produce unlikely plots or dramatic, heroic turns of events, prompting us to ask, "what happened to reality, where is common sense?").

### *5. Foundation for Creation is a Creator God*
We have seen the main character in L'Amour's *Lonesome Gods* holding to a type of pantheism (identifies God with the universe) with no transcendent Creator, with the ensuing exaltation of man himself. We find in Pope St. Clement I the full worldview, where God reigns absolutely and guides with His providence; and no one can dispute with Him or escape Him:

> *By the word of his power he established all things*, and by his word he can reduce them to ruin. Who shall say to him: What have you done? Who shall stand up against the power of his might? He will accomplish everything when he wills and as he wills, and nothing that he has decreed shall pass away. All things stand in his presence, and nothing lies hidden from his counsel, if the heavens tell forth the glory of God, the firmament reveals the work of his hands, day speaks to day, and night shares knowledge with night; there are no words, no speeches, and their voices are not heard. Since all things lie open to his eyes and ears, let us hold him in awe and rid ourselves of impure desires to do works of evil, so that we may be protected by his mercy from the judgement that is to come. *Which of us can escape his mighty hand?* What world will give asylum to one who deserts him…. Where, then, can one go, where can one escape to, from the presence of him whose hands embrace the universe?[4]

St. Leo the Great teaches that "For every believer regenerated in Christ… breaks with that ancient way of life that derives from original sin, and by rebirth is transformed into a new man." John's Prologue's depiction of St. John the Baptist goes counter to L'Amour's characters' self-exaltation (messiah-complex): "He was *not the light*, but came to bear witness to the light." When they asked the Baptist if he was the Messiah, he vigorously denied it, saying that he was merely His "voice" or "precursor," that the Messiah "would baptize with the Spirit and with Fire" (Mt 3:11). All true children of God similarly point away from themselves to God's Son.

---

[4] Pope St. Clement I, *Letter of Pope Clement I to the Corinthians*, Office of Readings for October 26, 2021, Universalis.com, accessed Oct. 26, 2021, https://universalis.com/readings.htm.

> The true light that enlightens every man was coming into the world. He was in the world, and the world was made through him, yet the world knew him not. He came to his own home, and his own people received him not. But to all who received him, who believed in his name, he gave power to become children of God; who were born… of God. (Jn 1:9-12)

We see the stark contrast too in Gregory Lekhtman, a gifted Russian émigré inventor and founder. He had an early interest in how things work and applies common sense, asking why things can't be better. When asked, "Where do your ideas come from?", he replied, "From God. I ask and I receive." Not only does he believe in God and attribute inspirations to Him, he is writing a book on philosophy to answer life's questions: "What is the purpose of life? What is the purpose of existence? Why are we here?"[5] These questions, or at least the answers, seem to be beyond L'Amour's ken.

## B. The Call to Evangelization: Failures of L'Amour

### *What is Damning is that L'Amour Proscribes Evangelization*
In *Lonesome Gods*, L'Amour says that we should not seek to convert the natives, while also implying that they have superior knowledge. "'*We do wrong,' he said, 'to try to convert them to our beliefs'*"; "sometimes [we] forget there are other ways, sometimes forget the Lonesome Gods of the far places, the gods who live on the empty sea, who dance with the dust devils and who wait quietly in the shadows under the cliffs…" (*Lonesome Gods*, Ch 29). He claims that the natives already knew what Christians know and they know even better than the Christians! Msgr. Rossetti, an exorcist, says these "gods" are evil spirits and points to signs of being led by them: narcissism, pride, disobedience, rejection of Christ and the Church (cf. *Diary*, 215, 229-230). To L'Amour's quotation below, we provide a response (Sermon):

> The Indian gestured with his pipe. "I was guide for a missionary when small. He was a kind, sincere man, trying to teach Indians something *they already knew better than he*, although the words were different…." "He asked me one time why I never went to church, and I told him that I went to the mountains. I told him my church was a mountainside somewhere to watch the day pass and the clouds. I told him, 'I will go to your church if you will come to mine.' I think by the time he left us he liked mine better." (L'Amour, *Son of a Wanted Man*, 117)
> It is one of God's greatest mercies to us that we, being alive, do not sacrifice to *dead gods or worship them*, but *through Christ* we have come to know the Father of truth. That knowledge consists *in not denying Christ* through whom we know the Father. (OOR, Monday 32nd OT, Year II)

---

[5] "How this Man Escaped Soviet Union and Became a Canadian," *National Post*, January 6, 2022, A3.

## 1. Fundamental Flaw of Nominalism, with Being Sage and not Prophet

An archbishop giving a retreat highlighted two missteps that may cut to the underlying error in L'Amour's characters. The first is the prevailing culture today of Nominalism. Its leading proponent was a fourteenth century Franciscan scholar, William of Ockham. He denied the reality of universals in the world: no structure nor objective truths (they are convenient labels, but don't exist). One can imagine the host of consequences that follow: we cannot know God, where we stand with Him since He acts arbitrarily, and must rely upon subjective experience and interpretation. "We therefore cannot reliably use reason or logic to discern good from evil, justice from injustice—and therefore we cannot freely and reliably choose what is good."[6] He prioritized the will over the intellect. There is not only no universal reality nor universal truths. What matters is how we act. Anarchy, including moral relativism, follow from unhinging the will from reason.

A second distinction made that connects with Nominalism is the distinction between the sage (reason, wisdom) and the prophet (divine faith). In the Old Testament, the sage represents the "Wisdom literature" (Job, Ecclesiastes, Proverbs, Wisdom Psalms). He is the wise one using human wisdom as a teacher and parent, who knows how to convey wisdom and seeks to dialogue to persuade others on the common ground of a universal wisdom of the ages. The sage says, "Have you noticed...", while the prophet speaks in God's name as from above, "The Lord says..." The sage looks more at what is happening in the now, while the prophet does discern the present but is always looking to the future coming of the Lord.

To sum up, L'Amour's characters appear to be Nominalist in their outlook, always questioning accepted wisdom and focusing on the will, e.g., that what matters is taking responsibility and what a man makes of himself. These are essentially sages and not prophets. The characters' constant questioning of truths recalls Pilate's words, "What is truth?", this while Pilate was standing before Truth Himself. Combine this apparent Nominalist approach (no universal realities or truths) with taking on the "sage" persona who knows everything through much travel, reading, thinking, and consultation, it is no wonder that this outlook is not open to the "prophet," the divine (e.g., through obedience to Church and Scripture). As the far-seeing archbishop noted, we need both the sage and the prophet, the human and the divine. We find in Balaam one who is a prophet hired to curse Israel, but ends up even prophesying the Messiah. For unlike the mere sage ("wise" one), he sees with God's eyes as a prophet (Num 22-25):

---

[6] Gerald Korson, "Nominalism," catholic.com, accessed February 9, 2022, https://www.catholic.com/magazine/print-edition/nominalism.

The oracle of Balaam son of Beor, the oracle of the man whose eye is clear, the oracle of one who hears the words of God, and knows the knowledge of the Most High, who sees the vision of the Almighty, who falls down, but with his eyes uncovered: I see him, but not now; I behold him, but not near — a star shall come out of Jacob, and a sceptre shall rise out of Israel. (Num 24:15-17)

## 2. L'Amour's Reason & Experience to be Purified and Elevated by Grace

Johannes Lotz, SJ, sheds light on the need for religious experience today. As overall context, he distinguishes three stages by which God reveals Himself: reason; religious experience; and divine revelation.

He first explains that non-Christian religions, lacking divine revelation, are founded on religious experience (possibly L'Amour's instinct). Religions act through religious experience, that moves them tremendously to God. The Vatican II document on relations with non-Christian religions, *Nostra aetate*, acknowledges their positive dimensions: all peoples "form but one community"; "His providence, evident goodness, and saving designs extend to all men"; "results in a way of life that is imbued with a deep religious sense"; "[Christianity] rejects nothing of what is true and holy in these religions." Religious experience prepares for its encounter with Christian revelation. Yet, it needs Christian revelation to complete what is incomplete, perfect what is imperfect, and eliminate error. For whatever comes from below and not directly from God is a constant searching and unceasing human experimentation that *needs purification and elevation*. Lotz perceives that many of their orientations do produce misinterpretations, or even the destruction of religious experience, leading to pantheism or atheism. This shows that they need redemption.

Thus Christianity contains in a complete and perfect form what remains fragmentary and imperfect in non-Christian religions. If Christianity does not hold to a source over and above the sources of other religions (God descending to become man), its claim would be incomprehensible and presumptuous. The source of religions is religious experience, which Vatican II calls the "experience of God" (*Gaudium et spes* 7), accessible to all individuals and peoples. "In contrast, Christianity lives from 'divine revelation,' for which the Council offers its own Dogmatic Constitution" *(Dei verbum)*. Revelation reaches its climax in Christ, and it is entrusted to the Church, which transmits it to us and interprets it for us, which in turn produces an historical development with manifold expressions.

### Healing and Elevating Grace

St. Thomas helps clarify the healing grace of faith. While humanity is capable of reaching God by reason, given the present fallen condition, without divine revelation, few can reach it without excessive difficulties, with full certainty, and without any error. So there is not absolute but moral necessity for this help, for *man's existential capacity is impaired* since Adam's legacy of original sin and concupiscence. Returning to Lotz's thesis, faith as healing grace is ordered to elevating grace. Humanity's ascent is based on God's descent (Incarnation), inasmuch as this is the only way in which a person can be capable of reaching God: "For the Son of God became man so that we might become God" (St. Athanasius). Healing grace purifies religious experience so as to lead us to elevating grace, to transform us for our divinization destiny in the Trinity (elevating).[7] Yet, Luigi Giussani makes a key distinction. While there is danger of experience leading to subjectivism and sentimentalism, he insists that our faith nevertheless derives from a *lived experience* of encounter with Christ.

> Now for traditionalists, the nexus [link to] with experience is an unacceptable risk, while for Giussani, it was the one possibility.... I would add that Giussani never accepted a reduced concept of experience. He did not reduce experience in the immanentistic, subjectivistic, and sentimental sense. He forcefully stressed that every proposal should be evaluated in terms of the heart's needs, and in this he was profoundly modern, but these needs are an objective and "infallible" criterion, or in other words, an original structure with which everyone is endowed that enables the recognition of the truth.... As Ratzinger said, "We can recognize only that which finds a correspondence in us." (*Where is God?*, 118)

But Christianity grows from the dynamic of an encounter with Someone who responds to the deepest needs of our hearts, crying, "He's the one!" Christianity derives from a lived encounter. Chiara Lubich too insists that Jesus "was present when we could *experience* him.... No! if Jesus is among us, he makes himself felt; we can experience him" (*Jesus in our Midst*, 56).

### 3. Rising Above Motive to Purpose of Creation
Beyond avoiding the Nominalist sage and divinizing religious experience, a helpful theological distinction is the truth that God created us from the *motive* of love, but the *purpose* of creation is adoration of the Trinity.

> This motive of love includes the idea of dialogue with the creature, that the Lover (God) has the power to reach out towards the "thou" [you]. Such a dialogue finds its foundation or flows out of the inner Tri-Personal life of the Trinity, the dialogical life of God lived in Trinitarian form with infinite intensity. The new dialogical situation with the creature is achieved through

---

[7] Johannes B. Lotz, "Christianity and the Non-Christian Religions in their Relationship to Religious Experience," in *Vatican II: Assessment and Perspectives: Twenty-Five Years After (1962-1987)*, ed. René Latourelle, vol. Three (New York: Paulist Press, 1989), 161-183.

the utterance of His divine Word— His Son — through whom the Father utters Himself, pours out of Himself, in a non-divine reality, an adequate self-expression of the Father in the Son.

We cannot say that the *purpose* of creation is man's happiness, which would subordinate God to a created reality. Everything, including man and all man's activity, leads upwards to glorifying God (absent from L'Amour).

> The purpose of creation is the Glory of God. Glory refers to a manifestation of the divine presence and the excellence and total perfection of God, it is His whole essence (sanctity, beauty, etc.), His shining brilliance, the awesomeness and overwhelming impact of his infinite being. All creation is made to praise the Lord. We see this in Scripture: in Dan 3:54 ("Bless the Lord, all things that grow on the earth, sing praise to him and highly exalt him for ever"); and as the Psalms especially proclaim, from the cherubim down to the most humble and insignificant worldly object. St. Francis of Assisi expresses this in his Canticle of the Sun: "Most High, all-powerful, all-good Lord, all praise is Yours, all glory, all honour and all blessings.... Praised be You my Lord with all Your creatures, especially Sir Brother Sun"....
>
> There are heresies that contradict the truth that the world was made for the glory of God (Denzinger n. 1805).... *It is essential that man not be teleologically enclosed within himself, but that he should turn towards God*: man should know that he was created for God (Vatican I). In terms of the order of the goals, *the primary purpose of creation is the glorification of God*; and *to that the happiness of the human being is directed.*[8]

## C. The Church's Mandate to be Missionary in her Essence

Epiphany, the feast day of the visit of the three wise men (Magi) is our feast day. It is the arrival of the Messiah long prophesied and with whom Jesus identified at Nazareth, fulfilling Isaiah 6. We are the Magi, we relive their search, discovery, and adoration.

> Today the Magi find, crying in a manger, the one they have followed as he shone in the sky. Today the Magi see clearly, in swaddling clothes, the one they have long awaited as he lay hidden among the stars. Today the Magi gaze in deep wonder at what they see: heaven on earth, earth in heaven, man in God, God in man, one whom the whole universe cannot contain now enclosed in a tiny body. As they look, they believe and do not question, as their symbolic gifts bear witness: incense for God, gold for a king, myrrh for one who is to die. So the Gentiles, who were the last, become the first: the faith of the Magi is the first fruits of the belief of the Gentiles. (St. Peter Chrysologus, OOR of First Monday after Epiphany)

---

[8] Attila Miklósházy, "Theology of Creation," in the "Creation Anthropology, Sin" Lecture.

## 1. Mandate of "Evangelii Nuntiandi" and Other Missionary Documents

St. Francis of Assisi perceived the Christian's mission: "You have been called to heal wounds, to unite what has fallen away and to bring home those who have lost their way." The Church is missionary in her essence (*Ad gentes; Redemptoris missio*); she would no longer be herself if she were not missionary. "How beautiful upon the mountains are the feet of him who brings good tidings" (Isa 52:7). Pope Paul VI's *Evangelii nuntiandi* describes how there is a line of continuity between Christ, the Church, and evangelization (n. 16). Evangelization is simply what Christ did, proclaiming the good news of the Father's plan for our liberation (especially from sin) and being made into a people of God (n. 17). But this very people, having been evangelized and continually being converted, must in turn become the "evangelizers." By their exemplary witness, that is, *by the very everyday holiness that Christians live*, questions are engendered in those who do not know Christ, in baptized who do not practice, and in nominal Christians. For today's culture needs to be permeated and evangelized (nn. 19-21).

But beyond Christian witness, our faith also has to be explained, justified, and made explicit. And it must be Christ and the kingdom that must be proclaimed (kerygma, preaching, or catechesis, n. 22), but which is only completed when it brings about a transformation in the hearer and when he in turn goes on to evangelize others (nn. 23-24). "Evangelization… is a complex process made up of varied elements: the renewal of humanity, witness of explicit proclamation, inner adherence, entry into the community, acceptance of signs, apostolic initiative" (n. 24).

## 2. Evangelization Flows from an Encounter with Christ

There is an irreducible link from Christ to Christians today. It is captured by Luigi Giussani's famous homily in which he describes Andrew and John, after John the Baptist pointed out Jesus to them, being transformed after spending time with Jesus, and how they shared the experience with this "Exceptional Presence" with others, who in turn shared, until we too have met Christ. There were exceptional "witnesses," who had encounters with Christ that seared their souls, becoming mystics in the world, possessing the capacity to touch hearts: C. Lubich with Christ abandoned on the cross and in our midst; St. Escrivá and St. M. d'Youville with God's paternity; Mother Teresa with Christ's thirst on the cross and in the poor. The conversion of Kiko Argüello, co-founder of the Neocatechumenal Way, is enlightening: "God permitted me to experience the absurd – atheism – until He had mercy." He was influenced by Sartre (life is absurd), but when nothing satisfied, he felt he would end up killing himself. He was saved by reading Henri Bergson, who taught that intuition is a way "deeper than reason itself, of arriving at truth" (see www.camino-neocatecumenal.org).

... my artist's intuition did not accept the absurdity of existence; I was aware of the beauty of a tree, of the beauty of things... Then if the absurd is not the truth, if there is a reason for being... the next step was: then somebody created us.... At that moment... something in me told me that God existed... that God loved me... that I was a son of God. And with great surprise I found... that this God that appeared in my heart, in my deepest soul, was Jesus Christ, the Jesus Christ of the Catholic Church.

Pope Francis offers a keen point within Giussani's charism: the focus remains always on this encounter with Christ, not on spiritual progress.

My first thought goes to your Founder, Msgr. Luigi Giussani, remembering the 10th anniversary of his birth in Heaven. I am grateful to Don Giussani for different reasons. The first and more personal is the good that this man did for me and for my priestly life, through the reading of his books and articles. The other reason is that his thoughts are deeply human and reach the most intimate yearning of mankind. You know how important the experience of encounter was to Don Giussani: the encounter not with an idea, but with a Person, with Jesus Christ. Thus he educated in freedom, leading to the encounter with Christ, because Christ gives us true freedom....

Everything in our life, today as in the time of Jesus, begins with an encounter. An encounter with this Man, the carpenter from Nazareth, a man like all men and at the same time different. Let us consider the Gospel of John, there where it tells of the disciples' first encounter with Jesus (cf. 1:35-42). Andrew, John, Simon: they feel themselves being looked at to their very core, intimately known, and this generates surprise in them, an astonishment which immediately makes them feel bonded to Him.... Or when, after the Resurrection, Jesus asks Peter: "Do you love me?" (Jn 21:15), and Peter responds: "Yes"; this yes was not the result of a power of will, it did not come only by decision of the man Simon: it came even before from Grace, it was that "primarear," that preceding of Grace. This was the decisive discovery for St Paul, for St Augustine, and so many other saints: Jesus Christ is always first, He *primareas* [takes the initiative with] us, awaits us, Jesus Christ always precedes us; and when we arrive, He has already been waiting. He is like the almond blossom: the one that blooms first, and announces the arrival of spring....

After 60 years, the original charism has not lost its youthfulness and vitality. However, remember that *the centre is not the charism, the centre is one alone, it is Jesus, Jesus Christ! When I place at the centre my spiritual method, my spiritual journey, my way of fulfilling it, I go off the itinerary*. All spirituality, all charisms in the Church must be "decentralized": at the centre there is only the Lord!... Never forget this, to be decentralized![9] (emphasis added)

---

[9] Pope Francis, "Address of his Holiness Pope Francis to the Communion and Liberation Movement," vatican.va, accessed Dec. 28, 2021,

We highlight the noteworthy example of John Paul II whose inaugural address of his pontificate reveals his attachment to Christ: "Open wide the doors to Christ." Christ is the answer to all our desires: "Do not be afraid. Open, I say open wide the doors for Christ."[10] In his inaugural encyclical, *Redemptor hominis*, he notes that we are made for love, and that it is only Christ who fills the void in our hearts. Scripture says of evangelizers: "The learned will shine as brightly as the vault of heaven, and those who have instructed many in virtue will shine like stars for all eternity" (Dan 12:3). S. Hahn's doctoral thesis undergirds this vision with the five Old Testament covenants culminating in Christ's worldwide kingdom. It is spiritual and sacramental, with heavenly authority more powerful than military might: "My kingdom is not of this world." It doesn't derive its authority from majority vote, the end of a gun, or the sword's edge (*Kinship by Covenant*).

### 3. Pope Pius X's Paradigm for Evangelization in the French Church

We look at the powerful efficacy of faith. H. Daniel-Rops writes that Pius X affirmed that "The policy of the Church is to take no part in politics."[11] This is a surprising maxim, especially in light of his diplomat predecessor, Leo XIII. Daniel-Rops explained that Pius X was a mystic living in the world and clearly subordinated all human reality to the divine, and placed primary emphasis on the spiritual elements, such as evangelization, holiness, and formation of priests. Yet, in the eleven years of his pontificate, he was called upon to resolve problems that were strictly political and often very difficult, to which he devoted as much attention and care as he did to the life of souls. In *E supremi apostolatus*, which declared the aims of the new pope and the general spirit of his pontificate, he writes with clarity: "The Sovereign Pontiff cannot separate politics from the magisterium he exercises over faith and morals." He never missed an opportunity to cite his predecessor's *Immortale Dei* to support the Vicar of Christ's right to intervene to serve "the interests of God" (*A Fight for God*, 210-211).

Before resuming our discussion of Pope Pius X, let us pause to explain the Church's understanding and balanced approach. As we saw with Pope John Paul II's dealing with early Liberation Theology proponents, the ordained ministers are not to leave their ministry to become politicians, much less to incite violence or bear arms. This, of course, is distinct from bearing arms to

---

https://www.vatican.va/content/francesco/en/speeches/2015/march/documents/papa-francesco_20150307_comunione-liberazione.html.

[10] Pope John Paul II, "Homily of his Holiness Pope John Paul II on the Inauguration Address of his Pontificate," Vatican.va, accessed October 26, 2021,
https://www.vatican.va/content/john-paul-ii/en/homilies/1978/documents/hf_jp-ii_hom_19781022_inizio-pontificato.html.

[11] Henri Daniel-Rops, *A Fight for God*, vol. 1 (New York: Image Books, 1967), 210.

defend one's country in a just war (even here, we are to consider the Church's path of dialogue). The Church does not even allow her ministers to tell their people which parties to vote for. We see the wisdom of Escrivá and Giussani, who both strongly protected the personal freedom to choose.

Returning to Pius X's vision, the French Church was faced with a ruling party who wished to destroy the Church. Then, dealing with a second ruling party and a liaison who was more moderate, the pope appeared intransigent when he commanded the French Church to refuse the modified offer (having the *associations culturelles* take control over the French Church's goods and property, and even influence the nomination of bishops). After consultation with the French hierarchy and after much agonizing and prayer, he came down firmly on rejecting the Government's offer. This meant that the French Church lost all her property and even moneys, and the clergy subsisted solely on the material sustenance of their flock. The liaison minister came to see the sublime wisdom of the saintly Pope Pius X:

> Pius X was the winner from every point of view, and he well deserved to be.... Marvellous, that's what the Pope was! I did not always fully understand him. It's only now, looking back, that I can see the whole thing in focus. He was the only one who saw clearly. Often and often in the Chamber, when I had to face up to both sides, left and right, I longed to tell them that they were all a poor lot, that there was only one man who saw clearly, who has a consistent policy and was working for the future— the Pope. He didn't want to die slowly, peacefully. He wanted the Church to live, and life is adventure.... His sacrifice was necessary: it has borne its fruits.[12]

The pope's divine wisdom in intervening in the French Church was validated by her fruits. There was a revitalization of the French Church. It underwent the stern school of poverty and a crisis of vocations, which excluded those who entered the seminaries with less than spiritual motives:

> It [the Church in France] was about to receive an impulse that would make her one of the best in the world, and certainly the least subservient to material interests and secular authority. More united, more homogeneous, more disciplined and more heroic, she would prove itself increasingly apostolic, while the faithful in turn would understand better the real ties that bound them to their priests. The separation, whereby the anticlericals had expected to accomplish the total ruin of Catholicism in France, *was on the contrary the starting point of an extraordinary revival within the very bosom of the Church.*[13]

---

[12] Ibid., quoted on p. 222.
[13] Ibid.

### *4. Context for Evangelization: Mercy with Understanding and the Cross*
The new evangelization presupposes the Eucharist as its key power. We note three key contexts. (1) Perhaps the greatest need of our time for evangelization is mercy. Julián Carrón notes that Christian principles are no longer self-evident because of the Enlightenment's detaching of values from their Christian origins (see next talk). The Catechism of the Catholic Church, reproposing Vatican I, affirmed: "The precepts of natural law are not perceived by everyone clearly and immediately. In the present situation sinful man needs grace and revelation so moral and religious truths may be known 'by everyone with facility, with firm certainty and with no admixture of error'" (n. 1960). Carrón validates this by the example of Paul, who could not see the error of his ways, until everything changed when he met the living Christ. Christians, like Paul, need to "read the signs of the times": "Christianity is not a new moralism, but the introduction of a new factor into reality that enables a new meaning for the life of everyone, for facing evil and suffering, a factor that is the answer to the need of the heart, to the need for meaning and affection" (*Where is God?*, 45). He highlights *Dei verbum*'s teaching that Revelation is not only a set of truths, but that "deeds and words have an inner unity." Jesus did not do a pre-evangelization: "He presented Himself, His presence, His way of acting, His way of looking, of embracing, of welcoming. This began to arouse interest in Him, so much so that those who were a thousand miles away in terms of perception of things, in the desert of those times, began to seek him out" (ibid, 48). Thus, he reiterates the call of the recent popes for mercy, for those who live in the desert of our times without a Christian context and self-evident principles, so that our look of mercy, as with Jesus', will reach hearts. (2) We also highlight Pius XII's insight: "It is the mysterious law of salvation-history, that many are saved by the few! The individual Christian is responsible for the salvation of others, of the 'many'" (*Mystici corporis* 44).

(3) Carl Sundell summarized Satan's strategy for the Third Millennium in Peter Kreeft's *The Snakebite Letters*. The key is that the devil lost the First Millennium because he created martyrs ("the blood of martyrs is the seed of Christianity"). For the Church prospers under persecution: "If Hell lost the First Millennium to Christ, it was because of the blood of the martyrs. But Hell won the Second Millennium because the Church got fat and luxurious and lazy. Now comes the strategy for winning the Third Millennium…"[14] We perceive how great movements have arisen from the ashes of destruction, such as the Focolare charism (World War II bombing, lack of understanding within the Church). With the Opus Dei charism, there were intense trials

---

[14] Carl Sundell, "Screwtape, Wormwood, Snakebite, & Braintwister," Semper Fi Catholic, accessed July 7, 2020, https://www.semperficatholic.com/forum/viewtopic.php?p=34781.

suffered by Alvaro del Portillo (and St. Escrivá), especially during the Spanish Civil War: e.g., arrested, father missing and then dying, asylum in embassies, crossing frontline to escape, all amidst attacks on the Church, with execution of 6,500 priests from 1936-1939.[15] We note also early opposition to Communion and Liberation.

We may find uplifting and consoling the words of St. Catherine of Siena on the power and beauty of the Church: "I saw how the Bride of Christ can give life, having in herself such vital force that no one can stay her; I saw that she shed forth strength and light, and that no one can deprive her of it; and I saw that her fruit never diminishes, ever increases."[16] In the vision of Nebuchadnezzar that is interpreted by Daniel (2:26-47), Daniel interprets a statue of a man with different composition beginning from the top to the feet (gold, silver, bronze, iron, mixed iron and earthenware) that depicts Nebuchadnezzar's empire and those that followed. But the Spirit, through Scripture, is providing a vision that prefigures all empires of human history. And Christ's empire will destroy all others and will remain forever. Many empires rise to disturb mankind (e.g., Roman Empire, Communism), but and will always be an ultimate One whose kingdom reduces all to nothing.

## Conclusion

L'Amour's characters may represent today's horizontalism that involves deeper moral and spiritual issues that may be culpable: quasi-worshipping of personal experience (idolatry); an exaltation of self (grandiosity); a glorification of the warrior with exoneration of its violence; a Nominalist sage's questioning of universal truths; a sniping against Christ's Church. We find present Satan's three temptations of Jesus: to use His divine power for food (e.g., personal gain, knowledge); to seek self-glorification (applause); and to desire what the world offers, and not giving God, who created all, due worship. It is sad that these represented don't experience: the filiation of the Father, the friendship with Christ, and the union of the Spirit; the Church as our unfailingly loving mother; the love of our Lady and the aid of guardian angels; the communion of the Eucharist, the forgiveness of Confession; the glow of prayer before the Blessed Sacrament and the mysticism of the Easter Triduum; the communion with angels and saints; the richness of and guidance by Scripture, Tradition, and the Magisterium; the leading of the Spirit that impels to the Trinity and to co-redeem the world as another Christ in the path of the Beatitudes. We see the fruits: L'Amour sought to be a good citizen and pantheistic storyteller; John Paul II to bring the world to Christ; Mother Teresa to be one with Christ's poor.

---

[15] John F. Coverdale, Saxum: *The Life of Alvaro del Portillo*, 19-29.
[16] Margaret Roberts, *St. Catherine of Siena and her Times* (New York: Putnams, 1906), 296.

# Retreat 3: Ecclesial Preparations for Mystical Transformation

## Conference 4
## Church Renewal: Marian Profile & Sacraments of Initiation

**A. Crisis in our Times**

A seminary faculty priest asked of his spiritual group of seminarians the question, "Is the priesthood today in a state of crisis?" He proceeded to enumerate evidence to confirm the existence of a crisis: e.g., (i) the mass exodus of priests following Vatican II, over 62,000 over 30 years; (ii) the Congregation of the Clergy's clear sense of the need of reform of seminary formation, which led to the implementing of a new 2016 *Ratio Fundamentalis Institutionis Sacerdotalis* (Vatican document on priestly formation); (iii) the ghastly Report by an independent Commission that over 330,000 children were victims of sex abuse in the French Church. There were an estimated 3,000 child abusers, two-thirds of them priests, in France over seven decades, and an estimated 216,000 were victims of clergy.

*1. Call for Massive Reform of the Church in our Times*
When horrendous actions are done by priests (and others) in regard to sexual abuse, then the Lord calls for a massive renewal. The abuse of children calls for great remorse and contrition, that must be expressed by much "reparation" (tears, prayer, penance, amendment of lifestyle) and much intercession for the Church. Each Catholic is to say to the Lord as did St. Catherine of Siena, "Lord, visit the wounds of your Church on my body," let me vicariously expiate for sins. Beyond expiation, there is need for holiness, the lack of which is the root cause of all the Church's crises.

The tragedy arises in part from the wrong steps taken after Vatican II. Cardinal Ratzinger, like Fulton Sheen, diagnosed a sociologization of the Church. He pointed to the blurring (admixing) by Hans Kung of *Ekklesia* (the Church) and *Concilium*, treating the Church as a permanent Council. The conciliar image "People of God" thereby "slipped into a *solely sociological significance outside the mystery of Jesus Christ*": "The Bishops' Synod of 1985 attempted a new beginning, putting the word *communion* at the center, which brings the Eucharist back to the center of the Church and therefore the understanding of the Church as the intimate place for the encounter between Jesus and men, in the act of His gift to us."[1] Within America, George Weigel's *Courage to be Catholic* provides a timely, rigorous and objective analysis of the causes of the sexual abuse crisis of 2002. He goes back to the roots of

---

[1] Antonio Socci, "Cardinal Ratzinger on the Church as Communion," *Inside the Vatican*, (August-September 2002): 11.

theological confusion and an erroneous pastoral approach that has now come home to roost. On the one hand, there was the misconduct of certain priests and the improper apostolic responsibility of bishops. But underlying all this is *a culture of dissent, and ultimately, a lack of fidelity*. For Weigel, the only response **is a call to holiness** (Appendix 3).

## *2. Specific Root Lacuna is Lack of Marian Holiness*

Bishops' exhortations to priests to fidelity to prayer, ministry, and obedience and to avoid living double lives are necessary, but fail to address the root cause. Priests often live only by the objective conformation to Christ with priestly powers (*ex opere operato*), but not by its subjective assimilation in holiness (*ex opere operantis*), to become Christ Himself. Weigel synthesizes this perfectly: "The Church has never been reformed by 'Catholic Lite,'" with "an insufficiency of saints" (*catholicculture.org*).

> The only adequate response to the crisis of 2002 is the response that is always called for when the Church is bottoming out. The call to holiness must be lived more intensely by every member of the Church, in whatever state of life. Everyone. The crisis of 2002 is, in this respect, like every other crisis in the Church's history. It is a crisis caused by **an insufficiency of saints**. That is a wake-up call for every Catholic— a call not to "take back" what is not ours to begin with, but to live holier lives.[2]

Let us attempt to validate this point through two examples used in one of the author's previous works. The first example is with St. Francis of Assisi. His times needed great reform and God called a humble beggar, but who was known above all as being the one most Christ-like.

> He [Francis] couldn't look away as feelings of doubt and fear, guilt and desire welled up within him. "Lord, what do you want me to do?" he asked. "Show me what you want me to do with my life." And the Lord answered! A voice as clear as the day responded: "Francis, go and rebuild my church which, as you see, is falling down."[3]

Later, when appealing to Pope Innocent III for approval of the new Franciscan foundation, the pope had interior doubts about this beggar, but revealed that God gave him a vision of Francis' work (captured by Giotto's "Dream of Pope Innocent III," Upper church of St. Francis in Assisi). In a dream, Innocent III saw St. John Lateran Basilica (cathedral of the Roman

---

[2] "George Weigel Extended Interview," *Religion & Ethics Newsweekly*, May 10, 2002, https://www.pbs.org/wnet/religionandethics/2002/05/10/may-10-2002-george-weigel-extended-interview/11686/. See *Courage to be Catholic* (New York: Basic Books, 2002), 190.
[3] Church of St. Francis of Assisi, accessed October 17, 2021, https://stfrancisnyc.org/francis-rebuild-my-church/.

Pontiff) collapsing on itself, only to be straightened up again by St. Francis. He understood that God was entrusting to St. Francis of Assisi the task of rebuilding the universal Church, for which the pope proceeded to approve the Franciscan rule and Order. We note here that it was not the pope and bishops (Magisterium) or great theologians who were to rebuild the Church, but a humble layman (later, a deacon) who espoused Lady Poverty; it was through a humble charism from below sent by the Holy Spirit. St. Francis of Assisi's holiness has since radiated through the Church: through being perhaps the most esteemed of Catholic saints; St. Clare and the Poor Clares; his Order which for some time was among the largest in the Church; has given rise to many new communities, e.g., Franciscan Friars of the Renewal, Franciscan Missionaries of the Eternal Word (Mother Angelica's Congregation); influenced lay people like the Martins (parents of St. Thérèse) and Pope Francis, and giving us saintly spiritual children, like Padre Pio of Pietrelcina and St. Maximilian Kolbe.

We need a reform on the scale of the Catholic Reformation. The schism within the Church arose in large part because of the decadence within her; she greatly needed reform. But the Council of Trent, while greatly assisting, was not the main catalyst for reform in the Church. It is saints who reform; sanctity begets sanctity. What was God's main response to the decadence within the Church (e.g., clergy, bishops, and religious who did not live their promises or vows of poverty, chastity, and obedience) and the Protestant Reform? God sent a plethora of saints to sanctify the Church: St. Philip Neri to reform Rome, the heart of the Church; St. Ignatius of Loyola to reform the entire Church (e.g., Trent, education, missions, and disciples like St. Peter Faber, St. Peter Canisius); St. Teresa of Jesus and St. John of the Cross to give a spiritual charism for renewal; and a host of other saints (e.g., Pius V, Robert Bellarmine, Charles Borromeo, John Fisher and Thomas More, Matteo Ricci, not to mention many lesser known saints, like Camillus of Lellis, Peter of Alcantara), and saints of the seventeenth century, like St. Francis de Sales, as well as new religious foundations (e.g., Jesuits).

### *3. Cognizance of Two Contemporary Issues*
First, we must be aware of the conflict and dissent that followed the Second Vatican Council that we must combat. Here is Coverdale's description:

> The French Dominican theologian Yves Congar, whom St. John Paul II would name a cardinal, entitled his book about the situation of the Church in 1969 *In the Midst of the Thunderstorm*. Pope Paul VI lamented: "Through some crack, the smoke of Satan has entered the temple of God." He described the state of the Church as one of "doubt, uncertainty, puzzlement, disquiet, dissatisfaction, and confrontation." Instead of the sunshine hoped for after the council, the Church experienced, the Pope

observed, "a day of clouds, of storms, of darkness, of searching, and of uncertainty." In the same vein, Escrivá described the decade following the close of the council as a "time of trial" for the Church.

The history of the post-conciliar era is complex, but certain elements stand out. Some who applauded the Second Vatican Council as a revolutionary break with Church history rather than a development of Christian tradition openly denied key Catholic beliefs, such as the real presence of Christ in the Eucharist or the permanence of marriage. Rejection of traditional teaching and papal authority was dramatically visible in the negative reception of Pope Paul VI's encyclical on birth control, *Humanae Vitae*. Even among some who did not directly contradict Church teaching, a corrosive relativism drained it of content. In many countries, Marxist concepts of class struggle and conflict were preached instead of Christian charity and unity.

Many religious orders suffered both a sharp drop in new members and a mass exodus of existing members, leading in some cases to something approaching collapse. Large numbers of priests left the ministry and the number of seminarians declined dramatically.... In the face of such circumstances, [Alvaro] del Portillo, like Escrivá, prayed fervently and did penance, asking our Lord to bring to a swift end the Church's time of trial.[4]

Second, in our times, Julián Carrón points out that only a few key authors (Montini, de Lubac, Giussani, Guardini, von Balthasar) perceived early that our secularized context has been stripped of previously self-evident principles, foundational convictions, such as "freedom of expression and of association, the right to publicly profess your faith, protection of work and the family, etc." (*Where is God?*, 9). Quoting Henri de Lubac, he notes that this arose from the attempts of the Enlightenment's thinkers who "often preserved a number of values that were Christian in origin; but, having cut off these values from their source [Christianity], they were powerless to maintain them in their full strength or even in their authentic integrity.... [separated, they] become... empty forms. Soon they are no more than a lifeless ideal."[5] Evangelization needs to understand this new context. From within the contemporary charism of Communion and Liberation, Julián Carrón thus affirms: "The power of numbers, of means, of structure or marketing strategies serves nothing. Everything happens through the power of truth [Christ], through the attraction it [He] exerts. We see this in the saints, women and men whose lives radiated the beauty of Christianity, who changed the existence of many people and thus also history" (ibid, 112). The renewal of the Church goes not through the Petrine but the Marian Principle of holiness (B); and the power of the sacraments of initiation (C).

### B. Reform Principally through Living the Marian Principle

---

[4] John F. Coverdale, Saxum: *The Life of Alvaro del Portillo*, 125-127.
[5] Henri de Lubac, *The Drama of Atheist Humanism* (San Francisco: Ignatius Press, 1995), 70.

## 1. Living Mary and with Mary

*Living Mary*: We would propose that the renewal of the Church takes place through living the Marian Principle. As John Paul II noted, the Marian Principle synthesizes the deepest contexts of Vatican II's renewal: e.g., the primacy of baptismal holiness and the central role of the laity in evangelization; the priority of holiness and contemplation over ministry; the kneeling theology that is a dialogue with the Bridegroom; facilitating ecumenical work (conviction of Cardinal Ouellet) and relations between the Magisterium and theologians; and being led by the Spirit within the Church.

*Praying to Mary*: We must not forget that we should go through Mary in evangelization: "It is the will of God that we should have nothing which has not passed through the hands of Mary" (St. Bernard, *Sermon 3*, 10). De Montfort teaches in *True Devotion of Mary* that evangelization is far more efficacious through Mary. As someone noted, "Why is it that more people do not come to Christ? It is because they have not gone through Mary." *Lumen gentium* affirms that Mary's prayer is more powerful than that of all the angels and saints, and that where devotion to her is spread, believers are drawn into closer union with her Son and the Father (n. 65). The solemnity of the Immaculate Conception is appropriately celebrated just before the birth of Christ as the first shoot that anticipates the fruit (John Knox). Pope Pius IX's *Ineffabilis Deus* acknowledges that Mary's "participation in God's divine nature exceeds that of all the angels and saints together. Her life reflects so great a fullness of innocence and sanctity that a more exalted creature cannot be conceived of, except by the Creator himself."

*Imitating Mary: Essence is Simply to be Instruments of God*: His spiritual director once shared with the author this essence of holiness. It is to maintain the presence of God in a specific sense: *to be merely an instrument, to allow God to act through us*. We often forget God and think primarily of our own efforts and actions. Mother Teresa's understanding of herself as a pencil of God is everything. Thus when we work or rest, whether we correct or hold back till a more propitious moment, whether we pray or do ministry, it all does not matter if we see that through it God's grace flows and acts through us; we are transmitters of God's secret grace. This is a new way of seeing and living the spiritual life. Besides being a fount of grace as instruments, it is also a way of *always maintaining our peace*. When we correct, it is God desiring it and acting in us; we don't have to be scrupulous about whether we should have corrected or if we were too harsh in our correction. The 99% is God's action; what I do is the 1%. This is the Marian path.

## 2. Marian Profile also Represents the Laity's Holiness for Evangelization

Holiness is simply the interior journey depicted by St. Teresa and St. John of the Cross. That is, holiness is attained in the Unitive Mansions through the increasing purification and possession by the Spirit, until there is spiritual marriage to become Christ's Bride and Body. Christ descends anew to take hold of our humanity to relive His life and His mysteries in each of us (Gal 2:20). The world begins to change, for Christ lives again. As new Christs, we allow the Spirit to overflow our souls anew into the world. We look at contemporary figures to see the power of Christ in mere humans, like Gianna Beretta-Molla, Pier Giorgio Frassati, Chiara Badano (Focolare), Guadalupe Ortiz de Landázuri (Opus Dei), and Henri de Lubac.

## 3. Holiness is a Fire that Propels Evangelization through the Cross

How do we explain the radical fruitfulness of the saints to evangelize? We can use an image from the expulsion of demons by our Lady during an exorcism: "The room grew silent, and Jason said, 'She is here.' As the Virgin quietly moved closer, the demons began to thrash wildly. She said nothing, but the radiant light of Christ shining through the humble handmaid of God was overpowering" (S. Rossetti, *Diary*, 275). St. Catherine of Siena explains this: that the soul becoming empty of self becomes transparent to God's glory. When Jesus teaches Mother Teresa to "Come, be my Light," as she grew holier, she became the lamp which allowed Christ the Light to shine through her onto Christ's poor in India. He calls Himself the light of the world (Jn 1:4-5, 8:12, 3:19). His light, which would be insufferable torture for demons, as from our Lady, is intense in saints, and they draw souls to Him. But this light grows more intense with the cross. We see this in St. Vianney: academic failure, parishioners' opposition, devil's attacks, 15 hours daily of hearing Confession; St. Pio: stigmata, devil's attacks, shut down by the Vatican for a few years; St. Newman: difficult journey to the Church, rejection from outside and within the Church. One model of renewal was Fr. Hugo (a light for Dorothy Day).

> Of Father [John] Hugo himself, Dorothy wrote in *The Long Loneliness* that he "was a brilliant teacher and one could see he was taking great joy in his work." In the Catholic Worker in 1978, she wrote, "I must not forget the influence of Fr. Hugo in my life. He gave retreats in the early days of the Worker…. He was young and preached so thrillingly a doctrine of 'putting off' the world and 'putting on' Christ'".… "The shepherds are not feeding their sheep" (*Dorothy Day*, by William Miller).… He chastised the priesthood, calling them back to holiness. Some listened, many turned and attacked him, calling him a "rigorist."[6]

---

[6] Rosemary Hugo, "Fr. John Hugo, Spiritual Director to Dorothy Day, calls us to follow Jesus," *Houston Catholic Worker* (Vol. XVI, No. 2, March-April 1996), accessed Dec. 19, 2021,

A second example of holiness is of the scholar, Cornelius C. a Lapide (1567-1637), a Flemish Jesuit and exegete. After studies in philosophy and theology at Jesuit Colleges, Universities of Douai and Leuven, he entered the Society of Jesus. Please note his wonderful prayer at the end.

> [After ordination]: After teaching philosophy for half a year, he was made professor of Holy Scripture at Leuven in 1596 and next year of Hebrew also. Twenty years later, in 1616, he was called to Rome in the same capacity, where, on 3 November, he assumed the office which he filled for many years after. The latter years of his life, however, he seems to have devoted exclusively to finishing and correcting his commentaries. He died at Rome. During his professorship at Leuven he liked to spend his holidays preaching and administering the sacraments, especially at the pilgrimage of Scherpenheuvel (Montaigu). He portrayed himself in a prayer to the Prophets at the end of his commentary on the Book of Daniel: "For nearly thirty years I suffer with and for you with gladness the continual martyrdom of religious life, the martyrdom of illness, the martyrdom of study and writing; obtain for me also, I beseech you, to crown all, the fourth martyrdom, of blood. For you I have spent my vital and animal spirits; I will spend my blood too." (Wikipedia, s.v. C. Lapide)

## *4. Marian Profile in the "New Springtime" of the Ecclesial Charisms*

Within the Marian Principle, we highlight finally the precious gift of the Spirit in the new ecclesial charisms. As the Mendicant Orders renewed the Church of the early Middle Ages, John Paul II saw these lay movements as a "new springtime brought forth by the spirit" to revitalize the Church today (Rome, Pentecost 1998). We highlight a few: the Charismatic Renewal's renewed focus on the Spirit; Focolare's "Jesus in our midst," uniting cultures, and "Economy of Communion"; Neocatechumenal Way's renewal of the baptismal vocation; Communion and Liberation's response of the human heart to Christ's Exceptional Presence; Opus Dei's sanctification of work and daily life; Taizé's ecumenical unity; Community of Sant'Egidio's work of reconciliation; Madonna House's Nazareth charism. Many of these have given birth to movements for social justice, culture, education, etc. What figures like Josemaría Escrivá, Luigi Giussani, and Chiara Lubich teach is that living Christian witness should cause people in society to ask what makes them different, what is the wellspring of their joy. Pope Benedict XVI wrote: "Watching them [charisms], I had the joy and the grace to see how, at a moment of weariness in the Church, at a time when we were hearing about 'the winter of the Church,' the Holy Spirit was creating a new springtime,

---

https://cjd.org/1996/04/01/fr-john-hugo-spiritual-director-to-dorothy-day-calls-us-to-follow-jesus/.

awakening in young people and adults alike the joy of being Christian" (*Meeting with the Bishops of Portugal*, May 2010).

## C. New Evangelization Founded upon the Sacraments of Initiation

It is the sacraments of initiation (Baptism, Confirmation, Eucharist) that make us children of God and give us the mission to evangelize the world (royal priesthood). Baptism remits our sins, introduces divine life, makes us children of the Father, and members of Christ's Body. But the early Church discerned that, after Baptism, they had not yet "received the Spirit," Confirmation: "For it had not yet fallen on any of them, but they had only been baptized in the name of the Lord Jesus. Then they laid their hands on them and they received the Holy Spirit" (Acts 8:16-17, cf. Acts 19:5-6).

What Confirmation, the second phase of initiation, brings is a greater infusion of the Holy Spirit for witnessing. We see this in the transformation in Jesus after His Baptism and in the apostles after Pentecost (their Confirmations). But both Baptism and Confirmation that completes it find their culmination in the Eucharist. This trajectory mirrors the three stages of Jesus' life. His Baptism is really the overshadowing of the Holy Spirit at the Incarnation, where He received the Spirit for His personal sanctification. His Confirmation took place at His "Baptism" at the river Jordan, where He received the Holy Spirit a second time, for His public ministry but especially to become a vessel of the Spirit to be poured out at Calvary (His "Eucharist"). And in a third moment, the Spirit led Him to the cross from which the Holy Spirit was then poured out from His sacred side.

This pattern is repeated in the Early Church. They were incorporated to Christ and became children of God at Baptism. But their transformation became very manifest at Pentecost, when the apostles were sent out and when many Christians, being persecuted, fled and brought the faith to many. Finally, their persecutions and martyrdoms became their Eucharist. Our times view Confirmation merely as a rite of passage or graduation, failing to recall the transformation attained by early Christians at Pentecost. And we have to see the Eucharist as configuring us to the Crucified in Calvary perpetuated at Mass. In the two appendices to follow: (1) we highlight the missionary theology of the sacraments of initiation for evangelization; and (2) provide a profile of the reform of the Church in France in the seventeenth century by the great St. Vincent de Paul. The latter gives us some indication of the scope and the method needed for such a vital reform today, especially of the clergy. (3) We include an interview excerpt with George Weigel on his analysis of the causes and the reform needed with the dissent culture and sexual abuse crisis.

## Appendix 1: The Sacraments of Initiation for Witnessing
**Confirmation gives us deputation to action (*agere in Christo*)**
The Incarnate Christ receives His task, His deputation to salvific, messianic activity in the world, through the Holy Spirit (at the Jordan, and at the Transfiguration). After the first stage of Baptism (existential at conception), now comes the second (functional: missionary) of Confirmation. In Confirmation the baptized Christian receives his deputation to salvific work with Christ for the salvation of the world. He is transferred from "being-in-Christ" to "acting-with-Christ."

**The Eucharist is the messianic office in operation**
Christ fulfills His messianic office primarily through the Paschal mystery. He is truly Messiah (Prophet, King, Priest) on Calvary: in His Passion, Resurrection, Ascension, and in sending the Holy Spirit, and in instituting the Church.
The Christian fulfills his messianic task by celebrating the Paschal mystery, primarily in the Eucharist, which makes the mystery fully present. This, of course, includes witnessing and preaching as well.
The special functions of the Holy Spirit seem to be the following, Eucharist being the highest:
- producing a more perfect image of the Lord Jesus in us,
- consummating, completing, perfecting the work of the Lord, uniting us with God and with one another in the Mystical Body (κοινονια, communion),
- making us more spiritual (interiorization),
- preserving and increasing faith,
- being the promise of immortality and incorruption (pledge of eternal life),
- preaching the Word of God with boldness (παρρησια, parresia),
- but most of all, by doing the will of the Father, exercising the priestly ministry by making present the sacrifice of the cross. [Summit]

**Integrating Baptism, Confirmation, Eucharist**
In Baptism we are conceived by the Holy Spirit to a new life.
In Confirmation, we are consecrated to a priestly ministry, assuming the obligation to do always the will of the Father. The principal act of this messianic mission is the sacrifice of the cross (Eucharist).
In the Eucharist, the Church is built up and constituted, redemption is proclaimed, and the pledge of immortality becomes present. In the Eucharist, Baptism and Confirmation are actualized. [Eucharist= Christ's cross] Thus, the special effect of Confirmation seems to be deputation to the messianic, priestly office, i.e., to the sacrifice of the cross. Through this sacrifice (primarily in the Eucharist), witness is given to the world, salvation is proclaimed, the pledge of immortality is present, and the Church is being built up.
Summary: In the sacrament of Confirmation, the gift of the Holy Spirit is given to the baptized so that, configured to Christ, they may fulfill their priestly office and messianic mission in the world **through witnessing, based on inner holiness.**[7]

---

[7] Attila Miklósházy, "Confirmation," Sacramental Theology I Lecture.

## Appendix 2: St. Vincent de Paul's Reform Initiatives

In my judgment, one of the first things that Vincent did was to found his own Congregation.... To make his group succeed, to be faithful to his original inspiration, he wanted to make his Missioners (what he regularly called the members) *models of priestly life*. The men were to live in common, pray and work together, and be nourished together through external supports. One of these was his habit of giving spiritual talks—we call them conferences—to his men every week. He hammered away at his favorite themes for more than thirty years, so it is no wonder that his followers developed *a sense of their own identity and purpose*. In particular, he praised the priesthood and urged his men to respect and support priests in their simple, humble, gentle, self-denying but zealous way. When they gave missions in rural parishes, *they often used their time to help the local clergy through retreats*.

An outgrowth of the parish missions and clergy retreats was the association called the *Tuesday Conferences*. These were meetings of *interested clergy who voluntarily agreed to bind themselves to a reformed way of life and to be nourished by the support of weekly conferences and discussions* of spiritual and pastoral topics. The amount of reform these conferences accomplished is *incalculable*. The initiative, it should be mentioned, came from the clergy themselves. Vincent was like their sponsor or godfather. - Seminaries were another such development. They were preceded by specialized brief programs to prepare candidates for ordination. Actual seminary programs were of various types and achieved only modest success in earlier times, but Vincent and others in his period began the laborious task of founding or refounding seminaries and *imparting the lessons that the directors and teachers had learned and assimilated in their own lives*.

With the death of Louis XIII and the accession of his mother, Anne of Austria, to the regency of the kingdom— quite against the king's own wishes— new winds of ecclesiastical reform began to blow in France. The queen regent expanded the purview of the council of ecclesiastical affairs, popularly known as the Council of Conscience. Formerly it had dealt with the appointments of bishops and abbots, but she added the supervision of all other religious affairs of the kingdom, such as ecclesiastical discipline, the repression of abuses, and even the encroachment of Protestantism... but it is known that Vincent de Paul was the secretary for about ten years, 1643-1653. He tried to ensure that *appointees would be good churchmen, pious and dedicated*, and not simply men using the office of bishop to enrich themselves and to enhance their families' honor.

*His extensive correspondence with individual bishops*, particularly Alain de Solminihac of Cahors, shows his attention to the details of clerical life.... The reforming activity that most endeared him to the Church in later years, however, was his *rejection of Jansenism*. This term describes a tendency in the theology of the period *to exalt the omnipotence of God at the expense of human freedom*. As with many similar movements, this one became involved in politics, not only in Vincent's lifetime but a century later. In recognition of his stand against this movement, the Church took Vincent de Paul as a model. The text of his canonization document, for example, concentrates on this rather than on his many works of charity, although these were not neglected. When all this is considered, however, we readily see that *Vincent was a leader in the reform of the Church in seventeenth century France*. He well deserved the praise lavished on him on 23 November 1660 by Bishop Henri de Maupas du Tour, bishop of Le Puy. He gave Vincent's lengthy funeral oration in which he exclaimed, "**He nearly changed the face of the Church.**"[1]

---

[1] John E. Rybolt, "Vincent de Paul and the Reform of the Clergy" (2010), in *Selected Works of John E. Rybolt*, 6-7, bepress.com, accessed Dec. 25, 2021,

## Appendix 3: George Weigel's Analysis of Current Crisis in the Church

Weigel on dissent culture that was a catalyst to sexual abuse crisis and on reform.[2]

Q: How would you describe the crisis itself?

Weigel: There are three parts of the crisis. There is the crisis of clergy sexual abuse, of which the most prevalent form is the homosexual abuse of teen-age boys and young men. There is the crisis of failed episcopal leadership. And, at the bottom of the bottom line, there is the crisis of discipleship. Sexually abusive priests and timid or malfeasant bishops are, first and foremost, inadequately converted Christian disciples. That's why the crisis is a call to everyone in the Church to live lives of more radical discipleship. As Father Richard Neuhaus and others have pointed out for months, the primary answer to **a crisis of infidelity is fidelity. Period.**

Q: *The Courage to Be Catholic* also describes what the crisis is not. Why did you do that? Weigel: Because confusions about what the crisis is and isn't get in the way of genuinely Catholic reform. This is not a crisis of celibacy; it's a crisis of men failing to live the celibate vows they pledged to Christ and the Church. It's not a crisis caused by the Church's sexual ethic, which flatly condemns all forms of sexual abuse. It's not a crisis caused by "authoritarianism," because the Church isn't an authoritarian institution — it's a community formed by an authoritative tradition... And it's not a media-created crisis.... It's a very serious mistake not to realize that this is a crisis that Catholics created and that only Catholics can fix.

Q: How? Weigel: The first step toward fixing what's broken is to recognize the spiritual roots of the crisis. Like every other crisis in 2,000 years of Catholic history, the current crisis is caused by **an insufficiency of saints**....

*The Courage to be Catholic* includes three chapters of recommendations on specific reforms: in vocation recruitment, in seminaries, in the priesthood, in the way bishops are chosen, in the exercise of the episcopal office, and in the way the Vatican gathers its information and relates to local Churches in crisis. Those recommendations are based on my own experience, on extensive discussions with some of the most effective reformers in the Church today, and on intense conversations I had in Rome last February and April....

I think the episcopal failures of recent decades have been similar to the failures of priests: It's fundamentally a failure in self-understanding. If a priest thinks of himself as simply another "minister," facilitating the "ministry" of others, he isn't going to think of himself as what the Church teaches he is — an icon, a living re-presentation of the eternal priesthood of Jesus Christ. And if he doesn't think of himself as **an icon of Christ**, he's going to be tempted to act in ways that contradict the commitment he's made to Christ and the Church. The same dynamic applies with bishops. Bishops who think of themselves primarily as managers — or worse, bishops who think of themselves as discussion-group moderators whose primary responsibility is to keep everyone "in play" — are going to be unlikely to act like apostles when the crunch comes.

---

https://works.bepress.com/john_rybolt/56/.

[2] "George Weigel on the Church Crisis in the U.S.," *catholicculture.org*, accessed Dec. 10, 2021, https://www.catholicculture.org/culture/library/view.cfm?recnum=4417.

# Retreat 3: Ecclesial Preparations for Mystical Transformation
## Conference 5
## Recovery: Church as Communion; Divine Filiation; & Marriage

It is proposed that the path to Church renewal entails recovery of three key areas: (I) Church as communion, (II) our divine filiation identity, and (III) marriage as anticipation of Christ's mystical marriage. These have as point of reference the Trinity, Father, Son respectively.

### *I. Recovery of the Church as Communion (Patristic Image)*

We highlight key points of the spirituality of communion. John Paul II taught in *Novo millennio ineunte* (NMI) that the greatest challenge for the Third Millennium is to "make the Church the home and school of communion" (n. 42). Scholars, like Joseph Ratzinger and Walter Kasper, had already noted that the image of Church as mirroring the Trinitarian Communion (*communio*) was already implicit in the Vatican II documents, confirmed by the Final Report of the 1985 Extraordinary Synod: "The ecclesiology of communion is the central and fundamental idea of the Council's documents."[1] David Schindler noted its ramifications: "The *communio* ecclesiology of the Second Vatican Council carries within it an astonishing *shift in the way we understand the world and the Church's mission in the world*"; *communio* is now understood as the primary meaning of the Church.[2]

This turn is a recovery of the patristic image (*koinonia*): the love of the Father through the Son in the Holy Spirit creates, redeems, and draws us to ultimately participate in their Trinitarian communion of love. Walter Kasper notes that the focus on Church as communion, accomplished through the Eucharist, is full of promise for ecumenical dialogue with the Orthodox Church (one bread making one Body, 1 Cor 10:16), and for understanding the close link between Church and the Eucharist. This is a recovery of an ecclesiology rooted in the best traditions of the undivided Church. There have since been two deviations. He finds that the Church as Trinitarian communion has been degraded to human "community" (through individualism and subjectivism) that led to a neglect of adoration and the dimension of sacrifice.[3] Second, Edward Oakes, understanding that all

---

[1] *The Final Report of the 1985 Extraordinary Synod of Bishops,* Rome, 1985 (Washington, DC: US Catholic Conference, Inc), C, 1.
[2] David L. Schindler, Preface, *Heart of the World, Center of the Church:* Communio *Ecclesiology, Liberalism, and Liberation* (Grand Rapids, MI: Eerdmans, 1996), xiii.
[3] Jeremy Driscoll, "Eucharist: Source and Summit of the Church's Communion," *Called to Holiness and Communion: Vatican II on the Church* (Chicago, IL: University of Scranton Press, 2009), 107-127.

theology, including communion, is based on a sound Christology, found a dilution of christocentrism. He notes that Dutch Evangelical, Klaas Runia, perceived that two prominent Dutch Catholic theologians diminished "confessional commitment to the Lordship of Christ," and two other theologians were corrected for their diminution of Christ's divine identity.[4]

Cardinal Ouellet noted that John Paul II's NMI "reminds us that only a spirituality of communion can contribute to the revival of the Church's holiness." We are to immerse the Church in the mystery of "her Trinitarian origin" (von Balthasar, *Dans l'engagement de Dieu*, n. 49). Chiara Lubich's profound "The Spirituality of Unity and Trinitarian Life" depicts how the Trinitarian Persons pour themselves out to become "non-being," creating a unity of Three, and this communion of self-giving is to be transplanted into the world. This God-given charism is to impregnate all sectors and fields of life: "There is no salvation in this world without a new culture" (Taiwan).

> Vatican II teaches that the new commandment of love is "the fundamental law" not only "of human perfection," but also "of the transformation of the world." The [Focolare] Movement has experienced this in various fields: politics, economics, culture, art, healthcare, education, media and so on. I will briefly mention just a few.
> [Nations, Society]: It has always been our conviction that if the relationship between Christians is mutual love, the relationship between Christian peoples and nations should also be mutual love. In fact the Gospel calls every nation to go beyond its own boundaries and look to broader horizons. Indeed it urges us to love the homeland of others as we love our own. Politicians who embrace the spirituality of unity live for this goal. They also try to practice the apparent paradox of loving the political party of the others as they love their own, for they are convinced that the good of their country depends on the contribution of all. Moreover they sense that if mutual love is practiced among those who are elected—even during their electoral campaigns—and the citizens of a particular region, this can be a path for overcoming the gap between society and politics….
> [Economy]: However in 1991 a new initiative emerged: the Economy of Communion. It aims to set up enterprises managed by competent people, who are able to run them efficiently and profitably. The profits are put in common; part is used to help those in need, to help support them until a means of employment is found. Another part is used to foster the growth of structures and programs to form people in ways of carrying out economic activities based on love and communion. Finally, part is used to further the growth of the business itself. Interpersonal and social relations can be viewed in a "Trinitarian" perspective which derives from the spirituality of unity and which forms the foundation of the Economy of

---

[4] Edward T. Oakes, *Infinity Dwindled to Infancy: A Catholic and Evangelical Christology* (Grand Rapids, MI: William B. Eerdmans, 2011), 405-417.

Communion. Some economists see in this a new paradigm to interpret economic theory and practice and enrich the understanding of economic interactions. They also see how it can contribute towards overcoming the individualistic framework which still dominates the field of economics.

All this presupposes that we cling to the Church, the sacrament of Christ (and mystically united with the Trinity), which is never lacking the Spirit:

> She [Church] is the tabernacle of his [Christ's] presence, the building of which he is both Architect and Cornerstone. She is the temple in which he teaches and into which he draws with him the whole Divinity. She is the ship and he the pilot, she the deep ark and he the central mast... She is paradise and he its tree and well of life; she is the star and he the light that illuminates our night. He who is not, in one way or another, a member of the body does not receive the influx from the Head; he who does not cling to the one Bride is not loved by the Bridegroom.... If we profane the tabernacle, we are deprived of the sacred presence, and if we leave the temple, we can no longer hear the Word.[5]

## II. Recovery of Divine Filiation Identity

### A. Crisis from Losing our Identity as God's Children (J. Philippe)

Troubles can overwhelm us, becoming mountains when they are but molehills. It is our divine filiation, our greatest gift, that is our rock. Jacques Philippe perspicaciously diagnoses that we have taken on false identities and that we need to recover, through the dark nights of a deep sense of our spiritual poverty, our identity as children of God (*Interior Freedom*, Section 5).

#### 1. The Need for Purification from our False Identities
Fr. Philippe's profound insight of our taking on false identities has far-reaching consequences. He teaches that we all have three basic needs: love, truth, and identity (who we are for ourselves and before others). These three in fact correspond to the three faculties of intellect, will, and memory respectively, and we attain them by the three corresponding theological virtues of faith (truth), love (communion with God and others), and hope (our security and identity in God). We shall address only the issue with identity. Before the Fall, Adam found his identity in God. Now, we identify ourselves with fashion fads, possessions (wealth, talents, good looks), works (e.g., religious and laity finding their identity in serving the poor). These identities create problems because we can become proud and intolerant of others (e.g., we complain that others do less or are less virtuous than us). *Not Recognizing the False Identities in Ourselves*

---

[5] Henri de Lubac, *The Splendor of Christ*, 209-210.

The problem is that we often do not recognize these false identities in ourselves. (i) Regarding ministry, we can become attached to serving the poor, or simply feeling self-satisfied from many good works. (ii) A second relates to Pelagianism. Bishop Miklósházy once told a class that we were all Pelagians because of our belief that God loves us more the more Rosaries and adoration we pray. (iii) A third regards friendships. A priest once expressed a sense he had of another priest: "He seems to be collecting special friends," friends who had good reputations or were highly esteemed. (iv) A fourth concerns one-sided piety, because of which a superior general of a religious congregation counselled her Sisters to keep their piety in their back pocket, that is, to be natural, and not be one-sidedly pious. (v) A fifth concerns attachment to human gifts, like our voices. Regarding the latter, we have been edified by encounters with Cardinal Ouellet, who greets you in a warm natural way like an old friend, and preaches with the same simplicity with no affectation in his voice.

Fr. Philippe identifies at least three problems with false identities: (i) pride; (ii) taking much energy to keep up the façade and going into a tailspin if this false identity is attacked; (iii) and most importantly, we are associating our identity with our doing instead of our being. For we are more than the sum of the good that we do:

> Human beings are more than the sum of the good they can accomplish. They are *children of God*, whether they do good or cannot yet manage to do anything. Our Father in heaven does not love us because of the good we do. He loves us for ourselves, because he has adopted us as his children forever.
> This is why humility, spiritual poverty, is so precious: it locates our identity securely in the one place where it will be safe from all harm. If our treasure is in God, no one can take it from us. Humility is truth. I am what I am in God's eyes: a poor child who possesses absolutely nothing, who receives everything, infinitely loved and totally free. I have received everything in advance from the freely bestowed love of my Father, who said to me definitively: "All that is mine is yours." (p. 124)

Beyond what we do or fail to do, God had us in mind from eternity, created us in the image of Christ to come, and then, through Christ's Paschal mystery, has made us children of God in Baptism. To understand the depth of this, we can look at the parable of the Prodigal Son. The father loved the prodigal son with such abandon, for he was not a mere stranger or worker— he was his own son! We too are truly, ontologically God's sons and daughters by Baptism. And the heart of life is to realize that I am "a poor child who possesses absolutely nothing, who receives everything, is infinitely loved and totally free." Even when we sin, we are to know this unconditional love (as discovered by the prodigal son): to know that He loves equally before we sin, while we sin, and after we sin.

## 2. Recovery of Identity through Purification in the Dark Nights

Jacques Philippe teaches us that only God can free us from these false identities by taking us through the Dark Nights (depicted by John of the Cross). He says that what we need to learn above all is the first Beatitude: "Blessed are the poor in spirit." It is helpful to offer further background. The Beatitudes are the new charter for the kingdom (building upon the Ten Commandments), as well as a portrait of Christ. But the Beatitudes constitute a building sitting on its foundation, the first Beatitude: "Blessed are the poor in spirit." Compromising this foundation of humility and self-knowledge is to undermine the entire structure of our Christian life (the rest of the Beatitudes). When our very foundation is compromised, only God can correct it, and He does so by sending trials and failures of the Dark Nights, that will take away our dependence on ourselves, gifts, and good works. It is an immense gift to receive this self-knowledge of our total poverty, for only then will we be truly free. Then we discover that we are loved, not for what we do, but for who we are as God's children. This is the treasure, receiving God's love, that no moth nor rust can consume (Mt 5:19-20). When the dross is removed, only God's love is left.

## B. Facilitating Recovery of Identity through Poverty of Spirit

### 1. Self-Knowledge

St. Teresa teaches that our divine filial identity leads us to be generous:

> We must seek new strength with which to serve Him, and endeavour not to be ungrateful, for that is the condition on which the Lord bestows His jewels. Unless we make good use of His treasures, and of the high estate to which He brings us, He will take these treasures back from us, and we shall be poorer than before, and His Majesty will give the jewels to some other person who can display them to advantage and to his own profit and that of others. For how can a man unaware that he is rich make good use of his riches and spend them liberally? It is impossible, I think, taking our nature into consideration, that *anyone who fails to realize that he is favoured by God should have the courage necessary for doing great things.* For we are so miserable and so much attracted by earthly things that only one who realizes that he *holds some earnest of the joys of the next world* will succeed in thoroughly abhorring and completely detaching himself from the things of this earth.[6] (emphasis added)

---

[6] St. Teresa of Jesus, *The Life of St. Teresa of Jesus: The Autobiography of St. Teresa of Avila*, trans. E. Allison Peers (New York: Image Books, 1960), 10.3.

That the awareness of our divine filiation needs to be recovered through the Nights can be seen in the saints. St. Angela of Foligno taught that the height we wish to attain is measured by the depths to which we descend:

> The more the soul is afflicted, stripped and keenly humiliated, the more it acquires, with purity, an aptitude for the heights. The height that it becomes capable of [reaching] is measured by the *depth of the abyss* where it has its roots and foundations. (*The Book of Visions and Instructions*, Ch. 19)

She expressed it thus: "I consider that the day when the humble revelation of ourselves has brought us many afflictions and sorrows, is a greater grace from God than many full days of prayer"; "The whole edifice of prayer is founded on humility and the more a soul abases herself in prayer, the higher God raises her" (*Autobiography*, Ch. 22). Mother Catherine Mechtilde de Bar (Catherine Mechtilde du Saint-Sacrament, 1614-1698), teaches us the insight that lack of humility prevents the Spirit from invading to possess us:

> God asks for nothing better than to fill us with himself and his graces, but he sees that we are so full of pride and self-satisfaction that it prevents him from communicating himself to us. For if souls are not founded upon true humility and self-contempt, we are incapable of receiving God's gifts, because our self-love would devour them. So God is obliged to leave us in our poverty, darkness, and sterility to make us realize our nothingness. This is how necessary the virtue of humility is. (*Adorer et adhérer*, 113)

St. Thérèse also explains how greatly humility attracts God's grace:

> Ah, let us then keep far away from everything that shines, let us love our littleness, let us love to feel nothing, and then we will be poor in spirit and Jesus will come to look for us, however far off we may be, and will transform us into flames of love. (*Letter*, 97)

## *2. Degree of Trust Determines how much we Receive*

One of the key fruits of the Dark Nights is to reveal to us our utter incapacity to attain God. This humbling self-knowledge is the foundation for our spiritual edifice. The humbler one is, the more one hopes. And what we hope for is what we shall obtain, as St. John of the Cross stated: "One obtains from God as much as one hopes for" (*Dark Night of the Soul*, I 2. Ch. 21). Jesus taught Faustina that if we hope for much, we shall receive much. The more we trust in God, the more we are confident, the more we will receive His grace. God is giving us grace, not according to our works but our faith. The problem in the spiritual life is our self-reliance; we rely on self and not on God, diminishing our faith and hope. The more we trust, the more we receive, as our Lord taught Sister Faustina:

> The graces of My mercy are drawn by means of one vessel only, and that is trust. The more a soul trusts, the more it will receive. Souls that *trust boundlessly are a great comfort to Me, because I pour all the treasures of My graces into them.* I rejoice that they ask for much, because it is *my desire to give much, very much.* On the other hand, I am sad when souls ask for little, when they narrow their hearts. (*Diary* 1578)

Thus, imitating St. Thérèse, one of the most powerful ways to receive God's grace is to learn to trust. Where God finds the faith of a child that looks to Him as Father, He can do much; without filial faith, He can do little. And perhaps, like Peter, after we have repented, "Depart from me, for I am a sinful man," we will hear Jesus call us, "Do not be afraid; henceforth you will be catching men" (Lk 5:8,10). Our Lord will pick us up from our ashes and clothe us with His grace as an apostle for His new evangelization.

### 3. Transformation through Fixing Gaze on Jesus and not on Self

After reading of a saint like John the apostle, our common inclination is to express a desire in prayer to love God as he did. St. Francis of Assisi teaches us a higher way: not to focus on acquiring gifts, but to simply rejoice in God's goodness, or to focus like Jesus on pleasing the Father. Here is an episode from one of St. Francis' Dark Nights. The Franciscans at that point had splintered into different groups and he was wondering whether it [Order's foundation] was all a big mistake. One day, while he was walking with Brother Leo, St. Francis gives a clear-sighted explanation of purity of heart through God and not through self-achievement: "Purity of heart does not rely in our being pure but in delighting in God being pure."

> One day Saint Francis and brother Leo were walking down the road. Noticing Leo was depressed, Francis turned and asked, "Leo, do you know what it means to be pure of heart?"
> "Of course. It means to have no sins, faults or weaknesses to reproach myself for."
> "Ah," said Francis, "now I understand why you're sad. We will always have something to reproach ourselves for."
> "Right," said Leo. "That's why I despair of ever arriving at purity of heart." [This self-focus on failing in spiritual life is a common pathology.]
> "Leo, listen carefully to me. Don't be so preoccupied with the purity of your heart. Turn and *look at Jesus. Admire Him. Rejoice that He is what He is— your Brother, your Friend, your Lord and Savior.* That, little brother, is what it means to be pure of heart. And once you've turned to Jesus, don't turn back and look at yourself. Don't wonder where you stand with Him."
> "The sadness of not being perfect, the discovery that you really are sinful, is a feeling much too human, even *borders on idolatry.* Focus your vision outside yourself, on the beauty, graciousness and compassion of Jesus Christ. *The pure of heart praise Him from sunrise to sundown.*"

"Even when they feel broken, feeble, distracted, insecure and uncertain, they are able to release it into His peace. A heart like that is stripped and filled— *stripped of self and filled with the fullness of God*. It is enough that Jesus is Lord."

After a long pause, Leo said, "Still, Francis, the Lord demands our effort and fidelity."

"No doubt about that," replied Francis. "But holiness is not a personal achievement. It's an *emptiness* you discover in yourself. Instead of resenting it, you accept it and it becomes the free space where the Lord can create anew. To cry out, 'You alone are the Holy One, you alone are the Lord,' that is what it means to be pure of heart. And it doesn't come by your Herculean efforts and threadbare resolutions."

"Then how?" asked Leo.

"*Simply hoard nothing of yourself*, sweep the house clean. Sweep out even the attic, even the nagging, painful consciousness of your past. Accept being shipwrecked. Renounce everything that is heavy, even the weight of your sins. *See only the compassion, the infinite patience and the tender love of Christ. Jesus is Lord*. That suffices. Your guilt and reproach disappear into the nothingness of non-attention. *You are no longer aware of yourself*, like the sparrow aloft and free in the azure sky. Even the desire for holiness is transformed into a pure and simple desire for Jesus."

Leo listened gravely as he walked along beside Francis. Step by step he felt his heart grow lighter as a profound peace flooded his soul.[7] (emphasis added)

*Eyes on Eternity*
St. Thérèse was able to fix her gaze on Jesus through her reading of the Last Things. It is keeping our eyes on eternity that transforms our vision:

> In my new desire for knowledge at the age of fourteen, God found it necessary to join to the "*pure flour*" some "*honey and oil in abundance*." This honey and oil He showed me in Abbé Arminjon's conference on the end of the present world and the mysteries of the future life....
>
> This reading was one of the greatest graces in my life. I read it by the window of my study, and the impressions I received are too deep to express in human words.
>
> All the great truths of religion, the mysteries of eternity, plunged my soul into a state of joy not of this earth. I experienced already what God reserved for those who love him (not with the eyes, but with the heart); and seeing the eternal rewards had no proportion to life's small sacrifices, I wanted to love, to love Jesus with a passion.... I copied out several passages on perfect love, on the reception God will give his elect at the moment he becomes

---

[7] Eloi Leclerc, *The Wisdom of the Poor One of Assisi* (Pasadena, CA: Hope Publishing House, 1991), 82-86.

their reward, great and eternal, and I repeated over and over the words of love burning in my heart.[8]

At fourteen, St. Thérèse read a book her father had borrowed. The book, *The End of the Present World and the Mysteries of the Life to Come*, now translated into English, consisted of nine conferences given at the Chambery Cathedral by Fr. Charles Arminjon, held in high regard by bishops and Cardinals. As her words above indicate, reading this book touched the depths of her soul: "This reading was one of the greatest graces in my life"; "the mysteries of eternity, plunged my soul into a state of joy not of this earth"; "seeing the eternal rewards had no proportion to life's small sacrifices, I wanted to love, to love Jesus with a passion." Soon after, she would ask her father permission to enter the cloistered Carmel at Lisieux.

### III. Renewal of Human Marriage in Light of Christ's Mystical Marriage

### A. Marriage is the Foundation for the Family

The renewal of the Church and world depends in large part on the strength of the family, which is the basic cell of society. And the health of the family is built upon the unity of marriage. As marriage goes, so does the family; as the family goes, so does society (we recommend Carl A. Anderson's "The Family: Sign of Communion in the New Evangelization").

Francis Fernandez presents the Holy Family as model for Christian family life in an uplifting meditation. He notes that Pope Paul VI points to Nazareth's roots to understand Jesus, who would have learned everything from Joseph and Mary (Homily, Nazareth, 1964). The pope asks whether we Christian parents fulfill our duties of teaching our children to pray, to prepare them for the sacraments, to pray with them, especially the Rosary, to invoke Mary and the saints, and to accept suffering (quoted in *Familiaris consortio* n. 60). For the family is a "domestic church," a school of love and virtue.[9]

But marriage's highest model and source is Christ's marriage to the Church as its model; it is the sacrament by which God reveals Himself as love. Marriage as a sacrament is so central that it was anticipated right at the beginning with Adam and Eve (Gen 1, "two become one flesh"). Marriage founders when the primacy of this "loving existence for the other" is lacking. Here is a brief theology on marriage:

---

[8] St. Thérèse of Lisieux, *Story of a Soul,* trans. John Clarke (Washington, DC: ICS Publications, 1996), Ch. V, 102-103.
[9] Francis Fernandez, Feast day of the Holy Family, *In Conversation with God*, vol. 1, 229-235.

## Attila Mikloshazy's Handout on Marriage

Marriage is a stable union of a man and a woman who give their mutual consent to live a common life. As such, marriage is a natural (secular) institution, based on natural law, and rooted in man's bi-sexual polarity (male-female) and in his capacity of socialization. Marriage was instituted also by a positive divine law (Old Testament), such that God becomes the witness and guarantee of the marriage-covenant. By their inner finality, all non-Christian marriages tend towards Christian marriage for their full meaning. The internal, dynamic tendencies of grace are already present in non-Christian marriages too (natural sacrament).

The sacraments are revelations of God, epiphanies of God. *In the sacrament of marriage, God wanted to reveal Himself as Love.* Christian marriage reveals God as a loving God. God found it, however, necessary to explain the way He understands marriage and love: He refers to it therefore as *Christ's love for the Church.* Love is in this light a divine thing in its greatness, faithfulness, and permanence. Marriage makes visible God's universal love both for the whole Church and for the human race. The sacramental expression of conjugal love represents and concretizes this love.

### *1. Christ Incorporates Marriage into His Person and Mysteries*

Non-Christian or natural marriage is already inviolable before God. But Christ's sacrifice has also drawn this mystery of marriage into Himself. Marriage between Christians (baptized) is a sacramental mystery, and the foundation of the sacramentality of marriage is the mystery of Christ and His Church. In Baptism, Christ had the spouses already incorporated into Himself; now *He assumes their unique marital bond also into the life of His Mystical Body.*

Christ continues to act historically in a visible way through the sacraments, which are visible (tangible) gestures, and which express and actualize God's infinite love. In marriage, it is Christ who joins man and woman together, so that through this union God is communicated to the spouses. Here the spouses, as ministers of the sacrament, act with the activity of Christ, appropriating Christ's eternal commitment to his people: "Through the sacrament of matrimony the *Savior comes now into the lives of married Christians. He abides with them thereafter,* so that just as He loved the Church and handed Himself over on her behalf, the spouses may love each other with perpetual fidelity through mutual self-bestowal" (GS 48), also re-presenting the Paschal mystery. Because of their Baptism, the spouses participate here in a special way in Christ's priestly office. Just as Christ is priest and victim at the same time, so the spouses are *both offerers and gifts at the same time: they give themselves, as Christ does in the Eucharist.*

Thus the lasting and ecclesial effect of marriage (*res et sacramentum*) is, as Augustine taught, the marital bond (*res*), which is also a "*sacramentum*," a "sacred sign." It is both an effect and also a further sign of the invisible reality ("quasi-character"). "In a way, the spouses are consecrated by the sacrament," so that they always remain *the living image (sign) of the fruitful union of Christ and His Church. So they become a sign of Christ's faithful love to His Bride, the Church.* A concrete image of this reality is given in Sheen's work, *Three to Get Married*, that in Christian marriage there is not just the romance between two spouses, but that Christ, who is Love, becomes a third partner; or as his audio book title goes, *The Two shall become One in Christ*.

## 2. Marriage as Covenant *(beyond Contract)*

Marriage is made through the mutual consent exchanged, which consists in the act of will by which both parties transfer and receive the perpetual and exclusive right to live a common life and to perform acts which are apt in themselves to generate children. But, while it has the element of a human contract, it goes far beyond to that of a **covenant**. Christian marriage is a graced covenant of love and fidelity between two baptized believers, which when ratified or sealed in flesh, has God as author, witness and guarantor of the indissoluble bond.

| Contracts | Covenants |
|---|---|
| - deal with things; | - deal with people; |
| - engage service of people; | - engage persons; |
| - are made for a stipulated period of time; | - are made for ever; |
| - can be broken, with material loss; | - cannot be broken; if violated, they result in personal loss and broken hearts; |
| - are secular affairs, belonging to the marketplace; | - sacral affairs, belonging to the hearth, temple, Church; |
| - are understood by lawyers; | - appreciated better by poets and theologians; |
| - witnessed by people, the State being its guarantor; | - witnessed by God as guarantor; |
| - can be made by children who know are the value of a penny. | - can be made only by adults who mentally, emotionally, and spiritually mature. |

The marital bond (*res et sacramentum*) is what gives the sacramental grace and enables the partners to indissolubility and fidelity (*res tantum*, or the grace effect). The sacrament opens up a *treasure of sacramental grace* from which the spouses draw supernatural power for the fulfilling of the rights and duties faithfully, holily, perseveringly unto death. *It increases sanctifying grace, adds particular gifts by elevating and perfecting the natural powers, and enabling the spouses to bear the burdens of their state with ease* (*Casti connubii*, n. 40).

## 3. Marriage as Loving Existence, Existence for the Other

Since marriage is a social sacrament, the meaning of marriage is *loving existence for the other: a service to the other spouse, to children, to the Church, and to mankind in general*. To exist for one another means giving oneself in love and joy, but also in renunciation, self-denial, and sacrifice (cf. Lk 9:23-24). This is the new wisdom of the cross (1 Cor 1:25). Love must help the beloved to become what he/she must become. The unfolding and growing Christian love must not remain just between the I and Thou, but must become a **We** (one flesh, one life), and so it will be *the best school for the love of others* as well. The higher meaning of marriage is the family with the procreation and the education of children, the fulfillment and crown. To this higher meaning (= family) is the mutual love of the spouses subordinated.[10]

## B. The Contribution of John Paul II's Theology of the Body

As a side note, we point first to the keynote contribution to communion by the new ecclesial charisms (e.g., Andrea Riccardi, Br. Roger of Taizé). John Paul II's Theology of the Body offers deeper insights, especially of the heart of human life as self-gift. Michael Waldstein identifies the fundamental source of John Paul II's vision of love as St. John of the Cross. He applies St. John's vision of love between God and the soul to human marriage, that can be synthesized in a triangle of three points: gift of self; paradigm of married love; and model and source is the Trinitarian communion.

> (1) Love implies a cycle of mutual giving, supremely the gift of self. (2) The paradigmatic instance of such self-gift in human experience is the spousal relation between man and woman. (3) The Trinity is the archetype of such love and gift from which the love between God and human persons as well as love between human beings derives as an imitation and participation.[11]

John Paul II teaches that the very foundation of what it means to be human is the gift of self, that mirrors the Trinitarian *ecstasis*, the eternal and infinite Trinitarian outpouring of Persons to each other. Made in the image of God who is Trinitarian love, we are made to receive love and to give love. All history is a love story. But it begins with the unconditional gift of self between spouses, from which comes the greatest fruit of children. Both are anticipations of the longing of the human heart for divine espousals with Christ and the love of the Father, through the Living Flame of Love. We can allow our Blessed Mother to form our marriages and families.

> May the Virgin Mary, who is the Mother of the Church, also be the Mother of "the Church of the home." Thanks to her motherly aid, may each family really become a "little Church" in which the mystery of the Church of Christ is mirrored and given new life. May she, the Handmaid of the Lord, be an example of humble and generous acceptance of the will of God. May she, the Sorrowful Mother at the foot of the Cross, comfort the sufferings and dry the tears of those in distress because of the difficulties in their families. May Christ the Lord, the Universal King, the King of Families, be present in every Christian home as He was at Cana, bestowing light, joy, serenity and strength. (*Familiaris consortio*, n. 86)

---

[10] Attila Miklóshazy, "Matrimony," Sacramental Theology II Lecture.
[11] John Paul II, *Man and Woman He Created Them: A Theology of the Body*, ed. Michael Waldstein, rev. ed. (Boston: Pauline Books & Media, 2006), 29.

## Retreat 3: Ecclesial Preparations for Mystical Transformation

### Conference 6
### Horizon of Grace: The Five Existential States of Grace

*(Charles Cardinal Journet's The Meaning of Grace; see New Evangelization)*
*Journet reveals how Christ's grace from the cross flows backwards and forwards in history to all. We see the far more surpassing covenanted "sacramental grace" within the Church that makes us like unto Christ and impels us to the Trinity and to co-redeem the world. Hahn's thesis offers a converging vision of Old Testament Covenants that lead to Christ.*

The eagle eye view of Journet's Thomistic "The Five Existential States of Grace" shatters the culture of human self-reliance and self-sufficiency, to reveal a vast panorama of Christ's grace flowing from Christ's cross into human history. In Journet's vision, there are five existential states of grace: A. grace deriving directly from the Father before the Fall; B. grace from Christ in anticipation of His coming; C. grace by derivation by His arrival; D. grace by contact (covenanted graces within Church) and at a distance (uncovenanted outside visible Church); and E. beatifying grace in heaven (not treated here). This horizon also gives clarity regarding whether one needs to belong to the visible Church to be saved (e.g., whether my Buddhist grandfather can attain salvation, what happens to Catholics who have abandoned the faith).

**A. Grace Flowed Directly from the Father before the Fall**

Adam and Eve already possessed original justice: the uncreated grace of the indwelling Trinity and sanctifying grace (created effects), as well as preternatural gifts (harmony of different levels). It was truly a paradise, when man was directed towards God, his entire being was in harmony with various subordinations, and the universe was subordinate to man. Then they lost all through their personal sin. Their state can be compared to the man in the parable on the way to Jericho who was robbed of gold (indwelling Trinity and sanctifying grace) and silver (preternatural gifts). After Adam sinned, he lost the gold, which results in the loss of the silver of the preternatural gifts: his mind and will are no longer subordinated to God, nor his five senses and sense faculties to the mind and will, nor the body to the soul, nor the universe to Adam. It allowed concupiscence, evil, suffering, and death to enter the world. The world now needed mediation.

**B. Grace after Fall by Anticipation of Christ**

As St. Augustine already understood, grace was poured forth backwards from the cross in anticipation, like a dawn anticipating the noon day sun. There were two economies: that of natural law, whereby man was guided by conscience (he also had creation, culture, guardian angels); and that of the Mosaic Law with its Covenant, by which they were guided by the Torah and fed by the anticipations of sacraments (circumcision for Baptism and sacrifices for the Eucharist). The grace of the Mosaic Law from divine revelation was greater than that of the natural law and thus more was expected from the chosen people. Yet the grace they received, though grace from Christ, was not as powerful or intimate as the New Testament grace. St. Augustine said that St. John the Baptist was far greater than he but that his Christian dispensation was greater than that of John, with the least of the New Testament receiving more than those in the Old Testament.

## C. Grace by Derivation from Christ within Church: Covenanted Grace

Christ established grace by contact with His Incarnation, and the Church at the beginning comprised only Mary and was never so holy; the Church thus has a Marian complexion. Because Adam after sin was now under the dominion of the senses, God's plan was that man would be healed through the senses by a God-man, who would give grace through His humanity, that is conjoined to the divine Person of the Son ("conjoined instrument").

Using an analogy of Christ healing the blind man by contact, Cardinal Journet teaches that those accepting Christ in the Church receive grace "by contact." The reason for its fullness and efficacy is that, given through Christ in the Church, grace is prepared in the heart of Christ which is close to the divine Person. As such, (i) it has three qualities of being connatural (belonging naturally), filial (Christ's sonship), and plenary (7 sacraments); (ii) it makes us like unto Christ; and (iii) it impels us to the Trinity and to co-redeem the world. Those receiving grace outside the Church (grace at a distance) receive *sanctifying grace but not sacramental grace*. Those who live in the sphere of Christ's coming receive greater (more powerful and intimate) grace than those in the Old Testament; but those who do not receive grace by contact receive grace but not in its fullness of those in the Church.

Grace received within the Church essentially comes directly from Christ, but through the Church's hierarchy. This grace is both (1) oriented by jurisdiction (teaching guided by the hierarchy) and (2) sacramental. Grace needs to be guided because one led by grace desires to know how to give himself to God and conform to grace, and for this the hierarchy (Magisterium) guides both dogmatically as by the voice of the Bridegroom or prudentially as by the voice of the spouse of the Bridegroom. But essentially it is still Christ speaking, clear and emphatically in the former, more muted but still His voice in the latter. Refusing to listen to the former is a heresy or schism against faith;

refusal to the latter is a moral disobedience against prudence. The sacraments are essentially encounters with Christ and flow from Christ, in order to lead us to become Christ (ipse Christus). The sacraments can be categorized under different forms: birth (Baptism), growth (Confirmation), and nourishment (Eucharist); sacraments of the living (Initiation) and the dead (Confession, Anointing); sacraments that impose character for worship (Baptism, Confirmation, Holy Orders); sacraments for order (Marriage, Holy Orders). The seven sacraments give a full blossoming of grace.

## D. Grace by Derivation outside the Church: Uncovenanted Grace

After the Paschal mystery and Pentecost, grace flowed from Christ to the world (backward to creation and forward to the eschaton). It was intended to be the full outpouring of "Covenanted grace" or "grace by contact." But the forces of evil as well as numerous obstacles opposed this tide. These obstacles comprise at least the following: (i) lack of witness by Christians (see example of witness by French woman after robbery that converted the Chinese communist, who also became a priest) and (ii) the rise of paganism (e.g., pantheism, polytheism). There are also fresh obstacles of: (iii) Judaism, which branch did not recognize the flower it bloomed and turned back to its root; and (iv) Islam, an acolyte of Judaism, but derived from a Judaism that was ossified and closed to the Incarnation and the Trinity; as well as (v) Protestantism and Evangelicals, whose leaders were likely heresiarchs and certainly schismatics (Journet's assessment); and finally (vi) atheism that has become a tempest with a wholly deliberate act of choice, an inverted act of faith, a truly religious commitment in reverse.

Faced with these oppositions and obstacles, God, who is Love, enters into a dialogue with each soul in these worlds where truth and error, light and darkness, are entangled together, sending grace "at a distance." They are truly "grace by derivation," still superior to grace of the age prior to Christ's coming and that directly prepare a soul for heaven. But they are given in a roundabout way, which is a sign both of God's love and the power of evil in the world. He set up a regime in which the Church does exist there but in a rudimentary or abnormal and restricted way, *an imperfect regime of uncovenanted graces*. These graces are given independently of the Church, yet it is the Church who intercedes for them. Those who receive these graces are *truly part of the Church but in a rudimentary, restricted fashion*. They live in various religions or denominations (e.g., Judaism, Islam, Protestantism), and the Church finds hidden allies among them. There are examples of these Christian graces arising in Judaism (e.g., among the Hassidim) and Hinduism, the rising of a co-redemptive and victim love. However, these cultures are often inimical to the Christian ethos. Uncovenanted graces are found in different "zones." The key to determine the efficacy of these uncovenanted graces is the zones that are determined, given the absence of the hierarchy. They are discerned by the criteria of the lack of (i) orientation through the hierarchy's teaching and (ii) the sacraments. They comprise the following groups: the Orthodox Church: teaching oriented with exception of the pope, but has all seven sacraments; Protestantism: lacks the Magisterium (teaching) and has only the two sacraments of Baptism and Marriage (with focus on Scripture); Judaism has the Old Testament and is faithful to the proclamation of God's transcendence to the world, and this is also true of Islam. India has a general climate of near pantheism.

But divine grace is strong enough to overcome all obstacles. Only God knows if the division of graces of contact and at a distance will persist till the end of time. For Judaism has lasted for two thousand years, Islam for fifteen centuries, Orthodoxy for nine centuries, Protestantism for four centuries. We have seen a whole vision of Christ's work from after Adam's fall and how consoling it is to see God's solicitude. [Summary of C. Journet]

### Appendix 1: The Suffering Church Awaits General Judgment

#### *1. All Nations and Persons will be Judged*
Evil always seems to have the upper hand. Daniel describes four beasts arising from the sea (lion, bear, leopard, beast), representing the four kingdoms of Nebuchadnezzar, Medes, Persians, and Alexander. But they also represent various kingdoms of history. The Fathers associate the horn that comes out with the beast (the instrument of the Dragon in Rev 13, 17, 19). What follows below is a vision of God (as Ancient One) and the Son of Man, and a judgment in which the beasts are thrown into the fire. While the Son of Man is identified in Dan 9 as God's people, the Jewish people saw a figure of the Messiah to come. Jesus, replying to Peter's identification of Jesus, *identified Himself as the Son of Man who is to suffer* (Daniel, Isaiah).

The Book of Daniel, mirroring the Book of Revelation, presents the proper background for viewing history. Applying the theology of the parousia (Christ's second coming) offers clarity to two dimensions. On the one hand, Jesus does not come into power only at the eschaton. Already after the Ascension, He sits at the right hand of the Father, possessing all power in heaven and earth (Eph 1:20-22), and is *already Lord* of cosmos and history. As Lord, He is also head of the Church, dwelling on earth in His Church, which is the kingdom of Christ already present in mystery (LG 3 & 5; Eph 4:11-13). Since the Ascension, God's plan has already entered into its fulfillment, already at the last hour, the final age, that is imminent.

> As the visions during the night continued, I saw One like a son of man coming, on the clouds of heaven; When he reached the Ancient One and was presented before him, He received dominion, glory, and kingship; nations and peoples of every language serve him. His dominion is an everlasting dominion that shall not be taken away, his kingship shall not be destroyed. (Dan 7: 9-14)

Most Christians are unaware that Christ has drawn all creation and history into Himself (von Balthasar, *Theology of History*). Chiara Lubich depicts it thus: "After the resurrection, Jesus is totally different. His relationship with the cosmos changed radically, so much so that he is no longer contained within time and space... Instead, he is the one who contains within himself space and time; the physical universe and all of humanity is within him."[1]

In this recapitulation, the suffering Servant has to relive His passion in us, making up what is lacking in the passion of Christ (Col 1:24). The human race is still under attack by evil powers, but it will be defeated definitively by Christ's Passover at the end. Until then, the Church will bear the mark of this world, groaning in travail with creation, sustained, above all, by the Eucharist. It is the time of the Holy Spirit and of witness, and also of waiting and watching, giving us the grace to bear the trials.[2] The Book of Revelation offers additional light, as recent scholarship sees it as intended "not so much as a prediction of future events at the end of history, but as a mystagogical commentary on the Divine Liturgy or the Mass" (see Stratford Caldecott, *The Book of Revelation as Liturgical Commentary*; see also Scott Hahn's *The Lamb's Supper* and *A Father Who Keeps His Promises*). Simply put, the Book of Revelation sets our turbulent history within the Mass we celebrate here and in heaven. Each Mass is already a proleptic second coming of Christ. Each age lives its proleptic final trials, but they are set within the all-powerful Paschal mystery of the Mass on earth and in heaven.

## 2. The Cross will be Established as the Standard of Judgment

Furthermore, Fernandez explains how Christ's cross will be established at the standard, and good and evil works will be judged by it before all:

> Then there will appear in heaven the sign of the Son of Man— the Holy Cross. That Cross so often despised, so often abandoned, a stumbling block to Jews and folly to Gentiles, which had been considered as something senseless; that Cross will appear before the astonished gaze of men as the sign of salvation.... All men since Adam will be there. And now they will all understand with complete clarity the value of self-denial, of sacrifice, or

---

[1] Chiara Lubich, *Jesus in our Midst*, 133.
[2] Attila Miklósházy, "Eschatology," Grace and Glory Lecture. *New Christ: Priestly Configuration* devotes Part III (pp. 243 ff.) to the "Last Things" from Miklósházy's lecture handouts.

surrender to God and to other people. At Christ's second coming the honour and glory of the saints will publicly be made known; for of these many died unknown, despised, misunderstood, and now they will be glorified in the sight of all. The spreaders of heresy will receive the punishment that they accumulated throughout the centuries, as their errors passed from one person to another, and were an obstacle that prevented many from finding salvation. Likewise, those who gave the faith to other souls and enflamed others with the love of God will receive the reward for the fruits that their prayer and sacrifice produced down the ages. They will see the results that the good each one of their prayers, their sacrifices and their vigils produced.[3]

## *3. Jesus Forsaken Unifies All (Trinitarian Communion)*

The centrality of Jesus Forsaken is illuminated in Chiara Lubich's core spirituality. She was granted mystical experiences in the summer of 1949, in which she saw how Jesus became a worm for us, reflecting on Isaiah 53:2, of the servant of the Lord "who had no beauty or majesty to attract us to him" and more on Ps 22:6, "I am a worm and not a man." This Jesus Forsaken will lift up all reality with His radiance:

> For her, Jesus was Jesus Forsaken, and she recognized his presence everywhere and in everything. God is love, and so is the Son made man. On the cross, in the painful cry by which he took upon himself all the sufferings of humanity and of creation, the greatest love was manifested. Jesus, love, is Jesus Forsaken, the greatest love, which made him give up his life and his unity with his father.... "Around us everything is Jesus Forsaken. Therefore, everything is loveable, because beneath everything and everyone, we see the *spouse of our soul*.... He, who is the worm of the earth, who is ugliness, who is a mixture of blood and tears and pain, is God. He divinized everything, he gave being to everything."

What may not be united here on earth will find Trinitarian unity in heaven. Through Christ, "everything is love, everything is unity and harmony."

> Divergent rays seemed to come out of the Father, reaching out to all creation and giving it unity, so that the presence of God can be discerned under every single thing. The idea of all created things is in the Son, and the Father projects these outside of himself, giving order to all, which are life, love and truth. Everything was conceived in the Word and everything was created in him. In the Word made man, in Jesus, the Father reaches every creature. In their origin, all things are united. At the end of times, Jesus will bring everything back within himself, in the Word, and therefore, in the heart of the Father, from where everything started.[4]

---

[3] Francis Fernandez, *In Conversation with God*, vol. 1, 146, 147.
[4] Fabio Ciardi, "To Paradise and Back," *Living City*, vol. 59, No. 02 (February 2020): 18-19.

## Appendix 2: Breadcrumb Trail Leads to Church and Trinity

Louis L'Amour's characters, like the Apaches, are able to follow a trail that is as clear to them as writing in a book. The Church Fathers too perceived a clear typology in which Old Testament prefigures the New Testament, pointing to Christ, His cross, release of the Spirit, and establishing of the Church. Christ's cross fulfills all the Old Testament prefigurations.

> The Holy of Holies was now just one more place, because the real Holy of Holies was on Calvary. There, too, was the real ark of the covenant, the one containing all the treasures of God: the real Victim obtaining divine propitiation: "God was in Christ reconciling the world to himself" (2 Cor 5:19). Aaron's staff has been substituted by the tree of the cross. The tablets of the Law has been superseded, their contents perfected and surpassed, by the new commandment of Jesus: love. The manna was now just something of a souvenir; the real Manna was the Body and Blood of Christ, the really sweet and fortifying nourishment for those making their pilgrimage through this world.[5]

Scholars find Israel as the Church in preparation, with "breadcrumbs" pointing to the *Church*: People of God (Church as the New Israel); 12 tribes reconstituted in the 12 apostles; holy remnant and diaspora after two exiles (early Christians fled persecution into the diaspora, are now in the diaspora of the world); worshipping community (the Torah, circumcision, and Passover fulfilled in the Beatitudes, Baptism, and Christ's sacrifice respectively); Holy City (Church symbolized as new Jerusalem: "And I saw the holy city, new Jerusalem, coming down out of heaven from God, prepared as a bride adorned for her husband," Rev 21:2); two houses of Israel (represents the split between Catholicism and Protestantism); kingdom of God (Christ began with "The kingdom of God is at hand").

The breadcrumbs lead to the Church. The Church has *Israel's mission*: a people from the nations (Christians are found in every society); a people for the nations (Church brings world to Christ); Israel was to lead nations to God but failed, which is now accomplished by the Church. The breadcrumbs lead to the Holy Spirit, seeing in Luke's vision of Pentecost a fulfilling the covenant in Sinai: both involving 50 days, the Holy Spirit as the New Law (e.g., Rom 8), and Pentecost fulfilling Sinai in its three fruits: giving of the Law, making a new covenant, and making a chosen people. Those who have eyes to see can perceive the Spirit realizing a new, divinized creation begun in Baptism and the *Trinitarian family* fulfilling our greatest relations: the family (mirroring the Trinity), marriage (with Christ), and filiation (to the Father), and bond of love (Spirit).

---

[5] Luis de la Palma, *The Sacred Passion*, 200-201.

# PART III

# AIDS: BUILDING BLOCKS

But, in no way, does the creature receive such a taste of the truth, or so brilliant a light therefrom, as by means of humble and continuous prayer, founded on knowledge of herself and of God; because prayer, exercising her in the above way, unites with God **the soul that follows the footprints of Christ Crucified, and thus, by desire and affection, and union of love, makes her another Himself....**
In several places we find similar words, by which we can see that it is, indeed, through the effect of love, that the soul becomes another Himself. He used to say: "Open the eyes of your intellect, and gaze into Me, and you shall see the beauty of My rational creature. And look at those creatures who, among the beauties which I have given to the soul, creating her in My image and similitude, are clothed with the **nuptial garment** (that is, the garment of love), adorned with many virtues, by which they are united with Me through love. And yet I tell you, if you should ask Me, who these are, I should reply" (said the sweet and amorous Word of God) "they are another Myself, inasmuch as they have lost and denied their own will, and are clothed with Mine, are united to Mine, are conformed to Mine." It is therefore true, indeed, that the soul unites herself with God by the affection of love.[1] (St. Catherine of Siena)

---

[1] *The Dialogue of the Seraphic Virgin St. Catherine of Siena*, Algar Thorold, trans., Catholic Planet.com, accessed Oct. 31, 2021, p. 14,
https://www.catholicplanet.com/ebooks/Dialogue-of-St-Catherine.pdf.

## III. AIDS: BUILDING BLOCKS
1. Eucharist: Calvary as Heart of Liturgy and Christian Life
2. Confession: Fruitfulness of Frequent Confession
3. Sacrament of the Sick: Mirroring Christ's Extensive Healing
4. Ascetical Mansions: Foundation Stones for Holiness
5. Ascetical Mansions: Begging Divine Mercy for the World (St.
6. Faustina)
7. Ascetical Mansions: Method of Mental Prayer (St. A. de Liguori)
8. Mystical Mansions: Abandonment Synthesized (J.-P. de Caussade)
9. Mystical Mansions: Texts by Saints & Model of Bl. Dina Bélanger
10. Spiritual Warfare: Discernment of Three Spirits
11. Spiritual Warfare: Jesus' 25 Rules to St. Faustina
12. Spiritual Warfare: Exorcist's Counsels for Everyday Life
    Spirit's Gift: Lay Charisms as a New Springtime in the Church

1. Two Aids for Renewal
2. Life of Grace: Infused Virtues & Gifts with Actual Grace
   Priesthood Renewal: Jesus' Appeal in *In Sinu Jesu*

These "Aids" or "Building Blocks" comprise the (1) three sacraments, (2) Ascetical and Mystical Mansions, and (3) Spiritual Warfare, as well as the role of renewal through the new ecclesial charisms. We incorporate as well (4) two Aids for renewal in the Church: life of grace and priesthood.

(1) The two daily sacraments of the Holy Mass and Confession go hand in hand, are not to be separated. It is vital to recover the heart of the Mass as making present the sacrifice of Calvary (beyond heavenly liturgy, real presence, and banquet). And modern saints have experienced the great efficacy of weekly Confession as a means of holiness (beyond remission of sins). We plead for extensive use of the Sacrament of the Sick (e.g., for mentally ill, evil infestation).

(2) St. Teresa of Jesus distinguishes between the Ascetical or human Mansions (Purgative stage) from the Mystical Mansions (Illuminative and Unitive stages). The Ascetical Mansions focus on the duties of our state of life, and various aids are provided to live it (e.g., prayer program, method of meditation, ecclesial charisms). The Mystical Mansions see the beginning of the entry of, and possession by, the Holy Spirit of our faculties and soul, leading to spiritual marriage. Provided are several texts by saints on the required abandonment, and Blessed Dina Bélanger as model.

(3) The key to ascending these Mansions to union with Christ is spiritual warfare. It begins with the discernment of three Spirits: rising beyond the human and evil spirits to the divine Spirit. Added to this collection are Jesus' 25 rules of spiritual warfare explained to St. Faustina, and an exorcist's counsels for daily deliverance and healing.

# AID 1

## Eucharist: Calvary as Heart of Liturgy and Christian Life
(Agreement with, and Surpassing of, David Fagerberg's Article Points)

### A. David Fagerberg: "It [Liturgy] is the Trinity"

Dr. David Fagerberg's fine article begins by assisting us to confirm a truth that we generally assume: that all religions, because they tend towards God (perhaps arising from our being made in the image and likeness of God, Gen 1), have temple, altar, priesthood, sacrifice, etc. Then he establishes three key points. (i) The specific distinction with Christian liturgy is that while it is primarily the work of God Himself: "Liturgy is not a human product, even if it is a human activity."[1] And (ii) then he goes on to pinpoint the specific cause of the divinization of Christian liturgy: it is based upon the hypostatic union (union with God and man in Christ), which distinguishes it from all human worship.

> All things must pass through the hypostatic union before they are of any use in liturgy. All religions have a temple and altar, a priesthood and sacrifice, sacred books and art, but in Christian liturgy this religious paraphernalia has been taken up by Christ to be wielded by his hand, and not ours.[2]

That is, what distinguishes Catholic or Orthodox liturgy is that it is based upon Christ, who is the Kingdom of God in person: "He is the new temple and new altar, the new priest and the final sacrifice, the word of life and the icon of the Father."[3]

(iii) He then explains that liturgy is all about Christ's offering worship to the Father: "The origin and the terminus of liturgy is the Trinity."[4] He explains with Pius XII's *Mediator Dei* n. 20: "The sacred liturgy is the public worship which our Redeemer as head of the Church renders to the Father, as well as the worship which the community of the faithful renders to its Founder, and through Him to the heavenly Father." Thus liturgy is the worship of the Son to the Father as well as our worship in and to the Son. Given the state of the liturgy in our times, where we get taken up by community and social justice on the one side and rubrics and liturgical rites on the other, we find in Dr.

---

[1] David Fagerberg, "The Liturgist Stands Beside Christ," *Inside the Vatican* (Sept.-Oct. 2021): 42.
[2] Ibid.
[3] Ibid.
[4] Ibid.

Fagerberg the clear focus on worship of the Father and a Trinitarian context. The human dimensions do have a place but constitute, as it were, the 10%; worship is the foundation and the principal focus of liturgy (90%). This means the Mass is not principally a meal but adoration.

Thus Dr. Fagerberg discerns the origin of the liturgy in the Trinity: "Liturgy's origin is not religious purity rituals, the human need for fellowship, Israel's temple, or ancient history. It is the Trinity."[5] It has two purposes: the glorification of God and the sanctification of man. He takes it further: that the liturgy has been in the mind of God, as we see in Eph 1, Eph 3, and Col 1. Jesus as man is now seated at the right hand of the Father and through the liturgy *carries us up with Him to the throne of the Father in every liturgy*. Christ's mysteries have passed into the sacraments (see St. Leo the Great). "The liturgist stands beside Christ, before the Father, in the Holy Spirit." All the mysteries of Scripture become actualized or fulfilled in the liturgy:

> For the Christian, the altar is the tree of life for Adam and Eve, the ladder for Jacob, the burning bush for Moses, the mercy seat of the ark of the covenant, the holy of holies in Solomon's temple, the still, small voice for Elijah and then his fiery chariot, the Jordan for John the Forerunner, the cross and empty tomb for Christ. When we stand before the altar we are standing before all these places. The mystery that unfolded across historical time now intends to invade our souls, if we let it.[6]

Going further, Dr. Fagerberg makes a key conclusion, the outcome. He insists that the liturgy is not just a rite but must be connected to life:

> The liturgy celebrated and the liturgy lived must be connected. So must be cult and cosmos, sacred and profane, Church and world, the sacramental Christ and our spiritual conversion, the eighth day and our ascetical discipline. The visit to heaven dispels the enchantment of worldliness, his descent opens our ascent, his *kenosis* achieves our *prokope* (elevation).[7]

Dr. Fagerberg highlights several notable aspects of the liturgy. But he seems to miss the central mark, the way Scott Hahn initially believed that the heart of Scripture is the Covenant (doctoral thesis), only to later realize that it is the Paschal mystery. Dr. Fagerberg's presentation bypasses this heart of earth and heaven— the sacrifice of Christ perpetuated in the Mass and celebrated eternally in heaven— as well as Holy Communion as an anticipation of the embrace of divine marriage.

---

[5] Ibid., 43.
[6] Ibid.
[7] Ibid.

One example of going deeper is John Cardinal O'Connor's article on seeing with inspired clarity that the Eucharist is the heart of priestly renewal. While he acknowledges dimensions necessary for continuing formation, he is convinced that renewal means a return to the *focus on the Eucharist's transforming the priest into Christ*. At priestly ordination, a man becomes priest through an objective transformation into an "another Christ," acting in the person of Christ, with the priest being nothing but "God." But it is by the continual celebration of the Eucharist that he is subjectively transformed in this progressive, lifelong process into Christ, using the powerful image of scrap metal (priest) dropped into a furnace (Eucharist).

> This is what it seems to me the Eucharistic Christ does to and for us, His priests. He so "melts" us into Himself, that it is difficult to discern where He "leaves off".... Christ does not merely enter into us in His Eucharistic presence. Far more, He sweeps us up into Himself. He divinizes us.... It [Eucharist] reaches out into the universe to feed and clothe and house and comfort the multitudes, bathing them in the love of the Crucified and Risen Christ, that love for which they are starved.[8]

Cardinal O'Connor makes the key contribution of its making us into Christ, but does not treat of the nuptial nor the all-important sacrificial dimension.

## B. Dr. Fagerberg Overlooks the Nuptial Dimension

Dr. Fagerberg's article bypasses the key path of spousal relationship to Christ (*Mystical Incarnation*, 285-290), that for which our hearts long. "The Word of God came down to earth to unite Himself to His bride, willingly dying for her, to make her glorious and immaculate in the bath of purification [Baptism]" (Methodius of Olympus, *Banquet* 3.8). We find in the entire catechetical tradition of the early Church the nuptiality of the Song of Songs employed as a figure of Christian initiation. The nuptial aspect of the Eucharist appears in the interpretation of some verses of the Song of Songs in which not only the wedding-feast, but the marriage union itself, prefigures the union of Christ and the soul consummated in the Eucharist.[9] St. Ambrose interprets the first verse of the Canticle, "Let him kiss me with the kiss of his mouth" (Song 1:2), as the kiss given at Communion of the Eucharistic banquet. In our era, Cardinal Ouellet captures the spousal dimension of the Church in "Witnesses of Love":

---

[8] John Cardinal O'Connor, "The Necessity of Continuing Formation for the Priest," https://www.vatican.va/roman_curia/congregations/cclergy/documents/rc_con_cclergy_doc_18061996_intr_en.html.
[9] Ibid., 204.

> ... the Church, mystery of communion, receives and realizes her most profound essence at the *Eucharistic banquet*, where the mystery of the wedding of the Lamb has already taken place and where the holy City, the new Jerusalem, descends from heaven like a bride adorned for her Bridegroom.... "The mystery is great," says the Blessed Saint Paul exalting this union. It is the much celebrated marriage to which the Bridegroom leads the Church as an espoused Virgin.

The Wedding Feast of Cana can help illuminate our nuptial destiny. Here we take up the three-step paradigm of Mary as virgin, bride, mother (von Balthasar). (i) First, we see that the transition from water to the New Testament wine has clear allusions to Christ's blood at Calvary. Calvary is perpetuated in the Mass, which unites us to Christ to become Christ (Body). (ii) But the Eucharist accomplishes this through a spousal union with Christ, so that "two become one flesh" (Gen 1). Before Mary became Christ's mother, she was "virgin" (availability) and "bride" (conception in her heart). (iii) Mary is both the model and the *facilitator* as the Mother of the Church and as the spouse of the Spirit. The shortcut is Mary, through whom we conceive (bride) to become (body) and give Christ to the world. This is all the work of the Spirit, but He accomplishes it through the Mass.

## C. Dr. Fagerberg also Bypasses the Apex and Core: Paschal Mystery

Beyond Dr. Fagerberg's vision, we root firmly first and foremost the Mass as Calvary's sacrifice perpetuated, that entails a nuptial communion with Christ (bride). For the height of the spiritual life is "to be crucified with him, to be another Christ... to renew in souls the mystery of the cross" (L. Martinez, *The Sanctifier*, 346), accomplished principally through Calvary represented, the Mass.

### *1. Fathers See Two Dominant Elements of Sacrifice (Calvary, Heavenly)*

We recall in *Mystical Incarnation* that Jean Daniélou's research finds in the Church Fathers two dominant images of the Eucharist as sacrifice: as a sacramental representation of the Paschal mystery and of the sacramental participation in the heavenly liturgy (see *New Christ: Divine Filiation*).

> If we go through the principal eucharistic catecheses, we feel that two chief themes constantly recur in explaining the primary significance of the sacrament: the Mass is a sacramental representation of the sacrifice of the Cross and the Mass is a sacramental participation in the heavenly liturgy. These two essential themes run through the whole eucharistic liturgy. They are explained mainly in connection with *the very heart of that liturgy*.[10]

---

[10] Jean Daniélou, *The Bible and the Liturgy* (Ann Arbor, MI: Servant Books, 1979), 128.

Thus, we need to re-establish Christ's sacrifice on Calvary as the center of history: "The Passion of Christ is the greatest and most stupendous work of divine life. The greatest and most overwhelming work of God's love" (St. Paul of the Cross). This was developed in *New Christ: Divine Filiation*: the world waited for His sacrifice prior to His coming, His sacrifice sends forth grace backwards and forward in time, and it is now celebrated in the eternal Mass in heaven and here on earth, Dom Casel's "mystery presence" teaches that Christ's sacrifice has truly become in human history the Mass, the real, though bloodless, sacrifice made present, for the Mass and Calvary are one and the same sacrifice (*Catechism of the Catholic Church*). Thus there is no heavenly liturgy nor real presence nor banquet without the Paschal mystery, which is its source and foundation. We might also add that the Paschal mystery is not really complete until the Ascension to the Father's right hand and in the releasing of the Holy Spirit onto mankind at Pentecost.

## 2. Loaves Miracle Signifying the Eucharist Points to Longing for Christ

The miracle of loaves prefiguring the Eucharist is noteworthy. There are three levels of being fed. (i) The first is feeding the hungry. The Church has always been at the side of the poor, sick, troubled, uneducated. (ii) But there is a greater need for teaching, the food of our souls: "he had compassion for them, because they were like sheep without a shepherd; and he began to teach them many things" (Mk 6:30-34). Perhaps the most crystallized form of teaching is Scripture. But Scripture is really Christ; it is the verbal incarnation of Christ, it is Christ's incarnation into a verbal body. Fr. Cameron teaches that Scripture proclaimed is to facilitate an encounter and dialogue with Christ. (iii) But the third feeding is prefigured by this miracle, the Eucharist. And here we find Christ's greatest incarnational form.

But the key to all three feedings is that we are made for Christ (Col 1) and long for Him. Even the crowds long, not so much for bread or teaching, but for being "with" Christ. Consider Mary's deep solitude during the first Easter Triduum and the remaining years of her life on earth, being separated from the "sun" of her life. Christ's teaching is in a certain sense His presence, especially in Scripture, but also in the teachings of the Church's Magisterium, doctors, and mystics. But all this longing converges in the Eucharist. In Christ in the Eucharist, we have everything: (i) we ascend the one Bridge to heaven and we have the only worship that the Father accepts, the sacrifice of the Son on Calvary made eternal; (ii) we receive all of Christ's attributes: light, life, way; (iii) we are assimilated to Christ in a mystical incarnation that Baptism begins; (iv) we have the beginning of spousal union, a foretaste in the kiss of the Bridegroom described by the Song of Songs (the Eucharist is an anticipation of the heavenly wedding banquet); (v) we receive the "Bread of Life," that responds to all our needs: food, worship, healing, sanctity, union, mystical incarnation, sacrifice. It is only the Eucharist that can feed the inner hunger in this life demonstrated strikingly in the saints, and in Scott Hahn, who longed for the Eucharist.

### 3. The Eucharist Conforms us to Christ Crucified (A. Miklósházy)

The Church was born from the pierced heart of the Lord. This sacrifice of Calvary, which has become the Mass, must lead to our own sacrificial existence. As there is no redemption without sacrifice, so there is no redeemed existence without being a sacrificial existence for every Christian, which is realized precisely in the Eucharist. Being a victim is an essential characteristic of this Redeemer God, and so is essential also for Christians. It is the Eucharist that conforms us to the Crucified. Sharing in Christ as Victim obliges us to do the same for others. Miklósházy, a liturgist, teaches that the Mass re-presents Christ's sacrificial state and not His risen state.

> This visible ritual action is a sacrifice, therefore the Mass is a visible sacrifice on the level of liturgical rite. The sacrificial character, however, must be visible in the liturgical rite itself: in the destruction, in the separation of the two species, in transubstantiation, in oblation, in communion, etc. Because the actual liturgical rite has such reference to the sacrifice of the cross, the Mass becomes a re-presentation of Christ's sacrifice by its structural elements (meal actions and prayers) as well as by its whole scope (preliminaries and consumption of the meal).
> (i) The preliminaries of the meal are shaped by the idea of sacrifice. All is done *"in memoriam passionis Domini"* and is meant to symbolize this. In the gifts the Church offers up itself in sacrifice at the same time.
> (ii) This offering of the Church, which at first is only symbolic, becomes essentially identical with the offering of Christ on the cross by the transubstantiation of the Church's sacrificial offering into Jesus' offering. The double consecration, whether it is regarded as the separation of the body from the blood of Jesus or as the re-presentation of the bloody fate of Jesus' person, *at all events re-presents Jesus' death*, because it renders present the person of Jesus *in the state of His passion and death*.
> (iii) The meal-sacrifice so constituted tends to its appropriate completion in the sacrificial meal. The purpose of the meal is to be eaten. The special feature of the Eucharist is that in it Jesus' offering on the cross is rendered present by His presentation as food to be consumed. Every sacrifice expresses communion with God. Jesus mounted the cross to restore this not for Himself, but for those he represented. To the nature of the Mass as a manifestation of the *"pro nobis"* ["for us"] of the sacrifice of the cross, there corresponds the visibility of the union with God in communion. Through this the Church has offered itself and which, by the consecration, *has become one with the Victim "Jesus."* So the Church is carried up to God by Christ and Him alone, and built up into Christ's Body in an ultimately real sense.

As a result, Christian existence is also a *sacrificial existence*.

Christian existence is sacrificial existence: The Eucharistic event is the mystery of *Christ's* redemptive act, the Paschal mystery, His death and Resurrection. He prayed: "I consecrate myself" (becoming a sacrificial gift, Jn 17:19). *Being a victim is an essential characteristic of this Redeemer God, and it is essential also for Christians.* The Church was born from the pierced heart of the Lord (*ex corde scisso*), so it belongs to the essence of the Church to become victim (= sacrificial gift) in the Eucharistic sacrifice for her own sins and for the sins of the world. There is no redemption without sacrifice, so there is no redeemed existence without being a sacrificial existence, which is realized precisely in the Eucharist. This sacrificial existence may have occasional moments of glory or transfiguration, *yet the daily Christian existence remains the sacrificial existence of Christ* (cf. Gal 1:24). [A professor of theology erroneously taught that the Eucharist is only about joy, not the cross]

Finally, this implies *our own victimhood*, ascending the cross with Christ.

In the [Mass] consecration text, the "given for you" has a double meaning: given for you as food now at the meal, but also "given up for you" to die on the cross. This would be parallel to the blood which is "poured out for you." Sharing in Christ Himself as Victim *obliges us to do the same as He has done, giving up ourselves to the Father as a gift* (Rom 12:1), as a sweet fragrance (Eph 5:2). It entails a purpose: the sacrifice is not an empty ceremony. The fundamental purposes are: expiation for sins, reconciliation with God, forgiveness of sins; but also worship, adoration, acknowledgement of God and restoring or achieving communion of life with Him.

It also entails a sacrificial attitude: It does not consist merely in a subjective feeling of mind and heart, but much more in one's objective self-understanding in faith. Components of this attitude are: awareness of being a creature, a sinner, God's child, and living the life of Christ (cf. Gal 2:20; 2 Cor 3:15). In today's theological understanding, however, we must say that in *the Victim of the Mass [Christ] is also the Church, as the Body and Bride of Christ*, and through the Church somehow the whole universe is included. The whole Church, therefore, in union with Christ in His role as *Priest and Victim*, offers the sacrifice of the Mass and is offered in it. By offering this sacrifice, the Church learns to offer herself as a sacrifice for all (cf. *Mysterium Fidei*). The priests especially, who re-present the person of Christ in a special way, are invited to imitate Christ the Victim, by seeing to it that every part of their being be dead to evil habits and desires (cf. *Presbyterorum ordinis* 13.4).[11] (emphasis added)

---

[11] Attila Miklósházy, "Eucharist," Sacramental Theology I Lecture.

# AID 2

## Confession: Fruitfulness of Frequent Confession

"Confession heals, Confession justifies, Confession grants pardon of sin. In Confession there is a chance for mercy. Believe it firmly. Hope and have confidence in Confession" (St. Isidore).

Many are unaware that frequent Confession aids in attainment of holiness (*Reconciliation and Penance*). We rightly see Confession as a means for remitting sin. But more deeply, it "ensures more rapid progress in the way of perfection." The New Rite of Penance (NRP) notes that it is a "serious striving to perfect the grace of Baptism, to conform more closely to Christ and to follow the voice of the Spirit more attentively." This conforming to Christ and listening to the Holy Spirit is the work of the higher Mansions, and Confession greatly assists this. The NRP shifts from a purely juridical act that infuses grace to focus on *repentance, healing, reconciliation after our sins wounded the Church, and the prodigal child restored to the Father*. The priest should "diagnose the sicknesses of the soul and provide remedies," revealing the heart of the Father and the likeness of Christ the Good Shepherd in his own bearing. Aid 2 draws from Attila Miklósházy's lecture on Penance.

## Elements within Confession

The spirit of the *New Rite of Penance* (NRP) ought to influence also individual celebration of Confession:

### Method of Confession

(i) Regarding Confession itself, it is important that the external accusation be made in the light of God's mercy.

(ii) Confession should not be conceived as a mere recitation of sinful acts, but much more as a spiritual conversation in which the penitent should indicate his state of life, the time of his last Confession, his difficulties in leading the Christian life, etc. [i.e., his journey to holiness]

(iii) The priest should help the penitent to make a complete Confession, encourage him to have sincere sorrow, offer his suitable counsel, instruct him in the duties of Christian life, and impose penance which should serve not only to make up for the past but to help the penitent to begin a new life and provide him with an antidote to weakness (NRP 18).

(iv) The absolution is given with the new Trinitarian formula of mercy. The words should be accompanied with the imposition of hands, a sign of imparting the Holy Spirit (NRP 19).

(v) Finally, both the priest and penitent ought to be aware that they are celebrating Christ's victory over sin, proclaiming the mercy of God, and thanking Him for the gift and experience of conversion.

## Mortal Sin

But we acknowledge the reality of people committing mortal sins or who are in the state of mortal sinfulness. Even if we described mortal sin as changing one's fundamental option, this rarely occurs in a cold-blooded choice of rejecting God. Mortal sin is not so much a particular act (though it can be) as it is *the culmination of a process, the final conclusion of a long drift away from God*, brought about over a period of time. People in mortal sinfulness are mostly those (presented earlier):

- who do not accept faith as the practical norm of their lives;
- who systematically refuse to apply the moral categories of good and evil to their actions;
- who abandon the use of means which help Christians to live the life of grace (prayer, sacraments, Church, etc.).

## New Approach in Confession for Conversion and Holiness

Today, integral Confession should be more concerned about the species rather than on the numbers. A better understanding of man's sinfulness as a *state*, rather than just individual acts, directs our attention to *the standing of the penitent before God, the areas of his life where he is weak or wounded, and the relationship between his baptismal commitment and present lifestyle.* This requires more presenting **a picture of one's spiritual life**, rather than merely enumerating sins. Such a presentation is not easy, requiring more preparation and time to explain.

In the Early Church, Confession first was considered primarily in order to determine the proportionate satisfaction for sins. In the Middle Ages, when absolution was viewed more as a juridical act, the "*cognita causa*" (confessing of sins) was the main reason for Confession. Today, with the emphasis more on *true contrition*, Confession should be viewed more as *a spiritual direction and healing* in which the penitent receives valuable help from a priest. A Christian (who has spiritual priesthood) is to become a better Christian. In this dialogue (conversation), priest and penitent together celebrate the mercy of God and make Christ present in their midst.

## Many Fruits of Frequent Confession that Aid in Attaining Holiness

Frequent Confession is useful and beneficial, especially for those who sincerely strive towards perfection. It effects:

- the remission of venial sins;
- the lessening or blotting out of temporal punishments;

- the increase of sanctifying grace;
- the correction of bad habits, the strengthening of virtues;
- the growth of genuine self-knowledge and Christian humility;
- the developing of the discernment of spirits;
- salutary self-control is obtained by resisting tepidity;
- the conscience is purified, the will is strengthened;
- ensures more rapid progress in the way of perfection.

According to the *New Rite of Penance*, the frequent (especially weekly) and careful celebration of Confession is not a mere spiritual repetition or psychological exercise [e.g., psychotherapy cannot remove guilt], but a serious striving to perfect the grace of Baptism, to conform more closely to Christ and to follow the voice of the Spirit more attentively (NRP 7.b).

## Necessity of Confessing to God but through the Church

Many Christians have doubts today about the usefulness and convenience of frequent Confession. They claim that it does not achieve its purpose. The arguments run in this way: "I don't know what to confess"; "I always confess the same things"; "I feel myself a hypocrite," etc. Objections cannot be raised against frequent Confession on the ground that it was not practiced in the early centuries. There has been a *legitimate development* under the influence of the Holy Spirit from public to private Confession, and to more frequent Confession of sins that do not have to be confessed. Furthermore, there is no doubt that frequent ("devotional") Confession has an important place in the spiritual life of saints and in many faithful.

The real reason for frequent Confession, however, is to be sought in *sacramentality*. That is, God works through mediation (Church), as with Christ's Incarnation. The sacrament is the place wherein the inter-personal action of God and man and all the essential mysteries of salvation converge in a *concrete and historical way*. The salvific will of God is realized here in concrete historical tangibility. Frequent Confession does not communicate something that could not be obtained otherwise; *but only here is attained the encounter between God and man to that perfect form and tangibility which is characteristic for the Christian salvation economy (through a priest, sacrament, Church)*.

If one claims that forgiveness can be obtained in many other ways, and for this reason he would neglect frequent Confession, one will manifest only that one did not understand the nature of this grace of forgiveness. Grace has always **a Christological and ecclesial character**, and *it is thus always meaningful that this finds its incarnational tangibility*. Thus, in Confession we find expressed and realized in a tangible way, as is clear from these reasons:

- that forgiveness is always the pure grace of God;
- the dialogue character of man as person (through a priest);
- the ecclesial character of sin and forgiveness;
- the intercessory power of prayer and penance by the Church;
- the trust in a higher power even in the most intimate matter of conscience;
- the insufficiency of self-evaluation in front of the merciful judgment seat of God;
- the rejection of all subjective, feel-good sentimentalism and of a vague, undefined, merely spiritual attitude.

There are, of course, other advantages of frequent Confession (see earlier list). *But all these are centered around the sacramental operation of Confession.* And through it we are elevated to the height of true Christian spirituality, which is the *integration of our whole life into the Paschal mystery of Christ.*[1]

## Practical Suggestions

We offer some elaboration to give further clarity. The first is that it is the sin of Adam that shut heaven from us and that only God can forgive sin (against an infinite God). Thus, our salvation depends on remission of sin, which we cannot trivialize and make purely personal. Second, Christ makes forgiveness of sin ecclesial (mediated through the Church) when he breathed on the apostles in a proleptic Pentecost and deputed, "If you forgive the sins of any, they are forgiven; if you retain the sins of any, they are retained" (Jn 20:23). Confession and forgiveness of sins go through the Church and are not a purely personal matter.

Here we consider examples of how we need the Church and others. David would have remained in his sin if God did not send Nathan to correct him, and David would not have been assured of his being forgiven until God assured him through Nathan. Robert Hugh Benson, in *Friendship with Christ*, teaches that heretics and schismatics may attain the Illuminative stage of the spiritual life, but, becoming proud of, and self-reliant on, their own interior lights, they make the critical error of not turning outwardly to Christ in the institutional or hierarchical Church. This was the path taken by Martin Luther, who relied on his interior lights, in contrast to John Henry Newman, who, while holding to the priority of conscience, always looked to the Church as mother (e.g., the key role of the Roman pontiff). To see the Church's power through the priest, let us share the unfortunate experience of a young man who, having expressed doubts about the then-questionable reputation of his diocese's seminary in the postconciliar period and cited the example of

---

[1] Attila Miklósházy, "Penance," Sacramental Theology II Lecture.

the questionable orthodoxy of a known theologian, was screamed at uncontrollably by a volatile interim vocation director and was told that he was going to hell (this theologian was a friend). The young man immediately rushed to Confession and a good confessor in just one brief counsel was able to reassure him (mediation).

Thus mediation is the key, all-important economy. Without God acting through a confessor, we can falter or doubt: not knowing whether a particular fall is a sin, how to overcome that sin, needing counsel. Without frequent Confession, a person with a bad habit (e.g., judging others, anger of impatience, failure in purity) may not perceive its sinfulness, can develop more ingrained bad habits, and fall into worse sin. The one who goes to frequent Confession often feels an infusion of peace (almost as if one's feet are lifted off the ground), is more assured of a good conscience, is strengthened by sacramental grace, receives counsel from the confessor, goes forward with renewed confidence. Above all, he wishes to be docile to Christ's Church that teaches to go to this sacrament "frequently and regularly," and finds that it is the way of the saints, as it was for John Paul II and Mother Teresa. Like the little child on the street who never veers far from the skirts of his mother, Christ's little one returns frequently to the skirts of holy Mother Church to be reassured.

A seminarian was inspired during his diaconate ordination retreat to make a General Confession to bury his past (especially for lack of cooperation with grace or sins of omission) and receive a new beginning and new impetus for his priestly life that he now renews each year. We find it consoling to know that one can also make an annual General Confession, and only have to confess those sins committed since the last one. An easy way to prepare for this is if we acquire the good habit at the end of each year of taking stock of and reviewing the sins of the past year (as well as the blessings), after which we are already prepared to make the annual General Confession.

Beyond making a General Confession, we might seek to look upon our sins through the lens of God. When we Confess and express our sorrow ("For these sins and all the sins of my life I am truly sorry"), God forgives not only the sins confessed, not only the sins I may have forgotten, but all the sins of my life. Especially with serious sins, say, if someone confesses committing abortions, then God forgives all these sins once and for all, and He also "forgets" them. The blood of Christ poured over them destroys the guilt and if the devil accuses us of them at our judgment after death, the Father can reply, "What sins? They no longer exist." In fact, Bishop Attila Mikloshazy went so far as to say that, if we have deep contrition, then we can find after confessed mortal sin that, not only have the lost sanctifying grace, infused virtues, gifts, and merits been restored, but we are raised to a higher level than before our sin. Consider what Jesus said of the sinful woman who wept at Jesus' feet in Simon's house: "Therefore I tell you, her sins, which are many, are forgiven, for she loved much; but he who is forgiven little, loves little" (Lk 7:47). At the end, it is love that counts.

Finally, we might bring a truth from eschatology, the theology of the "Last Things." God has already made His judgment on us at Baptism, at which He said, "You are my child, the beloved"; and if we sin mortally, Confession, a second Baptism, restores us. Baptism makes us God's children, and we are treated like the Prodigal Son. We remember too that Jesus does not judge (Jn 3:16), for He is "sheer salvation." Perhaps the biggest trap regarding our sins is to see them in isolation and not against the infinite mercy and merits of Jesus on Calvary. The saints understand this infinite disparity. St. J. F. de Chantal taught a troubled man to fall back into the infinite ocean of God's love, a counsel which greatly consoled him.

## Points to Address Scrupulosity

### Is Contrition Difficult?
*It is not the feelings that determine contrition but the will*
Perfect contrition is possible for everyone. Under the influence of grace, we can move towards loving God above everything. *But it is not necessary to feel this perfect love; it resides in the election of the will* with its practical judgment of the intellect. Generally, what often happens is that we are moved gradually from lower motives (gratitude, etc.) to the Infinite Goodness and Love.

**The Virtue of Penance** (*metanoia*= conversion, change of heart, contrition)
The virtue of penance is the right attitude towards sin. This virtue (habit) is achieved by many repeated acts of penance (mortification), especially by the central act which is contrition (conversion, repentance). But beside this central act, the virtue of penance has several other components as well:
- the courage to fear God and to face one's own existence by taking a stand to one's past;
- the willingness of letting the grace of God destroy our pharisaic self-righteousness;
- the hatred of sin and the willingness to fight against it through mortification (vigils, prayer, fasting, alms);
- sincere desire for amendment, trusting in God's gracious help;
- fighting against concupiscence and the fallen "world";
- readiness to regularly avail oneself of the sacrament of Confession;
- readiness to accept the consequences of sin (punishment, satisfaction, reparation);

- becoming co-responsible in fighting against sin in the Church and in the world;
- willingness of carrying the burden of sin in the misfortunes and miseries of human existence, etc.[2]

**The importance of Confession for removing the burden of guilt**: Here is a text from John Paul II regarding the burden that Confession takes away:

> Those confessionals scattered about the world where men declare their sins don't speak of the severity of God. Rather do they speak of his mercy. And all those who approach the confessional, sometimes after many years weighed down with mortal sins, in the moment of getting rid of this intolerable burden, find at last a longed-for relief. They find joy and tranquility of conscience which, outside Confession, they will never be able to find anywhere. (Homily, 16 March, 1980)

## Helpful Saint's Texts for this Area

### 1. We Experience Temptations throughout our Lives (J. M. Escrivá)

*There is a temptation to think that, if we make progress in our spiritual life, we will be protected from temptations. St. Escrivá teaches that we will all have temptations till we die. The lives of the saints suggest that temptations and troubles may increase with spiritual growth, as we find in the Dark Nights. This is a very salutary insight.*

> Let us not think that because we are on this road of contemplation our passions will have calmed down once and for all. We would be mistaken if we thought that our longing to seek Christ and the fact that we are meeting him and getting to know him and enjoy the sweetness of his love, makes us incapable of sinning. Though your own experience will tell you, let me nevertheless remind you of this truth. Satan, God's enemy and man's, does not give up nor does he rest. He maintains his siege, even when the soul is ardently in love with God. The devil knows that it's more difficult for the soul to fall then, but he also knows that, if he can manage to get it to offend its Lord even in something small, he will be able to cast over its conscience the serious temptation of despair.
>
> If you want to learn from the experience of a poor priest whose only aim is to speak of God, I will tell you that when the flesh tries to recover its lost rights or, worse still, when pride rears up and rebels, you should hurry to find shelter in the divine wounds that were opened in Christ's Body by the nails that fastened him to the Cross and by the lance that pierced his side. Go as the Spirit moves you: unburden in his Wounds all your love, both human and… divine. This is what it means to seek union, to feel that you are a brother to Christ, sharing his blood, a child of the same Mother. (*Friends of God*, n. 303)

---

[2] Ibid.

## 2. "No Temptation is a Sin" (M. Kolbe)
*Many are troubled by temptations. St. Maximilian Kolbe insists that temptation, when not given into, is not sin, and that we should not be troubled by temptations.*

> No temptation is a sin. No matter how long the temptation might last, it is not a sin, but much depends on how the soul reacts before it becomes a field of merit. As to the method of the battle, do not begin to doubt or fall into nervousness, but peacefully have recourse to the Immaculata and make nothing of it all, and simply do not have the time for it. Keep busy with something else. Sometimes people worry or fret. There is no need for it, for Satan uses it to tire a soul. I repeat, therefore, no temptation in itself does any harm to a soul, as long as, on our part, there is no consent. (Address given on August 16, 1936)

## 3. Jesus' Teaching on Expiating Sin through Love (C. of Siena)
*Many can be burdened and troubled by the thought of past and present sins. There is, of course, the objective remission of sins through the sacrament of Confession as well as other secondary means (Mass, prayers, good works), all presuming contrition. But there is another dimension that can give much consolation: that we can make reparation that is pleasing to God, above all through acts of love, as was received by Jesus to St. Catherine of Siena, if we have "the condiment of the affection of love."*

> Then, the Eternal Truth seized and drew more strongly to Himself her desire, doing as He did in the Old Testament, for when the sacrifice was offered to God, a fire descended and drew to Him the sacrifice that was acceptable to Him; so did the sweet Truth to that soul, in sending down the fire of the clemency of the Holy Spirit, seizing the sacrifice of desire that she made of herself, saying:
>
> "Do you not know, dear daughter, that all the sufferings, which the soul endures, or can endure, in this life, are insufficient to punish one smallest fault, because the offense, being done to Me, who am the Infinite Good, calls for an *infinite satisfaction*?
>
> However, I wish that you should know, that not all the pains that are given to men in this life are given as *punishments*, but as *corrections*, in order to chastise a son when he offends; though it is true that both the guilt and the penalty can be expiated by the desire of the soul, that is, by true contrition, not through the finite pain endured, but through the infinite desire; because God, who is infinite, wishes for infinite love and infinite grief [sorrow].
>
> Infinite grief I wish from My creature in two ways: in one way, through her sorrow for her own sins, which she has committed against Me her Creator; in the other way, through her sorrow for the sins which she sees her neighbors commit against Me.

Of such as these, inasmuch as they have infinite desire, that is, are joined to Me *by an affection of love, and therefore grieve when they offend Me, or see Me offended, their every pain, whether spiritual or corporal, from wherever it may come, receives infinite merit, and satisfies for a guilt* which deserved an infinite penalty, although their works are finite and done in finite time; but, inasmuch as they possess the virtue of desire, and sustain their suffering with desire, and contrition, and infinite displeasure against their guilt, their pain is held worthy.

Paul explained this when he said: 'If I had the tongues of angels, and if I knew the things of the future and gave my body to be burned, and have not love, it would be worth nothing to me.' The glorious Apostle thus shows that finite works are not valid, either as punishment or recompense, without the condiment of the affection of love." (St. Catherine of Siena, *Dialogue on Divine Providence*)

## 4. The Shortness of Life and a Partial Examination of Conscience
*Francis Fernandez offers an Examination of Conscience for the last day of the year.*

*Shortness of Life*
The time each of us has at his disposal is short, but long enough to tell God that we love him and to accomplish the work he has given us. For this reason St. Paul warns us: *Look carefully then how you walk, not as unwise men but as wise, making the most of the time* [Eph 5:15-16], for soon *night comes, when no one can work* [Jn 9:4]. *Short indeed is our life for loving, for giving, for making atonement. It is wrong, therefore, to waste it or irresponsibly throw out of the window such a great treasure. We cannot squander this period of the world's history that God has entrusted to each one of us.* (Friends of God, 39).

*Examination of Conscience, Greater Cause for Thanksgiving*
On examining our conscience we will easily find that during this past year we have at times lacked charity, been too easy-going in our professional work, grown used to a certain spiritual mediocrity, and given little in the way of alms. We have been a prey to selfishness and vanity. We have not done any mortification in our meals. We have ignored the grace offered to us by the Holy Spirit. We have been intemperate, bad-tempered, and stubborn in character. We have more or less deliberately allowed ourselves to be distracted in our practices of piety.... So we have countless reasons for ending the year by asking God's forgiveness, by making many acts of contrition and atonement. Let us look at each one of those days.... Nevertheless, in both the human and supernatural realms, our reasons for thanksgiving are incomparably greater. We cannot count the movements of the Holy Spirit in our soul, the graces we have received in the sacrament of Confession and in Holy Communion, the times when our Guardian Angel has protected us, the merit gained through the offering of our work and hardships for others, and the times when others have helped us. (*In Conversation with God,* vol. 1, 279-280)

# AID 3
## Sacrament of the Sick: Mirroring Christ's Extensive Healing

It was not till the early Middle Ages that the Church discerned that we are to honour Christ's real presence in the Blessed Sacrament, and till the twentieth century with Pope Pius X to reduce the age of First Holy Communion and to encourage daily Mass and Communion. It has taken till the seventh-eighth centuries that Irish monks brought to the continent the Irish Penitential books for regular Confession and till the twentieth century to encourage the faithful to confess "frequently and regularly."

There may be need for a similar development regarding the Sacrament of the Anointing of the Sick. There has already been progress made with the *New Rite of Anointing* (1973), specifically in regard to correcting the erroneous conception that it is "Extreme Unction," primarily for the dying It is the opposite: it is for all sick who are ill with some risk (*periculose*, which does not include a cold, summer allergies), but not necessarily be in immediate danger of death. This has wide application: any one with sickness of some seriousness (e.g., cancer, heart condition); anyone going in for major surgery; elderly who are frail (e.g., regular anointings in senior's homes); people with chronic debilitating issues (poliomyelitis, chronic arthritis, handicapped, blind, incurable). This sacrament has other key benefits: it can give complete healing if God wills it; increase of sanctifying grace and sacramental graces to help strengthen and comfort, reduce temporal punishment, and even remit serious sin. Though the sacrament of the dying is primarily the Viaticum, note that when St. Escrivá was suddenly dying, he asked for Absolution, and A. del Portillo also gave Anointing.

The norm is Jesus' curing the sick and expelling demons without exception in Mt 4:23-24. The key to understand who qualifies is to look first at the key text of James 5:14-16 in light of Jesus' curing all the sick. A key criterion is to *alleviate burdens* (*alleviat et confirmat*). One theology handout prescribes that, of those who have mental illness, only those with manic depression qualify. But are not the many who have mental illness (e.g., severe depression) also sick and seriously burdened? A spiritual chancellor, a canon lawyer, agreed that this sacrament is for both bodily as well as mental illness, correcting a serious misunderstanding given in some theology. Furthermore, this chancellor agreed that, within inner healing ministry, people with serious infestation by spirits and those sustaining trauma (e.g., sexual abuse) can also qualify for this sacrament. We would argue that, while it is not meant to be given regularly, it can be given more than once when it becomes a burden (e.g., someone in palliative or long-term care), and not just in cases of a relapse or worsening condition.

# AID 4

## Ascetical Mansions: Foundation Stones for Holiness

As employed in this book, we find that it is very useful to distinguish in spiritual life or in the ascent of the spiritual journey two primary stages: Ascetical and Mystical Mansions, but that the latter also have two levels (Illuminative and Unitive), giving rise to three overall stages. These three stages appear to correspond to what St. Margaret Mary Alacoque teaches of three streams:

> From this divine heart [of Christ] three streams flow endlessly. The first is the stream of mercy for sinners; it pours into their hearts sentiments of contrition and repentance. The second is the stream of charity which helps all in need and especially aids those seeking perfection to find the means of surmounting their difficulties. From the third stream flow love and light for the benefit of his friends who have attained perfection; these he wishes to unite to himself so that they may share his knowledge and commandments and, in their individual ways, devote themselves wholly to advancing his glory.[1]

Within the Ascetical Mansions, a strong foundation must be established. Many foundation stones can assist: daily Mass (with a great love of the Blessed Sacrament) and weekly Confession, a spiritual director can greatly assist, affiliation with an ecclesial charism, a daily prayer program, choosing the very best of spiritual reading books (especially of the saints), accepting and giving fraternal correction, etc. While we have to go through the Ascetical Mansions to attain the Mystical Mansions, the Spirit desires to lead us beyond the former to union with Him in the Unitive Mansions. We recommend the booklet, *A Plan of Life* (and the longer *Norms of Piety*), by Fr. **Joseph M. Muntadas**. Both are available online. Here are his plan's nine points:
1. The Morning Offering
2. Mental Prayer
3. Holy Mass
4. Spiritual Reading
5. A Visit to the Blessed Sacrament
6. Devotion to Mary
7. Examination of Conscience
8. Frequent Confession
9. Throughout the Day (contemplation, sanctifying work)

---

[1] St. Margaret Mary Alacoque, Letter, OOR for feast day, Liturgies.net, accessed Oct. 20, 2021, http://www.liturgies.net/saints/margaretmaryalacoque/readings.htm.

## Cardinal van Thuan's Ten Norms for Sanctification
From his experience in prison of "You have only to choose God and not the works of God!", Cardinal van Thuan composed a program of ten rules:
1. I will live the present moment to the fullest.
2. I will discern between God and God's works.
3. I will hold firmly to one secret: prayer.
4. I will see in the Holy Eucharist my only power.
5. I will have only one wisdom: the science of the Cross.
6. I will remain faithful to my mission in the Church and for the Church as a witness of Jesus Christ.
7. I will seek the peace the world cannot give.
8. I will carry out a revolution by renewal in the Holy Spirit.
9. I will speak one language and wear one uniform: Charity.
10. I will have one very special love: The Blessed Virgin Mary.[2]

## Author's Suggested Womb for Attaining Holiness
1. Three Loves: Church, Eucharist, Mary
2. Two "Daily" Sacraments: Daily Mass, Weekly Confession
3. Two Identities: Filial Love of Father and Spousal Love of Christ
4. Marian Principle: Living Christ's Receptivity and Expropriation
5. Abandonment: Living the Sacrament of the Present Moment
6. Wombs: Turning to Ecclesial Charisms Provided by the Father
7. Mediation: Seeking Spiritual Direction
8. Discernment of Spirits: above Human and beyond Evil Spirits
9. Foundation: Self-Forgetfulness and Peace of Heart
10. Horizon: Eternity for Zeal for Souls and the Poor
11. Models: Imitation and Intercession of the Saints

*Note regarding ecclesial charisms.* Julián Carrón, responding to Andrea Tornielli's noting doubts that some have about these charisms, explains that past tensions between parishes and charisms is a misdirection. We are called, as Pope Francis exhorts, to "go out"; to reach those who do not know Christ is the real issue and goal; and today, we are often not reaching people. He refutes a second charge, that they are not elite crack troops, but are like Matthew in Caravaggio's painting asking, "You are calling me?", the tax collector given a gratuitous call to serve as an apostle (*Where is God?*, 106-108). As Ratzinger noted, it is wondrous that these instruments had no plans (e.g., Benedict, Dominic, Ignatius, Escrivá), yet helped to transform the world. The author sees lay charisms as successors to the Mendicant Orders, as great gifts for our times given by the Holy Spirit Himself.

---

[2] Francis Cardinal van Thuan, Duong Hy Vong: Nguyen van Thuan, accessed January 31, 2016, http://www.nguyenvanthuan.com/tenrules.html.

# I. *Daily Prayers & Counsels*
## Morning Offering and Prayer to Guardian Angel

Morning Offering
My Lord and my God, I offer you all my thoughts, words, and actions in union with Jesus and Mary. Help me to always want to do your will in all things.

My Queen, my Mother, I give myself entirely to you. And to show my devotion, I consecrate and give to you my eyes, my ears, my mouth, my heart, my whole body and soul. Dearest Mother, keep me ever yours. Guard me as your property and possession.

Prayer to Guardian Angel (before Morning Offering and before retiring)
Angel of God, my guardian dear, to whom God's love commits me here, ever this day ["night" for before bedtime], be at my side, to light, to guard, to rule, to guide.

**Prayers for Daily Meditation and Mass by St. Josemaría Escrivá**
Prayer before Meditation
My Lord and my God, I firmly believe that you are here; that you see me, that you hear me. I adore you with profound reverence; I beg your pardon of my sins, and the grace to make this time of prayer fruitful.
My Immaculate Mother, Saint Joseph my father and lord, my guardian angel, intercede for me.

Prayer after Meditation
I thank you, my God, for the good resolutions, affections and inspirations that you have communicated to me in this meditation.
I beg your help for putting them into effect. My Immaculate Mother, Saint Joseph my father and lord, my guardian angel, intercede for me.

Offertory
My Lord and my God: into your hands I abandon the past and the present and the future, what is small and what is great, what amounts to a little and what amounts to a lot, things temporal and things eternal.

Consecration of Host
'Holy Father, through the Immaculate Heart of Mary I offer to you Jesus, your beloved Son, and in him, through him, and with him I offer myself for all his intentions and in the name of all creatures.'

Spiritual Communion before Receiving Communion
I wish, my Lord and my God, to receive You with the purity, humility and love with which your Most Holy Mother received You, and with the fervor and spirit of the Saints. (See stjosemaria.org)

An Act of Spiritual Communion
My Jesus, I believe that You are in the Blessed Sacrament. I love you above all things, and I long for You in my soul. Since I cannot now receive You sacramentally, come at least spiritually into my heart. I embrace You as if You were already there and unite myself entirely to You. Never permit me to be separated from You. (EWTN, there are shorter versions available)

**Daily Prayers**
Prayer for Daily Neglects (see ourcatholicprayers.com)
Eternal Father, I offer Thee the Sacred Heart of Jesus,
with all its love, all its sufferings and all its merits.

First, to expiate all the sins
I have committed this day and during all my life. *Gloria Patri.*

Second, to purify the good I have done poorly this day
and during all my life. *Gloria Patri.*

Third, to supply for the good I ought to have done,
and that I have neglected this day and all my life. *Gloria Patri.*

Act of Contrition
O my God, I am sorry and beg pardon for all my sins, because I have deserved Your dreadful punishment, because I have crucified my loving Savior Jesus Christ, and most of all, because I have offended Your infinite goodness, and I firmly resolve, with the help of Your grace, never to offend You again and carefully avoid the occasion of sin.

St. Josemaría Escrivá
**17 Signs of Pride** (*Furrow* n. 263)

— Thinking that what you do or say is better than what others do or say;
— Always wanting to get your own way;
— Arguing when you are not right or when you are but insisting stubbornly or with bad manners;
— Giving your opinion without being asked for it, when charity does not demand you to do so;

— Despising the point of view of others;
— Not being aware that all the gifts and qualities you have are on loan;
— Not acknowledging that you are unworthy of all honour or esteem, even the ground you are treading on or the things you own;
— Mentioning yourself as an example in conversation;
— Speaking badly about yourself, so that they may form a good opinion of you, or contradict you;
— Making excuses when rebuked;
— Hiding some humiliating faults from your director, so that he may not lose the good opinion he has of you;
— Hearing praise with satisfaction, or being glad that others have spoken well of you;
— Being hurt that others are held in greater esteem than you;
— Refusing to carry out menial tasks;
— Seeking or wanting to be singled out;
— Letting drop words of self-praise in conversation, or words that might show your honesty, your wit or skill, your professional prestige…;
— Being ashamed of not having certain possessions.

## The Real 12 Days of Christmas (see vox.com)

A legend about Catholics in England not being allowed to practice their faith openly and learned through hidden meaning:
The partridge in a pear tree was Jesus Christ.
Two turtle doves were the Old and New Testaments.
Three French hens stood for faith, hope and love.
The four calling birds were the four gospels of Matthew, Mark, Luke, John.
The five golden rings recalled the Torah or Law, the first five books of the Old Testament.
The six geese a-laying stood for the six days of creation.
Seven swans a-swimming represented the sevenfold gifts of the Holy Spirit: prophesy, serving, teaching, exhortation, contribution, leadership, and mercy.
The eight maids a-milking were the eight beatitudes.
Nine ladies dancing were the nine fruits of the Holy Spirit: love, joy, peace, patience, kindness, goodness, faithfulness, gentleness, and self-control.
The ten lords a-leaping were the ten commandments.
The eleven pipers piping stood for the eleven faithful disciples.
The twelve drummers drumming symbolized the twelve points of belief in the Apostles' Creed.

## Mary's Significant Role in the Life of Blessed Dina Bélanger

The Mother of God plays a significant role in the mystic life of Bl. Dina Bélanger. Although Christ is at the center of her spirituality and she is transported into the heart of the Most Blessed Trinity, she never loses her focus on the Blessed Virgin Mary. To the last, the Blessed Virgin Mary keeps appearing in her autobiography. In 1924 AD, the Blessed Virgin Mary's motherly love is revealed to Blessed Dina. The most ardent and devoted love of an earthly mother is cold compared to the flames of love of the Immaculate Heart of Mary. On 4 August 1925 AD, Blessed Dina discerns the Blessed Virgin Mary's general role as mediatrix of all graces. On 18 January 1928 AD, she beholds how the Blessed Virgin Mary offers her Divine Son to the Heavenly Father with one hand and how with the other she dispenses the treasures of the Most Sacred Heart of Jesus to souls.

On 29 July 1925 AD, she is overwhelmed by the Blessed Virgin Mary's beauty that she is allowed to gaze upon. No masterpiece of human art can in any way compare to and convey the delight of her appearance, her kindliness, her compassion, the gracefulness of her smile. In a different part of her autobiography, Blessed Dina describes her interior disposition when receiving Holy Communion. She imagines receiving the Eucharistic Lord from the hands of the Blessed Virgin Mary. When making her thanksgiving, she has the Blessed Virgin Mary speaking while she herself is content with listening, with uniting herself to the Savior, to contemplate and love Him.

This practice is based upon a recommendation by St. Louis Marie de Montfort who writes in his *Golden Book*: "After Holy Communion, close your eyes and recollect yourself. Then usher Jesus into the Heart of Mary: You are giving him to his Mother who will receive him with great love and give him the place of honor, adore him profoundly, show him perfect love…" (p. 376).

(Engelbert Recktenwald, *Die Selige aus Kanada - Dina Bélanger und ihre Sendung*, 51-52, unable to locate English source).

## Blessed Dina Bélanger's Horror of Passing Judgment

I had an indescribable horror of criticism, of passing judgment on the actions of others. I was struck by the following truth which I heard expressed: As you have judged your neighbor, so will God judge you. Judge not, and you will not be judged.

It was a divine light, and with it, I received the strength to make a resolution always to judge others favorably, a strength that has enabled me to remain faithful to my resolution to this day. How admirable is the power of grace! In my thoughts, I attributed the best intentions to everyone, whether their actions were good or reprehensible. If their guilt seemed obvious, I found excuses. In speaking, I would defend those who were not present; how I suffered when of necessity I had to remain silent! If they were attacked in my presence, my face became serious; I would attempt by my silence to show disapproval of disparaging or unkind remarks and I would wait for a suitable moment to slip in a word and change the course of the conversation.

Yes, I have been and I still am very strict with myself on this point of fraternal charity. I was more concerned about the reputation of others than about my own. Of course, this involved sacrifice: a disregard for human respect, for what other people might say, the courage to hold to a different opinion. That is why I understand that it is God alone who acts in me and through me. Being of a shy and timid nature, how could I possibly have withstood uncharitable comments in public? No, I could not have done it, definitely not. God alone kept up the struggle. The light that was given me from above, as well as the help, are today my consolation and my hope. I have no fear of the judgments of the eternal Judge, for from that early age, I cannot remember having deliberately judged anyone. "Oh, Jesus, I beg you to continue to grant me this precious gift, and when the time comes for my soul to wing its way towards you, it will be immersed trustfully in your mercy, in spite of its many miseries."

(Blessed Dina Bélanger, *Autobiography of Dina Bélanger* (Québec City: Les Religieuses de Jésus-Marie, 1997).

## II. New Institutions, Ecclesial Charisms, Spiritual Direction

❖ Steubenville University has a strong spiritual and orthodox teaching program, along with courses during the summer. They offer retreats and an outstanding youth weekend program.
http://www.franciscan.edu/home2/Content/main.aspx

❖ Madonna House, Combermere (founded by Catherine Doherty whose cause of canonization has been introduced): one can attend programs or spend time working there, drawing from their spirituality and life of poverty. There is also opportunity for spiritual direction.
http://www.madonnahouse.org/

❖ Mariapolis with the Focolare Lay Movement (one of the great new movements in the Church), entailing a few days of workshops for youth.
http://www.mariapolis.focolare

❖ Militia Immaculata (MI), a lay sodality founded by St. Maximilian Kolbe, affords regular meetings with prayer and regular teachings given.
http://www.consecration.ca/

❖ For spiritual direction and retreats, a pre-eminent ecclesial charism is the Opus Dei. Their charism teaches how to be holy in the everyday life.
http://www.opusdei.ca/sec.php?s=228

❖ The Holy Spirit appears to be working fruitfully through the Charismatic Renewal in a way that is accessible to laity, to renew parishes, and that calls them to evangelization. We should note that Steubenville University follows this charismatic charism.

❖ For those struggling within the Church, an article by Jean Daniélou might be helpful: "I am in the Church" (available online). He describes his love of the Church. http://terryfenwick.blogspot.com/2014/04/i-am-in-church-written-by-jean-danielou.html

> Many Christians today give the impression that they do not feel at ease in the Church and that they only remain faithful to her with difficulty. I must say that my experience is contrary to theirs. The Church has never disappointed me. It is rather I who would be inclined to accuse myself of not having drawn profit enough from all that she had to offer to me.

## III. Spiritual Reading List
(Some notable works for daily spiritual life are bolded)
### Classics

St. Francis de Sales: *Introduction to the Devout Life*; *On the Love of God* (2 vols.)

St. John of the Cross: *Complete Works*; *Ascent of Mount Carmel*; *Dark Night of the Soul*

St. Teresa of Jesus: *Complete Works (ICS)*; *Life*; *Way of Perfection*; *Interior Castle*

St. John Henry Newman: *Apologia pro Vita Sua*; *Parochial & Plain Sermons*

St. Thérèse of Lisieux: ***The Story of a Soul*** (John Beevers' translation)

St. Ignatius of Loyola: *Spiritual Exercises*; *Autobiography of St. Ignatius of Loyola* (J. Olin)

St. Augustine: *Confessions*; *The City of God*; *Trinity*; *Sermons*; *Commentaries*, etc.

St. Catherine of Siena: *The Dialogue*

Jean-Baptiste Chautard: ***Soul of the Apostolate***

Adrienne von Speyr: ***John*** (Commentary on John in four volumes)

Jean-Pierre de Caussade: ***Abandonment to Divine Providence***

Thomas à Kempis: *Imitation of Christ;* Lorenzo Scupoli, *The Spiritual Combat*

St. Louis de Montfort: ***True Devotion to Mary***; ***Secret of Mary***

Luis de la Palma: ***The Sacred Passion***

Javiera del Valle: ***About the Holy Spirit***

Francis Fernandez: ***In Conversation with God*** (7-vol. meditation set)

### Recommended Works
Notable Authors: J.H. Newman, C. Marmion, R. Guardini, R.H. Benson, A. von Speyr, L. Giussani, J. Escrivá, C. Lubich, F. Sheen, R. Cantalamessa, J. Ratzinger

Jacques Philippe: (1) *Time for God*; (2) *Searching for & Maintaining Peace*; (3) *In the School of the Holy Spirit*; (4) *Interior Freedom*; (5) *The Way of Trust and Love* (St. Thérèse of Lisieux)

Timothy Gallagher (Ignatian charism): (1) *Discernment of Spirits*; (2) *The Examen Prayer*; (3) *An Ignatian Introduction to Prayer*; (4) *Spiritual Consolation*; (5) *Meditation and Contemplation:* (6) *Discernment of the Will of God*

Purity: *Virginity* (Raniero Cantalamessa); *God asks for an Undivided Heart* (Andrew Apostoli); *Every Man's Battle: Winning the War on Sexual Purity One Victory at a Time* (Stephen Arterburn, Fred Stoeker); *The Courage to be Chaste* (Benedict Groeschel)

Confession: *Guidebook for Confessors* (Michael Giesler); *Frequent Confession* (Benedict Baur); *Pardon and Peace* (Alfred Wilson)

Stages or Pillars of Interior Life: *Carmelite Spirituality in the Teresian Tradition* (Paul-Marie of the Cross); *I Want to See God: A Practical Synthesis of Carmelite Spirituality* (Marie-Eugène); *Fire Within* (Thomas Dubay); *Gospel of Contemplation* (Mary Niere); *The Impact of God: Soundings* (Iain Matthew); *Spiritual Passages* (B. Groeschel); *The 5 Pillars of the Spiritual Life: A Practical Guide to Prayer for Active People* (Robert Spitzer)

Spiritual Warfare: *Temptation & Discernment* (Segundo Galilea); *Deliverance Ministry* (ICCRS, Charismatic Renewal Doctrinal Commission); *An Exorcist Explains the Demonic* (Gabriel Amorth); *Deliverance from Evil Spirits* (Francis MacNutt); *Unbound* (Neal Lozano); *Exorcism & Church Militant* (Thomas Euteneuer); *Diary of an American Exorcist* (Stephen Rossetti); *Ransomed from Darkness* (Moira Noonan)

Education: *The Educational Philosophy of St. John Bosco* (John Morrison); *Don Bosco the Catechist* (Gian Carlo Isoardi); *The Intellectual Life* (A.G. Sertillanges)

Tradition: *Christian Spirituality in the Catholic Tradition; Spiritual Theology* (Jordan Aumann); *The Three Ages of the Interior Life* (R. Garrigou-Lagrange); **The Spirit of the Liturgy** (J. Ratzinger); *The Sanctifier* (Luis Martinez); *God or Nothing* (R. Sarah)

Books by/about Saints
**The Spirit of St. Francis de Sales** (Jean-Pierre Camus); **Life of Christ,** *Treasure in Clay*, *Seven Last Words* (F. Sheen); *Witness to Hope* (George Weigel's biography of John Paul II); **Union with God** (Columba Marmion); *Autobiography of Dina Bélanger;* **Conchita: A Mother's Spiritual Diary** (M.M. Philippon); **I Believe in Love** (Jean D'Elbée); *Testimony of Hope* (F.X.N. van Thuan)

Lives of the Saints
*Curé d'Ars* (François Trochu); *St. Dominic Savio* (St. John Bosco); **Lay Siege to Heaven**; **The Quiet Light** (Louis de Wohl); *The Man of Villa Tevere* (Pilar Urbano); *Saxum: The Life of Alvaro del Portillo* (J. Coverdale); *Journal of Gérard Raymond*

Marian: *True Devotion to Mary, Secret of Mary; Secret of the Rosary* (St. Louis de Montfort); **The Immaculate Conception and the Holy Spirit** (H. M. Manteau-Bonamy); **Mother Teresa: In the Shadow of Mary** (Joseph Langford)

Spiritual Direction: *Seeking Spiritual Direction* (T. Dubay); *Through Wind and Waves* (F. Fernández-Carvajal); *St. Francis de Sales, Jane de Chantal: Letters of Spiritual Direction*

Human Formation: *Getting Things Done* (David Allen books); *The 7 Habits of Highly Effective People* (Stephen Covey)

# AID 5

## Ascetical Mansions: Begging Divine Mercy for the World
*(Diary* of St. Faustina)

*This text is incorporated because it goes right to the priestly heart of Christ and of every true disciple of Christ, "to plead for mercy for the world"; and also, united with Christ's sacrifice, to be transformed into Christ.*

O my God, I am conscious of my mission in the Holy Church. It is my constant endeavour to plead for mercy for the world. I unite myself closely with Jesus and stand before him as an atoning sacrifice on behalf of the world. God will refuse me nothing when I entreat him with the voice of his Son. My sacrifice is nothing in itself, but when I join it to the sacrifice of Jesus Christ, it becomes all-powerful and has the power to appease divine wrath. God loves us in his Son; the painful Passion of the Son of God constantly turns aside the wrath of God.

O God, how I desire that souls come to know you and to see that you have created them because of your unfathomable love. O my Creator and Lord, I feel that I am going to remove the veil of heaven so that earth will not doubt your goodness.

Make of me, Jesus, a pure and agreeable offering before the face of your Father. Jesus, transform me, miserable and sinful as I am, into your own self (for you can do all things), and give me to your eternal Father. I want to become a sacrificial host before you, but an ordinary wafer to people. I want the fragrance of my sacrifice to be known to you alone. O eternal God, an unquenchable fire of supplication for your mercy burns within me. I know and understand that this is my task, here and in eternity. You yourself have told me to speak about this great mercy and about your goodness.[1]

---

[1] St. Faustina, Excerpt of *Diary* in Office of Readings for her feast day, accessed Oct. 5, 2021, http://www.liturgies.net/saints/faustinakowalska/readings.htm.

# AID 6

## Ascetical Mansions: Method of Mental Prayer (St. A. de Liguori)

*"The Lord is more pleased with one soul who strives for holiness than a thousand who lead imperfect lives"*

### *Preface*

What wisdom the saints possess! When a seminary priest was asked what he thought of a well-known speaker invited to talk about helping the poor, he surprised the questioner when he said that he thought it was just "okay," as a more positive reply was expected. He went on to justify his reaction by explaining that, being from India, he had met Mother Teresa of Calcutta three times, celebrating Mass for her once, and that when she spoke, he felt as if God Himself was speaking through her. A number of people were present for her visit to Toronto when her community opened their Toronto house, and the memory of her visit is still etched in the seminary priest's heart. He immediately noticed a difference with Mother Teresa: she was praying the Rosary before, during, and after the welcome rite in the Church; she spoke from the veranda about Mary and giving out Miraculous medals. We find a similar effect from reading St. Alphonsus de Liguori's explanation on Mental Prayer, in comparison to common talks heard on *Lectio Divina*, it was inspiring; it feels as if St. Alphonsus was speaking with the very mind of God, recalling remarks about Jesus' speaking with authority, unlike that of the scribes. *There is a depth and fire to his words that will be apparent to the reader.*

### *Necessity of Prayer*

To begin, we should consider first the importance of prayer in general. He teaches us that, with prayer, we defeat the devil, and without prayer, the devil wins. St. Teresa of Avila said: "I am convinced that the Lord will lead to salvation the soul that perseveres in prayer, no matter how many sins the devil will urge against her." Thus, the devil wishes above all else to prevent souls from devoting themselves to prayer. St. Teresa declares that the devil knows that he has lost the soul who perseveres in prayer. It is love which unites a soul with God but it is prayer or meditation which enkindles that love of God in souls. "In my thoughts a fire blazed up" (Ps 39:4). [p. 176]

One particular benefit of prayer is self-knowledge. St. Teresa of Avila wrote to the Bishop of Osma: "We may think we have no imperfections, but they will appear clearly as soon as God opens our eyes in prayer." St. Bernard wrote that those who do not meditate lack self knowledge and have no awareness of their own limitations. Prayer, he says, "orders our affection and directs our action." If people abandon prayer, they will soon cease loving

Jesus Christ. Prayer is like a hearth in which the fire of divine love is kindled and kept blazing. St. Catherine of Bologna teaches, "Anyone who does not devote time to prayer slips the leash that binds them to God, and when the devil finds someone like that cool in God's love, he has no difficulty in enticing them to eat the poisoned fruit." [p. 145].

### *I. Preliminary Points*

(1) <u>Location</u>: Prayer ideally should be prayed in the church, that is, before the Blessed Sacrament. If this is not possible, one can pray anywhere.

(2) <u>Time & Length</u>: The best time is in the morning, so that we can move from prayer to our duties. But ideally, we should pray both in the morning and in the evening. The length should be half an hour, and we can increase it if we like.

(3) <u>Themes</u>: St. Alphonsus' inspirations leap immediately to the heart of spiritual life. The most important theme we ought to dwell upon is *the Passion of our Lord*, a fount of wisdom, light, and strength. St. Francis de Sales calls Calvary "the hill of lovers." All those who love Jesus Christ often resort to this mountain where they breathe the very air of divine love. The second important theme to meditate upon is the *Last Things* (death, judgment, heaven, hell), to meditate upon eternity and our eventual death. It can be particularly useful to imagine ourselves on our deathbed, kissing the cross and on the point of entering eternity. We could add here the importance of meditating on *the love of God* as well. He insists that we should, like St. Teresa of Avila, bring a book with us.

(4) <u>Effects</u>: Love of God; knowledge of self; avoiding traps of the devil.

### *II. Structure and Method*
A synthesis of St. Alphonsus' teaching (with author's comments)

#### Two Types of Mental Prayer

(A) **Lectio Divina**:
    (i) *Lectio* (Reading)
    (ii) *Meditatio* (Meditating)
    (iii) *Oratio* (Praying, dialoguing with God)
    (iv) *Contemplatio* (Contemplation, God's action of "lifting" the soul to Himself)

(B) **Ignatian Meditation:** Enter the Gospel scene to identify with one of the characters with our imagination (e.g., becoming St. Mary Magdalene to understand something of the Resurrection; become a shepherd to enter into the Nativity mystery). St. Ignatius teaches us to compose the scene, and to remain in a mystery as long as it moves us.

#### Method

Like a book, a meditation is composed of three parts: "Preparation" (Introduction); "Meditation" (Body); "Conclusion" (Conclusion).

*1. Preparation*
- ❖ Humility: Act of humbling oneself
- ❖ Presence of God
- ❖ Petition to the Holy Spirit, Blessed Virgin Mary, St. Joseph, Guardian Angel, Patrons
- ❖ *Hail Mary* (for help of our Lady) and *Glory be* (acknowledgement)

*2. Meditation: Lectio Divina or Ignatian-Type*
- ❖ Reflection: This seems to encompass *Lectio* and *Meditatio*
  *Choose subjects most conducive to devotion, spend more time on texts that move us*
- ❖ 3 Great Acts: This encompasses both *Oratio* and *Contemplatio*: engage in acts of will, petition, or resolution
  - ➤ Affections
  - ➤ Petition
  - ➤ Resolution (important to put inspirations into practice)

St. Alphonsus de Liguori strongly encourages us to make these acts, even in natural contemplation (when we have active and not passive contemplation). These are exercises of our heart, and we also need to ask for graces; for only if we "ask" shall we receive.

*3. Conclusion*
- ❖ Thanksgiving
- ❖ Resolution: This is very important, for which resolutions must be very concrete
- ❖ *Pater Noster, Ave Maria*

What follows is how St. Alphonsus de Liguori enriches mental prayer by linking it with the stages of the interior life, correlating them with the interior journey of St. Teresa of Jesus and St. John of the Cross.

### III. Stages of Prayer, with Purifications

We begin with meditation and are gradually led to the superior contemplation, which is quite different. In meditation, we find God as a result of our mental efforts; in contemplation, God is present to us without these mental efforts. In meditation we employ acts of our own faculties; in contemplation it is *God who is active and we are the recipients of the graces which He pours into our souls without effort on our part*. The divine love and light which fills our souls disposes us to contemplate the goodness of God, who will bless us with His gifts.

## A. 3 Main Stages of Prayer in Ascent to God

### 1. Natural Recollection

There are two levels of Recollection. The first is also called (a) <u>active recollection</u>, and it is primarily, with the aid of grace, *what we can do ourselves*. The state of recollection occurs when one's intellect is able to ponder deeply some mystery or eternal truth, outside the soul, as it were. Without conscious effort, untroubled by external distractions and totally absorbed within itself, experiencing at the same time, a deep sense of serenity, the soul is able to concentrate on the mystery or the eternal truth in question.

(b) <u>Contemplative repose or loving attention to God</u> is virtually the same except that now the soul is focused on some spiritual thought and *absorbed in itself, feels itself gently attracted to God*. Against the advice of some mystics to leave aside meditation and not make acts of love, offering, or resignation to God's will, St. Alphonsus de Liguori strongly encourages that the person praying in this state of activity, while there is no need of "meditating" (second step), *should make acts of the will in this state of deep recollection* (unless one has achieved the exalted state of *passive contemplation*).

Fr. Segneri is quite correct when he insists that, when God takes the initiative in speaking and working in us, we should be *silent and leave aside our own efforts, doing nothing beyond turning ourselves willingly and lovingly toward Him*. But when God does not speak to us, *we must take whatever steps we can to unite ourselves with Him*, namely, by meditations, affections, prayers, and resolutions. But we should make those acts which flow from us gently and without doing violence to ourselves. St. Francis de Sales teaches us to make a number of acts of love within a determined space of time, St. Jane Frances de Chantal used to make 50 acts of love in a day.

### 2. Contemplation: God's power grasps us

There are two levels. *After the purification of the senses*, the Lord grants the soul the grace of <u>contemplation</u>. In *<u>affirmative</u> (positive) contemplation*, the soul *without any effort on its part through divine illumination perceives immediately some created truth*, such as the torment of hell or the happiness of heaven, or some uncreated truth, such as the divine attributes of mercy, love, power, or goodness. In the state of *<u>negative</u> contemplation*, the soul is aware of the divine perfections in a somewhat *confused and general way and not individually*, although this gift does convey knowledge of the divine goodness with much greater clarity.

- ❖ **Supernatural Recollection**: *God's illumination* is poured directly into our hearts.

This supernatural recollection comes from God by way of an extraordinary grace which leaves the soul in a passive state. This *infused* recollection brought about by an **illumination**, which the Lord pours into the soul, arouses in the soul a wonderful sense of love of God. The soul should not be forced to abandon that peaceful discursive communication which God's inspiration may suggest. Nor should the soul strive to reflect on anything particular or to make any resolutions, nor pray curiously into the nature of the recollection being experienced. *Rather the soul should allow itself to be directed by God to reflect on whatever He inspires, and to repeat these acts which the soul knows are due to divine inspiration.*

- ❖ **Prayer of Quiet**: *God's love* is poured directly into our heart, bypassing the senses.

**God's love** is communicated directly to the spirit in the *very center of the soul*. And this love is often so ardent that it communicates itself even to the external sense. Very often the soul possesses *the prayer of quiet without any external sense of sweetness*. St. Teresa of Avila says that not all the powers are suspended. Certainly, *the will is bound*, in the sense that it is *unable to love any other object except God* who draws the soul to Himself. The intellect and memory or imagination often remain *free* and can roam around. St. Teresa of Avila advises the soul not to be upset by this: "Let the soul make fun of these thoughts and reject them as foolishness and remain undisturbed in the set of quiet. Since one's will is dominant it will bring one's imagination under control without any further effort on the part of the soul." *But if the soul gives himself over to reflection, he will lose the prayer of quiet without any further effort. Souls should refrain even more in this prayer of contemplation from making resolutions or any other acts involving their own choice. They should only elicit those acts toward which God is gently attracting them.*

**3. Union. There are 3 levels** (developed in next pages):

- ❖ Simple

- ❖ Nuptials (betrothal, engagement)

- ❖ Spiritual marriage

## B. 2 Stages of Purification to Attain Prayer of Infused Contemplation

Before He leads a soul into the *prayer of contemplation*, the Lord usually permits a soul to be purified by undergoing a period of aridity or desolation which is called *spiritual purification*. This purifies the soul from any imperfections which would hinder the gift of contemplation. There are two types of aridity, one which affects our senses (Dark Night of the Senses) and one which affects the soul or spirit (Dark Night of the Soul).

### *1. Dark Night of the Senses*
There are two types of sensible aridity, *natural* and *supernatural*. (i) Natural aridity brings with it a certain disgust for spiritual matters, and a certain darkness or sense of obscurity which, however, is more or less of a transient nature (desolation?). (ii) Supernatural aridity leaves the soul in a deeper sense of darkness, which is of longer duration and seems to deepen with each passing day. These souls, though they have no desire for creatures and have their thoughts firmly fixed on God with a determination and a great desire to love Him above all, nevertheless feel themselves incapable of doing so on account of their imperfections, which seem to be the reason why they have become displeasing to God. They still endeavour to lead a virtuous life.

This troublesome supernatural aridity is, nevertheless, a movement of God's grace, a divine illumination which brings with it both suffering and darkness. These would desire to **unite** themselves with God spiritually, but are *unable to do so because their senses and their souls are not yet free from sensible attractions*. Natural imaginings, ideas, and representations fill their minds. This aridity, moreover, causes the soul painful obscurity which, at the same time, can be positively beneficial since it helps to detach the soul from all sensible pleasures, both natural and spiritual. In this state souls consequently acquire a deep awareness of their own *misery* and their inability to perform any good act by their own power. They acquire, at once, a reverential fear of God and a great veneration for Him.

The confessor should help these souls to *understand God's action within them and to see this as preparation for great graces*. They should not omit any form of discursive meditation and instead humble themselves in God's presence, offer themselves totally to Him, and resign themselves to accepting His will, which always works for our good.

### *2. Dark Night of the Soul*
After the purification of the *senses*, the Lord usually grants the grace of contemplation, sometimes called "joyous contemplation" or the grace of supernatural recollection, quiet, and union. However, after the grace of

recollection and quiet and before the gift of union, the Lord purifies the soul further by *aridity of the spirit* or desolation by which He leads the soul to the **death of all self**. The Dark Night of the Senses results in the lack of all *sensible devotions* (desires?).

The Dark Night of the Soul is a divine illumination which leads souls to recognize their own *nothingness*, with the result that they experience excruciating sufferings in themselves. Even though they are more determined than ever to overcome themselves in everything and to be ever attentive to please God, they become more and *more conscious of their own imperfections*. They feel *rejected* by God, even abandoned by Him, on account of their ingratitude for all the graces they have received. Their acts of devotion, their prayers, communions, acts of penance, bring *no sense of satisfaction*. Only with great difficulty and at the cost of overcoming themselves can they continue to perform these acts of virtue. Instead of feeling meritorious, these acts seem to be worthy of *condemnation* and seem only to render the soul more hateful in God's sight. It happens frequently that souls in this state feel that they hate God, who accordingly rejects them as His enemies. They experience the very pains of the *damned* since they feel rejected by God.

In addition, the Lord sometimes *permits a thousand other temptations to accompany this desolation of spirit, temptations to impurity, anger, blasphemy, disbelief, and above all despair*. In the midst of all this, these tortured souls are unable to realize that they have, in fact, rejected these temptations; they fear they have consented and so their sense of rejection by God increases. The spiritual darkness in which they find themselves *deprives these souls of all sense of being determined to resist temptations* or leaves them, at best, in a *state of doubt*. A confessor should counsel them to have no fear or timidity, but to trust ever more and more in God, quoting the saying of St. Teresa of Avila that *no one loses God without being aware of it*. He should assure the penitent that all those temptations to blasphemy, unbelief, impurity, and despair are not sins but suffering, *which, if patiently borne, bring the soul nearer and nearer to God*. St. Teresa of Avila says that *"It is in aridity and temptations that the Lord tests His genuine lovers. Even if aridity lasts the whole of their lives, these souls should not abandon prayer since the time will certainly come when they will be fully rewarded."* They should remain steadfast and look forward to special graces from God, who is leading them securely in the way of the Cross.

The confessor should encourage these souls to do three things:
(i) They should humble themselves before God by admitting that they deserve these sufferings on account of their past infidelities.

(ii) They should resign themselves entirely to the will of God and express their willingness to accept all these trials and even greater ones for as long as God wishes.

(iii) They should abandon themselves, as if dead to self, into the arms of Divine Mercy and commit themselves at the same time to the protection of our Lady, Mother of Mercy and Consolation of the Afflicted.[1]

## Appendix: Carmelite Method of St. Teresa of Jesus (D. Chowning)[2]

St. Thérèse wrote: "For me, prayer is a surge of the heart; it is a simple look turned toward heaven, it is a cry of recognition and of love, embracing both trial and joy." Thus prayer is primarily a surge or aspiration of the heart. It is in this sense that St. Teresa of Jesus sees that the greatest way of attaining union with Christ is through prayer. Fr. Daniel Chowning explains that methods of prayer (e.g., Ignatian) are not prayer itself. We have to remember that prayer is God's work, His action within us. St. Teresa sees mental prayer as "nothing other than the intimate sharing between friends; it means taking time frequently to be with the one we know loves us." Thus, prayer is essentially "**friendship with Christ**": it is becoming aware of His presence within or beside us; and is thus not a work of the head but of the heart, of love. She had great difficulty with discursive meditation until she was 23 years old when she read Francisco de Osuna's *The Third Spiritual Alphabet*, that taught her this simple method of centering on Christ. She understood that friendship requires time (fidelity), it is not for the perfect but everyone, and is about coming to experience God's love for us.

Thus, most important is presence to Christ: to cultivate a **sense of Christ's presence and to fix our hearts on Him**. The steps for mental prayer can be summarized as follows. *Preparation*: First, quiet our minds, letting go of our preoccupations. *Meeting the Lord*: Then quietly sit with Jesus, aware of His presence within. To remain attentive to Jesus' presence, we can use scenes from Scripture (or a good book), to recall that the same Christ is now present within us. Simply look at Him with the eyes of faith, and be aware that He is looking at us. *Intimate Sharing*: We may be moved to speak to Him, e.g., sharing our concerns or our love for Him. We may "experience a deep peace, or recollection, or communion with Jesus. Rest in this deep communion as long as it lasts. Do not cling to it." *Conclusion*: Thanksgiving, oblation, petition. Thus, prayer is essentially friendship or intimacy with Christ, which we try to extend to the rest of the day.[3]

---

[1] St. Alphonsus de Liguori, *Alphonsus Liguori: Selected Writings*, 143-150; 166-181; 302-312.
[2] For Ignatian and Carmelite schemas, see "Guide for Catholic Meditation," *Catholic Survival Guide*, accessed Dec. 19, 2021, https://catholicsurvival.guide/guide-for-catholic-meditation/.
[3] Daniel Chowning, "Created for Love: A Retreat on St. John of the Cross."

# AID 7

## Mystical Mansions: Abandonment Synthesized (de Caussade)[1]

### *I. Living the Path of Abandonment*

#### A. Living Abandonment in the Present Moment

*1. Three Duties of Each Present Moment:* (i) soul accepts the present moment events; (ii) fulfills the duty of the present moment; and (iii) acts on the inner promptings from the Holy Spirit.

*2. Slave, Forgets Self: The Servant-slave seeks only to please the Master (introduced in Section II).* Each baptized soul has been bought and has no rights. He is like a slave with his eyes only on the Master and gives no thought to himself. He finds delight only in God's glory and His will. He does not follow his senses or reason but his faith, which allows him to rise above the storms that seem to threaten to destroy his humanity.

*3. The 90%-10% paradigm applied here.* There are two levels: (i) our acting in God: foundation of our plan of life (10%); (ii) God acting in us: now we focus on the Holy Spirit's leading in each present moment (90%). The soul walks in the darkness of faith, with God leading Him by the hand moment by moment. This converges with St. Thérèse's path in her desire to be little so that the Father would take care of all for her.

#### B. Mystical Mansions have Different Focus from Ascetical Mansions

*1. Beyond heroism and asceticism:* St. Escrivá focuses on the small things:

> But, I must remind you, mortification does not usually consist of great renunciations, for situations requiring great self-denial seldom occur. Mortification is made up of small conquests, such as smiling at those who annoy us, denying the body some superfluous fancy, getting accustomed to listening to others, making full use of the time God allots us… and so many other details. We find it in the apparently trifling problems, difficulties and worries which arise without our looking for them in the course of each day. (*Christ is Passing By*, n. 37)

*2. It disregards all that is happening* around it and in the world, the way the Holy Family did at Nazareth. It is a hidden path. *God looks after the abandoned souls:* "To meet a simple soul is to meet God." God looks after everything, He guides the soul in darkness so that it does not fall into traps. And God brings him into His wine cellar (Song of Songs 2:4).

---

[1] Jean-Pierre de Caussade, *Abandonment to Divine Providence*.

*3. Prayer as Being in Love:* Alvaro del Portillo describes prayer not as a duty but as "the conversation of people in love: a conversation in which there is no place for boredom or distraction; a heart-to-heart talk to which we look forward impatiently, to which we go with a hunger to get to know Jesus better and really relate to him; a conversation conducted with the delicacy of a soul in love and which ends with a renewed desire to live and work only for the Lord" (Saxum, 148). This represents the higher Mansions.

*4. Summarizing this path in advice given to a fearful deacon:* A deacon expressed fear of giving his all to God by pointing to the analogy of the fear one might feel in jumping into a pool from a diving board. Several points were suggested to him: (i) when God takes away the natural (e.g., health), *He always replaces it with supernatural gifts*; (ii) Mary and Joseph are holding him by the hand, with his guardian angel leading the way; (iii) God prepares everything, he only has to allow himself to be led; (iv) this abandonment is living the filial sonship of Jesus to the Father (a son and not a worker); (v) he can contemplate the last things (e.g. imagine his death being imminent), which makes every hour precious, asking how to make it so.

## C. It Entails Focusing only on Acting on what the Spirit Indicates

A religious congregation sent a "word" from God to the author about fixing his gaze on the Spirit and not his doubts about writing this book. The call to be a pencil in the Spirit's hand encapsulates Aid 7's abandonment.

> May my son be patient in the duties that I entrusted you and be confident in the help of my Holy Spirit. You are a pencil in my Hand that must be docile to my promptings. Don't worry about the poverty of your writing but be confident in the power of my Spirit who opens the mind of my disciples to let them come into communion with my Love and be united to my will. Be happy to work for the works of the Lord because so you manifest concrete charity. Be happy to have at your side, my Mother who is your Mother, Mother of the Word. She will guide you and protect you. Word of the Lord to his little servant!

*1. Digression: Being Troubled by Small Issues but not Changing or Growing*
"There is only one thing necessary" (Jesus to Martha). In this path of abandonment in the present moment, all we have to do is to put into practice whatever the Spirit is inspiring in us in that moment. When one is constantly troubled about some area, it may mean that that person is constantly examining himself and having self-recriminations and self-accusations, but not changing, growing. This common habit of being troubled but not being docile to the Spirit is the failure to do the "one thing necessary," to act as Jesus' disciple: "Therefore, everyone who hears these words of Mine, and

acts on them, will be like a wise man who built his house on the rock" (Mt 7:24; cf. Lk 6:47-49). The presupposition is that God is the Architect who is providentially guiding all the events of life to guide and form us and that our responsibility, like that of a little child with his Father, is simply to be led by the hand each moment. In doing this, he is not to focus on how he is doing or on his weaknesses but to simply put into practice that which is being shown that will lead him to sanctity. It is a trap therefore to be constantly examining one's conscience, when *all that is needed is to act upon* that which God is pointing out.

*2. People do not Submit to God, Holding on to their Way*
Going to spiritual direction without the primary focus on acting on the Spirit's counsels can lead to little progress. One revered senior priest told seminarians, "If you change one thing each year, you will become a saint." Sr. Madeleine of St. Joseph gets to the heart of why many fail to climb the Mystical Mansions: a lack of denial of self. The soul is tempted to focus on *actions* and not on the interior act of *subordination* to God, "love is a submission."[2] It does not matter how many weaknesses we have, the only thing that matters is submission. It seems that people do not change! We are to have no opinions but the Spirit's opinions, no desires but the Spirit's desires (penance, apostolate, reading), no hopes but the Spirit's hopes, no plans for the future but the Spirit's plans; and thus to be like Christ.

We can learn from the wisdom of Dietrich Bonhoeffer about "cheap grace" and "costly grace." One of the most quoted parts of the book *The Cost of Discipleship* (*The Cost of Following* in the German original) deals with the distinction which Bonhoeffer makes between "cheap" and "costly" grace.

> Cheap grace is the preaching of forgiveness without requiring repentance, baptism without church discipline, Communion without confession. Cheap grace is grace without discipleship, grace without the cross, grace without Jesus Christ.
> Cheap grace is to hear the gospel preached as follows: "Of course you have sinned, but now everything is forgiven, so you can stay as you are and enjoy the consolations of forgiveness." The main defect of such a proclamation is that it contains no demand for discipleship.
> In contrast to cheap grace, costly grace confronts us as a gracious call to follow Jesus, it comes as a word of forgiveness to the broken spirit and the contrite heart. It is costly because it compels a man to submit to the yoke of Christ and follow him; it is grace because Jesus says: "My yoke is easy and my burden is light." (Wikipedia, s.v. "The Cost of Discipleship")

## D. Concrete Examples of Living the Higher Path

---

[2] Sr. Madeleine of St. Joseph, *Within the Castle*, 48.

## *1. Concrete Examples*

On the spiritual level, there are two basic sets of Mansions: Ascetical and Mystical. The Ascetical focuses on duty, asceticism and austerity, and heroism; the Mystical focuses on living as a son or daughter of God by abandonment and being led by the Holy Spirit, as Jesus did. This is the path of St. Francis de Sales, treated in *Mystical Incarnation: "You are my Son, the Beloved"* and already covered in Homily 7. St. Francis de Sales looked upon fasting, heroism, asceticism, and great missionary works for God like great virtues that hovered over the cross at Calvary and that attracted much attention. But his virtues of preference were the "little virtues" that are like shrubs found at the bottom of the cross, fertilized by the blood flowing from the cross: humility, meekness, gentleness, patience, cheerfulness, self-forgetfulness, etc. These enabled him to be full of charity and understanding of others, to be always available. He would even unvest before Mass in order to see someone who wanted his attention. This Nazareth path allowed the Spirit to live in him in all things, as with Jesus.

Concretely, this path entails a dispossession of oneself, such that one is led by the Spirit. It is to have no hopes or plans, no desires, no ideas, but only the Spirit's plans, desires, and reasoning. It means that, apart from the necessary human planning, a principal, priest, superior, or bishop allows Mary (spouse of Spirit) to be the principal, pastor, superior, or bishop, and each be merely the secretary. This means that, instead of our usual moving ahead with our own good ideas, it entails a constant listening to what Mary and the Spirit are saying and acting only on these inspirations. For daily life, it is to live like Fr. Cantalamessa, consulting God in everything we do (making a trip or purchase, p. 83). In inner healing ministry, it is to consult the Spirit even at *each step*, "What next, O Holy Spirit?" So we "hear" and then "act," over and over again. A radical example of its sublime power is the Spirit "possessing" St. Matthew to produce the "Word of God" (Gospel of Matthew) that feeds the Church and is employed in the liturgy.

## *2. Specific Aspects of Abandonment: Self-Forgetfulness, Cross, Charity*

An exercise for following this path of abandonment is to focus primarily (90%) on higher aspects. These comprise especially self-forgetfulness, so as to be concerned about, and to be available for, helping others;, e.g., to give them understanding, excusing weaknesses. Instead of focusing on poverty, a simplicity of lifestyle may be superior. The latter entails, like a large family with one income, buying not the cheapest but what is good quality and value, and then making things last and taking care of one's possessions. A good Catholic mother can offer some small mortification in Lent, but St. Escrivá proposes putting much greater priority on making her home a pleasant and happy place as proposed by one saint (well-ordered, full of cheerfulness, good meals, and full of understanding). We find that those attached to their own ideas will doggedly argue for their rights, that "there is a both/and" (e.g., making a crusade about anti-vaccinations while Ukraine is being attacked), forgetting that docility to the Spirit is 90%.

The lower Mansions focus on having good health and energy to do many things for God; the abandoned soul, living in the Mystical Mansions, accepts crosses, like sickness and humiliations. The abandoned one, who is often in poor health, sees this as the will of God, and trusts Him. When a few of St. Thérèse's sisters expressed concern for her health as she was dying, she told them that God the Father knew what was best. Blessed Alvaro del Portillo had a similar sentiment: "'God knows better.' We men have little understanding of how his fatherly and gentle care leads us towards him" (Preface, *Friends of God*). St. M. Kolbe taught that the infirmary was the heart of his City of the Immaculate in Poland and that the sick did the most to promote the cause of evangelization.

Those in whom "God lives" at the Unitive Mansions encounter trials that mirror St. Thérèse's: death of her mother and departures of her sisters to Carmel, serious illness in adolescence, extreme sensitivity, initially unable to enter Carmel, mission precludes becoming a missionary, her volunteering to join a new Carmel in Vietnam not accepted, health woes, falling asleep during her daily meditations, dementia of her father, early death. The robust apostle of Christ can have solid health, travel much for evangelization, is able to assist the poor or sick, engages busily in apostolate; the abandoned soul often lacks good health, may be unable to sleep well, can be restricted in apostolic work and feel useless. The latter profile may describe the retired Pope Benedict XVI in his frailty and contemplative prayer for the Church, yet which may far surpass his past fruitfulness as former-reigning pope.

The abandoned soul also lives universal charity. For "Charity is the soul of faith, makes it alive; without love, faith dies" (St. Anthony of Egypt). We are not be concerned about what we eat or drink (Jesus' words) nor about the future, but with sanctifying our work today to contribute to the salvation of souls and to be at the side of those living their Calvaries on earth. We ought to imitate Dorothy Day, who understood that the "Church was the Church of the poor," and that we are not to see charity as merely handouts, but a solidarity owed to the poor in their worth and dignity (*The Long Loneliness*). We rise above concern for our family to have compassion on God's children whose lives are endangered (e.g., millions of refugees; those in famine or war-torn areas; children with AIDS or child soldiers).
Jean-Pierre de Caussade, in *Abandonment to Divine Providence*, identifies the heart of abandonment: pure love through detachment (Ch. 4, n. 2, p. 74):

What we learn by these teachings [of God] is that there is nothing good except God. To know this *we must get rid of all we hold dear. We must strip ourselves of everything.* We cannot be settled in the state of pure love until we have experienced a lot of setbacks and many humiliations. We must reach the state when all that *the world contains ceases to exist and God is everything to us.* Now for this to happen, God destroys all our personal affections [e.g., devotions, guidance of others, our plans]. (emphasis added)

Thus, this path is that of "pure love" that presupposes losing all so that God becomes everything: "there is nothing good except God." We must strip ourselves of all attachments, "we must get rid of all we hold dear." We have to experience "a lot of setbacks and many humiliations," such that "all that the world contains ceases to exist and God is everything for us…. Thus we have two duties to fulfill: we actively seek to carry God's will into effect and passively accept all that his will sends us" (n. 3, pp. 74, 75).

## II. "Sold as Slaves without any Rights to Please the Master"

This text is presented because it identifies the secret of attaining holiness through abandonment only, thus allowing God to do the rest. But who can live this abandonment? "A holy soul is one which, by the help of grace, has freely submitted to the will of God…" *God arranges everything as an architect plans a building,* and all we need is "complete and utter abandonment to the will of God." De Caussade uses a helpful image of seeing ourselves *as sold as slaves* and having no rights. This means that we are free to forget ourselves and only seek to please God, once we have done the duties of our state of life. Elsewhere, de Caussade uses the same image of a slave, who only thinks of the Master's interests and nothing of his own.

> "Offer sacrifice in the right spirit and trust in the Lord" (Ps. 4:5). Which is to say that the great and firm foundation of the spiritual life is the *offering of ourselves to God and being subject to his will in all things.* We *must completely forget ourselves,* so that we regard ourselves as an object which has been sold and over which we no longer have any rights. We find all *our joy in fulfilling God's pleasure* — his happiness, his glory and the fact that he is our great and only delight. Once we have this foundation all we need to do is spend our lives rejoicing that God is God and being so wholly abandoned to his will that we are quite *indifferent* as to what we do and equally indifferent as to what use he makes of our activities. Our main duty is to abandon ourselves, once we have faithfully discharged all the proper duties of our state of life, of course, for the way in which we fulfill these duties will be the measure of our holiness.

But how can we not be troubled by the crosses of life? De Caussade teaches us that we must rise above the inevitable fears and troubles of life and "soar like an eagle above these clouds, with our eyes fixed on the sun and its rays, which are our duties." We are not to be governed by our feelings but by faith through which we rise above these things.

> By that I mean *we should never think of ourselves but be continually occupied with loving and obeying him*. We must put aside all those fears, those uneasy broodings, those qualms of conscience, and those anxieties which can arise from the concern we have for achieving holiness and our salvation. As God wants to look after all our affairs, let us leave them all to him so that we can concentrate our whole attention on him.... Let us take good care not to get foolishly involved in all those fears and doubts, like paths leading nowhere, only tempt us to wander on and on until we are hopelessly lost. Let us leap over this maze of self-love instead of trying to explore its alleys.
>
> So come! Never mind weariness, illness, lack of feeling, irritability, exhaustion, the snares of the devil and of men, with all that they create of distrust, jealousy, prejudice and evil imaginings. *Let us soar like an eagle above these clouds, with our eyes fixed on the sun and its rays, which are our duties*. We cannot help being aware of all these evils, of course, and we cannot be indifferent to them, but let us never forget that ours is not a life governed by our feelings. We must live in those upper reaches of the spiritual life where God and his will are active in a process which is eternal and unchanging. There, he who is uncreated, immeasurable and cannot be described by human words, will keep us far removed from all the shadows and turmoil of the world. We shall feel through our senses countless disturbances, it is true, but they will all disappear like the clouds in a windswept sky. God and his will are the eternal objects who captivate every faithful soul; and when the day of glory arrives they will be our true happiness. Here on earth we suffer— to use the language of allegory— the attacks of monsters, owls and savage beasts. But terrible though these attacks are, *behind them God is acting and giving something of the divine* which will give us the brilliance of the sun, for here below both body and soul are *refined and fashioned like gold and iron, linen and gems*.... The truly faithful soul, well versed in all the secrets of God, lives in peace, and, instead of being frightened by what happens to it, is comforted, for it is quite, quite certain *that God is guiding it. It accepts all things as a manifestation of God's grace, ignores itself and thinks only of what God is doing. Love inspires it to perform its duties more carefully and faithfully*. A soul completely abandoned to God sees nothing clearly except the action of grace, apart, that is, from the slight defects which grace can turn to good account.[3] (emphasis added)

---

[3] Jean-Pierre de Caussade, *Abandonment to Divine Providence*, Ch. IV, 73-74.

# AID 8

## Mystical Mansions: Texts by Saints & Model of Bl. Dina Bélanger

### I.    *Quotations for Abandonment in Higher Mansions*

#### 1. Spiritual Counsels (St. Claude de la Colombière)

*Saint Claude de la Colombière ranks among the masters of the spiritual life as a director of souls, including St. Margaret Mary Alacoque. Jesus told her, "Father Claude is my perfect friend and servant. His gift is to lead souls to God." This is an opportunity to tap into the wisdom of this outstanding Jesuit. His is a wisdom that goes beyond a legalist mode of determining our degree of sinfulness to the deeper path of the heart that we find in figures like St. Francis de Sales.*

### Humility and Simplicity

Anyone who thinks of what he is, what he has been, and what he can do of himself will find it difficult to be proud. To shatter pride it is enough to remember that the first sign of real virtue is to consider self as nothing at all. We have only to look at Jesus Christ who, emptying himself, gave all glory to his Father.

If people praise me, it is a mistake, an injustice done to God. People do not think so highly of us as we imagine: they know our faults, even those we do not see ourselves.

If God uses me for great things, he should be praised and thanked for making use of such a poor instrument, but I myself am not on that account any better; it might even happen that I shall be damned after having helped to save others.

We should imitate Our Lady: she acknowledged that God had done great things for her and that all generations would call her blessed, but instead of attributing anything to herself she says: "Magnificat anima mea Dominum" (Lk 1:46)....

We have no reason to despise anyone. A humble man sees only his own faults. It is a sign of little virtue to notice the imperfections of others. A person may be imperfect today who in a little while, recognizing this, may rise to great sanctity.

It is very necessary to walk with great circumspection, humility, and distrust of self in directing others and in one's own spiritual life. We must be detached from our natural desire to make great progress; that leads to illusions and may make us indiscreet. Love of humility and abjection and a hidden and obscure life are the great remedies....

Once God is master of a heart, he does not remain idle. If you saw that you always remained the same, it would not be a good sign even though things seemed to be going on fairly well. When the world is entirely satisfied and even in admiration, a soul that is really enlightened from above finds a hundred things still with which to reproach itself and can only wonder at those who admire its virtue. I do not think there are any souls in the world with whom God is less pleased than with those who imagine they have reason to be pleased with themselves. As soon as we begin to see how lovable Our Lord is, we should have very hard hearts if we did not love him greatly; and when we love greatly, we think we have never done enough for him.

You must overcome everything by humility and simplicity. These virtues are not, as some think, the virtues of stupid people: on the contrary, stupid people are not capable of practicing them. We require a great deal of light to know ourselves and much strength to despise all that is not God so as to abandon ourselves to him and to those who govern us in his name. People who are less docile and who count on themselves because they think they know better are really greatly to be pitied. It would be a strange blindness to think there is any knowledge or prudence above the knowledge and prudence of God, so that we could be dispensed from following the teaching of the Gospel.[1]

### The Vows of Religion on Obedience

Our fervor, love of retreat and solitude, of prayer and of austerity must all be ruled by obedience. Make sure that before doing anything extra you do all that God wishes: make yourself dependent from morning till evening, and be quite certain that the most specious and holy things in appearance are horrible in God's eyes as soon as our own will is found in them. A soul which is not submissive in everything like a child is exposed to all the deceits of the devil, who has never deceived and never will deceive a truly obedient soul.

I place so much value upon this virtue that the others seem to me valueless unless they lead to it. I would rather give up all mortifications, prayers, and good works that swerve in a single point, I do not say from the orders, but even from the will of those who govern me, however slight might be the indication of that will. How can we have a single moment of repose if we do our own will? How can we live, even if all we do be holy, if we do not know if what we do be pleasing to God? And how can we know this unless all we do is ordered or approved by Superiors? I say approved and found good: for one can extort permissions and think one is doing marvels when one has forced the lot to give in to our fervor. (Letter 105, London, 1678)

The flight into Egypt, from the point of view of mere human prudence, seemed very hard and unreasonable. What was to be done among an unknown and

---

[1] This is drawn from "The Spiritual Direction of St. Claude de la Colombière," pp. 189-191, World Wisdom Online Library, accessed Oct. 5, 2021,
http://www.worldwisdom.com/public/viewpdf/default.aspx?article-title=The_Spiritual_Direction_of_Saint_Claude_de_la_Colombiere.pdf.

idolatrous people? Yet it is the will of God and therefore must be expedient: to argue about obedience, however unreasonable it seems, is to mistrust the prudence of God and to believe that with all his wisdom he gives orders which cannot be for his glory and our benefit. When orders are given in which humanly we can see no sense, a man of faith rejoices in the thought that it is God who commands and who prepares graces for us which we can only receive in secret ways unknown to us. (Retreat Notes. Lyons, 1674)

Sometimes I have felt great repugnance in obeying, but by God's grace I have conquered. I reflected that it is dangerous to make plans for oneself even in things of little importance, unless we are ready to throw them all up in order to obey or to practice charity. There is danger of being humanly attached to any occupation that it costs us to leave off, or that we would rather do than something else, or even rather do than doing nothing. We must consult God about our plans. (Retreat Notes. Lyons, 1674)

We may well admire the obedience of Saint Francis Xavier: he is told that he is to make a journey of six thousand miles: he replies that he is ready to start immediately; he did not hesitate a single moment when Saint Ignatius spoke to him— yet he had to leave relations, friends, and country for a foreign land. He did not require to be persuaded. He went without luggage, even without books. He left all joyfully, happy that Saint Ignatius had chosen him. He looked upon it as an opportunity of gaining great merit and believed that God had spoken to him through his Superior.

We, on the contrary, complain if we are asked to do things that are difficult or contrary to our inclinations; we grumble in doing them and think the Superior does not like us. Yet we ought to look upon it as a grace. If we obey only when we like what is commanded, we do it to please ourselves and not for the sake of obedience. Saint Francis Xavier submitted his judgment. He had little hope of being recalled to Europe, for he was the Apostle of the Indies, the support of religion in half the known world; besides, there seemed no reason to recall him, and he did not expect it.

When we are in a place we like and in which we think we are doing good, where we are successful in our work and useful to the house, what do we say about an order which calls us elsewhere? But it is just then that we ought to obey: it is God alone who acts against all our human reasoning perhaps, but for reasons which are unknown to us, but which will be very advantageous for us. The worst of it is we will not trust him. But the climate! the Superior! the work! Never mind. Go in God's name: "Cast all your cares upon him, for he has care of you" (1 Pet 5:7). (Retreat Notes, Lyons, 1674)[2]

---

[2] St. Claude de la Colombière, *The Spiritual Direction of St. Claude de la Colombière*, M. Philip, ed. (Ignatius Press, San Francisco, 2018).

## 2. Confidence in God
## (St. Claude de la Colombière)

*This prayer of "Perfect Confidence" was one of Bishop Attila Miklósházy's favourite prayers.*

My God, I believe most firmly that You watch over all who hope in You, and that we can want for nothing when we rely upon You in all things; therefore I am resolved for the future to have no anxieties and to cast all my cares upon You. "In peace in the self-same I will sleep and I will rest; for You, O Lord, singularly have settled me in hope."

Men may deprive me of worldly goods and of honors; sickness may take from me my strength and the means of serving You; I may even lose Your grace by sin, but my trust shall never leave me. I will preserve it till the last moment of my life, and the powers of hell shall seek in vain to wrest it from me. "In peace in the self-same I will sleep and I will rest."

*Let others seek happiness in their wealth, in their talents; let them trust in the purity of their lives, the severity of their mortifications, in the number of their good works, the fervor of their prayers; as for me, O my God, in my very confidence lies all my hope.* "For You, O Lord, singularly have settled me in hope." This confidence can never be in vain. "No one has hoped in the Lord and has been confounded." I am assured, therefore, of my eternal happiness, for I firmly hope in it and all my hope is in You. "In You, O Lord, have I hoped; let me never be confounded."

I know, I know but too well, that I am frail and changeable. I know the power of temptation against the strongest virtue. I have seen Satan fall from heaven, and pillars of the firmament totter; but these things alarm me not. While I hope in You I am sheltered from all misfortune, and I am sure that my trust shall endure for I rely upon You to sustain this unfailing hope.

Finally, I know that my confidence cannot exceed Your bounty, and that I shall never receive less than I have hoped for from You. Therefore I hope that You will sustain me against my evil inclinations, that You will protect me against the most furious assaults of the Evil One, and that You will cause my weakness to triumph over my most powerful enemies. I hope that You will never cease to love me, and that I shall love You unceasingly. "In You, O Lord, have I hoped; let me never be confounded." Amen.

## 3. Self-Forgetfulness is the Secret of Peace and Happiness
## (St. Elizabeth of the Trinity)

*Blessed Elizabeth of the Trinity, writing to Mme. Alges suffering depression and other things in her life, gives a good idea of the spirit with which she faced her illness and the depth, wisdom, and authority her suffering gave her.*

> I believe that the secret of peace and happiness is to forget oneself, to cease to be concerned with oneself. That doesn't mean not feeling one's physical or mental suffering; the saints themselves passed through these crucifying states. But they did not dwell on them; they continually left these things behind them; when they felt themselves affected by them, they were not surprised, for they knew "they were but dust"... it seems to me that God is asking you for abandonment and unlimited trust during the painful times when you feel those terrible voids. Believe at those times *He is hollowing out in your soul capacities to receive Him* [teaching of St. John of the Cross], capacities that are, in a way, as infinite as He Himself. Try then to will to be *wholly joyful under the hand that crucifies you*; I would even say that you should look at each suffering, each trial, "as a proof of love" that comes to you directly from God in order to unite you to Him.
>
> ... It seems to me that the weakest soul – even if it is the most guilty – is just the one that has the best grounds for hope, and this act by which it *forgets itself, to throw itself into the arms of God, glorifies him more and gives him more joy* than all the falling back upon self, and all the self-examination that makes it live in its wretchedness, while in its centre it possesses a Saviour who comes at every moment to cleanse it. (Letter 249)
>
> Jesus wants you to go out of yourself, to leave all preoccupations, in order *to withdraw into the solitude he has chosen for himself in the depths of your heart. He is always there, although you don't feel it; he is waiting for you and wants to establish a "wonderful communion" with you*... He, through this continual contact, can deliver you from your weaknesses, your faults, from all that troubles you... Nothing should keep you from going to him. *Don't pay too much attention to whether you are fervent or discouraged*; it is the law of our exile to pass from one state to the other like that. *Believe that he never changes, that in his goodness he is always bending over you* to carry you away and keep you safe in him. If, despite everything, emptiness and sadness overwhelm you, unite this agony with that of the master in the Garden of Olives... Think about this God who dwells within you, whose temple you are; Saint Paul speaks like this and we can believe him. *Little by little, the soul gets used to living in his sweet company, it understands that it is carrying within it a little heaven where the God of love has fixed his home. Then it is as if it breathes a divine atmosphere; I would even say that only its body still lives on earth while the soul lives beyond the clouds and veils, in him who is the unchanging one.* Do not say that this is not for you, that you are too wretched; on the contrary, that is only one more reason for going to him who saves. We will be purified, *not by looking at this wretchedness, but by looking at him who*

*is all purity and holiness*. In the saddest times, think that the divine artist is using a chisel to make his work more beautiful, and remain at peace beneath the hand that is working on you.[3]

## 4. St. Faustina on Abandonment

In a spirit of faith, St. Faustina perceived in each moment the unique treasures of divine grace and that we have already here on earth the beginning of eternal life in the human soul. She wanted to evaluate all events in life, especially difficult moments, and neighbours, in the spirit of faith, to see them as God sees them. One biographer writes:

> The spirit of faith gradually led St. Faustina to a total surrender of her whole self to God. This total gift of self and of her autonomy arose from the conviction of the merciful love of the Heavenly Father, in whose protective arms we may peacefully place ourselves.... Accepting everything from Him, she drew closer to Him through everything.... The desire to accept everything from the fatherly hand of God led Sister Faustina to complete abandonment in every circumstance in life.

This abandonment engendered in St. Faustina's heart was clearly evident on various occasions:

> I accept everything that comes my way as given me by the loving will of God, who sincerely desires my happiness. And so I will accept with submission and gratitude everything that God sends me. (*Diary* 1549).

> My most sweet Master… I will put Your gifts to the best use of which my soul is capable. Living faith will support me. Whatever the form might be under which You will send me Your grace, *I will accept it as coming directly from You, without considering the vessel in which You send it.* (*Diary* 1759).

> I have come to know Him well. God is love…. I have placed my trust in God and fear nothing. I have given myself over to His holy will; *let Him do with me as He wishes.* (*Diary* 589)[4]

---

[3] Elizabeth of the Trinity, trans. Anne Englund Nash, *The Complete Works of Elizabeth of the Trinity, Vol 2: Letters from Carmel* (Washington DC: ICS Publications, 2014), Ltr 249.
[4] *In St. Faustina's School of Trust* (Cracow: The Congregation of the Sisters of Divine Mercy, 2002), 24-25.

## 5. St. Francis de Sales
## "Be untroubled by public opinion"

Consideration of what will be said or thought of you is contrary to simplicity. This virtue, as we have said, *looks only to pleasing God*, not creatures at all.... After the simple soul has done the action that it considers it ought to do, it thinks no more about it. And if it should occur to the person what will be said or thought of him, the soul checks the thought instantly, because it will allow nothing to divert it from its one aim, namely, of dwelling on the thought of God alone, that it may love Him more and more.... We must not perpetually fear trouble, either for ourselves or for others, for trouble of itself is not sin. If I know that by going into certain society, I shall expose myself to the risk of hearing something said to me that will trouble and disturb me, I ought not to avoid going into it; but I ought to do it, armed with confidence in divine protection, certain that it will strengthen me so that I may overcome my own nature, against which I desire to make war.... But where do you think this trouble comes from, if not from a want of simplicity and especially because we often waste our time conjecturing "What will they say? What will they think?", instead of thinking only of God and of what will render us more pleasing to His goodness?... make up your mind quickly and waste no time in considering whether you ought to say it or not. We are not meant to give an hour's consideration to all the small actions of our life.

Simplicity does not meddle with what others are doing or will do; it thinks of itself. But even as it regards itself, it dwells only upon really necessary thoughts, and always turns quickly away from any others. This virtue has a close affinity to humility, which does not allow us to have a bad opinion of anyone but ourselves.

You ask how you must observe simplicity in conversation and recreation. I reply: as in all other actions, although in this particular one there should be a holy freedom and frankness in conversing upon such subjects as to serve to foster a spirit of joy and recreation. We should be quite unaffected in conversation, but at the same time not inconsiderate, for simplicity always follows the rule of the love of God. But should we happen to say some little thing that seems to us not to be received as we would wish, we must not on that account waste time in weighing and searching into all our words. No, it is indeed self-love, undoubtedly, which makes us inquire so closely whether our words and actions have been well received or not. (St. Francis de Sales, *The Art of Loving God*, 117)

## II. Model of Abandonment
## "About Blessed Dina Bélanger"

*This online summary of this remarkable mystic was added because she can be a tremendous guide to all Christians. After she graduated to become a concert pianist, Jesus called her to enter a specific religious congregation. Entering at the age of 24, she died at 32, attaining remarkable sanctity. Fr. François-Marie Léthel, professor at the Teresianum in Rome and a retreat director to the papal household, raves about her. One commentator believes that, formed by St. Thérèse, she has gone beyond her teaching. (cf. Bl. Dina Bélanger, The Autobiography of Dina Bélanger, 3<sup>rd</sup> ed.)*

Like St. Thérèse, she was asked by her superiors to write the story of her life. She obeyed quite simply, but it was a heroic effort of which she would later say: "That act cost me more than any other in my life." It is in this manuscript that we find three important practices that formed her spiritual life: The True Devotion to Mary of Louis de Montfort, the Little Way of Spiritual Childhood of St. Thérèse, and her great devotion to Jesus in the Eucharist.

During her novitiate, she formulated her ideal: "The most perfect union with God." To achieve this ideal, she cultivated interior silence and recollection, as well as the practice of constant little acts of mortification (in order to subdue her nature). She also strove to practice perfect abandonment, recognizing the Holy Will of God in all the events of life. She relied on the Virgin Mary to unite her to Jesus because she saw in Her the "quickest way to be immersed in Jesus" (149). Her motto came to be: "Love and let Jesus and Mary have their way!" Furthermore, in her efforts to achieve her ideal of perfect union, she considered it necessary to stay not only aware of Jesus' presence within her, but to allow Him to act in and through her. For this she found it necessary to strive after purity of intention: "to act out of love for Jesus alone; not seeking myself or any created thing." She also saw the need of doing all her acts in union with Jesus and thus began, at her particular examinations of conscience, to ask herself questions such as these: "Have I allowed Our Lord to act through me?" And: "Have I striven to act with the gentleness, kindness and love of Jesus? In this way, I made my small contribution to the work at hand." (155).

Her efforts were greatly rewarded by her Divine Master. As she attested: "At first it seemed He was at my side, that He was walking close by me. Then I found He was within me. I loved to speak to Him interiorly when I was out alone in the street. Then He gave me His spirit in place of my own; His judgment so that I might appreciate things, happenings, people in the way He wished. After that, He replaced my will with His own; then I felt a great strength which urged me on towards good and compelled me to refuse Him nothing" (104-105).

This mystical gift of the exchange of wills in her, Jesus called Divine Substitution. This gift consisted of Jesus substituting Himself for her in such a way, that she lived the life of Heaven while He lived in her place on earth. Her will had become so united to His that He was able to freely act in and through her as though she was another humanity for Him to operate in on earth. Thus her acts took on the value of His. The Divine Substitution seems to be a similar or the selfsame gift as seen in other modern mystics such as Venerable Concepción Cabrera de Armida of Mexico, who received the gift of Mystical Incarnation, and the Servant of God, Luisa Piccarreta of Italy, who received the gift of Living in the Divine Will.

Blessed Dina came to understand that Our Lord is seeking to bestow such gifts on other generous souls: "The Trinity of Love is seeking souls on whom It can bestow Its Divine Treasures. Infinite Goodness needs to give, to give Itself. Few are those souls who abandon themselves totally to the Sovereign Will. If God is to pour a profusion of graces on a human soul, He must find Jesus living there. A soul is too finite to contain the ocean of infinite favors; but Jesus, the Illimitable, taking the place of what is limited, can satisfy in some way the immense desire of the Heavenly Father" (212).

Our Lord also revealed: "Apart from the eternal and perfect happiness that I enjoy in my Father and in Myself, my happiness is to reproduce Myself in the souls that I created out of love. The more a soul allows Me to reproduce Myself faithfully in her, the more joy and contentment I find. The greatest joy a soul can give Me is to allow Me to raise her up to my Divinity. Yes, my little Bride, I take immense pleasure in transforming a soul into Myself, in deifying it, in absorbing it wholly into the Divinity" (335). On September 4, 1929, in the thirty-third year of her life, consumed not only with tuberculosis, but also with intense desire to be united eternally to her divine spouse, she was freed from the shackles of this earthly dwelling and that desire was forever fulfilled.[5]

Addendum: We wish to highlight that, for the Christian path to holiness, the model is that lived by the Holy Family. St. Thérèse, who lived Nazareth, revealed that she has never received any visions. She lived instead a spousal union with Christ, conformity to His will, and zeal for reparation for the love He did not receive and salvation of souls. Nevertheless, great souls, especially with universal missions, can be given mystical experiences: e.g., St. Escrivá's revelations about Opus Dei in 1928 and living in Christ's pierced right hand; Chiara Lubich's at Loreto and Paradise '49.

---

[5] "For Consecrated Souls," Sicut in Caelo, accessed October 12, 2021, http://www.sicutincaelo.org/downloads/FCS_Read.pdf. Permission was granted to reprint these pages from the Soeurs Religieuses de Jésus-Marie at Sillery in Québec City, Canada.

# AID 9

## Spiritual Warfare: Discernment of Three Spirits

Fr. Garrigou-Lagrange, in *The Priest in Union with Christ*, offers much wisdom and clear-sightedness in delineating the three spirits active in our lives: human, evil, and good spirits. The difficulty is that we can be dedicatedly serving God, and yet be following the wrong spirit. We perceive that one of the greatest needs of the Church today is *discernment of which spirit guides us*. Clearly, we discern that we must avoid being led by the evil spirit. But perhaps the main issue within the Church today is a tendency to rely, not on the Holy Spirit, but on human wisdom (human spirit), which is necessary at the natural level, but is only the foundation for the infused theological virtues and, even more, for the gifts of the Holy Spirit. Instead of following the Pharisees' predilection for living religion in a primarily human and external fashion (e.g., today's horizontalism), we should imitate St. John, the Eagle, to see things divinely (e.g., Prologue of John).

What we find amazing is how much L'Amour's novels' characters, used to represent today's predilection to the horizontal, conform not just to the human spirit, but especially to signs of the evil spirit: pride, lack of faith (with distorting truths of God), presumption of spiritual progress, touchy-feely sentimentality, seeking extraordinary phenomena, with fruits of the evil spirit (e.g., self-absorption, pride, discord, disobedience, agitation).

### *1. Divine Spirit*
Fr. Garrigou-Lagrange elaborates upon Tradition's understanding of the three spirits. He defines "spirit" as that which "signifies a special way of judging, loving, willing or acting, a mental attitude or inclination— for instance, to prayer, to penance or to contradiction…" (p. 228). We highlight a key point: "This spirit of God is at first latent in beginners and becomes **more manifest in Proficients [Illuminative] and in the perfect [Unitive].**" A key principle is that the Spirit is active primarily in the Mystical Mansions.

> In the spiritual life we have to distinguish between three kinds of spirits. The spirit of God, the spirit of the devil and the spirit of human nature…. The spirit of God is an internal prompting or tendency of the soul to judge, love, will and act in a supernatural way…. This divine spirit is, therefore, particularly evident in the promptings of the Holy Ghost which correspond to the seven gifts. This spirit of God is at first latent in beginners and becomes more manifest in Proficients [Illuminative] and in the perfect [Unitive], who are more docile to the Holy Ghost…. (p. 228. There is no need to develop this spirit, as most of the book treats of it)

## 2. Fallen Human Spirit

Let us look at the spirit of human nature in two aspects that may be prevalent in people today (describes today's horizontalism very well).

> Opposed to the spirit of God is the spirit of human nature which is characterized as an inclination to judge, will and act in an excessively human nature, following the lead of fallen nature which tends towards its own ease and advantage. (p. 228)

First, there is a tendency towards a feel-good sentimentalism and making everything about "community," "compassion" (buzzwords). This spirit, which always leads to tepidity and eventually sloth, can have this character:

> Sometimes it has a peculiar affectionate character revealing itself in sentimental attachments to creatures, in an emotional love for them which takes the place of that genuine love existing in the will. And it is but a step from romantic sentiment to carnal prudence and stupidity, even of divine things— so that he only regards their capacity to satisfy his senses or his pride. (p. 229)

Second, the spirit of human nature does not seek the heights of the spiritual life, choosing mere philanthropy and much activity:

> A soul which is influenced by this spirit will cease to make further progress and abandon the spiritual life once it has encountered its first difficulties or period of aridity. It hides its inattention to the interior life under the cloak of an energetic apostolate, devoting all its energy to external activity, which has ceased to be supernatural and has become entirely superficial. Such a person is confusing charity with philanthropy, humanism and liberalism. Gradually this natural activity loses its initial drive; it begins as a burst of energy, changes into a general hurry, and finally slows down to a leisurely pace. (p. 233)

Herein we find the great weakness, blindness, and tepidity that can infect the Church when she gives in to following the human spirit.

## 3. Evil Spirit: Devil

Now let us look at signs of the evil spirit. (i) The first of these is *pride*, especially of a sense of superiority or even false humility. The following can apply also to consecrated souls:

> *Humility* is never encouraged by this spirit, for it gradually distorts the soul's vision to see itself as greater than it really is, greater than anyone else. Almost unconsciously it makes the prayer of the Pharisee its own: "O God, I give thee thanks that I am not as the rest of men..." This spiritual pride

goes hand in hand with a false humility, which accuses itself of some evil so as to avoid being accused by others of even greater faults and in order to make them think that we are truly humble. Sometimes the evil spirit leads us to confuse humility with faint-heartedness, which is the daughter of pride and fears to run the risk of contempt [some fear their faults being revealed]. The evil spirit is also an enemy of obedience, prompting us either to open disobedience or to servility according to circumstances. (p. 239)

(ii) A second area concerns the virtue of *faith*. One of these is to distract us from the more profound truths of the faith, such as those contained in the Our Father or in the mysteries of the Rosary. It encourages us to focus on what is extraordinary, as the devil himself tempted Jesus to cast himself down from the parapet of the temple so that many may see and applaud (p. 239). With similar intent, the devil frequently suggests desires contrary to our vocations (e.g., St. John Vianney being tempted to become a contemplative). One particular and common temptation is to seek *doctrinal novelties* that do not conform to the Church's teaching (e.g., immediate resurrection after death, suppressing Christ's centrality that led to the Church's issuing *Dominus Jesus*), or the opposite temptation to hold on to archaic traditions. Here is a very striking text of Fr. Garrigou-Lagrange:

> The devil is only too well acquainted with the principle— *corruptio optimi pessima* ["The corruption of the best is the worst"]— and so he strives unceasingly to pervert a man's faith. He realizes that there is nothing worse, nothing more dangerous, nothing more worthy of condemnation than a false brand of Christianity which nevertheless retains a faint resemblance to the truth. That is why he sometimes disguises himself as Christ before revealing himself in his true character as the archenemy of Christ. (p. 240)

Fr. Garrigou-Lagrange condemns especially the falsification of the supernatural truth, as we find in *heresies and schisms*: "No one but the devil is responsible for this. Such falsification of divine faith must be likened to the act of picking up the sword to slay oneself and one's own brothers— an act of suicide and fratricide" (p. 241). These are very subtle but common temptations.

(iii) Regarding the virtue of hope, there is *presumption of spiritual progress*, bypassing self-conquest, resulting in annoyance with self and even despair:

> It is easy to find an example of this [presumption] in the desire of some people to find a quicker route to holiness than that provided by the normal development of the spiritual life through the various stages and who wish to avoid the way of humility and self-conquest in their effort for perfection. He is also quick to make us annoyed with ourselves when we realize clearly our many imperfections, and then sorrow gives way to anger— the off-

spring of pride and an effective barrier to sorrow. Presumption in its turn leads to despair, when a man recognizes the inadequacy of his own efforts for attaining the end he desires. (p. 241)

(iv) The following temptation, in the area of *charity*, is one that is prevalent today— sentimentality, being "touchy-feely," and the opposite, finding fault in others:

> As regards the virtue of *charity*, the evil spirit tries to foster other qualities which bear a misleading resemblance to that virtue. Adapting his tactics to our varied and conflicting natural inclinations, he encourages in some a false charity of sentimentality, humanitarianism, liberalism, which cloaks its excessive leniency under a guise of mercy and generosity; in others he nourishes a zeal for souls which is forever discovering faults in other people but never in themselves, always seeing the speck of dust in their brother's eye but never the beam in their own... (p. 241)

(v) There is a special area of which we must be vigilant, the seeking of any *extraordinary phenomena*. Garrigou-Lagrange warns: "It would be presumptuous on our part to crave for extraordinary graces, such as revelations or interior conversations [interlocutions].... There is a special danger in revelations which seem to refer to future events or to questions of doctrine, since they so easily give rise to deception."

In contrast, the soul that lives simply is guided deeply by the Spirit:

> But a soul which lives and perseveres in humility, self-denial and almost continual recollection often receives in accordance with the seven gifts of the Holy Ghost special inspirations which result in a wonderful blending of simplicity and prudence, humility and zeal, firmness and gentleness. The harmony and blending of the virtues are a sure sign of the presence of God's spirit. (p. 244)

(vi) *Fruits of the Evil Spirit*: The result of following the evil spirit are several. First, there is *discord and destruction of peace*, but worse yet is self-absorption, and being formed in the image of Satan in *despair and pride*:

> The man who is influenced by this spirit [Satan] chafes at every contradiction. So absorbed has he become with his own self that he practically denies the existence of anybody else and unconsciously exalts himself above all his neighbours, like a statue on a pedestal. If such a man commits a serious sin which he finds impossible to hide from others, he is upset, angry, desperate. Eventually his mind is darkened and his heart hardened. But notice the cunning of Satan.... After the sin he troubles man's conscience with thoughts of God's relentless justice, so as to drag

him down into the depths of despair. And thus he forms souls after his own likeness— despair following on pride. (pp. 241-242)

Fr. Garrigou-Lagrange points to key overall signs of the evil spirit:

Consequently, if anyone is granted sense consolations in prayer but comes away with increased self-love, higher in his own estimation than those around him, with less obedience toward his superiors and less simplicity in accepting the advice of his spiritual guide [director], that is a certain indication of the presence of the evil spirit in his sense devotion. The absence of humility, obedience and brotherly love is always a sign of the absence of the spirit of God. (p. 242)

He gives yet another three ways to discern which spirit we are following. First, "*acts which a man is suddenly called upon to perform* are a good guide to the nature of the spirit in that individual, whereas we must be careful in drawing conclusions from acts that are the result of mature deliberation." We see that the sinful woman's spontaneous act at Simon's house contrasts to the Pharisees' scheming (e.g., whether the Baptist's work was divine or human). Second, "*Suffering* is also a trustworthy guide to the secrets of a man's heart. That is why false friends never stand the test of adversity… 'The furnace tests the potter's vessels, and the trial of affliction just men' (Eccles 27:6)." Third, "*authority* reveals a man for what he is…. Now he has to show wisdom and prudence without the mediocrity of the opportunist or utilitarian, charity for all, justice, fearless courage in correcting evildoers, kindness in helping his faithful subjects" (pp. 245-246).

Msgr. Rossetti confirms that demons bring narcissism, pride, paranoia, rage, lies, discord, and despair. He has seen in possessed people demonic traits: "a snarky arrogance, a look of rage, and a narcissistic self-focus." Demons feed on our anger, unforgiveness, arrogance, disobedience, self-hatred, fear, desire for respect, which makes deliverance difficult (*Diary*, 272, 229, 223).

Resistance is the key obstacle to opening our hearts to God. Jesus condemned the Pharisees for their hardness of heart, for resisting the Holy Spirit (Mk 3:5; Acts 7:51). It is highlighted in Saul's experience when persecuting the Christians: "It hurts you to kick against the goads" (fight against God's will, Acts 26:14). Whenever we have interior resistance, we are kicking "against the goad," fighting God's will, and thus lose peace. The moment that we give in, peace floods again into our souls and a sweet surrender is experienced, a resting once more in God's arms. A sign that we are following the Holy Spirit and not the evil spirit is this acceptance of the events of life, willingness to be corrected instead of fleeing God as Adam and

Eve did, and a docility that quickly puts into practice what our spiritual directors, superiors, or Holy Spirit indicate.

### 90% vs. 10% Test of our Centre of Gravity

Let us apply another test that we have used earlier but not explained. We have come up with a rough rule of the human cooperation representing 10%, the Holy Spirit's work representing 90%. This outwardly resembles the famous 80%-20% Pareto Principle ("for many outcomes, 80% of consequences come from 20% of the cause"), but differs in the internal dynamism. This paradigm comprises two different agents, one being God.

This paradigm is an over-simplification, as it is clearly 100% of both sides but with God's action infinitely surpassing man's action. The use of the 10% rule is to employ a simple imaginative tool to point out the necessity of a both/and path that requires human cooperation, while highlighting the greater truth that it is a negligible contribution relative to God's divine work (see St. Augustine). For it is more deeply God who does everything in us: perhaps beginning with the illumination, followed by concomitant and then subsequent actual graces. So, while simplistic, the two levels paradigm of the human 10% and divine 90% can be a rough rule to discern what is our center of gravity in what we do: does our seeking to guide others to Christ rely 90% on our efforts and only 10% on God, or the reverse? Our center of gravity is the major criterion for spiritual efficacy. Again, the example of the apostles is salutary. Before Pentecost, we see the failure in St. Peter's presumption, relying on himself:

> Peter declared to him, "Though they all fall away because of you, I will never fall away." Jesus said to him, "Truly, I say to you, this very night, before the cock crows, you will deny me three times." Peter said to him, "Even if I must die with you, I will not deny you." And so said all the disciples. (Mt 26:33-35)

What a transformation took place after Peter's fall. Mainly fisherman and simple men, as the Sanhedrin came to see in Peter and John, with the Holy Spirit, they came to conquer the world. Their actions were 1% relative to the 99% of the Spirit. When Jesus asked him three times if he loved Him with *agape* (God's divine, unconditional love), Peter, having learned his lesson, could only reply that he would give him *philia* (brotherly love). Notice here that Jesus' foundation is one of love, it is love that makes one available. Similarly, Jesus could only use the apostles after they had run away at Gethsemane and abandoned him, and Paul after he had persecuted Christians. *There must be no self-reliance, but reliance only on Divine Love, the Spirit.*

# AID 10

## Spiritual Warfare: Jesus' 25 Rules to St. Faustina

Jesus' exhortations on "spiritual warfare" in St. Faustina's *Diary* are an aid to spiritual progress. We thank Kathleen Beckman for her kind permission to reprint her commentary. But the author has decided to insert his own commentary so as to focus on spiritual warfare as framed in St. Ignatius' discernment of spirits (i.e., as diverting us from holiness). We do include Beckman's introduction (in italics). See also catholicradioassociation.org.

*In Cracow-Pradnik, June 2, 1938, the Lord Jesus directed a young Polish Sister of Mercy on a three-day retreat. Faustina Kowalska painstakingly recorded Christ's instruction in her diary that is a mystical manual on prayer and Divine Mercy. Having read the Diary a few times in the past 20 years, I had forgotten about the unique retreat that Christ gave on the subject of spiritual warfare.... Here are the secret whispers of Jesus to his little bride Faustina on how to protect herself from the attacks of the devil. These instructions became Faustina's weapon in fighting the good fight. Then, Our Lord began, saying: "My daughter, I want to teach you about spiritual warfare." What followed were 25 secrets of spiritual warfare revealed by Christ to Saint Faustina. (1760).*

1. **Never trust in yourself but abandon yourself totally to My will.**

As *The Spiritual Combat* teaches, God looks with horror at our self-reliance. We follow Christ's filial obedience to the Father through docility to the Spirit, accepting what the Father permits, for He knows what is best for us.

2. **In desolation, darkness, and various doubts, have recourse to Me and to your spiritual director. He will always answer you in my name.**

We can experience in desolation (caused by the evil spirit) or in Dark Nights (caused by Holy Spirit) darkness, doubts, temptations, dryness, and obsessions. In the midst of these, God gives us a bulwark, manifesting His will in a privileged way through superiors, directors, and confessors.

3. **Do not bargain with any temptation; lock yourself immediately in My Heart.**

Eve's principal error was dialoguing with Satan. Spiritual writers teach us to resist temptations at the very outset, to allow no entry into the castle. St. Escrivá teaches us to find shelter in the wounds (or Sacred Heart) of Christ.

4. **At the first opportunity, reveal the temptation to the confessor.**

Transparency breaks the power of Satan's troubling the soul, as with Adam's revealing his sin (for "confession of sins leads to salvation"). Just opening up ourselves to Jesus through a representative can illuminate our darkness. It is for the author the first and key rule of spiritual warfare.

5. **Put your self-love in the last place, so that it does not taint your deeds.**

St. Catherine of Siena teaches that self-love is what undermines all spiritual life. The opposite is total self-forgetfulness to live the First Commandment, to love God above all things and for Himself. The merit of our acts derive from the degree of love contained therein. We cannot take our good actions to heaven, but our love, which is eternal.

6. **Bear with yourself with great patience.**

Bearing with ourselves with patience flows from self-knowledge, knowing ourselves as God sees us. It is the first pillar of St. Catherine of Siena, "You are she who is not, I am He who is." The adult becomes impatient with self; St. Thérèse teaches that, while learning to walk, a child will constantly fall.

7. **Do not neglect interior mortifications.**

Saints teach us that we are to value exterior mortifications (e.g., fasting), but that interior mortifications (docility to God's will) are superior, reflecting the higher Mansions. St. Francis de Sales prefers the "little virtues."

8. **Always justify to yourself the opinions of your superiors and of your confessor.**

Jesus taught St. Faustina, "He is the veil behind which I am hiding. Your director and I are one; his words are My word" (*Diary* 1308). In other episodes of her life as well, Jesus taught her that obedience is supreme.

9. **Shun murmurers like a plague.**

St. Francis de Sales teaches us this insight about avoiding murmuring at all costs. For He lives primarily, not by asceticism, but like our Lord by docility to the Father's *will*, which are partly manifested in the events of life.

10. **Let all act as they like; you are to act as I want you to.**

Most people are troubled by what others do or by what is happening in the world. Unlike the devil, we do not seek to control, dominate, or possess, but give each his freedom. St. F. de Sales never acted when he encountered closed hearts, but moved heaven and earth to help open hearts.

11. **Observe the rule as faithfully as you can.**

Reginald Garrigou-Lagrange teaches that a religious who is very faithful to her rule of life will be able to accept martyrdom if offered. The lay person who sanctifies the daily little things, especially the duty of the moment, can attain holiness and help sanctify the world (St. Escrivá).

12. **If someone causes you trouble, think what good you can do for the person who caused you to suffer.**

Jesus returned hate with love (e.g., Calvary), and asks us to forgive and ask for blessings for the perpetrators. St. John of the Cross counselled self-emptying love: "Where there is no love, put love and you will find love."

13. **Do not pour out your feelings.**

The superficial soul lives by feelings, as in post-Vatican II confusion, with its feel-good sentimentality ("community," "compassion"). But Jesus teaches us to show our love by action (St. Teresa), and to primarily turn to, and find our rest in, Him (and his wounds) in the solitude of our trials.

14. **Be silent when you are rebuked.**

We imitate Jesus: "And as a sheep is silent before the shearers, he did not open his mouth"(Isa 53:7). Jesus' disciples have his brandmark, and learn to silently accept corrections, and even humiliation. "When you experience something unpleasant, look at Jesus Crucified and be silent" (J. of Cross).

15. **Do not ask everyone's opinion, but only the opinion of your confessor [director]; be as frank and simple as a child with him.**

A director represents God, and his counsel should dominate and, amidst multiple appeals, choosing God's will given through him. Jesus taught St. Faustina to be transparent to him like a child as she would to Jesus Himself.

16. **Do not become discouraged by ingratitude.**

Most of us desire gratitude and appreciation and become troubled when the recipients of our kindness do not reciprocate. Jesus' higher way was lived by Francis de Sales, who taught a bishop to expect ingratitude. "Don't say 'that person bothers me.' Say, 'That person sanctifies me.'" (St. Escrivá).

17. **Do not examine with curiosity the roads on which I lead you.**

Mary lived simplicity, not focusing on others' questioning her divinely caused pregnancy but only on doing God's will in each moment. We are to be held in God's arms without concern. Saints live neither in the past or future, but in the eternity of each present moment (John of the Cross).

18. **When boredom and discouragement beat against your heart, run away from yourself and hide in My heart.**

Jesus implies that aridity and discouragement come from self-reliance and self-focus. The devil too brings him certain dispositions: self-absorption, isolation, pride, idleness, veering from the present moment, etc. Jesus exhorts us to hide in His heart, where peace reigns. "Peace I leave with you; my peace I give to you; not as the world gives do I give to you. Let not your hearts be troubled, neither let them be afraid" (Jn 14:27).

19. **Do not fear struggle; courage itself often intimidates temptations, and they dare not attack us.**

Fear often arises from our anticipating difficulties, and may underlie all sin. Fear is from the devil (full of rage); God is love and "love casts out all fear." Contrary to the devil's dominant traits of pride and disobedience, we learn from St. Catherine of Siena that *humility* gives us the strength to tackle anything for Christ, and St. Teresa that *obedience* to His will gave strength for her mission despite her illnesses. Christ teaches us that His servants will face trials, which are actually great blessings and will constitute our crown.

20. **Always fight with the deep conviction that I am with you.**

Marijana, a seer at Medjugorje, earlier saw God as judging her and being far away in heaven, and then learned the great truth that He loves her unconditionally like a good Father and is always close to her. When a priest joked that Jesus never listens to him, Sr. Briege McKenna pointed to his side and said, "Jesus is right here."

21. **Do not be guided by feeling, because it is not always under your control; but all merit lies in the will.**

This is a key truth, for many today are led by feelings (human spirit). Jesus responded to St. Teresa of Jesus's question about why He needed our actions: "To see your will." Many express their love for Jesus but do not express it in action (e.g., sanctifying work, listening to the Spirit's calls to change). God only knows if we love Him when He sees our love in actions.

22. **Always depend upon your superiors, even in the smallest things.**

An efficacious way to grow in holiness is to "always consult." And God normally works through others (incarnational economy, by which He uses the whole family). Since the Holy Spirit works through others (e.g., parents, teachers, bishops), obedience to them is obedience to Him. A seminary priest here consults his superior and director in everything he does (e.g., which summer project to take on and extracurricular requests to accept).

23. **I will not delude you with prospects of peace and consolations; on the contrary, prepare for great battles.**

Jesus often teaches saints this truth, that this life is not for rest but for battle. Thérèse, from reading *The End of the Present World*, learned how short life is for serving God and how tremendously He rewards our little efforts.

24. **Know that you are on a great stage where all heaven and earth are watching you.**

Like St. Thérèse above, we all see the brevity of this life by living against the horizon of eternity. The angels are in awe of the sacrifices of martyrs. Our own glory is not so much in heaven as it is in the hidden sacrifices of life (the Canadian martyrs' glory was already manifest in their torture).

25. **Fight like a knight, so I can reward you. Do not be unduly fearful, because you are not alone.**

Our Lord's sole weakness is that He does not like to be outdone in generosity. Those who serve Him with generosity will be served by Christ for all eternity; seating us at the Wedding Banquet and putting on His apron. But here in our Dark Nights, we go out into the night to find Christ our Spouse, as St. John of the Cross teaches.

# AID 11

**Spiritual Warfare: An Exorcist's Counsels for Everyday Life**
(Permission granted Oct. 11, 2021)

*These are notes summarized from an exorcist's conference to seminarians on healing, deliverance, and exorcism. We also recommend Stephen Rossetti's illuminating* Diary of an American Exorcist *for more hands-on or practical insights into this area.*

**Key Insight**: Deliverance and exorcism are always subcategories of healing, which is a subcategory of discipleship of Christ.

**Distinction between Healing and Deliverance**: Since it is important to get deliverance right, we must therefore avoid two extremes: past centuries' approach to find evil spirits in everything; and the modern approach in science that everything can be explained humanly. We shoot for the middle-ground. Scripture itself has no problem *in making a distinction in Jesus' life between healing and expulsion of demons*. For example, we have exorcism in Mk 1:21: "I know who you are …. Be silent, come out," and right after that, Jesus healed the fever of Peter's mother-in-law (no exorcism involved). Later that day, people brought all who were sick or had demons, and Jesus healed the human elements and expelled demons, and Jesus clearly knew the distinction. Yet in Mk 9:14, the chapter title reads, "The healing of a body with a mute spirit," indicating that the modern commentator seems embarrassed by evil spirits (that is, perhaps it was just a sickness, like epilepsy).

**We should have no Fear of Exorcism**: In today's terminology, deliverance is a term for *minor exorcism*, while exorcism is for *major exorcism*. Many avoid use of the word "exorcism" because of the catechizing influence of Hollywood movies, e.g., "The Exorcist," which makes us afraid to become exorcists. That is not true, because the **fruit of exorcism is peace, never fear**. When the fruit is not peace, then it wasn't an exorcism. Hollywood wants to generate fear in movies to attract our attention (sensationalism). *We need to be re-catechized by holy Mother Church.*

**Unhealed Wounds Likely Main Cause of Uncharacteristic Outbursts**: We are still talking a lot about the lower level of infestation. *If you get the small stuff right, you will get the big stuff right.* For example, if in a conversation I exploded in anger, I may apologize. But when I reflect upon it later, I realize more fully that I really blew it, and I recall a lot of memories— this is the true source of the problem. I can then pray, "Lord, could you take me back, I need to work through some anger of the past." The unhealed wounds or memories can explain about 40-50% of our emotions according to the assessment of modern thinking. When we take time to discern, we discover that these **unhealed wounds are the cause of about 90% of our emotional disturbances**; and only 5% was added by ourselves. Then the light dawns upon us, "So that is how that works." If we don't bring a magnifying glass to examine it, then we don't see that "little bug." Where we have a wound, the devil loves to come and infect it, but again it is only the extra 5%.

**Delving into the Occult is Breaking the First Commandment**: Another area is the tremendous importance of the first commandment. The first commandment is that "you shall have no other gods before me" (Exod 20:3). Many people turn to Tarot cards, psychics, Ouija boards, horoscopes, etc. If you go into a Barnes & Noble Bookstore in the US, you will find a section on witchcraft that is larger than the entire section on religion. *If you call on powers that are not explicitly from Jesus, they tend to respond.* There are only two realms of power, good and fallen angels (demons). There is no such thing as a neutral realm, it does not exist (e.g., "white magic"): *there are only good or bad angels.* Those with a South American background might be familiar with faith healers, who might use herbs but can also add incantations. They usually feel better initially but end up much worse, with deeper infections. In many cases with people from *India*, he finds that their ancestry involves so many spirits (some infested people take on the form of the Hindu gods), and praying basic deliverance brings relief.

**The Masonic Society (Freemasons)**: The entire American country has been dedicated to Masonism. The Masons have 33 degrees, and, at each degree, *they take an oath that they will never break the oath, invoking a curse on themselves and on their progeny in the name of Egyptian gods* if they do break it. This has been going on for centuries. While the average card-carrying Masons are not the problem, *they do take these oaths.* At the first degree, they strip down, take off their wedding ring, and make the oath (taking off clothes represents losing my proper right, taking off the ring indicates that this is more important than my spouse). By the time they are in the high 20 degrees, there are rituals that involve stepping on the Bible (affiliation is more important than Scripture). And yet in the US, except for Kennedy and Obama, every president was a Mason.

One example of Masonic background is that of a man who came and shared unusual experiences he had been having since the age of eight. When he touches areas in buildings, he can see what has happened there in the past, e.g., he once saw someone hanging as from suicide, and checking it out confirmed what he saw. The exorcist interviewed him before starting deliverance, and found out that there was Masonic background in the family and that the father was still an active member. They prayed a long time over him and he was finally healed. He was not possessed nor oppressed. He was a Catholic but this had not been addressed. There are no traditional categories for his case.

**Confess and also Renounce**: *So the rule of thumb is that spirits tend to respond when you call on them.* For example, those who have used a Ouija board will have a little infection, but it is still a bug. So it is important to confess this sin in Confession. *But we have to close a door as well, by **renouncing** in Jesus' name what we did and renounce any spirits who have come in.* You are saying to the devil, "No, I am not of your kingdom, I reject you." So we have to remove the infection (Confession), but also close the door that we opened. We do this renunciation of the devil each year at the Easter vigil.

**Infestation is Similar to an Infection**: Evil spirits work the way infections do in a wound. When you go to emergency at a hospital with a wound (e.g., cut), they will check for infections. No one thinks doctors and nurses are neurotic when *they are constantly cleaning everything*. We too should be doing things by which we are constantly "cleansing" our spiritual infections. The evil spirits love to get in there and make it worse, because the enemy is the enemy of human nature (God is the friend of human nature).

**Wounds Come from Three Places**:
*My Sins*: Sin harms myself, others, and my relationship with others. The devil likes to come into these wounds and infect. Consequently, one of the most important things is to go to Confession, from which there is always a partial indulgence, a partial remittance of temporal punishment, so a *partial healing of the wound that the sin has caused*. So as you heal, there is not so much area for infection to go in. Thus, Confession is one of the main instruments of Exorcism. **One good Confession is worth a hundred deliverances**.
*Forgiveness of Sins that Others do against us*: There is an analogy with physical injury. If someone hits me with a car and hurts me, it really wounded me. So sins done to me are also areas where spirits can infect. For this, we encourage people *to forgive; until they forgive, the spirits hide in that unforgiveness.* This is not just intellectual forgiveness but forgiveness from the **heart**. *This is the main way to overcome this infection.*
*The Remnants or Consequences of Ancestors' Sins*. The exorcist illustrates with a personal example. His grandfather was a raving alcoholic, and the result was that his own father did not bond with his father, and subsequently, ended up being a very distant father to the exorcist. The grandfather may himself have been abused. This is now affecting the exorcist in his daily life. The solution is to pray for healing of our ancestry, as we are connected to our ancestors. We should *specifically offer Masses for our ancestors, who, if they do not need purgation, may need healing*. There was the experience of a woman with southern Baptist background who experienced great joy after praying for her mother for a week after her death, perhaps because her prayers allowed her mother to go to heaven. This did not happen as easily with her father,

who was a tough nut. The prayer team suggested that she offer three Masses for him, after which she experienced joy at the third Mass and the priest celebrating that Mass also had a sensation of a soul being freed.

**All the big stuff is an exaggeration of the little things.** There is great need for priests to pray for people and not just provide the sacraments. We should never want to do exorcisms, unless the bishop asks us.

## Questions

1. **Deliverance in Confessions and cleansing before and after hearing Confessions**: The priest has a proper authority in the area of deliverance and healing, even if he doesn't have a charismatic charism. The powers that he invokes are much more powerful by his priestly office. St. Alphonsus de Liguori told his priests that, in the confessional, if they have any inkling that spirits may be involved, say *sotto voce*, "In Jesus' name, I bind and cast out spirits." When priests are dealing with wounds, they sometimes encounter infections in wounds. A priest should pray before and after he enters the Confessional, just as a surgeon scrubs up before and after surgery. This exorcist sometimes before hearing Confessions just says one Hail Mary slowly before the tabernacle and three after hearing Confessions. This is because he is called to do penance for and with penitents. Our Lady is very good with these details. Since there can be some transference, why not go before the Blessed Sacrament: "Lord, I am human, I hear a lot of things in the Confessional, heal me."

2. **The Old Rite of Blessing of Holy Water is powerful**: It is a bit of an act of war, remembering that God honours the intention. In the past, the old rite was used for everything: many blessed their homes, some blessed their crops (one time a tornado took out all the other farms but did not touch the farm of the man who blessed it with holy water). So in the old rite, there were constant minor exorcisms happening. As in hospitals, we should cleanse ourselves, why not bless the offices every day. On this low level, why not, what is it going to hurt? If the exorcist uses an office, he blesses it. Or if he has had a hard day, he blesses himself with holy water, and usually feels a lifting of heaviness. St. Patrick's breastplate prayer is a very powerful prayer; he was fighting against wizards, witches, druids, etc.

3. **Praying the Our Father every day**. We are doing deliverance on a regular basis by saying "deliver us from the evil one." Throw out that mini kingdom of the devil. The Our Father is a wonderful deliverance prayer.

4. There are several things that are good in the ***Manual of Minor Exorcisms*** for priests who don't think they know this area. It includes: prayer of St. Basil (used for centuries); prayer for homes, prayer for inner healings, etc. Many

priests focus on talking problems out, but the problem is that this is remaining at the level of concepts. But the moment you pick up a book like the *Manual* and start to pray with parishioners, the Lord **speaks to their hearts**. With a woman whose 30 year old daughter was dying, they went to pray in the Church. The woman came out saying how wonderful it was. If there is something that might be infected, then take authority over it, since he/she is your parishioner (jurisdiction, authority).

**What to do at the parish level?**
If someone says that they have an infection, speak to them, get to know them. Even after they see an exorcist, they need an authentic community, which can be very healing. The parish priest can have them do the following three things: 1. Go to Confession. 2. Go to Mass. 3. Pray the deliverance prayer card that they can pray themselves before the tabernacle (see *Manual*). You will find that half of these cases clear up; partly because there was pastoral love, they were heard and taken seriously. Most priests to whom this has been explained are happy to follow this instruction.

Serious cases should be referred to the diocese, but ensure they have substantial claims. Some people may want attention or have a neurological condition. On the other hand, some people do have issues, some don't know they have them, and some can have a combination of both. For example, one lady who was really overweight, with no family, and whose only relationship was one with a murderer in prison, while not a candidate for major exorcism, was a border line case. She had been to many psychiatrists and given medication, but the voices in her head did not stop. She had a combination of both psychological condition and need for evicting spirits who were hindering the effect of the medicines. After receiving deliverance, with a return to a psychiatrist and with medicines given, the voices in her head stopped.

**How much do we need to know about a wound to pray over it?**
The actual wound is usually deeper than the person and the priest knows. So the priest should pray and ask what is happening. It can take a few days before the cause dawns upon the priest. This is also because of the promise, "Where two or three are gathered in my name, there I am." *And many times, in the next day or two, something comes supernaturally and it is most often right.* This is an ordinary grace, and it involves the humility of asking the Lord, where many with wounds going to a psychologist may not be healed.

**What does the exorcist do during those hours of deliverance?**
Some people have charismatic gifts of discernment, but you need someone to *confirm* their discernment. Some things need to be *renounced*, and specific

ones need to be *renounced three times*, because the devil likes to mimic God's economy (e.g., Trinitarian formulae).

## A Hindu becoming Catholic may need to renounce pagan gods

This is almost always not addressed at all in the RCIA. It may take care of a lot of things, because Baptism is like a seed in soil but the seed may not germinate. You may call on that germination, and you may have to cleanse the soil of these pagan cultures in Jesus' name (this cleansing applies to other religions besides Hinduism, like Islam). But with Hinduism, some might be projections of human experiences, but certainly some of them can be spirits; in fact, some infested people can take on *the poses of a Hindu god, because there are evil spirits in the form of that god.* The exorcist is amazed at how our present liturgical rites have been disarmed (need to "re-weaponize" the texts, so to speak). We used to have nine exorcism prayers which have been taken out from one rite. So Baptism really is the life of God, but *weeds can overgrow that life, so we need to call on that power.* But the Anglo-Saxon mentality is not open to that, saying that deliverance belongs only to fictional movies.

## Inter-generational sins. Doesn't Baptism remove all sins?

Yes, Baptism does remit all sins, but there is another element to consider. For example, you can have crack babies and some alcoholism pre-disposition from alcoholic parents, which is not just but which happens. Yes, Baptism has the power, but until we call on that power, *it does not become activated.* This applies especially with Voodoo. The exorcist can't find one Irish person without some witchcraft in his past. In the distant past (e.g. Druids), when in doubt, the Irish went to the witch doctor. And so, until someone commands, "In Jesus' name, depart," this influence will continue. The exorcist has often seen people come in with a very strained face and after deliverance leave with a humanized face. *Jesus did not start with the Eucharist, but began instead with the basic things, like healing and deliverance.*

## How do we distinguish real from false charisms?

We can test these gifts by their fruits. Priests have the grace of priestly office. There are differences between clairvoyance and real discernment: with discernment there is a peace, while clairvoyance has both a peace and something wrong with it. Many people have received charisms as they needed them (e.g., healing, discernment, a word of prophecy). But those with charisms have to be obedient, that is, to be subservient to the Church that Christ established. The disobedient spirit is always from the evil one, the good spirit always leads to obedience.

## What is the role of St. Michael and the Archangels?

The person who casts out the devil is **first Jesus, then Mary, and then St. Michael**. The short prayer is always good to use, but you can add "in Jesus' name." *Priests have the right and authority to pray the long St. Michael exorcism prayer (Leo XIII)*. While anyone could pray it previously, Cardinal Ratzinger limited it to priests. This exorcist likes the children's prayer to the guardian angels. The exorcist used a prayer for inner healing from the *Manual of Minor Exorcisms* on the seminarians.

### How much sickness is caused by spirits?
Most sicknesses seemingly are physical, but there may be about 10% that are demonically inspired or demons manifesting themselves. In a charismatic centre, a Jesuit looks after people who are living in a dump. He has them drink holy water and about 10% need not go for regular modern medicine. Sirach teaches what to do with someone who is sick: he should first pray; then give up his faults (by going to Confession); offer a sweet-smelling sacrifice sacramentally (Mass?); give the physician his due place at the human level. Sirach's teachings are precisely the program followed at the *Lord's Ranch Clinic* in El Paso, Texas. Sometimes, people don't have to go to the clinic after these steps, but those who go might heal better.

### Question about Neal Lozano? A Father's Blessing
Neal Lozano is good but he is introductory. His is a very valid way, for he understands that it is a subcategory of healing, which is a subcategory of discipleship in Christ. A father's blessing is a good thing. One element in Neal Lozano's book is to encourage fathers to give a father's blessing, for many people feel that they have been rejected, it feels like a cause. Many need to be blessed by a father, it has the effect of a deliverance. The exorcist said that there is an efficaciousness that is much higher for them to hear him speaking as a father, "I bless you…"

If you find a good charismatic or priest with true gifts, it is good to have them pray over you, for we all have afflictions. *This exorcist has prayed over many priests and sisters who had no clue that there was anything there*. Then they realize that the problem wasn't them or their sins. Confession takes care of many things, but you still need some additional help. Never ask to become an exorcist. Nevertheless, deliverance from evil spirits is part of the work of every priest. This exorcist enjoys seeing the fruits of the ministry of exorcism; but he does not like the work nor even talking about it, nor even thinking about the enemy. A key insight from another exorcist is relevant here: "If someone tells you categorically that he is possessed, he is probably not. But if he acts truly surprised at his bizarre symptoms, he just might be" (S. Rossetti quoting an experienced exorcist in *Diary*, 38).

# Appendix

Here is a dialogue between Fr. Amorth and a devil about our Lady:

> Father Amorth: "What are the virtues of the Madonna that make you angriest?" Demon: "She makes me angry because she is the humblest of all creatures, and because I am the proudest; because she is the purest of all creatures, and I am not; because, of all creatures, she is the most obedient to God, and I am a rebel!"
>
> Father Amorth: "Tell me the fourth characteristic of the Madonna that makes you so afraid of her that you are more afraid when I say the Madonna's name than when I say the name of Jesus Christ!" Demon: "I am more afraid when you say the Madonna's name, because I am more humiliated by being beaten by a simple creature, than by Him…"
>
> Father Amorth: "Tell me the fourth characteristic of the Madonna that makes you most angry!" Demon: "Because she always defeats me, because she was never compromised by any taint of sin!"
>
> Father Amorth: "Satan told me, through the possessed person, 'Every Hail Mary of the Rosary is a blow to the head for me; if Christians knew the power of the Rosary, it would be the end of me!'"[1]

A dialogue between St. Dominic and the devil in a possessed Albigensian.

> Devil: "Then listen well, you Christians: the Mother of Jesus Christ is all-powerful and she can save her servants from falling into Hell. She is the Sun which destroys the darkness of our wiles and subtlety. It is she who uncovers our hidden plots, breaks our snares and makes our temptations useless and ineffectual. We have to say, however reluctantly, that not a single soul who has really persevered in her service has ever been damned with us; one single sigh that she offers to the Blessed Trinity is worth far more than all the prayers, desires and aspirations of all the Saints. We fear her more than all the other Saints in Heaven together and we have no success with her faithful servants. Many Christians who call upon her when they are at the hour of death and who really ought to be damned according to our ordinary standards are saved by her intercession. Oh if only that Mary…. had not pitted her strength against ours and had not upset our plans, we should have conquered the Church and should have destroyed it long before this; and we would have seen to it that all the Orders in the Church fell into error and disorder. Now that we are forced to speak…. nobody who perseveres in saying the Rosary will be damned, because she obtains for her servants the grace of true contrition for their sins and by means of this they obtain God's forgiveness and mercy."[2]

---

[1] Gabriel Amorth, *Last Exorcist*, in Gelsomino Del Guercio, "Devil Admits to Exorcist: 'I am Afraid of the Madonna,'" *Aleteia*, accessed Dec. 19, 2021, https://aleteia.org/2017/07/02/devil-admits-to-exorcist-im-afraid-of-the-madonna/.

[2] St. Louis de Montfort, *Secret of the Rosary* (Rockford, IL: TAN Publns., 1976), 33rd Rose.

# AID 12

## Spirit's Gift: Lay Charisms as a New Springtime in the Church
*The divine graces poured forth into the Church through the twentieth-century lay ecclesial charisms are astounding. Here we present Pope Benedict XVI's address that introduces the charism of Communion and Liberation, while clarifying the fruitful collaboration between the Church's hierarchy and ecclesial movements.*

My first thought goes to your Founder, Mons. Luigi Giussani, to whom many memories bind me and who became a true friend of mine.... Through him, the Holy Spirit raised in the Church a Movement, yours, that would witness to the beauty of being Christian in an age when the opinion was spreading that Christianity is a difficult and oppressive way to live. Fr. Giussani then committed himself to awaken in youth the love for Christ, "Way, Truth and Life", repeating that only he is the way towards the fulfilment of the deepest desires of the human heart, and that Christ does not save us regardless of our humanity, but through it. As I was able to recall in his funeral homily, this courageous priest, who grew up in a home poor in bread but rich in music, as he himself liked to say, from the beginning was touched, or rather wounded, by the desire for beauty, though not any sort of beauty. He sought Beauty itself, the infinite Beauty which is found in Christ.... The event that changed the life of the Founder has also "wounded" a great many of his spiritual sons and daughters, and has given way to multiple religious and ecclesial experiences which form the history of your vast and well-organized spiritual Family. Communion and Liberation is a community experience of faith, born in the Church not by the will of an organized hierarchy but originating from a renewed encounter with Christ and thus, we can say, by an impulse derived ultimately from the Holy Spirit....

The reality of ecclesial movements, therefore, is a sign of the fecundity of the Lord's Spirit, because it manifests in the world the victory of the Risen Christ and it accomplishes the missionary mandate entrusted to the whole Church.... the Servant of God John Paul II had this to say: that there is no conflict or opposition in the Church between the institutional and the charismatic dimensions, of which the Movements are a significant expression. Both are co-essential to the divine constitution of the People of God. In the Church the essential institutions are also charismatic and indeed the charisms must, in one way or another, be institutionalized to have coherency and continuity. Hence, both dimensions [hierarchy and charisms] originate from the same Holy Spirit for the same Body of Christ, and together they concur to make present the mystery and the salvific work of Christ in the world....

I said that if the Lord gives us new gifts, we must be grateful, even if sometimes they may be uncomfortable. At the same time, since the Church is one, if the Movements are really gifts of the Holy Spirit, they must, naturally, be inserted into the Ecclesial Community and serve it so that, in patient dialogue with the Pastors, they can be elements in the construction of the Church of today and tomorrow.

(*Address of his Holiness Benedict XVI to the Members of Communion and Liberation Movement on the 25th Anniversary of its Pontifical Recognition*, Vatican.va)

# TWO AIDS FOR RENEWAL

## Life of Grace and Priesthood

This treasure of humanity enriched by the inexpressible mystery of divine filiation and by the grace of "adoption as sons" in the Only Son of God, through whom we call God "Abba, Father," is also a powerful force unifying the Church above all inwardly and giving meaning to all her activity. Through this force the Church is united with the Spirit of Christ, that Holy Spirit promised and continually communicated by the Redeemer and whose descent, which was revealed on the day of Pentecost, endures for ever. Thus the powers of the Spirit, the gifts of the Spirit, and the fruits of the Holy Spirit are revealed in men. The present-day Church seems to repeat with ever greater fervour and with holy insistence: "Come, Holy Spirit!" Come! Come! "Heal our wounds, our strength renew; On our dryness pour your dew; Wash the stains of guilt away; Bend the stubborn heart and will; Melt the frozen, warm the chill; Guide the steps that go astray." (John Paul II, *Redemptor hominis* 18)

## TWO AIDS FOR RENEWAL

These two final Aids are devoted to renewal in life of grace and the priesthood. They relate to some degree to all consecrated souls.

1. Life of Grace: Infused Virtues & Gifts with Actual Grace (Reginald Garrigou-Lagrange). For those seeking divine union, this might enable understanding of how the Holy Spirit, the personal love of God, works through the infused theological and moral virtues, the gifts of the Spirit, and actual grace that calls us to cooperation.

2. Priesthood Renewal: Jesus' Appeal in *In Sinu Jesu*.
   *In Sinu Jesu*, recommended by one of the best-known spiritual writers of our time, is a rather unique work. The anonymous monk author presents private revelation in the form of interior interlocutions addressed primarily to priests and consecrated souls. Jesus desires a renewal in the priestly and consecrated life through a recovery of the love of the Blessed Sacrament, a return to the saints, becoming other Johns (beloved disciple), and many other helpful insights.

# RENEWAL 1

## Life of Grace: Infused Virtues & Gifts with Actual Grace

### (Synopsis of Reginald Garrigou-Lagrange)[1]

Christians know the word "grace," but may think of it primarily as some "thing" infused into us through the sacraments. To understand grace, we can turn to the theologian of grace in the New Testament, St. Paul. The key to Paul is that he did not know Christ during His lifetime, but "encountered" Him as "grace." On his way to Damascus, Christ revealed Himself to Paul, who came to understand three truths: that Christ is the living Lord; is united to His Mystical Body ("why do you persecute me?"); and is utter gratuitous love in transforming him from a condemned persecutor to a prince of the Church. Thus, the heart of Paul was his being loved: "He loved me, and gave Himself up for me" (Gal 2:20). To describe this great discovery, he took a common word *"charis,"* meaning "favour," to express God the Father's unutterable love for us (the first grace); that led Him to give us the unspeakable gift of His Son and His cross (the second grace); from which water and blood (representing the sacraments) caused the uncreated grace of God (the third grace of indwelling of Spirit); which created incorporation to Christ (the fourth grace): that comprises both (i) divinizing of our souls through sanctifying grace (remission of sins, divine life, divine filiation) and (ii) divinizing our faculties (infused virtues, gifts of Holy Spirit, fruits of Holy Spirit, and Beatitudes). But for Paul, all redemption and sanctification are given in Christ; *grace is the Person of Christ*. After a brief preface on uncreated-created grace, this synthesis focuses on introducing the reader primarily to the elevation of the faculties through the infused virtues, the gifts of the Holy Spirit, and the action of actual grace.

### I. Uncreated (God) and Created Grace (Sanctifying Grace) in Brief

Water (Baptism) and blood (Eucharist) flowed from the side of Christ (together: sacraments). Baptism causes two main effects: indwelling of the Trinity (uncreated grace) and an incorporation into Christ which causes the created effects of divinizing the soul (sanctifying grace) and the faculties.

### A. Uncreated Grace: Indwelling of Trinity & Incorporation to Christ

The primordial principle to understand how God is personally communicated and dwells in man is the Incarnation of God's Son in Christ.

---

[1] Reginald Garrigou-Lagrange, *The Three Ages of the Interior Life*, 48-96.

For the indwelling of the Trinity cannot but take its point of departure from the economic Trinity operating in salvation history, and, more particularly, in the Incarnation. In this "personal union," the divine Word (John's Prologue) stands in personal relationship with the humanity of Jesus in such a way that the God-man loves the Father with the same love of the eternal Son. This love or bond of unity between the Father and the Son is the Holy Spirit. It is through the Spirit that Christ obeys, loves, and unites Himself to the Father (Lk 1:35, etc.). The indwelling in the baptized is attributed to the Spirit; but all three are present, for they are three Persons in one God.

*Incorporation to Christ*
As the Holy Spirit overshadowed Mary to incarnate the Son of God as man, so Baptism through the overshadowing of the Spirit causes a mystical incarnation of Christ in the baptized in germ, to become "another Christ, Christ Himself." We add that St. John of the Cross teaches that the Father is pleased to the degree He finds the image of Christ in us: "My Son… whoever resembles you most satisfies me most, and whoever is like you in nothing will find nothing in me. I am pleased with you alone, O life of my life!… My Son, I will give myself to him who loves you and I will love him with the same love I have for you, because he has loved you whom I love so" (*Romance on Prologue*). Being made "just" before God in Baptism, he participates in the eternal filiation of the Word incarnate, sustained, vivified, and animated by the Spirit (the "Paraclete" in Jn 14-16). The Spirit is the bond of communion and communication between the Father and the Son. Through Baptism (Rom 6:3-5) and the Eucharist (1 Cor 10:16), we begin to live inseparably in communion with the Son and the Spirit.

*Holy Spirit's Work*
This divine work is all accomplished through the Holy Spirit. The sending of the Spirit at Pentecost brings the redemptive and divinizing work of Christ to its realization. As the Spirit of the risen One, His mission is to render all humanity sharers in the sonship of Jesus Christ, *rendering Christ present in all times and in all places of history*! It is clear therefore that the missions of the Son and of the Spirit, though distinct, cannot be separated.

## B. Created Grace: Sanctifying Grace

What remains to be explained in the Trinitarian indwelling is the relation between the uncreated gift ("Holy Spirit") and the created gift ("sanctifying grace"). The adoption of man through the work of the Spirit of Christ in Baptism implies a supernatural elevation. Although the transformation depends totally on the indwelling of the Spirit who incorporates man to Christ, the nature of the effect or change is *proportioned to the openness* of the creature who enjoys the indwelling. To explain this fact, theological reflection has introduced the notion of uncreated grace and created grace.

For Thomas Aquinas, it is clear that the reality of the communication of God (uncreated grace) comes prior to the created effect (sanctifying grace). It is therefore the **indwelling divine Persons who produce this transformation in man**. This transformation is sanctifying grace, the seed of glory, that introduces him into this higher order of truth and life. It is an essentially supernatural life, *a participation in the intimate life of God, in His divine nature*, since it even now prepares us to see God someday as He sees Himself and to love Him as He loves Himself.

Grace can be described in many ways. In simple words, it is the gratuitous love of God, a special love-relationship which is brought about by the Holy Spirit dwelling in our hearts. All sacraments give the uncreated grace of the indwelling of the Trinity, that brings an infusion of the divinization of the soul of sanctifying grace. As a parent loves and gives himself and all his possessions, so the Father pours out all to us. Let us illustrate the power and richness of sanctifying grace as given through the sacrament of the Sick, with the sick person's relationship with the three divine Persons:

> 1. The indwelling **Holy Spirit** brings with Himself His special gifts that are so much needed in sickness: courage, trust, harmony, peace, confidence, hope, love, obedience to the will of the Father, even joy, etc.
>
> 2. He assimilates, configures us to the suffering **Christ,** so that sharing in Christ's sufferings we may share also in His Resurrection, thereby providing us with the true meaning of our sickness.
>
> 3. He enables us to accept the will of the **Father** with loving obedience in this time of trial, as the test of our loyalty and faith, and to prepare us for our complete surrender to Him.

Here we see the union of the Father, Son, and Holy Spirit with the sick person, that manifests their closeness to and mercy for him. In this way the sick person can experience truly that God did not abandon him in the time of trial, but through the Holy Spirit sends to him His Son, Christ, who comes in the sacrament to heal and to console. It is Christ who is present and administers the sacrament in the person of the priest and in the midst of the believing community, the Church. Grace is Christ.

## II. Introduction to Infused Virtues and Gifts through Actual Grace

### Background

The primary focus in this brief synthesis is to describe how, along with the sanctifying grace that elevates the soul, the divine cortege of infused virtues and gifts of the Holy Spirit, along with actual grace, elevates our faculties so that we can live our divine filiation.

If we are to live not just at the natural level but at the supernatural level of divine grace, it is incumbent upon us to understand its inner workings. Many are not conscious of the presence, beginning with Baptism, of the indwelling Trinity within our souls (uncreated grace), which brings about a created transformation of (i) soul (sanctifying grace: remission of sins, participation in God's divine life, divine filiation) and (ii) of faculties (e.g., infused virtues, gifts of the Holy Spirit). Concretely in daily life, many are not aware that the infused theological virtues (faith, hope, and charity) tower over the intellect, through which we can bridge the infinite chasm to arrive at the inner sanctuary of the Trinity. But the theological virtues must be perfected by the gifts of the Holy Spirit, through which we are led, as was Jesus, by Him in daily life. But the dynamism for these virtues and gifts is actual grace, the constant inner divine impulses from the Holy Spirit (e.g., inspirations). This last means that, given the foundation of sanctifying grace, what matters most is cooperation with actual grace, the consequence of which neglect Reginald Garrigou-Lagrange describes as "hail falling upon seedlings," that is, killing the life of grace.

### The Natural and Supernatural Life of the Soul

Here we examine how the human organism is elevated divinely to be possessed by the Holy Spirit. Reginald Garrigou-Lagrange, with his Scholastic background, distinguishes explicitly the natural level from the entirely gratuitous gift of God that is grace. In the human soul, there are two natural faculties that are already quite different. (1) The sensitive (senses) part is common to men and animals, and includes the external (five senses) and internal (imagination, emotions, sense memory) senses.

(2) The intellectual towers above the senses. For the soul is spiritual, and it does not intrinsically depend on the body, and will thus be able to survive the body after death. And from the essence of the soul spring our two higher faculties, the intellect and will. The intellect knows not only sense qualities like colour, but also being, the intelligible reality, of necessary and universal truths, such as "we must do good and avoid evil." Animals, possessing only the sensible faculty, can never attain to this knowledge. Since the intellect is

capable of knowing the good in a universal manner, it follows that the will can love this good, will it, and accomplish it.

(3) Yet, while the intellect and will can develop greatly, as seen in men of genius and superior men of action, they can't attain to the knowledge and love of the intimate life of God, which is of another order, entirely supernatural. While man can know God from his reflection on created beings, he cannot attain the essential and formal object of the divine intellect. It is sanctifying grace, the seed of glory, that introduces us into this higher order of truth and life. It is an essentially supernatural life, a participation in the intimate life of God, in the divine nature, since it even now prepares us to see God someday as He sees Himself and *to love Him as He loves Himself.* Sanctifying grace is like a divine graft received in the very essence of the soul to elevate its vitality and to make it bear no longer merely natural fruits but supernatural ones, meritorious as that meriting eternal life. This divine graft of sanctifying grace is therefore an essentially supernatural life, immensely superior to a sensible miracle.

Even in this present life, divine grace develops in us under the form of the infused virtues and of the seven gifts of the Spirit. As the intellectual and sense faculties spring from the very essence of the soul, the infused virtues and the gifts of the Holy Spirit spring from sanctifying grace, received in the essence of the soul— the virtues and gifts, with sanctifying grace, constitute the *supernatural organism*, which were given to us in Baptism and restored by Absolution if we have the misfortune to lose it. The transformation is already a "beginning of glory": "the same supernatural life, the same sanctifying grace, is in the just on earth and in the saints in heaven" (p. 36).

## A. The Theological Virtues

The theological virtues are infused (divine) virtues which have for their object *God Himself*, our supernatural last end; the infused moral virtues have for their object the *supernatural means* proportioned to our last end. Among the theological virtues, infused faith, which makes us believe all that God has revealed because He is Truth itself, is like a higher spiritual sense which allows us to hear a divine harmony that is inaccessible to every other means of knowing and of which God is the composer. This higher musical sense permits us to hear the voice of God through the prophets and through His Son before we are admitted to see Him face to face. The one with the musical ear of faith alone grasps both the meaning and soul of the symphony, even though the one without faith can hear the symphony as well. The perfect chords of the symphony are called the mysteries of the Trinity, the

Incarnation, the Redemption, the Eucharist, and eternal life. By this superior sense of hearing man is guided toward eternity.

Thus, there is an immense difference between a man of faith and a very learned man who sincerely makes a historical and critical study of the Gospels and its miracles without ever coming to the point where he believes. "Faith… is the gift of God," says St. Paul. It is the basis for justification, for it makes us know the supernatural end toward which we must tend. It makes us, in fact, adhere supernaturally and infallibly to what God reveals to us about His intimate life, according as the Church proposes it to us: "With it, the scholar will drop on his knees; feeling the wretchedness of man, he lifts his hands out in seeking mercy. Then the scales drop from his eyes, he is changed, a man, meek and humble of heart; he can die, he has conquered the truth" (Lacordaire; see A. Frossard).

To tend effectively toward this supernatural end and to reach it, man has received two helps, hope and charity, which are like two wings. Without them, man could make progress only in the direction indicated by reason; with hope and charity he flies in the direction pointed out by faith. Just as our intellect cannot know the supernatural end without the infused light of faith, so *our will cannot tend toward it* unless its powers are augmented to a higher order with infused or supernatural hope and love.

First, by hope *we desire to possess God*, and in order to attain Him we rely, not on our natural powers, but on God Himself who always comes to the assistance of those who invoke Him. Second, charity is a superior and more disinterested love of God. It makes us *love God*, not only in order to possess Him some day, but *for Himself and more than ourselves, because of His infinite goodness*. It ordains to Him the acts of all the other virtues, which it vivifies and renders meritorious. *It is the great supernatural force, the power of love, which permitted saints to overcome all obstacles in persecution.*

*Thus a man illumined by faith advances toward God by the two wings of hope and love.* As soon as he sins mortally, he loses sanctifying grace and charity, since he turns away from God, whom he ceases to love more than himself. But divine mercy preserves infused faith and hope in him as long as he does not sin mortally against these virtues. Such are the superior functions of the spiritual organism: the three theological virtues (elevate the soul) which grow together, and with them, the infused moral virtues (elevate the faculties) that accompany them. Like Paul, the baptized senses that the wonderful plan ("good news") of God has broken upon him and laid hold of him. Grace results in intimate attachment to Christ, and the Person and act of Christ fills his vision. Grace discloses a new world.

## B. The Moral Virtues

Here we must first clearly distinguish the infused moral virtues from the merely acquired moral virtues. The *acquired* moral virtues are acquired by the repetition of acts under the direction of more or less cultivated natural reason. The *infused* moral virtues are thus called because God alone can produce them in us, and are received not from repetition but at Baptism (or restored after mortal sin by Absolution in Confession). The acquired moral virtues, known to the pagans, have an object accessible to natural reason; the infused moral virtues have an essentially supernatural object commensurate with *our supernatural end*, an object inaccessible without the infused light of faith in eternal life, the gravity of sin, the redemptive value of our Saviour's Passion, and the value of grace and the sacraments.

This subject matter is important since some people consecrated in their *youth* did not give sufficient importance to the moral virtues. That is, they seem to have the three theological virtues, but almost lack the moral virtues of prudence, justice, fortitude, and so on. Similarly, they may have the infused moral virtues, but not the corresponding acquired (human) moral virtues in a sufficient degree. Older people see the importance of the moral virtues in social life, yet do not sufficiently value the theological virtues, which are incomparably higher, since they unite us to God. How are the two sets of virtues exercised? The acquired virtues are subordinated to the infused virtue as a *favorable disposition*. The acquired virtues can be compared to the agility of a pianist through repetitions of acts, while the infused virtues can be compared to the musical art in the artist's intellect. While he may not be able to practise his art if he loses the use of his fingers, his art (music), however, remains in his intellect.

These moral virtues consist in a happy medium between the two extremes, extremes manifested by the excess on the one hand and deficiency on the other. However, we must not misunderstand this mean as mediocrity, as a halfway between good and evil, as opposed to a mean between two contrary evils. That is, it is also a summit (like a mountain between two valleys), e.g., fortitude being superior to fear and temerity; prudence to imprudence and cunning. In addition, this happy medium tends to rise without deviating to the right or the left in proportion as the virtue grows.

## C. The Gifts of the Holy Spirit

The gifts of the Holy Spirit are the perfection of the infused virtues. Pope Leo XIII, in *Divinum illud munus* (n. 9, see Vatican.va), captures the sublimity of the gifts of the Holy Spirit that make us docile to Him:

> By means of them the soul is furnished and strengthened so as to obey more easily and promptly His voice and impulse. Wherefore these gifts are of such efficacy that they lead the just man to the *highest degree of sanctity*; and of such excellence that they continue to exist even in heaven, though in a more perfect way. By means of these gifts the soul is excited and encouraged to seek after and *attain the evangelical beatitudes*, which, like the flowers that come forth in the springtime, are the signs and harbingers of eternal beatitude. (emphasis added)

We recommend Francis Fernandez's discourse in *In Conversation with God* in which he offers fulsome meditations on each of the seven gifts of the Holy Spirit, for which reason we need not go over them in detail.[2] We reprint here his summary so that we can see in general the specific value of each gift of the Holy Spirit:

> The gift of understanding shows us the riches of the Faith with greater clarity. The gift of knowledge enables us to judge created things in an upright manner, and to keep our heart fixed on God, and on things insofar as they lead us to him. The gift of wisdom enables us to comprehend the unfathomable wonder of God, and it urges us to seek him in preference to all other things, amid our ordinary work and obligations. The gift of counsel points out the paths of holiness to us — God's Will in our ordinary daily life — and encourages us to choose the option which most closely coincides with the glory of God, and the good of our fellow man. The gift of piety inclines us to treat God with the intimacy with which a child treats his father. The gift of fortitude uplifts us continually, helping us to overcome the difficulties which we inevitably meet on our journey to God. The gift of fear induces us to flee the occasions of sin, resist temptation, avoid every evil which could sadden the Holy Spirit, and to fear above all the loss of the One whom we love, and who is the reason of being of our life. [3]

Fr. Fernandez explains that we must rid our souls of any possible obstacles through purification to allow the Holy Spirit to invade us through these gifts.

> When a Christian fights to acquire these [acquired and infused] virtues, his soul is preparing to receive the grace of the Holy Spirit fruitfully. The Third Person of the Blessed Trinity, the soul's sweet guest (Sequence, "Come Holy Spirit"), pours out his gifts: wisdom, understanding, counsel, fortitude, knowledge, piety and the fear of the Lord (cf. Is 11:2).[4]

---

[2] Francis Fernandez, *In Conversation with God*, vol. 2 (New York: Scepter, 1993), n. 83 (pp. 513-518); nn. 87-93 (pp. 537-586).
[3] Ibid., 515-516.
[4] St. Josemaría Escrivá, *Friends of God*, 92, quoted in ibid., 517.

We would like to add a clarification to Reginald Garrigou-Lagrange's stating that the infused theological virtues are "superior" to the gifts of the Holy Spirit:

> The theological virtues, which unite us to the Holy Ghost, are superior to the seven gifts, although they receive a new perfection from the gifts; thus a tree is more perfect than its fruit. These virtues are the rule of the gifts, in the sense that the gifts make us penetrate more deeply and taste with greater delight the mysteries to which we adhere by faith; but the immediate act of the gifts is the special inspiration of the Holy Ghost.[5]

Reginald Garrigou-Lagrange's insight conforms to the teaching of St. John of the Cross. Infused contemplation accomplishes a divinization of the soul by grace and of its faculties through the infused virtues by the actualization of the Gifts of the Holy Spirit. The divinized operation of the faculties takes place above all through the theological virtues of faith, hope, and love, "which are the true principles of this transformation and of its passage to the mystical life."[6] Garrigou-Lagrange's analogy of the theological virtues as a tree clearly indicates that "a tree is more perfect than its fruit." While accepting that fact, is not the purpose of the tree its fruits? Jesus taught that he comes to look for fruits in us (Mt 7:19; cf. Jn 15:2; Mk 11:12-14). Garrigou-Lagrange himself says that saints are like great ships with large sails (gifts of Holy Spirit). We are to be possessed by the Spirit by these gifts of the Holy Spirit to enable a mystical incarnation (Gal 2:20): "God provides the wind, you must raise the sails" (St. Augustine).

Why we are taking pains to highlight the gifts of the Holy Spirit as the perfection of the infused virtues is manifest in different ways. These gifts are key to living out of sanctifying grace. It is necessary, because the infused virtues, which though divine, work under the control of our reason and therefore at the natural level. The gifts of the Holy Spirit in contrast work extrinsically under the control of the Holy Spirit, as long as we look to His inspiration ("unfurling" the sails that are the gifts of the Holy Spirit). These gifts of the Holy Spirit also help ward off the seven Capital sins and the attacks of the evil spirit. The gifts of the Holy Spirit and the infused virtues perfected by the gifts together bring an anticipation of the heavenly "beatitudes" by the acts of the eight Beatitudes, as well as the fruits of the Holy Spirit (actions that reveal a life led by the Spirit, following Christ's words, "You will know them by their fruits"). The gifts are like "virtues," *dispositions* to live the good life, the fruits are their *actions*. Of such perfection are the gifts of the Holy Spirit that Reginald Garrigou-Lagrange describes saints as big (unfurled) sailing ships, moved by the breath of the Holy Spirit.

---

[5] Reginald Garrigou-Lagrange, *The Three Ages of the Interior Life*, 78, footnote 45.
[6] Paul-Marie of the Cross, *Carmelite Spirituality in the Teresian Tradition*, 76.

## D. Actual Grace

### 1. The Necessity of Actual Grace

Reginald Garrigou-Lagrange also explains that, while the natural order is necessary (though needs the cooperation of God even at that level), a divine impulse (actual grace) is required to produce acts of infused virtues or of the gifts of the Holy Spirit. As against Pelagianism and Semi-Pelagianism, the Church teaches that on our own we can neither dispose ourselves positively to conversion, nor persevere for a notable time in good, above all, until death. Without actual grace, we cannot produce the slightest salutary act nor reach perfection: "Without me you can do nothing" (Jn 15:5); "for God is at work in you, both to will and to work for his good pleasure" (Phil 2:13). God actualizes our freedom without violating it, disposing us to habitual grace and to act meritoriously. As St. Augustine says, when He crowns our merits, it is still His own gifts that He crowns.

This is why we must pray. Except for the first grace, which is gratuitously given to us without our praying for it, *prayer is the normal, efficacious, and universal means by which God wishes that we should obtain all actual graces we need.* This is why our Lord inculcates so often the necessity of prayer to obtain grace: "Ask, and it will be given you; seek, and you will find; knock, and it will be opened to you" (Mt 7:7). This is especially true when we must resist temptation: "Watch and pray that you may not enter into temptation; the spirit indeed is willing..." (Mt 26:41). We must find consolation in Augustine's words: "God never commands the impossible, but in commanding He tells us to do what we can, to ask for that which we are not able to do, and He helps us in order that we may be able." By His actual grace He even helps us to pray. There are consequently actual graces which we can only obtain by prayer. We must not become imbued with the Semi-Pelagian spirit, imagining that everything can be attained with will and energy, even without actual grace.[7] This may be the problem of our times, epitomized by Louis L'Amour's novels' characters. We must ask for grace to keep to His precepts, especially that of the love of God and of others.

### 2. The Different Actual Graces

Actual grace presents itself under different forms. (i) It is often given as a light or interior *illumination,* e.g., when we receive an interior light in listening to the Gospel of the day at Mass. (ii) It is followed by a grace of *inspiration*

---

[7] Semi-Pelagianism was not as extreme as Pelagianism, but it still denied important points of the faith. Its basic claims were: (1) the beginning of faith (though not faith itself or its increase) could be accomplished by the human will alone, unaided by grace; (2) in a loose sense, the sanctifying grace man receives from God can be merited by natural human effort, unaided by actual grace; (3) once a man has been justified, he does not need additional grace from God in order to persevere until the end of life.

*and attraction*, by which we are strongly led with a disinterested love for the Saviour to love and to action. (iii) At times it even brings one to *give oneself fully to God, to suffer, and if need be, to die for Him*— this is not only a grace of attraction, but a grace of strength.

Actual grace moves the will in two ways: proposing an object which attracts the will, or by a motion or interior impulse which God alone can give. As to the first, God can propose heavenly happiness to us, but a mother too can propose a sensible object to attract a child, as can one's guardian angel suggest good thoughts. But God alone can move our will to good by an interior impulse, for He is closer to us than we are to ourselves (we see God's closeness in preserving us in existence (*conservatio*) as well as the collaboration in our actions (*concursus divinus*)). He can move our soul and faculties from within according to their natural inclination by giving us a new energy. Just as a mother can lift up a child in the natural order, God can lift us up in the spiritual order, lift up our will to good. He is the very Author of our will; and in consequence, He alone can move it from within, acting in the very inmost depths of our will, to will and to act.

Actual grace is called prevenient grace when it arouses a good thought or feeling in us when we have done nothing to excite it in ourselves. If we do not resist this grace, God adds to it a helping or concomitant grace. Finally, God sometimes moves us to act by deliberation according to our human mode (e.g., I see the hour has arrived to do my Examen Prayer and am led by deliberation to do it— this is called a cooperating grace), and at other times, by special inspiration to act in a superior mode without deliberation (I immediately say a received aspiration to God without deliberation). It is important to note that God works in the first manner according to the human mode with the infused virtues (with deliberation, our cooperation); *in the second manner of superhuman mode with the gifts of the Holy Spirit*. Under the latter, we are more passive than active, and our activity consists especially in *consenting freely to the operation of God, in allowing ourselves to be led by the Holy Spirit, in promptly and generously following His inspirations*.

## 3. Fidelity to Grace

Fidelity to grace is of the utmost importance, and especially so is increasing fidelity to the actual grace of the present moment, that we may correspond to the *duty of that moment, which manifests the will of God in our regard*. As Augustine says, "God who created you without yourself, will not sanctify you without yourself" (*Sermon* 15.1). Actual grace is constantly offered to us for the accomplishment of the duty of the present moment, just as air comes constantly into our lungs to permit us to breathe. As we must inhale in order to breathe, so we must receive with docility the grace which renews our spiritual energies in the journey toward God. He who does not receive grace with docility will eventually die from spiritual asphyxiation: "and we do exhort you that you do not receive the grace of God in vain" (2 Cor 6:1).

Without a doubt, God takes the first step toward us by his prevenient grace, then He helps us to consent to it. He accompanies us in all our ways and difficulties, even to the moment of death. We must be faithful to these prevenient graces by: (1) joyfully welcoming the first illuminations of grace; (2) then by following its inspirations with docility in spite of obstacles; and (3) *finally by putting these inspirations into practice no matter what the cost.* Then we shall cooperate in the work of God, and our action will be the fruit of His grace and of our free will. It will be entirely from God as first cause, and entirely from us as second cause. The first grace of light, which efficaciously produces a good thought in us, is sufficient in relation to a voluntary good consent; however, **resistance** to sufficient grace falls like hail on a tree in bloom. Efficacious grace is offered us in sufficient grace, as the fruit is in the flower. If we do not resist sufficient grace, actual efficacious grace is given us, and by it we advance surely in the way of salvation. *Sufficient grace thus leaves us without excuse before God, efficacious grace does not allow us to glory in ourselves*; with it we advance humbly and generously.

We should not resist the divine prevenient graces of Him who has given us sanctifying grace, the infused virtues, and gifts of the Holy Spirit, and who daily draws us to Himself. We would not be content with living a mediocre life and with producing only imperfect fruits, since our Saviour came so that from within us "shall flow rivers of living waters" (Jn 7:38).

There are three aspects to be considered with respect to fidelity: (a) first of all, that we may preserve the life of grace by *avoiding sin*. The life of grace is incomparably more precious than that of the body, the unveiled splendour of sanctifying grace would cause us to be ravished; (b) second, *fidelity* is required to merit and obtain the increase of the life of grace; (c) third, the necessity of *sanctifying* each and every one of our acts, even the most ordinary, by accomplishing them with *purity of intention, for a supernatural motive, and in union with our Lord*. If we were thus faithful from morning to evening, each of our days would contain hundreds of meritorious acts of love of God and of neighbour, and our union with God would be more intimate and much stronger.

# RENEWAL 2

## Priesthood Renewal: Jesus' Appeal in
## *In Sinu Jesu* (with brief introductions)

*One of the best known and esteemed spiritual writers of our time shared how he was influenced by "In Sinu Jesu," with which we were till then unfamiliar. Trusting this spiritual writer, the author himself read the book and was quite taken by it. We encourage readers to take up this fine work, as it can be invaluable for renewing our faith.*

*The author (i) has selected what he discerns as major common themes from the vast material, with selections to illustrate these major themes, while (ii) adding brief introductions. These excerpts are taken from "In Sinu Jesu: When Heart Speaks to Heart: The Journal of a Priest at Prayer by a Benedictine Monk" (Angelico Press, 2016). We thank Angelico Press for giving permission (granted February 3, 2022).*

### The Need for Renewal in the Church

**Private Revelation**: We note that public revelation has ceased and the Church leaves it up to us to choose if we wish to accept particular private revelations. Yet, if the Church approves a revelation or a saint, we ought to have openness to the Holy Spirit working in it. For example, now that the Church has approved of Lourdes and Fatima, it is good to show openness to them. We find this openness in John Paul II, who believed that it was our Lady who redirected a bullet that would have killed him during the failed assassination attempt, and felt impelled to go to Fatima to express his gratitude to her. We can imitate the faith and devotion of this pope and hearken to the messages (private revelation) from our Lady to the three children at Fatima. Likewise, we can trust the private revelation of a doctor of the Church like St. Catherine of Siena, whose *Dialogues* comprise primarily God's words to her in visions.

Regarding *In Sinu Jesu*, the author trusts the highly esteemed spiritual writer who recommended it to him. The book does have an *imprimatur* and a *nihil obstat*, which indicate that there is nothing in it that is contrary to the faith. The author's own sense, from the parts he has read, is that the words of this book indeed reflect the voice of the Shepherd (the Lord told us that His sheep listen to His voice as Shepherd), and in fact resonate with key convictions that he holds (e.g., importance of our Lady and the saints, that the priest is to live between the altar and the tabernacle, that the Mass is primarily a sacrifice). The primary overall insight that resounds in this book is that Jesus is calling for a renewal in the Church through a renewal in the priesthood.

> **Texts from *In Sinu Jesu* (with Introductions)**

## 1. The Secret of Priestly Holiness: Becoming John
Jesus teaches that John, the Beloved Disciple, is the model for priests. (May 8, 2008, p. 61)

> Yes, I have called you to become another John.
> I want you to gaze upon my Face
> with all the tenderness and adoration
> that the Holy Spirit gave him during the years he spent in my company.
> Even after my Ascension
> he discerned my abiding presence in the Sacrament of my Love and
> learned to contemplate there the glory of my Eucharistic Face.
>
> John was the friend of my Heart.
> When he saw my Heart pierced on Calvary, his own heart was pierced too.
> This created between him and my Most Holy Mother the deepest of bonds.
> This it was that sealed the covenant of filial and maternal love
> that I established between them
> by the virtue of my words from the Cross.
> It was this that made their life together
> after the birth of my Church at Pentecost
> a model of perfect unity and of burning charity.

## 2. Friendship With Jesus
John and the apostles were formed for their task by being with Jesus and being formed by Him to become first His "friends." (May 28, 2013, p. 240)

> Watch and Pray with Me. The first thing I asked of my priests, my newly-ordained apostles, and of these, the three closest to My Heart, was to watch and pray with Me. I did not send them out immediately, nor did I entrust them with any priestly task apart from keeping watch with Me in prayer, lest they fall in the hour of trial.
> I wanted them close to Me to console Me, to comfort Me in My agony by their union with My prayer of obedience and abandonment to the Father. This was their first priestly action, their first mandate as priests of the New Covenant: not to preach, not to teach, not to heal, nor even to baptize, but to watch and pray with Me.
> When will my priests begin to pray as I have asked them for so long -- lo, all these centuries -- to pray? I want priests who will watch and pray with Me. I need such priests. Without their prayer, my mystic agony will be prolonged and be without consolation from the friends whom I have chosen to abide with Me in the trials that will soon beset My Church, my

poor, frail Bride. The crisis in My priesthood will continue and will even grow worse unless My priests -- the chosen friends of My Heart -- forsake this passing world's vanities and empty pursuits to become adorers in spirit and in truth.

I wanted them to understand by this that unless a priest keeps watch and perseveres in prayer, all else will be in vain. He will dispense the substance of My mysteries, but without the sweetness of a heavenly unction, without the fire and light of a personal experience of My Divine Friendship. This is why I beg My priests to become adorers: to begin to keep watch and pray close to Me in the Sacrament of My Love…

## 3. Priests are to Have a Preferential Love for Jesus
Jesus must be our first love bar none. (January 31, 2008, pp. 31-32)

> This is the root of the evil that eats away at the priesthood from within: a lack of experiential knowledge of my friendship and love. My priests are not mere functionaries; they are My chosen ones, the friends whom I chose for myself to live in such communion of mind and heart with Me that they prolong My presence in the world. Each priest is called to love My Church with all the tender passion of a bridegroom, but to do this, he must spend time in My presence. He must experience Me personally as the Bridegroom of his soul.
>
> Never miss an opportunity to greet Me, to adore Me, to remain with Me, even if only for a moment, in the Sacrament of My love. In eternity, you will see the inestimable value of every moment spent in My Eucharistic presence.

## 4. The Secret of Jesus' Saints and Priests must be Sanctity
This book has reiterated multiple times the necessity of sanctity. (October 29, 2007, pp. 13, 15)

> This was the secret of my saints,
> of the holy friends whom I have made known to you:
> Dom Marmion, the Curé of Ars,
> Saint Peter Julian Eymard, Saint Gaetano Catanoso,
> Dom Vandeur, Father Marie–Joseph Cassant,
> all of these, priests according to My Heart.
> And there are so many others also
> who knew how to live between the altar and the tabernacle,
> that is, between their offering of the Holy Sacrifice
> and My abiding presence….
> My Heart thirsts for the love of saints.
> To those who come to Me, I will give love and holiness.
> And in this shall my Father be glorified.
> And this shall be wrought by the intimate action of my Spirit.
> Where I am present in the Sacrament of My Love,
> there also is the Spirit of the Father and of the Son.

## 5. Holiness through Adoration

To become John is to be a contemplative. Jesus reveals that the power of the apostles derived from the contemplative prayer of Mary and John. (December 20, 2011, pp. 208-209)

> Adoration is a furnace and a forge.
> The soul called to a life of adoration
> must expect to suffer the intensity of the fiery furnace,
> and the reshaping of all that is misshapen in her
> in the forge of My Divine Will.
> For this to happen,
> it is enough that the soul offer herself to My love,
> and remain humble, peaceful, and quiet
> as I purify and transform her in My presence....
> It is the simple prayer of adoration
> that renders a priest fit for the sacred ministry
> by giving him a pure heart
> and by correcting all that is incompatible with My Divine Holiness
> and with My Priestly Love in his life.
> This way of holiness through adoration
> is a secret revealed to My saints in ages past,
> and it is a gift that I am offering My priests
> in these times of impurity, persecution, and darkness.
> To overcome impurity, I will give them a shining purity
> that will blaze before the eyes of the world
> as a testimony to Divine Love.
> For persecution, I will give them a manly strength and a resoluteness of
> purpose that will confound those who plot their downfall.
> For darkness I will give them a clear light by which to order their steps
> and see what choices are pleasing to My Heart.

## 6. The Priest is to be always in Intercession before the Father

A priest of Christ is always in intercession mode, which was the mode of Jesus. From His beginnings, at prayer at night, and even on the cross, He was all intercession. How do we pray the Mass?: is there adoration and intercession? As Cardinal Arinze said, is there ACTS (adoration, confession, thanksgiving, and supplication)? (January 10, 2012, pp. 213, 215)

> It consists in placing oneself with Me before the Father,
> with a boundless trust in the merits of My Passion
> and in the wounds that I present to the Father
> on behalf of all who approach Him with confidence, through Me.
> I live in the Sacrament of My Love as I live in heaven,
> in a ceaseless estate of intercession
> for all who believe in Me

and come to Me with the weight of life's burdens and sorrows.
There is nothing that I will not do
for the soul who approaches Me with confidence....
The emptiness of My churches
apart from the hours of the liturgical offices,
is an indictment,
first of all, of My priests,
and then, of My faithful.
My Eucharistic Presence meets with coldness,
with indifference, and with a chilling ingratitude,
even on the part of My priests
and of consecrated souls.
They fail to recognize in the mystery
of the Most Holy Eucharist
the pearl of great price,
the treasure once hidden in the field,
but now offered freely
to all who would partake of its inexhaustible riches.

## 7. "The Night of my agony and betrayal. Nothing of my passion has passed away"

The holy one stays close to Christ, especially in His Passion. He told Blessed Dina Bélanger that many priests do not console Him in His Passion. What is the difference between Padre Pio and the good priest? Why do people flock to participate in Padre Pio's Mass, as did bishops during the sessions of the Second Vatican Council? Padre Pio does not get caught up with the congregation, music, rubrics, or busy thoughts, but penetrates the interior mystery, which is Calvary, and he also lives the mystery, becoming a crucified Christ; he becomes a living sacrament.

The teaching here is all christocentric. We find it in Cardinal Sarah's three counsels in a talk given to the seminarians at St. Augustine's Seminary in a visit to Toronto: friendship with Christ, conversation with Christ, and crucifixion with Christ. We see how Cardinal Sarah's points strike our hearts much more deeply than the frequently human focus of Sunday homilies (e.g., love each other, be encouraging, be patient).

> There is not a single moment of My sufferings that is not present in this the Sacrament of My Love for you. Here you will find Me in every detail of My Passion, for nothing of My Passion has passed away. All remains actual and efficacious in the mysteries of My Body and Blood given up for you. If you would be with Me in My sufferings, come to Me in the Sacrament of My Love. If you would keep watch with Me in Gethsemane, come to My altar, and abide there with Me. If you would accompany Me in My imprisonment, in My trial, in My condemnation, and in My being mocked, scourged, and

crowned with thorns, seek Me out in this Sacrament where I wait for a little compassion from those who profess to be My friends.

I am still carrying My cross, and the weight of your sins falls heavy on My shoulder, and crushes Me even to the ground. None of this is over and forgotten; it remains present in the Sacrament of My Passion, in the Mystery of My Sacrifice made present on the altar and remaining wherever I am: the pure Victim, the Holy Victim, the Spotless Victim, whom you contemplate in the Host....

This all my saints understood: the presence of My Passion in this Sacrament, and this Sacrament as the memorial of My Passion. This the Holy Spirit teaches even to the little and to the poor who open their hearts to My mysteries made present at the altar. This is the great reality that, today, so many have forgotten.

## 8. Reparation is the Exercise of Love
Those who are holy mirror St. Thérèse of Lisieux, who understood that the greatest tragedy in human history is that Jesus was not loved and spent her life trying to make reparation for the love Jesus was not receiving. (December 27, 2011, pp. 210-211)

>The Angels are like living flames
>who burn in My Eucharistic presence
>without ever being consumed.
>For all of this, My Angels cannot replace
>a single human heart in My presence.
>What I look for from men,
>what I wait for, above all, from My priests,
>my Angels cannot give Me....
>Again, it was John who offered Me faithful love
>in exchange for Judas; faithless betrayal.
>He made reparation to My Heart that suffered so grievously
>when Judas walked out of the Cenacle into the night.
>In that moment, John gave Me all the love of his heart,
>begging Me to accept it
>in reparation for Judas' cold and calculated plot against Me.
>
>Be another Saint John for My Heart.
>Offer Me reparation by offering Me yourself
>in the place of those who flee from before My Eucharistic Face;
>in the place of those who cannot bear to remain
>in my presence, close to My Heart;
>in the place of those priests of Mine
>who have time for all else save for Me.

## 9. A Priest is to Allow Christ to Live in him Ceaselessly

Jesus taught Blessed Dina Bélanger that "a priest is to be a replica of me," through a substitution of Christ (He takes over), as a perpetual oblation and victim. (November 29, 2008, pp. 94-95)

> Do not be fearful of preaching. Know that I will be with you to speak through you and to touch even the most hardened hearts. Abandon yourself to me in complete confidence and I will abandon myself to you so that your words will be my words
> and your presence my presence.
> This is what I long to do with every priest of mine.
>
> If only my priests would allow me to speak and to act through them!
> What miracles of grace they would see!
> A holy priest is quite simply
> one who allows me to live in him as in a supplementary humanity.
> In every priest I would speak and act,
> delivering souls from the powers of darkness and healing the sick;
> but most of all, I desire to offer myself in every priest
> and to assume every priest into my own offering to the Father.
>
> This I would do at the altar in the celebration of my Holy Sacrifice,
> but not only there;
> the life of a priest united to me is a ceaseless oblation
> and he, like me, is a *hostia perpetua*, a perpetual victim.
> You cannot imagine the fruitfulness of such a union,
> and this is the fruitfulness that I desire
> for my Father's glory and for the joy of my Bride, the Church.

## 10. The Priest is to Re-live Christ's Passion

A priest is to be both a priest and victim. Fulton Sheen notes that the Old Testament priest differs from the New Testament priest in that the latter priest is also the victim. He perceived that priests love the priesthood but don't necessarily want the victimhood: obedience to the bishop, making time for prayer before the tabernacle, putting the Eucharist in first place, living poverty, forgetting self and family, etc. (Mar. 1, 2010, pp. 145-146)

> Suffering and adoration are two expressions of the love that I desire to see burning in your heart. Suffer in love for Me, and adore Me out of love. It is love that gives suffering its value in my eyes and in the eyes of My Father, and it is love that makes adoration worthy of me and pleasing to My Heart. This is your vocation: to suffer and to adore, always in love. The love that reaches Me through suffering is a source of graces for the whole Church. The adoration offered Me out of love consoled My Eucharistic Heart and wins an immense outpouring of graces for the sanctification of My beloved priests.

Suffering, for you, is the humble acceptance of every limitation, fatigue, humiliation, disappointment, and sorrow. It is the joyful acceptance of infirmity and weakness. It is adhesion to all the manifestations of My will, especially those that you are incapable of understanding in the present moment. Suffering offered in love is precious in My sight. Accept the sufferings that I allow and I will for you; thus will you participate in My passion through patience and accomplish the mission that I have entrusted to you.

## 11. Our Lady is the Priest's Consolation and Help

Jesus teaches saints that the most efficacious way to go to Him is through our Blessed Virgin Mary. Many don't understand this secret. Vatican II teaches that she is the Mother of the Church, which means that she is the Mother of each, and has given spiritual birth to us, and accompanies us from conception to death. St. Louis de Montfort teaches that she is the mould of Christ, forming Christ in us, to the degree that we consecrate ourselves to her and turn to her. (February 21, 2008, pp. 43-44)

> My Mother's Sorrowful and Immaculate Heart
> is to be your refuge and your place of solace.
> Go to my Mother in all your needs....
>
> If all my priests knew this
> -- not merely with their minds, but in their daily experience --
> the priesthood would be transformed.
> My Most Pure Mother is the faithful and indispensable collaborator
> of the priest who represents me and pursues my work in the Church.
>
> My Mother is attentive to the ministry of the priest
> and to his personal spiritual needs,
> as she was attentive to my ministry
> and to all my needs during my life on earth....
>
> Never fail to recognize the mystical presence of my Mother in the Mass.
> She is there at your side.
> She rejoices in your distribution of the fruits of my redemption,
> and participates in it.
> The hands of every priest are, in some way, held in my Mother's hands.
> She acts with the priest.
> Her participation in the Holy Sacrifice renewed upon the altar is silent but efficacious.
> Her presence at the altar, though invisible, is real.
>
> My Church has long acknowledged the presence of my Mother
> at every offering of my Holy Sacrifice,
> but it is now more than ever necessary

that priests should deepen their awareness of this most precious gift.
She is the Coredemptrix.

Just as my Sacrifice is renewed mystically in every Mass,
her offering, her participation in my offering, is also renewed.
The priest who knows this and allows it to penetrate his heart
will be graced with a holy fervour in every Mass he celebrates.

## 12. The Joy of the Cenacle: The Eucharist is all about Love

We are to receive and give love, and the power to love comes from the Eucharist. Mother Teresa established in the Constitutions of her Order that her Sisters are to begin their day with the Eucharist to receive Christ so as to be able to love Christ in the poor. (citation uncertain)

> It is right that you should feel joy and peace
> in my presence here tonight
> because it is the presence of Love,
> infinite, living Love.
>
> So few souls understand that my Eucharistic Presence
> is all Love,
> and that when they approach my altar,
> or kneel before my tabernacle,
> or gaze upon my Sacramental Form,
> they are in the presence
> of Love so powerful and so gentle
> that nothing created can be compared to it.
>
> I instituted the Sacrament of my Body and Blood
> so that souls might eat Love, drink Love,
> and abide in Love's company.
> I did this for all souls until the end of time,
> but especially for my priests.
> My priests hunger for Love,
> my priests thirst for Love,
> my priests seek the company of Love,
> but so few of them come to me.
>
> You are experiencing joy in my presence tonight:
> that too is right for I intended,
> --from the night before I suffered, this night--
> that the Sacrament of my Body and Blood
> should be a fountain of pure joy
> set in the midst of my Church
> to irrigate the whole world.

## 13. The Priest is to Make God the Father Known

Jesus teaches us that God the Father is our ultimate goal. The Father was everything for Jesus, and He leads us to Him. St. Josemaría Escrivá and St. Marguerite d'Youville both received profound experiences of the Father's love and of their divine filiation (sonship and daughtership).

> Too often my Father is forgotten.
> He is acknowledged as God,
> but His Fatherhood remains unknown,
> and it was to reveal His Fatherhood
> that I came into the world….
>
> Learn to trust in my Father,
> for to trust in Him is to believe in His love for you.
> To trust in Him is to walk in imitation of me.
> To trust in Him is to obey the inspiration of the Holy Spirit….
> Nothing delights the Heart of the Father more
> than the abandonment to Him
> of a soul who believes in His love
> and trusts Him with all things great and small.
>
> My Father is unknown even now,
> after two thousand years,
> and because He is unknown,
> souls continue to live in fear, in bondage, and in darkness.
> Yes, a soul that has not learned to call God "Father"
> is still in darkness and in the shadow of death.
> Such a soul suffers the cold chill of alienation
> from my Father's Heart.
> Much of the suffering and scandal
> that wounds and disfigures my priests
> could have been avoided
> had they been taught in their formative years
> how immense a grace it is
> to live as sons cherished by my Father at every moment.

## 14. Priests are Sons and Fathers

Jesus teaches that the greatest need of our time is paternity and that priests are called to spiritual paternity. (March 15, 2011, pp. 173-174)

> *Spiritual Childhood and Fatherhood*: One who has not known the joys and the security in love of divine sonship cannot receive the grace of supernatural fatherhood. One learns to be a father by being a son and, even in the perfection of spiritual fatherhood, one remains a little child, a son beloved of my Father, full of confidence in His Providence and ready, at every moment, to embrace His Will as it unfolds.

*Wounded Sons*: So many of my priests are retarded in the exercise of their spiritual paternity because they are wounded in their identity as sons. I am about to heal many of my beloved priests who bear, deep within their souls, the wounds of a sonship that did not unfold as I would have wanted it to unfold because of the sins of fathers, and this over many generations....

*Paternal Generativity in the Church*: Those who will be healed in this way will become fathers of souls, participating in the tenderness and strength of the Eternal Father and sharing in the fatherhood that the Apostles recognized in me whilst I lived on earth among them in the flesh. I revealed the Fatherhood of God to my Apostles and graced them with a new birth into my own Divine Sonship. Thus were they rendered capable of a supernatural fatherhood that even today generates life in my Church.

## 15. Live Close to Jesus' Saints

Jesus teaches us that the way to Him is through His closest friends, the saints. Many Christians do not know this secret of the communion of the saints. When we look at the lives of the saints, virtually every one of them has a profound devotion to our Lady and has also been formed by other saints. In some cases, our Lord Himself assigned saints to become mentors/parents of budding saints (e.g., St. Mary Magdalene to St. Catherine of Siena, St. Jean de Brebeuf to Blessed Catherine of St. Augustine). This is also the pattern of the religious communities and lay movements, where the members imitate and supplicate the holy founders. (January 30, 2010, p. 143)[1]

> I have charged so many of My saints
> to walk with you,
> to attend to your needs,
> to obtain for you the graces of repentance,
> and illumination, and union with Me
> that My merciful Heart so desires to give you.
> Some of these saints, though not all of them, are known to you.
>
> They have adopted you, some as a brother, others as a spiritual son.
> Their interest in all that you do, and say, and suffer
> is continuous and they are, at every moment, attentive to you.
> Call upon My saints.
> Ask for their help.
> Walk in their company.
> Invoke those whom I have made known to you.
> Welcome those whom I will make known to you.

---

[1] A Benedictine Monk, *In Sinu Jesu*.

# Appendix 1: Theology of Ministerial Priesthood in Brief
(Attila Miklósházy)

*For the call to renewal in the priesthood, it may help to review in brief the theology of the priesthood.*

**The priesthood of Christ is absolutely unique**: He is Son of God, Incarnate Word, Image of the Father; the Church is His Body. He put an end to Old Testament priesthood, the new Israel begins with Baptism. Baptismal (offering themselves) and ministerial priesthoods share in Christ's one priesthood.

**Christ and Church**: Christ, Son of the Father, became a High Priest through Calvary, and He has associated the Church as the Universal Sacrament of Salvation (an extension of Christ in space and time), *a sacramental presence of Christ.*

**Apostolic College**: The apostles, **called personally by Christ**, *share Christ's mission as well as His triple office of priest, prophet, and king* "priests of sacred worship, teachers of doctrine, and officers of good order" (LG 20). This apostolic succession derives from Christ to the apostles and from the apostles to all bishops to the end of time. The apostolic ministry is, therefore, *the sacrament of the effective presence of Christ and His Spirit* in the midst of the people of God.

**College of Bishops**: Vatican II correctly points to the College of Bishops *sharing in the apostolic ministry* and receiving a call from Christ, moving away from the medieval focus on function (consecrating at Mass and Absolution). It is thereby not a call from the community nor a function. It is the College of Bishops who receive the fullness of priesthood, and from whom priests and deacons receive their participation in this order. Bishops, priests, and deacons all participate in Christ's ministry and share the apostles' ministry: *there is one apostolic ministry and one character passed on but in 3 grades*; the common ground is the active sacramental-personal presence of the risen Christ. The essential rite for all three ordinations: imposition of hands (matter) and epiclesis (form). The Church has added other non-essential elements (e.g., anointing). The character received at ordination constitutes the bishop *a member of the College, configures him to Christ, and enables him to act in the person of Christ* (LG 21-22). Because ordination is the expression of an infallible promise of God to mankind, the priesthood is *necessarily irrevocable; it is forever.*

The biblical image of *shepherd* seems to be the essential, constitutive factor: they should expound the whole mystery of Christ; they should guard the doctrine of the Church, but also adapt their presentation to the needs of the times; they should foster dialogue with all men (*Christus Dominus*). The sacramentality of this sacrament flows from the Church as Sacrament.

**Ordination Character Graces**: Ordination is the symbol of God's initiative, the character thus becomes a permanent source for graces needed for the office (*fons gratiae*). The sacrament increases grace that the individual may become a suitable minister, God touches the individual and confers the grace and virtues necessary to the office. *Its main effect is that it configures the person to Christ the High Priest,* and makes him in a certain sense "alter Christus." It is *a deepening and a re-orientation of baptismal grace* in view of the specific mission and service of the ordained minister. The primary effect of the sacrament is the definitive and effective insertion of the recipient into the apostolic ministry and Office of the Church, established by Christ for the Church. In the case of ordination, the natural power which man has to symbolize God is replaced by the *power which Christ has to symbolize God.*

**Priesthood**: Priesthood refers primarily to the episcopal office, presbyters *participate in (and inserted into) the episcopal office and ministry*. The Catholic priesthood is primarily a personal, **life-long, exclusive bond with Christ** (not an objective service, a job), which entails *celibacy*, not demanded by the very nature of priesthood, yet it accords with it on many scores. By their consecration (*ex opere operato*), priests are set apart in a certain sense, that they may be totally dedicated to the work of the Lord. A fruitful sacramental encounter requires *holiness in the minister* (*ex opere operantis*). Priests are consecrated to continue the 3-fold function of Christ: *to preach the Gospel, shepherd the faithful, and celebrate divine worship* (LG 28). The primary duty of priests is to proclaim the Gospel to all, not teaching their own wisdom but God's Word, and *to summon all men urgently to conversion and holiness* (PO 4). While all the baptized, as members of the Body, symbolize Christ's presence in the world, only the ordained symbolize Him as *Head of the Mystical Body*.

**Diaconate**: The deacon is part of the hierarchy or apostolic ministry and office: not of the "*sacerdotium*," but ordained to the "*servitium*."[2]

## Appendix 2: Alice von Hildebrand on Today's Attacks on our Faith

I wondered why Alice had chosen to focus almost exclusively on the years at Hunter in her *Memoirs of a Happy Failure*. She replied, "Because if you want to destroy a society you should aim... to destroy the family and to pervert education. We no longer educate children; we give them information perverted by relativism and subjectivism." She witnessed firsthand the deterioration of the culture and the despair of the young people who were not taught that there was anything such as absolute truth. We live now with the results of this lacking philosophy.

Dr. von Hildebrand elaborated to me on three such consequences, the first being feminism. "The devil has convinced some women that maternity is the one great obstacle to their attaining human fame, i.e. the one that has been the privilege of man from the beginning. When (Satan) succeeded in doing so (let us think of Simone de Beauvoir) the door was wide open to abortion, his greatest victory since original sin: the Mother of the Living (Eve) accepting to murder her children. All women, whether married or unmarried are called to motherhood; to denigrate motherhood is threatening the very foundation of society."

---

[2] Attila Miklósházy, "Holy Orders," Sacramental Theology II Lecture.

Secondly, she named relativism, "the intellectual cancer devastating our society…an intellectual revolt against key truths: metaphysical, ethical, religious. Science is accepted and glorified because it does not tell me how to lead a human life… there is no 'you should' or 'you should not'. Modern man does not want to obey. He escapes from moral obligations by claiming that it is all subjective: it is up to me to live as I please."

And finally, pornography: "the most disgusting presentation [distortion] of a sphere in which, in the most mysterious way, God and the woman collaborate to bring a new life into existence."

The idea of the universal maternity of womanhood is beautifully illustrated in Dr. von Hildebrand's own life. Although she did not have her own children, as I read her memoir, the word "fruitful" kept coming to mind, especially in her relationship with her students. She actually became godmother to several of them as they entered the Church. She names among her happiest memories "the incredible joy of seeing that several of my students came out of the dark of prejudice and error."

I wanted her thoughts on why there was such a pointed attack on Catholicism in particular at the college. Because Catholicism, she responded, is "the only religion that has an authority, a Magisterium, claiming that it is the only one founded by Christ. (This is a) key role of faith: my intellect kneels to revelation: Credo ut intelligam. (The Church has) authority [wording modified]… (She) keeps reminding man of his creaturehood, and a creature should listen and obey. Modern man wants to do as he pleases… The devil is very open-minded toward other religions: each has its own doctrine. [But] none has the divine seal of truth."

This attack has everything to do with what we see today. The natural results are "the sapping of man's relationship to God, and opening the door to any perversion." She pointed out the Supreme Court decisions which legalize "the murder of the Innocents (and which give) a perversion of the same dignity as marriage. May God have mercy. But He expects us to fight."[3]

---

[3] Claire Dwyer, "Alice von Hildebrand: 'A Happy Failure,'" spiritual direction.com. Permission granted by Claire Dwyer to reprint this excerpt on March 30, 2022..

# PART IV

# COUNSELS: TOOLS

Jesus in the midst… is Jesus! It's not that here among us we have a formula or a virtue, or some goodness or kindness, or a sense of the divine. Here with us is *a person*! We do not see him with our own eyes, but he hears us and scrutinizes our every thought, every throb of our heart, every consent of our soul. He's here! (C. Lubich, Loppiano, Nov. 27, 1975)

If we are united, Jesus is among us. And this is what is valuable. It is worth more than any other treasure that our heart may possess; more than mother, father, brothers, sisters, children. It is worth more than our house, our work, or our property; more than the works of art in a great city like Rome; more than our business deals; more than nature which surrounds us with fields, and flowers; more than the sea and the stars; more than our own soul. (C. Lubich, Meditation 1949)

Christ has made us his associates in the redemption of other people, because by living in us, it is always *Jesus acting in the person*. One by one, his words became ours. We too could say, "I am the light of the world" (Jn 8:12). In fact, from this cell of the Mystical Body that we formed, a light radiated so strongly that simple and good souls, sincerely desirous of God, like sinners humbled under the weight of their sins, recognized it as the light of Jesus. This light has such an impact on people, even those from an atheistic background, that it instantly brought about an inner conversion, in the sense that people who had been attached to a thousand things before, now felt that something else existed, something they had unconsciously yearned for, and that alone would fulfil their desires and totally satisfy them: Jesus.[1] (C. Lubich, *A Simple Harmless Manifesto*, Trent, 1950)

---

[1] Chiara Lubich, *Jesus in our Midst*, 37-39, 46-47.

## IV. COUNSELS: TOOLS

1 Counsel 1. Intellectual: Student Satisfied with Rote-Formula
2 Learning
3 Counsel 2. Human Growth: Troubled Woman with Human
4 Weakness
5 Counsel 3. Present: Seminarian Anxiously Anticipating the Future
6 Counsel 4. Spiritual Direction: Key Elements (R. Garrigou-
7 Lagrange)
8 Counsel 5. Spiritual Direction & Confession: Digressions
9 Counsel 6. Conscience: "Whether Mortal Sin is an Infinite
10 Offense?"
11 Counsel 7. Unity: Disquiet about the Holy Father
12 Counsel 8. Occult: Couple whose Son is Reading Occult Works
Counsel 9. Divine Joy: Christ's Three Dispositions during Trials
Counsel 10. Sacrifice: Offering Christ with His Mysteries
Counsel 11. Chastity: Seminarian's Desire to Protect Celibate Vows
Counsel 12. Struggles: Overcoming all through Jesus in our Midst

These "Counsels" are responses to various life questions or difficulties. Real-life questions often provide light and more clear-cut understanding of how to proceed in daily life issues. They are reprinted here to offer some clarity in following the path of Christ and avoiding digressions in the spiritual life that cause heartache and stress.

# COUNSEL 1

## Intellectual: Student Satisfied with Rote-Formula Learning (Ceases to Think for Himself and to Continue to Learn)

*Difficulty: Within the final comprehensive exam course for dogmatic theology, one seminarian complained that he did not understand the material. It soon became evident that he was merely giving an old Catechism rote-formula theology (e.g., Adam sinned, Jesus saved, etc.), remaining at the level of the time he entered the seminary. The difficulty is not growing, remaining in mediocrity.*

*Counsel: To (i) inculcate continuing to grow; and (ii) seek human perfection in seeing education as self-education, that is, to learn to think and to work at mastery in academics and our professions.*

To sanctify our work, St. Escrivá points us to the clear goal of human and Christian perfection, with the "greatest perfection possible":

> To sanctify our tasks we have to bear in mind that "a Christian should do all honest human work, be it intellectual or manual, with the greatest perfection possible: with human perfection (professional competence) and with Christian perfection (for love of God's Will and as a service to mankind). Human work done in this manner, no matter how humble or insignificant it may seem, helps to shape the world in a Christian way. The world's divine dimension is made more visible and our human labour is thus incorporated into the marvellous work of Creation and Redemption. It is raised to the order of grace. It is sanctified and becomes God's work, *operatio Dei, opus Dei.*" (*Conversations with Monsignor Escrivá de Balaguer*, 10)

### I. Three Presuppositions about Education

Let us begin with human perfection. Where he fails in faith and morals, L'Amour offers some helpful insights on human wisdom, especially on matters of education. Here are three key principles that can help direct us. The first is, "Do you understand that all education is self-education?"

> ... *all education is self-education.* A teacher is only a guide to point out the way, and no school, no matter how excellent, can give you an education. What you receive is like the outlines in a child's coloring book. You must fill in the colors yourself. (Louis L'Amour, "*Lonesome Gods*," p. 16)

The second point develops the first point, that we must learn to think. We can't simply sit in class without actively questioning, making connections:

> Much as I loved reading I was wary of it, for I soon saw that much that passed for thinking was simply a good memory, and many an educated man has merely repeated what he had learned, *not what he had thought out for himself.* (Louis L'Amour, *Bendigo Shafter*, Ch. 5, 78-79)

But most important is the need to continue to learn and that one learns by succeeding in small things and by overcoming failure— by pushing through to the next level. One student in that class, a chemist, related how he had to break through to a mastery of his science to be able to do research:

> Much of what I say may be nonsense, but a few things I have learned, and the most important is that *he who ceases to learn is already a half-dead man*. And do not be like an oyster who rests on the sea bottom waiting for the good things to come by. Search them, find them. (L'Amour, *Lonesome Gods*, Ch. 5, p. 50)

> Nobody ever told me life was easy, and for me it had never been, but I was, I think, the stronger because of it. One learns to succeed by succeeding in small things first. Mostly a person learns to succeed by simply overcoming failure. (L'Amour, *Passing Through*, Ch. 22, p. 209. One can find a number of his sayings online)

Without learning that all education is about self-education, that others only provide tools, that it is up to us to think and to assimilate, then we shall never get very far. But the main problem is that some do not strive to push through to the next level. The seminarians are taught to try to *excel* in their studies to the best of their God-given abilities.

## II. Benefit from Having a Course to Prepare for the Comprehensive Exam

The first thing pointed out to these students was how fortunate they were to have an entire course to help prepare them for their comprehensive exam, and to be tested by only one professor (no panel) for only half an hour. In contrast, a rector of a Redemptoris Mater seminary described the demanding comprehensive exam requirements for his licentiate degree in Canon Law at St. Paul's University in Ottawa. They were responsible for 15 fairly wide blocks of material and had to synthesize them on their own without a preparatory course. In addition, they were examined by two panels of three professors. Similarly, for the philosophy degree at the Toronto Oratory, each course professor submitted three questions for a total of 48 exam questions, and the students had to face a panel of three professors and write a three-hour exam, all without a preparatory course.

The second thing pointed out was the vast modification of this course. The previous recent tradition was to have the students present the lectures. To see its insufficiency, imagine medical students presenting final exam lectures to fellow students and basically being able to capture only the fundamentals, where a gifted and experienced professor with a comprehensive background is able to unify the spectrum and synthesize in-depth. For this course, there have been two major overhauls. First, the instructor has put together for you an altogether new course from scratch, synthesizing each of 19 themes in two questions. Subsequently, the instructor was asked to expand and complete his course synthesis by incorporating comprehensive theological elements to the synthesis questions (e.g., Scripture, Tradition, and Magisterium (e.g., Councils, heresies), theological developments, links to other theological disciplines, personal and pastoral learnings), for which the students complete a weekly worksheet. Thus, the refined course has both a "synthesis" of the most contemporary developments as well as a "comprehensive" command of wider dimensions.

The instructor goes to further lengths to help the students: a course Reader was distributed as well as early access to Quercus' online platform's reading material granted at the beginning of the summer; each theme is summarized for half an hour and students get a chance to rehearse giving their final exam, to which feedback is given. Given that the instructor is basically handing them everything on a silver platter, do the students do their part and fill out the colouring book; or do they just sit back without personal synthesis and just try to memorize the material at the end of the course?

## III. Seminarians' Part in Thinking and Synthesizing

### A. Remote Preparation
The above background begs the question of whether students are doing their part. If they find themselves struggling in this course, they can ask themselves key questions:
1. Does the student seek to make a personal synthesis in dogmatic theology, which is about integrating the various theological disciplines into a "system." For this "Theological Integration" comprehensive course is an opportunity to pull together the different dogmatic areas (e.g., Trinity, soteriology, sacraments, ecclesiology). Thus, he must distinguish Church history, which seeks to see patterns of events, from dogmatic theology, which requires an overarching systematic synthesis of "faith seeking understanding," as reflected in St. Thomas' vast *Summa Theologiae*.
2. The student is ultimately responsible if education is indeed "self-education." He can learn from an effective model of this self-education in the great works program at Oxford University (England) in which the student reads great works and meets periodically with a tutor to discuss the works. This requires much thinking and personal synthesizing of the books.
3. More remotely, do we read theology in the summers? One seminarian with a science background who struggled in theology took a night course on writing essays and began reading theology on his own during the four-month summer breaks. His theological acumen developed considerably.

## B. Immediate Preparation Suggestions

1. *Summer review:* The instructor prepared the material for you at the beginning of the summer, did you review the material during the summer?

2. *Synthesizing during lectures:* In class, do you actively "think" and try to synthesize, or do you just sit back and listen without thinking? If you imagine each theme as comprising three points, can you identify the three main points and express the subpoints, each in one sentence?

3. *Synthesizing material:* When you read the material (e.g., a chapter), do you close the book and try to synthesize it? A professor in Rome gave a student priest this key advice: "After you read a chapter, you should close the book and ask, 'What is the essential idea?'"

4. *Do you "confront" the insights presented and incorporate them into your previous understanding?* Do you realize that the lectures are key, that the professor is synthesizing the reading material and highlighting the most important points? If you miss his key points, what is the point of having lectures?

*Putting it Together*
In the larger picture, do you wish to excel in theology or just coast and get by? Do you remain as you did when you entered, or do you push through to a higher level? As one priest told seminarians, "if you change one thing each year, you will become a saint." Do you understand that all education is self-education, and that you must learn to synthesize in such a way that you can explain to a family member without notes in a way that they can understand? Can you synthesize what you have read into the "essential idea" and express it in one sentence? Can you identify the three subsections of a lecture or chapter, synthesize each in a sentence, and correlate them? Can you draw out a "genealogical tree" of your key points. This is the art of thinking and not merely parroting a few things one has memorized.

## C. The Systematic Nature of Theology and Scholarship in General

Theology is reason applied to faith; it entails scholarship. Scholarship is not about summarizing in a haphazard fashion. It is about relating all the materials to the essential idea; specifically a framework with which you can hang all the various particular elements (where it becomes like algebra: A + B = C). This will enable the priest, deacon, or lay person working in pastoral ministry to speak on questions about the faith (e.g., faith and evolution) in a synthetic and clear manner that feeds and inspires the people of God. When one bright student at an oral exam spouted many facts, the instructor at the end showed him how to integrate his points under major themes, and most especially how to preach from the heart to touch the hearts of the faithful ("head speaks to head, heart speaks to heart"). Here are two texts that illustrate the way of scholarship: A. G. Sertillanges' *The Intellectual Life* depicts the synthesis approach of scholarship of a genealogical tree; and John Henry Newman's description of the need for the Anglican Theology of his time to become a "systematic" theology:

A. G. Sertillanges, *The Intellectual Life: Its Spirit, Conditions, Methods*, 178-182.

> "Having settled on how much is to be remembered, we must think of the order to be adopted. One's memory must not be *chaos*. Science— *scientia*— is knowledge through causes.... Merely to accumulate recollections is to make them all unusable and inevitably to recover them only by chance....
> .... A well-ordered mind is like a **genealogical tree**, in which all the branches spring from the trunk and so communicate with one another; relationships of every degree appear clearly in it, showing family descent in all connections and as a whole.
> That means that, in memory, as in thought itself, we must bring everything into relation with what is *essential*. The primordial, the fundamental, the simple, when complexity arises step by step and through successive *differences*, is what supports memory, as it does knowledge, and makes it efficient at the moment when it comes into play....
> So when you want to remember, notice the connections and the reasons of things; analyse them, look for the why and wherefore, observe the genealogy of happenings, their order of succession, and their dependent consequences; imitate the procedure of mathematics in which necessity *starts from the axiom and arrives at the most distant conclusions*. Fully to understand a thing, then to learn and to introduce into one's mind not fragments, not loose links but *a chain*, is to make sure of the sticking quality of the whole."

*John Henry Newman on the Need for a Systematic Anglican Theology* (*Apologia pro Vita Sua* (New York: Norton, 1968), pp. 63-64).

> "It is proposed," I say, "to offer helps towards the formation of a recognized Anglican theology in one of its departments. The present state of our divinity is as follows: the most vigorous, the clearest, the most fertile minds, have through God's mercy been employed in the service of our Church: minds too as reverential and holy, and as fully imbued with Ancient Truth, and as well versed in the writings of the Fathers, as they were intellectually gifted. This is God's great mercy indeed, for which we must ever be thankful. Primitive doctrine has been explored for us in every direction, and the original principles of the Gospel and the Church patiently brought to light.
> But one thing is still wanting: our champions and teachers have lived in stormy times: political and other influences have acted upon them variously in their day, and have since obstructed a careful consolidation of their judgments. We have a vast inheritance, but *no inventory* of our treasures. All

is given us in profusion; it remains for us to **catalogue, sort, distribute, select, harmonize, and complete.** We have more than we know how to use; stores of learning, but little that is precise and serviceable; Catholic [universal] truth and individual opinion, first principles and the guesses of genius, all mingled in the same works, and requiring to be discriminated. We meet with truths overstated or misdirected, matters of detail variously taken, facts incompletely proved or applied, and rules inconsistently urged [applied] or discordantly interpreted. Such indeed is the state of every deep philosophy in its first stages, and therefore of theological knowledge. What we need at present for our Church's well-being, is not invention, nor originality, nor sagacity, nor even learning in our divines, at least in the first place, though all gifts of God are in a measure needed, and never can be unseasonable when used religiously, but we need peculiarly *a sound judgment, patient thought, discrimination, a comprehensive mind, an abstinence from all private fancies and caprices and personal tastes— in a word, Divine Wisdom.*"

## Addendum

The author counsels priests to be mentored by *one great saintly theologian* over an encyclopedic reading of diverse theologians. Not only should we choose from among the greatest, we ought to choose a saintly one— for we become what we read— whom we can discern by his fruits. With von Balthasar, for example, we find that John Paul II bestowed a Cardinal's hat for his theological contributions, Cardinal Ratzinger lauded his theological insights, Fergus Kerr called him the greatest theologian of the twentieth century, he collaborated with a mystic (von Speyr), and the causes of canonization of both have been introduced.

Yet, the author also counsels *openness to Holy Spirit wherever he is found.* This certainly applies to the teachings of Vatican II. But it may also apply to a theologian like Teilhard de Chardin, who was silenced but not condemned, who remained faithful to St. Paul, emphasizing Christ's cosmic dimensions. Pedro Arrupe SJ, General of the Society of Jesus, wrote: 'Teilhard's ideas proclaim the openness and concern with cultivating the world which characterized the teachings of the Council and of John XXIII and Paul VI and, today, John Paul II." While Teilhard is opposed by some, he is praised by intellectuals like J. Ratzinger, É. Gilson, F. Sheen, W. Kasper, and C. Schönborn. Siôn Cowell writes: "This [theological condemnation by some] is clearly not the view of Cardinal Casaroli writing on behalf of Pope John Paul II in 1981... Nor is it the view of Cardinals Henri de Lubac SJ and Jean Daniélou SJ or of a host of distinguished but objective theologians and thinkers..." (he lists 24 intellectuals from among others, see https://www.teilhard.org.uk/teilhard-de-chardin/the-man/).

# COUNSEL 2

## Human Growth: Troubled Woman with Human Weakness

*Difficulty: A woman came to receive the Sacrament of the Sick, but it was discerned that her underlying issues for being troubled may have been human and emotional.*
*Counsel: To proclaim the need to become human (e.g., natural, human virtues) as foundation for holiness. Attila Miklósházy taught that the holier we are, the more incarnate we become.*

### Being Human, Natural

Of all the things we talked about, I sense that this may help you the most. Holiness is built upon the human foundation. My experience has been that holy people are very human and natural, are very much themselves, comfortable in their own skin, and can also speak their mind, being very simple and transparent ("what you see is what you get" transparency). I have seen this in Sr. Briege McKenna, Fr. Andrew Apostoli, and Dr. Janine Langan. Being the opposite, that is, being excessively pious, perhaps also arising from my culture, made me the opposite (inscrutable, polite).

If you can entrust the growth of your human foundation to our Lady and St. Joseph and work at it incrementally, you will find that growing in being human and natural will make you more at ease and at peace in being yourself and comfortable in your own skin. If you wish to grow, you must begin with the human foundation. My experience in spiritual direction is that most problems arise from a weakness in the human. Here are three books that you might consider reading to strengthen the human foundation:

> Stephen Covey, *The 7 Habits of Highly Effective People*
> Jean-Pierre Camus, *The Spirit of St. Francis de Sales*
> David Allen, *Getting Things Done*

### Perfectionism

It is possible too that you may be obsessively finding your identity in your work. Not to play the psychologist, but experience shows that such a strong attachment to work may arise from some wound or failure from the past, because of which we end up trying to live up to the expectations of someone or some ideal. Our true identity is not found in what we possess (e.g., money, talents) or what good we do, but in being unconditionally and infinitely loved by God, like a newborn child in her mother's arms. Fr. Jacques Philippe with wonderful insight addresses this problem of finding our identity in our possessions and our good works comprehensively in *Interior Freedom* (Ch. 5, pp. 120 ff.).

## Allow our Lady and the Holy Spirit to Take Over

To help overcome the weight of the responsibilities that you carry, in whatever you do, especially your tasks, you can allow our Lady to take over and for you to be her assistant in all affairs: jobs, marriages, families, etc. For example, a priest can allow the Spirit to preach through him as an instrument and our Lady to "preside" at Mass in him; a principal can make Mary the principal and he be the secretary. This relieves the burden from your shoulders, alleviates the stress, and allows the work to become divine.

## Pandemic as Allowed by God in His Permissive Will

You feel fear and uncertainty during the pandemic. Try to see the pandemic, which in itself is a bad thing, as being allowed by God and therefore being within his permissive will. That is, it is God's will that "permits" it, but for a greater good. Thus, instead of being afraid of it, embrace it as a gift through which God is giving us many graces. Peter Kreeft disagreed with the title of a book, "*Why do Bad Things Happen to Good People,*" because, he understood that, if God allows these events, then there are thus no "bad" things. Fear is from the devil. We can periodically experience fear, but we can do what St. Thérèse did during the dark night in the last year of her life: make acts of faith, hope, and love when those temptations come to us. As Christians, we should normally be at peace: that is, the surface of our soul (sea) can be in the midst of troubles (trial, flu), as long as we maintain peace in the depths of our soul (bottom of the sea).

## Sins and Wounds do not Hinder Union with God if we Know how to be a Child before Him

Apart from daily falls of impatience and lapses, especially when we are busy, tired, carry many responsibilities, we can be troubled by our weakness, sometimes exacerbated by wounds. We tell ourselves that we should not be falling and feel that God is displeased with us. But the serious sins (e.g., abortion, promiscuity) move God's merciful heart as did the sinful woman at Simon's house. The key, as with this woman, is to learn how to unburden these weaknesses like a helpless child before her mother in our daily Examen Prayer. We can learn from the transformation in Fr. Michael Gaitley after Jesus asked, "Michael, what is wrong?" (we insert our name, "Susan, what is wrong?"). Fr. Gaitley broke out of the interior "vicious cycle" and looked *upward to God* and *unburdened* his troubles on Jesus. Jesus understood his weakness and dilemma. Imagine his tears of joy, and those of Adam after God led him to confess his catastrophic sin. Regarding sin, Jesus never accuses, He is "sheer salvation" (Jn 3:16).

# COUNSEL 3

## Present: Seminarian Anxiously Anticipating the Future

*Difficulty: A troubled seminarian visited twice: (i) he anxiously anticipated meeting someone; (ii) the issue turned out to be an attraction and the question of vocation.*
*Counsel: To teach the vital importance of avoiding anxiety while living in the present moment.*

The seminarian did not realize that the worst thing he could do is to worry about an imminent problem that may never happen and thus lose his peace. He ends up losing the Holy Spirit, who is a lover of peace, and worse yet, not finding Christ in each present moment. Here are two texts that capture this truth: "Anxiety is the greatest evil that can befall a soul except sin. God asks you to pray, but he forbids you to worry" (St. Francis de Sales); "The soul that has its hope in God has nothing to fear; for all obstacles and difficulties, God overpowers" (St. Teresa of the Andes).

### The Purely Human Level of the Present Moment

To address not anticipating the future, we begin with human wisdom, that has some limited value. Our human tendency is to be living in our heads (minds and memory), often going back to the past (e.g., sins and failures) or to be worrying about the future. Living this way in our heads leads to anxiety. It is when we stop, e.g., to be drawn by the beauty of a sunrise or sunset or absorbed in prayer, that we are truly alive. Then *our senses and our hearts* are deeply alert and aware, and gratitude and joy can fill us.

The theme of being alive to life, creation, and our senses is often found in Louis L'Amour's books. Here are a few examples.

> It is my great gift to live with awareness. I do not know to what I owe this gift, nor do I seek an answer. I am content that it be so. Few of us ever live in the present, we are forever anticipating what is to come or remembering what has gone, and this I do also. Yet it is my good fortune to feel, to see, to hear, to be aware. (Louis L'Amour, *Bendigo Shafter,* Chapter 45, 557)

L'Amour counsels us not to worry in anticipation of a bad outcome of which we have no control, as it is a waste of time and energy. Rather we act and act decisively when it is time to act, but not anticipate it.

> So what did that spell for Ange [who might have been killed]? Always she was there in my thoughts, but I kept shoving those thoughts of her to the back of my mind. There was nothing I could do to help her, or even to find her, until I could get a weapon and a horse. To think of her was to be

*frightened*, to let myself waste time in worrying— time that I'd best spend doing something. One thing I'd learned over the years: never to waste time moaning about what couldn't be helped. *If a person can do something, fine— he should do it. If he can't, then there's no use fussing about it until he can do something.* (L'Amour, *Sackett Brand*, Ch. 3, p. 29, emphasis added)

He makes clear that living in the moment does not preclude planning: "Hardy realized that he had learned some good things from pa; one was to do one thing at a time; not to cross bridges until he came to them, but at the same time to try to imagine how he could cross them when the time came" (*Down the Long Hills*). We must plan for the future and intermittently look to check where we are at; but we must not *live* in the future.

Living in the present is also possible because God in His divine providence has provided many "wombs" in our midst: Mother Church, Scripture and Tradition, saints, parents, teachers, mentors, the sacrament of the present moment. Within His family at Nazareth, Jesus too was always looking to His Father. It is a state of perpetual love and *dependence*; it is not so much about opening our minds but our hearts. "May the God of love and peace set your hearts at rest and speed your journey" (St. Raymond of Penyafort).

## Brother Lawrence's Presence of God and Katharine Drexel's Present Moment

But L'Amour's present moment is limited to this world. Brother Lawrence of the Resurrection teaches us how to live with a profound sense of God's presence in daily life (referenced earlier in this book):

> I flip my little omelette in the frying pan for the love of God, and when it's done, if I have nothing to do, I prostrate myself on the floor and adore my God who gave me the grace to do it, after which I get up happier than a king. When I can do nothing else, it is enough for me to pick up a straw from the ground for the love of God. The times of activity are not at all different from the hours of prayer… for I possess God as peacefully in the commotion of my kitchen, where often enough several people are asking me for different things at the same time, as I do when kneeling before the Blessed Sacrament.[1]

We find the duty of the present moment explained by St. Katharine Drexel:

> Peacefully do at each moment what at that moment ought to be done. If we do what each moment requires, we will eventually complete God's plan,

---

[1] Accessed January 2, 2005, http://www.theocentric.com/?p=187.

whatever it is. We can trust God to take care of the master plan when we take care of the details.

She was led by the Spirit to the goal of bringing souls to Christ:

> I looked up in wonder at God's wonderful ways and thought how little we imagine what may be the result of listening and acting on a desire He puts into the heart. Nourish before Him great desires… May our desire be to bring Him hearts, for all are His by right, having been purchased by every drop of His blood. I wish to be one who conscientiously takes part in the unfolding of God's plans, and eventually have a glorious part in the final unfolding of time into the glory of God's Kingdom in heaven. If we are disciples (of Jesus) we shall be happy to spend ourselves and be spent for the salvation of souls.[2]

**Real Issue was Attraction to a Woman and the Question of Vocation**

But the same seminarian asked for help again, this time going to the heart of his problem. Because of frequent difficulty with temptations against chastity, he had doubts about whether he should go on to the priesthood. In his heart of hearts, he did feel that he was called to the priesthood, a key point. But he tried to discern God's will by asking at Mass and expecting an immediate answer. But God does not normally work this way. The author offered four points to the seminarian, summarized here:

1. *Always consult externally*: This is what you did so well. I learned this great lesson only after years of running around trying to discern my vocation interiorly, instead of finding a director.
2. *Remove obstacle*: At the end, you came around to the key point that is troubling you, of the interior attraction to a woman. Here we learn the great rule: to "cut off" contact with anything that opposes our vocation, after which peace will return.
3. *Present problem to God but leave it to His timetable*: In your case, apply the principle of presumption: that you are being called in whatever state you find yourself, and, that if it is other, then God will make it abundantly clear; he will hit you between the eyes. Once presented to God, you are not to think about it; allow God to reveal what and when He wishes to in His way and time.
4. *Present moment*: After you have done all of the above, the main thing now is to find Jesus in, and do the duty of, the present moment (Madonna House's spirituality). That is, allow Jesus to take and lead

---

[2] St. Katharine Drexel Church, "Novena of St. Katharine Drexel," accessed November 29, 2021, https://www.skdparish.com/faith-enrichment/novena-of-saint-katharine-drexel/.

you by the hand in each hour. He is right there mystically, and that is all you really need to do in Christian life.

The immediate cause of his inner turmoil may have been his not cutting off relations with the woman who was attracted to him. The Church understands this truth, that we are to remove ourselves from the occasion of sin or temptation. As long as we are still embroiled in that situation, we are in "no-man's land," neither fully engaged nor fully detached, and always in inner turmoil. But in the larger scale of things, the key action was that he consulted a representative of God (see St. Ignatius' thirteenth rule)— this alone can be the catalyst for resolving the issue. Regarding discernment of vocation because of difficulties with chastity, once he has brought it out in direction, all he has to do is presume that God is calling him where he is, and expect that God will show him if it is otherwise. After doing all this, his main task as Christ's disciple is to be led by Him in each present moment.

**Living against the Horizon of Eternity**

Saints live the present moment through the horizon of eternity (Ch. 9, *Priestly Configuration*). They find life so short that it is almost passed and long for union with God: "We must see life in its true light… it is an instant between two eternities" (St. Thérèse); "Saint Agnes opened her arms and prayed: I pray to you, holy Father; behold, I am coming to you, whom I have loved, whom I have sought, whom I have always desired" (Vespers of Feast Day). Here is a news item on Alice von Hildebrand's death:

> Those who knew Lily [Alice] often heard her say that her candle was growing ever shorter. In fact, she yearned for death— to see the face of our Lord, to be reunited at last with her husband Dietrich, her parents, her dearest friend Madeleine Stebbins— with the peace that only true innocence and profound faith can grant. (info.hildebrandproject.org)

But we can find God in this life in the eternity of each present moment, to be held in God's arms, receiving and putting into practice whatever is given so as to please Him, that leads to a glorious destiny. The Fathers find Christ's mysteries present *hodie* (today). We can seek to live each day as if it were our last, perhaps with Ecclesiastes' reminder (11:7-12:14).

> God will bring you to judgement…. while man goes to his everlasting home. And the mourners are already walking to and fro in the street before the silver cord has snapped, or the golden lamp been broken, or the pitcher shattered at the spring, or the pulley cracked at the well, or before the dust returns to the earth as it once came from it, and the breath to God who gave it. Vanity of vanities, Qoheleth says. All is vanity.

# COUNSEL 4

## Spiritual Direction: Key Elements (R. Garrigou-Lagrange)[1]
(A Synthesis of a Section of *Priest in Union with Christ*)

*Moral Necessity of Direction*: Garrigou-Lagrange follows Tradition in teaching the necessity of spiritual direction to make spiritual progress: "Therefore, spiritual direction is one of the normal means of progress in virtue and of arriving at intimate union with God"; "No one is an impartial judge in his own case because each man judges according to his own particular inclination." Its necessity is greater with spiritual advancement (202-203).

*Qualities of a Good Spiritual Director*: St. Teresa of Jesus identifies three qualities: prudence, knowledge of the spiritual life; being learned (first two are primary). (i) His charity must lead the soul *to Christ* and not himself. Tauler describes the latter directors as hunting dogs who eat the hare instead of bringing it back to their master. (ii) Yet his "charitable kindness must not be allowed to degenerate into weakness or slothful leniency. It must be *firm, courageous, fearless* in speaking the truth, in order to be effective in leading souls to perfection. He must not waste time in useless conversation... but go straight to the point in directing a soul toward holiness of life" (205). (iii) "He must prudently discover in that soul the *predominant fault* which has to be destroyed and the special attraction [by Holy Spirit] which has to be encouraged" (206). (iv) He must not be *hasty* in leading souls too swiftly or indiscriminately to contemplative prayer nor consider it as a waste of time to consider this option (206).

*Qualities of a Good Spiritual Directee*: (i) The directee must show *respect*, sincerity, and docility with affection to the director, avoiding harsh criticism and over-familiarity. (ii) He must be sincere and perfectly *transparent* of everything, good and bad. (iii) He must be *very docile*, but can present concerns, obeying if the director does not change his mind. (iii) It is important to maintain *continuity* with a director. One should change a director if his advice is contrary to faith and morals, or "if his views are too natural, if he displays too much emotional affection, or if he lacks the necessary knowledge, prudence, or discretion." (iv) St. Louis of France counselled his son: "*Choose a wise and virtuous confessor* [director] who will tell you what to do and what to avoid, and give him complete freedom to reprove and correct you." (v) The director becomes "the instrument of the *Spirit in recognizing the promptings* to grace and in urging the directed soul to respond to those inspirations with increasing promptitude." (206-207).

---

[1] Reginald Garrigou-Lagrange, *Priest in Union with Christ*.

**1. Direction of Beginners** (grades are like children-teens-adults) (209-215) Garrigou-Lagrange notes three areas in direction: mortification, sacraments, and prayer. *Mortification*: He highlights that we must *not despise corporeal penances*: "A man who cannot restrain his appetite cannot attain perfection" (St. Philip Neri). This includes food and sleep. But the *higher is the interior mortification:* e.g., not replying to insults, not revealing things that make others think well of us, giving way to others, not hankering after things of this world, praise, and one's own will. The better forms of mortification are those that are negative in character: restraining our curiosity, being reserved in conversation, being content with food that is unpalatable, choosing things of lesser value, rejoicing even in lack of things we need, accepting daily annoyances (illness, calumny, misunderstanding). Attention should be given to the person's predominant fault. (209-211)

*Sacraments*: These are already covered in Aids 1 and 2. Besides recommending daily Mass and weekly Confession, we add the importance of preparing for, and making thanksgiving after, Mass (St. Teresa says that after Holy Communion, Jesus sits on His throne to enrich the soul with mercy, "What would you like Me to do for you?" We recommend St. Teresa's counsel to make a few daily Spiritual Communions. (211-212)

*Prayer*: A key principle is highlighted: "St. Teresa was quite certain that a person who persevered in prayer, no matter how violently the devil tempted him to sin, would assuredly be led by God to the harbor of salvation. For this reason, the devil is never so anxious as he is to obstruct this spiritual exercise, because he knows, as St. Teresa says, that *he has lost the soul which perseveres in prayer*" (213). Mental prayer for those able should be *half an hour* in duration. He recommends meditation on the Last Things and above all Christ's Passion. St. Teresa teaches us to bring a book each time we do mental prayer. Garrigou-Lagrange also teaches that "Meditation should not occupy the whole time of mental prayer. The soul must *turn aside from reflection to acts of the will, making a complete offering of itself* to God in acts of humility, confidence and love." We will conclude with a request for perseverance in conforming one's will to the divine will and also to make a practical resolution (e.g., avoiding a weakness, practice a virtue). While the beginner is granted favours and sense consolations to urge him on, God will bring him to *sense aridity* (dryness) to test his fidelity and to offer an opportunity of offering generous resistance and of acquiring new merits. The beginner is encouraged to remain faithful. Beginners must also be urged to *sanctify their daily actions, to be continuously recollected (e.g., avoid excessive interest in this world)*. St. J. F. de Chantal had the practice of making an *aspiration at the beginning of every hour* to consecrate it to God. He must set time for spiritual norms, e.g., prayer. (212-215)
*Retarded Souls* (215-217)

Garrigou-Lagrange describes many as "retarded souls" who do not progress to the Illuminative way of proficients. They end up not being beginners, proficients, or the perfect, but are more like spiritual dwarfs. The reason for this stunting can be various. First, *some pay little attention to the details of the service of God* (recalling Jesus' injunction about being faithful in the little things, Lk 16:10). "Eventually this negligent soul no longer seeks God in everything that it does but self; it loses all sense of the presence of God." He believes that a religious who is most faithful in observing his rule in all its details will accept the grace of martyrdom if God offers the occasion. Holy souls come to realize the *eternal significance of daily details*. A second reason for stunted growth is their unwillingness to offer God the demands he makes of them, refusing to make the effort, losing their seriousness of purpose and becoming spiritually slothful. "Perhaps that which prevents the soul from lifting itself up from earth to heaven is *an attachment to some useless frivolity* for the sake of the pleasure we derive from it, an attachment though it may be no stronger than a piece of thread is effective *in keeping our heart fixed on earth*." A third source can derive from making fun of the person of virtue (when we ourselves are unwilling to rise to this fidelity). (215-217)

## 2. Direction of Proficients (Second Conversion, 218-222)

According to St. John of the Cross, there are three signs which indicate the transition from discursive meditation (beginners) to the beginning of infused contemplation. This higher form of prayer is not attributed to the soul's efforts aided by sanctifying grace, but to the virtue of faith perfected by the gifts of the Holy Spirit; that is, it is moved by the Holy Spirit Himself. The three signs are: (i) sensible aridity, with *no consolation in divine things* or in any thing created (enables recognition of vanity of created things, not sufficient by itself); (ii) the soul *never forgets God*, retaining "a keen desire for perfection and feels that it is falling back in its service of God"; and (iii) it can no longer practice discursive meditation but finds pleasure in a *simple loving attention* directed toward God. Some manifesting these three signs are undergoing the Dark Night (passive purification) of the Senses, "during which they are weaned from all attachment to sensible consolations in order to come to a more spiritual and generous love of God." Only those who are *generous* in passing through this crisis will enter the illuminative way of proficients. Others less generous, retarded souls, will *return* to discursive meditation to accept the gift of initial infused contemplation, or accept it for a brief period.

The director must protect the soul from spiritual gluttony, the temptation during this aridity to return to *sense consolations*. A second temptation is to *return to discursive meditation*, running to a spring when they have already arrived at the spring of the water that flows into everlasting life (Jn 4:14). A third danger is to lose trust in God and despair or *cease prayer*, when prayer is never more fruitful than during this period of trial. This passive purification of the senses has to be endured here on earth, else it will have to be completed in Purgatory, but without merit. During this trial, the soul must rest content with a confused and general knowledge of God, but, in *affective love*, can make acts of confidence and love. The soul must be prepared to bear patiently *"temptations against purity, the loss of sensible comforts, ill-health, opposition from fellow men."* Habitual failings of the intellect include "a constant wandering of the mind away from God to creatures, unwillingness to forgo one's own opinion, an authoritative attitude in ruling others, or the opposite failing of extreme leniency toward those who oppress the weak. Faults to be found in the will are an innate love of self and unbridled attachment to spiritual consolations. Actual or occasional faults of the intellect are mistakes made in matters relating to the spiritual life [e.g., visions]. Actual faults affecting the will are presumption, ambition, pride or arrogance" [dissent]. (218-221)

**3. Direction of Perfect Souls** (Third Conversion, 223-227)
The soul passes from the Illuminative to the Unitive way through the Dark Night of the Spirit, which brings a new spiritual crisis. The soul is enabled by the gift of understanding to recognize *the grandeur of God and its own wretchedness*. "This new spiritual light reveals the splendor of God's holiness and at the same time all the hidden defects of the soul— even the most insignificant," which causes *extreme torment*, since the spiritual light from the gift of understanding is overpowering. The soul suffers *violent temptations against faith, hope, and charity*, since the devil is anxious to make use of this spiritual darkness to bring the soul to despair, and the soul responds by making extremely intense and meritorious acts of faith, hope, and love (e.g., as St. Thérèse did in her Dark Night). There are three signs of this passive purification: (i) "the soul is unable to accuse itself of committing fresh faults and yet it does not know whether it deserves God's love or His hatred"; (ii) "it continues for longer periods without committing even the smallest fully deliberate venial sin and has lost all desire for creating things, thus revealing its extraordinary habitual love of God"; (iii) "the soul now enjoys continuous contemplation and the highest love of God in spite of its spiritual aridity."

*Spiritual Direction*: Souls who have reached this stage have their will perfectly conformed to the divine will, and must now pray for the grace to persevere in this spiritual night of sorrow, enlisting the aid of the saints.

> They should not attack their temptations directly but, so to speak, ride over them, turning to God for the actual grace to overcome them. They must regard it a privilege to wage such a glorious struggle in the divine cause and one which is so highly profitable to the soul. Their love of God must be a *pure love of friendship, showing themselves ready to accept His good pleasure in all*

*respects*, following the example of Job: "After darkness I hope for light again" (Job 17:12). (224-225)

God calls them to *a life of reparation for sinners*, to endure great suffering, like St. Paul of the Cross, who attained transforming union when he was about thirty-one years of age and still had to continue his suffering till he was eighty-one. These reparative souls must be guided to a perfect conformity with Christ the Victim, often meditating on Christ's Passion, while "considering at the same time the heinous sins which tear individual souls and entire nations away from God and drag them down into paganism." To this end, they should unite their daily crosses to Christ's offering in the *Mass* that perpetuates Calvary, and have "frequent recourse to *Our Blessed Lady*, our co-redemptrix, whose secret influence leads souls to an intimate union with Christ." Generally these souls enjoy an infused contemplation enlightened by the gifts of the Holy Spirit, but find it difficult to realize this owing to long periods of both sensible and spiritual aridity. "Eventually they bear a *perfect resemblance to Christ crucified and are the means of saving many souls*. It is this **apostolate of suffering and prayer** which is the hidden source of the fruitfulness of the apostolate of preaching and instructing— a fact well known to God and the Angels."

## The Way to Perfection
(i) They must place all their trust in God and not in themselves nor their good resolutions, with complete confidence in His help, and then cooperating with all their power. (ii) They must try to avoid the slightest deliberate fault, for "The devil makes use of deeds of small importance to provide an opening for greater faults" (St. Teresa). In addition,

> "[iii] These souls must not be unduly upset after committing some fault, but should humble themselves immediately and turn to God by making a short act of contrition and renewing their determination, and thus return to peace. [iv] Close friendships with persons of either sex are to be avoided, no matter how holy those persons may be. [v] Let them destroy in themselves all tendency to self-esteem and rejoice in humiliations, taking a spiritual pleasure in being despised and ridiculed. [vi] They should always show prompt and willing obedience toward their superiors. [vii] They must constantly attend to the presence of God and resolve to please God and love Him courageously…. [viii] They must have a great love of prayer and an ardent desire for the kingdom of heaven…" (226-227).

# COUNSEL 5

## Spiritual Direction & Confession: Digressions

### *I. Digressions in Spiritual Direction*
*Synopsis of the Spiritual Struggles of Three Directees*

#### Directee 1: Lack of Knowledge, Docility, and Selfless Love

Permission was granted to anonymously share this profile (Oct. 26, 2021). A spiritual director has been directing a lay Catholic for about eighteen years. This man is very devout, a devoted husband and father, and a dedicated worker. He goes to daily Mass, weekly confession, monthly spiritual direction, and dedicates time to formal prayer each day.

Yet it began to become clear after many years that, beyond fidelity to a plan of life and carrying out of the duties of his state of life (as Christian, husband, father, professional), he was not making progress beyond this foundation (Ascetical Mansions). Since he sought to attain holiness, the director was surprised he had to remind him after a few years to attend daily Mass. More significantly, he made little progress in learning to become human (e.g., working on mastery of the English language, being informed about world affairs, being natural), self-forgetful, and gaining self-knowledge, basic courtesies like replying promptly to emails, let alone the deeper aspects of the Mystical Mansions. In addition, he seemed to have a high opinion of his spiritual progress and focused on acquiring spiritual knowledge to share with clients in his professional practice.

The greatest difficulty was probably learning to forget himself to think about zeal for souls and concern for those in great need. The director tried to teach him that at the heart of the spiritual life were the two great commandments of love of God and of neighbour. It took him many discussions on this topic before he really started to act upon it. But the director had to teach him to move beyond just praying for the few who were killed in floods, to greater needs, e.g., the hundred million persecuted Christians. And even after teaching him self-forgetfulness to think of God's children on their Calvaries, the topic of discussion would still revert to whether he was in consolation or desolation, or that he had grudges against others (surfaced multiple times). The director asked, "Why are you so focused on yourself? Your fundamental problem could be what Dom Marmion discerned was the main cause of most consecrated souls: 'They think too much about themselves and not enough about Jesus and souls.'" Here is the exchange that followed immediately.
    Directee: "Then what should I bring up in spiritual direction?"

Director: "Whatever the Holy Spirit reveals to you that you should bring up."

Directee: "But, Father, I talk to him all day and I still don't know what He wants me to address."

Director: "To think that you have continual dialogue with the Holy Spirit may be presumption, as only those in the highest Mansions attain that level of continual dialogue through possession by the Holy Spirit. Both your lack of knowing what the Spirit wants you to address and your being very slow to put into practice what He tells you suggest that you are not really listening to the Holy Spirit. In any case, the focus is not so much about *dialoguing* with the Holy Spirit as *to simply put into practice* whatever He is telling you to do: "My food is to do the will of my heavenly Father." People who love God put their love into *action*, otherwise God does not know whether we truly love Him (St. Teresa of Jesus). We want to become like John Paul II, to become so attuned to the Holy Spirit that everything he does and says flows from that union. Our task is not to know whether we are pleasing to God or not (taking our spiritual pulse); our only task is simply to put into practice whatever the Spirit is saying. And if we do not know what to bring up in spiritual direction, we can simply ask, "O Holy Spirit, it is almost the day for spiritual direction and I still don't know what to bring up. Show me what you want."

## 1. Lack of Self-Knowledge

We highlight four lacunae in this directee which may be found in many. There are indications here of issues. First, to say "Father, I am dialoguing with God all day" suggests a lack of self-knowledge. Holy people are intensely convinced of their lack of cooperation with God's grace. As we draw close to God the divine Sun, our spiritual "freckles" become more apparent, as our faces' freckles are seen more clearly outside in the noon day sun. Second, inculcating the concern for those in great need had to be explained over and over again. This begs the question of what may be the source of such an incapacity to see his weakness and to understand. It may be because many of us believe that we are "good" with a few weaknesses, and this is fundamentally wrong in the spiritual life (see the first pillar of St. Catherine of Siena of self-knowledge of my poverty and the first Beatitude, "Blessed are the poor in spirit"). God could only use Saints Peter and Paul after their falls and their subsequent knowledge of their deep woundedness. This was the case with the religious priest who knew that he was a "screw-up" and Fr. Gaitley who was in touch with his "brokenness." The Christian who believes he is good because he does some charitable works reflects the lack of self-knowledge typical of the lower Mansions. The degree to which one's heart is humble may determine the degree of its openness to God. When one's heart is open from self-knowledge, then grace works quickly and powerfully, as in the young soul of St. Dominic Savio.

## 2. Not Looking to the Spirit to Know what to Discuss

Second, faced with the directee's inability to know what to bring up, as he was always focused on himself, the director emphasized the principle of bringing up what the Spirit is suggesting to him. When he argued that he did not know what the Spirit is saying, the director asked him if he *asked* the Spirit to show him, and explained to him how the director himself would sometimes be pleading to the Spirit before an imminent spiritual direction. He had learned this lesson from a spiritual director during graduate studies: "You are faithful to spiritual direction, prayer, your studies, your plan of life. *But where is God meeting you?*" But there can be the opposite problem. Having been introduced to the practice of listening to the Spirit, someone at the early stages might fall into the trap of believing that everything they think is from Him, which happens at the highest Mansions.

## 3. Lack of Acting on Counsels

Third, for years the director counselled him on weaknesses, and years later, he is found to have made very little progress. Instead, when the director asked him during spiritual direction if he understood what was being explained, for the conversation was one-sided with only occasional grunts of assent, his reply was "I am trying to *understand*." The priority in spiritual direction is not understanding, but making a resolution to act quickly, spontaneously, and with alacrity and interest upon whatever directive is being given by the Holy Spirit. The focus was wrong.

The director sought then to highlight Jesus' key teaching that distinguishes his disciples, those who hear and act on His word. He did this by pointing to Jesus' own teaching that He must have lived: "Blessed rather are those who hear the word of God and keep it!" (Lk 11:28); "Every one then who hears these words of mine and does them will be like a wise man who built his house upon the rock…" (Mt 7:24). There is the very enlightening episode in St. Escrivá's life when he said to Jesus interiorly, "Lord, I love you more than these sisters to whom I am giving Holy Communion," to which Jesus responded interiorly, "Love is shown by action." There is also the example from St. Teresa of Jesus' question to Jesus, "Lord, why do you need our actions," to which He replied, "So that I can see your will." Unless our Lord sees our acts of love in action, then He does not see our love. Thus, the trap in the spiritual life is to be focused on having pious desires or being concerned about one's spiritual progress instead of being, like Chiara Lubich, a simple instrument in the hands of the Artist, or Mother Teresa, "I am a pencil in God's hands." We must live Jesus, who was led in every moment by the Father's Spirit to act on the Father's will: "My food is to do the will of him who sent me, and to accomplish his work" (Jn 4:34; cf. Lk 6:47; Jas 1:22-25).

This directee lacks excuse when we consider how God helped a seminarian with multiple weaknesses to overcome them. His director had diagnosed an excessive piousness with a need to learn to be more human, and over the years, the new priest learned to be natural. Having a speech impediment, he sought help from the University's Speech Pathology Department and, with the help of a kind professor, eventually learned to speak fluently. He also had a deficit in a few other areas: lacking know-how to write essays, he took a university course that greatly aided him; lacking confidence in preaching as a deacon, he found kind assistance from the homiletics professor; lacking confidence in singing, he gained a certain facility and confidence from the aid of a music teacher at the Choir School. When he found that his grasp of theology was weak, he began to read theological works during the summers.

## 4. Lack of Love (of God and Souls)

Third, even after many counsels about forgetting himself to think of God's children, he would still revert back to self, "Father, is spiritual life about my going to heaven?" Worse still, he focused on lesser issues, like floods. When he asked, "How can I love like this," the director replied: "Simply, love." Holy people's hearts respond to great tragedies. We can learn from Chiara Lubich in our responding to Russia's brutal annexing of Ukraine (2022).

> In November 1956, an uprising of the Hungarian people was brutally suppressed. Chiara responded by calling for an army of volunteers for the cause of God, "volunteers of God": "A certain society has attempted to erase the name of God, the reality of God, the providence of God and the love of God from people's hearts. There has to be a society that can put God back in his rightful place.... A society that witnesses to only one name: God." (*Città Nuova* (1957), anno II n. 1)

## 5. Diagnosis: Ultimate Enemy of the Spiritual Life is Self

We should do an examen to see, like this directee, if we fail to change, for there is no standing still in life; the likelihood is that we are sliding. We can ask: do we see ourselves as good people instead of sinners; do we ask (consult) the Spirit for guidance; do we act on His inspirations instead of focusing on understanding in life; and above all, are we wrapped up in self while God's children suffer (see Augustine's cities of God and self below)?

> Accordingly, two cities have been formed by two loves: the earthly by the love of self, even to the contempt of God; the heavenly by the love of God, even to the contempt of self. The former, in a word, glories in itself, the latter in the Lord. For the one seeks glory from men; but the greatest glory of the other is God, the witness of conscience. The one lifts up its head in its own glory; the other says to its God, "Thou art my glory, and the lifter up of mine head." (*Confessions*, Book XIV Chap. 28)

The last question is key: the ultimate goal of the spiritual life is accomplished in the Dark Night of the Spirit, where there is annihilation of the fallen self and self-love. We will be judged by love. Heaven is all about forgetfulness of self and love; hell is ultimate narcissism, forgetfulness of others to live in the isolation, glorification, and gratification of self.

### Directee 2: First Commandment, Restore Foundation

Permission was granted to anonymously share this profile (Nov. 14, 2021). The second directee is a priest, who has been going for spiritual direction for about fifteen years, as seminarian and then as priest. Among the issues that the directee feels plague him are:
- a strong desire to please others and to be liked, especially as he was loved in the parish to which he was assigned after ordination;
- an inability to say no, precisely because he wants to be liked;
- a strong attachment to knowledge of many human things (computers and any electronic gadgets, cars and bikes, city by-laws, etc.) and seems to be constantly acquiring information or knowledge of what is happening (e.g., in diocese);
- an anxiety about a medical condition, and constantly trying to find different remedies and testing different drugs;
- an inability to stay in the present moment, having a busy head.

We first make a general comment. The author finds a common failing in the spiritual life arising from *looseness* of some form: e.g., laity seeking to serve God with busyness but not consulting to see if it is God's will; priests who have a loose plan of life, which opens them up to many distractions.

This priest's looseness is failing to focus primarily on God's will. Jesus was rooted in Nazareth, daily fulfilling His Father's will in the Father's presence, sanctifying his work. This priest was often not present at meals and running off; he was not "at home." He manifests flightiness, opening himself up to every wind and attraction. St. Borromeo teaches instead to "keep the stove tightly shut so that it will not lose its heat and grow cold. In other words, avoid distractions as well as you can. Stay quiet with God. Do not spend your time in useless chatter" (OOR of his feast). His focus on his being troubled by others' actions indicate that he is focused on other's failing and not principally the fidelity to his vocation, thus missing the forest for the trees; as in Jesus' distinction between the camel and the gnat: "You blind guides, straining out a gnat and swallowing a camel!" (Mt 23:23-24). The priest fails to perceive his dominant fault, the "camel," and sees only the gnats. Jesus also taught, "For where your treasure is, there will your heart be also" (Mt 6:21). We will draw from sources used by Fr. Francis Fernandez. Fr. Tissot's examination of conscience reveals our treasure:

> At any moment, if I desire to know where I am, what is the state of my soul, what tone echoes within me I merely ask : *Where is my heart* ? By this question I seek solely to know what is the *dominant disposition* of my heart, which inspires and directs it, and keeps it as it were in its possession....
>
> This question causes me to cast a rapid glance into the innermost centre of my being, and I at once see the salient point; I give ear to the tone echoed by my soul, and immediately catch the dominant note. It is an intuitive proceeding, and is quite instantaneous. There is no need for intellectual inquiries, efforts of will, and ransacking the memory; I hear and see. It is a glance, *in ictu oculi*. It is simple and rapid....
>
> 33. Its object. — Sometimes I shall see that my dominant disposition is **the want of approbation or praise, or the fear of reproach**; sometimes, the bitterness that springs from some annoyance from some harmful project or proceeding, or else the resentment caused by some remonstrance; sometimes, the painfulness of being under suspicion, or the trouble felt through some aversion; or, it may be the slackness induced by sensualism, or the discouragement resulting from difficulties or failure; at other times, **routine, the product of carelessness, or frivolity**, the product of idle curiosity and empty gaiety, etc. Or else, on the contrary, it may be the love of God, the desire for sacrifice, the fervour kindled by some touch of grace, full submission to God, the joy of humility, etc. Whether it be good or bad, it is the main and dominant disposition that must be ascertained; for we must look at the good as well as the evil, since it is the state of the heart that is important to know. I must go directly to the **mainspring** which sets all the wheels of the clock in motion...[1]

We often stop at the details and remain at the circumference, and don't go straight to the centre. This state may derive from prolonged lukewarmness: "A house is not destroyed by a momentary impulse. More often it is because of an old defect in its construction. Sometimes it is the prolonged neglect by its inhabitants that permits water to get in, at first drop by drop, imperceptibly, the damp eating away of the woodwork and rotting even the structure of stone" (Cassian, *Conferences*, 6, in *In Conversation*, vol. 2, 242-243). Or it could be, as Georges Chevrot identifies, the problem of Peter following the arrested Jesus *from afar* (Lk 22:54), a lack of generosity:

> We need only change a pronoun in the short evangelical phrase in order to discover the cause of our own desertions, be they small errors or serious falls, fleeting relaxation of effort or lengthy periods of lukewarmness.... Men follow Christ with maddening lack of generosity and with grudging lack of commitment to their Lord. There are too many Christians who, if they can said to follow him at all, follow Jesus only from afar. (*Simon Peter*, quoted in *In Conversation*, vol. 2, 246).

---

[1] Joseph Tissot, *The Interior Life: Simplified and Reduced to its Fundamental Principle* (Burns Oates & Washbourne Ltd., 1927), 307-308. Reprinted by CreateSpace, 2013, Part III.

This priest should do an examen: what is his first love, his *mainspring*. Is it him or Jesus? L'Amour in *Killoe* portrays two half-brothers: Tap, always leaving home, a dashing gunfighter, egotistic, and "walking" with another man's wife while courting a young woman; Dan has always remained with his father, who seeks his counsel because of his solidity, maturity, and slow deliberation. If this priest is like Tap, all about himself, then it will manifest itself in his being all over the map and not grounded. Has he learned the "radicalism of love" that John Paul II used to describe C. Lubich's charism, or given himself to self-love and the *idolatry* of desiring esteem. If he learns to cleave to Jesus, he will find himself living the hidden fidelity of the duty of each moment. Tap is all about self and craving superficial gratification: "the sow is washed only to wallow in the mire" (2 Pet 2:22). The priest has to learn to be like the Holy Family, who put God first by living the duty of the moment. To uproot *false loves*, perhaps meditation on the Passion can aid in detachment from self-love and attachment to the crucified Christ.

> If you seek an example of despising earthly things, follow him who is *the* King of kings and the Lord of lords, in whom are hidden all the treasures of wisdom and knowledge. Upon the cross he was stripped, mocked, spat upon, struck, crowned with thorns, and given only vinegar and gall to drink. Do not be attached, therefore, to clothing and riches, because they divided my garments among themselves. Nor to honours, for he experienced harsh words and scourgings. Nor to greatness of rank, for weaving a crown of thorns they placed it on my head. Nor to anything delightful, for in my thirst they gave me vinegar to drink. (OOR, feast day of St. Thomas Aquinas)

**Directee 3: Temptation to Live by Feel-Good Sentimentality**

Permission was granted to anonymously share this profile (Nov. 20, 2021). The following can happen to a seminarian who is going to spiritual direction every two weeks. Given this frequent spiritual direction, he was counselled to bring up what the Holy Spirit is showing him, to focus on learning to quickly act on whatever the Holy Spirit is appealing to him to do, and thus aim for doing spiritual direction in about half an hour.

What can happen is that he can fall into deviations. Within the same session he can seek academic help in improving a class theological presentation which is better served outside of spiritual direction, as it is sacred and aimed at sanctification, and can end up delaying another seminarian waiting his turn. Second, he might ask questions about his ordination and his retreat for it, which is a fair topic, but he must keep these brief. The main concern is the sense that he enjoys spiritual direction as a friendly chat or conversation, the warm and pleasant sharing of spiritual things.

The director learned a great insight from a graduate thesis director with whom he shared his own doubts about being equipped to do seminary formation. The thesis director simply made one key point: "You cannot always be their friend, but you can be their father." Directees can easily slide into seeking only a friend, the warmth of affection, support, and unconditional acceptance, and not the discipline of a father. But it is the father who loves him enough to always want to make him rise to greater levels of love of Jesus and of sacrifice. Jesus formed the apostles according to His own path of sacrifice: of persecution and of being led to Calvary. We might be tempted to follow St. Peter's inclination on the Mount of Transfiguration to want to enjoy heaven on earth in this life (Mk 9:5). St. John Chrysostom sees Jesus pointing His apostles in the opposite direction: "You talk of sharing honours and rewards with me, but I must talk of struggle and toil. Now is not the time for rewards or the time for my glory to be revealed. Earthly life is the time for bloodshed, war, and danger" (OOR, feast day of St. James).

The two dimensions of guiding others by Alvaro del Portillo sheds light on this difficult area of formation. A father asked del Portillo how to combine strength with affection in raising his children, and the response included the need to be "demanding." We need both the paternal affection that the directees or children should receive, but also the loving demandingness of the director or parent, so as to lead them to human virtue and holiness.

> "Just let them see a smile on your face.... When you have to correct them, don't put on a long face. Say with a smile whatever needs to be said, and don't worry. When people know that you really love them, you can tell them anything, no matter how painful."
>
> He also asked his collaborators to practice "a demandingness that is full of affection, full of the respect and gentleness that our Father [St. Escrivá] asked of us in our treatment of others— but at the same time really demanding. We have to call a spade a spade. If we don't, we're not fulfilling our obligations."[2]

## II. Digressions in Confession

### Penitent 1: Pelagianism, Perfectionism

There is a trap to avoid in Confession. There can be a tendency to confess our sins in this way: "Father, I have *not* loved God as much as I should. I have *not* prayed as much as *I should have*. I knew I should have but I didn't. And I fell into this sin. I knew it was wrong, but I gave in any way. I knew

---

[2] John F. Coverdale, *Saxum*, 166.

that I should have gone to Confession immediately." Instead of a direct self-accusation (e.g., "I have judged others"), it is about myself normally being good and occasionally failing, expressed in the negative ("I have not..."). When one is convinced of one's deep sinfulness, it comes out in a manly accusation of sins, with only a few details to indicate its gravity or cause: "First, I have judged other priests a few times, perhaps because, out of pride, I thought myself better than them. Second..." St. Josemaría Escrivá used to give four helpful basic criteria: a good confession is concise, concrete, clear, and complete; no more is needed. That is, we confess to the best of our ability and our sorrow, expressed by our willingness to change. Thus, good Confessions involve being "direct" and to the point and accusing ourselves without too much explanation or excusing of self. When we are giving many details of why we failed, we may be excusing ourselves, falling into self-pity, or using Confession for sharing. However, in the confessional, we can raise concerns (informal direction).

There may be a greater incidence today of scrupulosity or perfectionism. When pathological, they can be helped much by a psychological support. The larger and spiritual issue is whether one is *focused on oneself*. The scrupulous person is all concerned about his "cleanliness" before God. Martin Luther had terrible torments about his sinfulness that recalls scrupulosity, and he appeared to fall into individualism (and not live the higher and more important communal dimension). In a standard act of Contrition, there are three levels of sorrow: (1) "for I have deserved your dreadful punishment"—this is about me. We must acknowledge our sins (10%) but focus primarily against offending the Beloved (90%); (2) "because I have crucified my loving Saviour, Jesus Christ, and (3) most of all, because I have offended your infinite goodness"; and because of this, "I firmly resolve never to offend you again and avoid the occasions of sin." The focus should be about the latter two of offending God: crucifying Jesus and offending God's infinite love.

Experiencing the love of God in Confession should lead me to want to *return love*, not just be feeling sorry for myself when I have fallen yet again. This way, God can express and give His eternal mercy over and over again, being pleased that the penitent is not selfishly thinking about his weakness but rather about his beloved Father's goodness to him. There is a world of difference between these two approaches. Perhaps an antidote to scrupulosity is not to take ourselves too seriously (to laugh at ourselves), imitating saints, who have a keen sense of humour.

> # 7. Holiness consists in having *a sense of humor*. Some people have added an eleventh commandment to the Decalogue: "Thou shalt be glum." In truth, they firmly believe that the more sour one's puss, the holier one must

be. How incongruous that is, however, especially when we note that Christians are commissioned to be messengers of the Gospel, that is, "good news." Now, this anomaly struck even so vehement an opponent of Christianity as Nietzsche, who quipped: "If Christians wanted me to believe in their God, they would have to look more redeemed!" The greatest saints, however, were not dour, depressing sorts. Saint Philip Neri was a practical jokester. Saint Teresa of Ávila often asked God to deliver her from would-be saints who made a career out of looking miserable. Good humor makes external various interior dispositions. Peacefulness, calmness, contentment, acceptance of God's Will in one's life – all make for genuine joy, which is not a cheap brand of hilarity or superficiality. Joy arises from the sure conviction that God is in charge, and that nothing will happen this day that He and I – together – will be unable to handle. Joy comes about because of the awareness *that the greatest battles in life – against the world, the flesh and the Devil – have been fought – and won – by Jesus Christ*; it but remains for us to claim the victory. This type of perspective on reality provides a person with a real sense of humor, which is a fitting and necessary pre-condition for entrance into a state of eternal joy.[3]

## Penitent 2: Confession not Viewed as Aid to Attaining Holiness

A devout husband, father, and professional who went to daily Mass and frequent Confession, had an approach typical of the older Confessions that was more juridical. He tended towards being punctilious about the species of sins and the number, but wanting only Absolution, without any counsel from the confessor, as if the confessor were primarily a dispenser of absolution and applier of a penance. The Church's *New Rite of Penance* moves beyond this juridical approach to one that is more pastoral and medicinal. It fits within the larger framework of continual conversion, with Confession offering spiritual direction, a significant aid to sanctity.

> Today, integral Confession should be more concerned about the species rather than the numbers (listing of sins). A better understanding of man's sinfulness as a state rather than just individual acts, directs our attention to the *standing of the penitent before God, the areas of his life where he is weak or wounded, and the relationship between his baptismal commitment and present lifestyle*. This requires more *presenting a picture of one's spiritual life*, rather than merely enumerating sins.[4]

---

[3] Peter Stravinskas, "'All the way to Heaven is Heaven': 7 basic steps to holiness," *Catholic World Report*, accessed Dec. 19, 2021, https://www.catholicworldreport.com/2017/11/29/all-the-way-to-heaven-is-heaven-7-basic-steps-to-holiness/.
[4] Attila Miklósházy, "Penance," Sacramental Theology II: SAT 2432HS Lecture (Toronto School of Theology at the University of Toronto, Toronto, Ontario, 1978).

# COUNSEL 6

## Conscience: "Whether Mortal Sin is an Infinite Offense?"
(Question from a Priest)

*Difficulty: A priest was troubled from reading that mortal sin is an infinite offense, was consoled to learn in watching one of the author's retreat talks on YouTube.*
*Counsel: We learn from St. Vianney, who taught that our sins are like a few grains of sand against the mountain of God's infinite mercy. More importantly, spiritual life is not primarily about avoiding sins but about transformation in Christ to co-redeem the world.*

Dear Father J,
So good to receive your question, happy to try to respond to it.
You raise a very good question, one that has troubled many people through the ages. To illustrate the consequences of this train of thought, let me mention to you what a fine priest whom I directed since seminary days revealed to me: that he lived in an anxious mode, and his greatest fear was the judgment that Jesus would levy against him at death. This shocked me, as I had taught him the very key point you raised about God's mercy. Let me begin with Jesus' forgiving mercy: "Truly, I say to you, the tax collectors and the harlots go into the kingdom of God before you [Pharisees represent those who think they are good]" (Mt 21:31).

**Immediate Issue: Gravity of Mortal Sin before God**

First, your intuition is correct about what I meant about God's infinite mercy. Your concern about mortal sin being an "infinite" offence, as you term it, is highlighted especially in Scholastic theology (but precedes it), and relates to our incapacity to expiate any offense against God, as all sins are offenses against the infinite God. Thus, mortal sins against an infinite God can only be expiated by an infinite God. This view of our incapacity for satisfaction is supported by St. Thomas in the *Supplement* to the *Summa Theologiae* (q. 13, ad 1): "Just as the offense derived a certain infinity from the infinity of the Divine majesty, so does satisfaction derive a certain infinity from the infinity of Divine mercy, in so far as it is quickened by grace, whereby whatever man is able to repay becomes acceptable."

I am not sure if a mortal sin is an infinite offense so much as it can only be repaid or expiated by God Himself; this is the key point. The thing is that sin is not a subsistent reality so much as it is a lack of the good; in any case, only God is infinite. It appears that no sin can be an infinite reality, otherwise it becomes God, and then we end up with the battle of two "gods," as in Gnosticism. Even Satan cannot be an infinite being with all his evil. As St. Thomas understood, sin is not a being; it is an absence of goodness that was there and should have remained, but for deviant free will of angels and man. St. Thomas affirms that "a sin incurs a debt of infinite punishment in the sense of 'unlimited' punishment'" (ST 2-2ae, q. 87, a. 5, ad 1). In any case, the concern of St. Thomas is about satisfaction made to God, and the merits of His Son on the cross that has "infinitely" paid for our sins. Even when we go to heaven, we will participate in God's eternity but we ourselves do not become eternal (become God). Only God is infinite and no creature, good or evil, can become inherently evil, but can have an aversion to the infinite good. But Aid 2 already responds to your concern. To St. Catherine of Siena was revealed that, with love from sorrow at Jesus being offended, we can repair the offense with infinite satisfaction.

**A Deeper Issue: are we Focused on Sin instead of Christ?**

The deeper issue is not the sin in itself; it is rather about how we perceive and approach it, and this in two ways: immediately and remotely. First and immediately, the entire human and Christian dispensations are built upon a "both/and" foundation. This can be summarized by what Jesus taught St. Catherine of Siena about the two pillars of Christian life: self-knowledge and Jesus' love. We always begin with the deep sense of our poverty and nothingness, but we are not to be fixated on it, but to look at Jesus ("Think of me and I will think of you"). So the huge mistake many make is to take their serious sins in isolation, instead of the "both/and" of setting them against the infinite love of Jesus on the cross.

Furthermore, this anticipates the remote problem. The trap in the spiritual life is to be thinking about myself in constant self-examination. If we forget about ourselves in love, by constantly seeking to love Jesus and constantly begging Jesus for salvation and help for all in the world, we should have no fear of death and judgment, Purgatory, or hell. Even Napoleon Bonaparte, who arrested and exiled two popes, reconciled with God and Church before his death. In a famous talk to her nuns (given in her *I Thirst* series), Mother Teresa told them that they did not understand the love of Jesus, so focused were they on their being troubled by their sins.

**Jesus' Merciful Gaze can Lift our Wounded or Sinful Hearts (Carrón)**

But we have to go more deeply to two issues: the problem of evil and of our own sins. We can be troubled by horrors committed (e.g., Holocaust, terrorism). How we can speak of mercy when our sense of justice desires severe retribution. Regarding accepting evil, we draw the example of a seven-year old Japanese girl who asked Benedict XVI about the devastation she had witnessed after a Tsunami, and he had no answer but Christ:

Dear Elena... I also ask the same questions: why is it this way? Why do you have to suffer so much, while others live comfortably? We do not have the answers, but we know that Jesus suffered like you, innocent, that the true God who shows Himself in Jesus is at your side. This seems to me to be very important, even if we do not have answers, if sadness remains: God is at your side. Be sure that this will help. One day we will also be able to understand why it was this way.[1]

Because evil can insert a wedge between ourselves and God (e.g., "How can God allow this to happen?"), Julián Carrón, who used the example above, substantiates this truth of Christ with real-life paradoxes. He gave the example of a woman gravely wounded in a terrorist attack who was able to say: "For years, when I woke up in the morning, my mind was always flooded with all the scenes of horror I had seen and always carried with me. But since I met you, when I wake up, the first thing that comes to my mind's eye are your glad faces ['the glad faces of her Christian friends prevailed and she changed']." We do not have ready-made answers, but know that God's Son became man and His Paschal mystery embraces everything; and know that His justice will be administered in the next life. Jesus was able to accept the world's evil and say, "Father, into your hands, I commend my spirit," maintaining His bond with the Father. Regarding our sins, we can be consoled by identifying ourselves with a prisoner, who, thanks to a Christian encounter, was able to say, "I'm certainly not happy about the harm I did when I committed that crime, but I am grateful because through this bad thing I did I was able to meet Christ."[2]

But the thought of Msgr. Giussani goes even deeper, one that corresponds to Pope Francis' *Amoris laetitia*. He argues that it does not matter how long it takes us to arrive at a morally good state, even if it takes "fifty years," and to leave the timetable of attainment to Him. And though we may be far from perfect and feel unworthy to receive Communion (e.g., after arguing with one's wife), we have to see this sacrament not "as a prize for the perfect but a powerful medicine and nourishment for the weak" (Pope Francis). What matters is to seek to correspond to that desire deep within our heart. Fr. Carrón illustrates this by pointing to three figures living in sin (Samaritan woman, adulteress, sinful woman at Simon's house) in which Jesus pierced through the mass of sins to see the good that lay therein, and his gaze of mercy and acceptance revitalized that desire. He points to couples who resisted marriage from bad experiences but who decided to marry when they encountered happy marriages, pointing to hope of change and need for Christian witness. Here is a profound text by Fr. Carrón.

---

[1] Benedict XVI, *A Sua immagine: Domande su Gesù*, Channel 1, Italy, 22 April 2011.
[2] Julián Carrón, *Where is God?*, 42.

When you see something beautiful, even if you cannot live it yet, you cannot help but desire it. You may be incapable of living it, but you are unable to not desire it. The question is whether I follow my desire for the beauty I see, the good I sense, the fulfillment to which I aspire. Even if I am bumbling in my way of achieving it, even if a moment later I err again, it is as if my own desire does not give up in me: saying yes to this desire, following it, is the simplest form of prayer. The desire becomes prayer and prayer is nothing other than the ultimate expression of our desire to live up to the fullness for which we were created and to which we are called. (*Where is God?*, 140)

## Being Forgiven and Loved Should Lead to our Self-Gift

St. John Vianney similarly taught: "You do not need to wallow in guilt. Wallow in the infinite mercy of God." Saints become wounded by God's love and fix their eyes on the Master, the Beloved. Hell is about self; heaven is about love, which is self-forgetfulness, to think only of God and others. We learn the proper disposition from St. Thérèse.

> "Even if I had committed all possible crimes, I would still have the same confidence; I would feel that this multitude of offenses would be like a drop of water thrown into the flaming furnace of God's love."
> 
> "I ask that from now on, you never let your past sins be an obstacle between you and Jesus. It's a ruse of the devil to keep putting our sins before our eyes in order to make them like a screen between the Savior and us."
> 
> "Think of your past sins to persuade yourself of your weakness; think of them to confirm your resolution not to fall again -- that's necessary -- but think of them mainly to bless Jesus for having pardoned you, for having purified you, for having cast all your sins to the bottom of the sea." "Do not go looking for them at the bottom of the sea! He has wiped them out; He has forgotten them."

We insist that the goal is to live by love and not simply to avoid sins, which is the level mainly of St. Teresa's first two Mansions (Interior Castle). Duty and works characterize the Ascetical Mansions, and love the Mystical. Love, not duty or works, is the apex that glorifies God and saves souls:

> St. Elizabeth of the Trinity was greatly consoled when she despaired of remotely attaining St. Teresa of Jesus' exalted works: "... it was said to me in the depths of my soul that St. Teresa's glory was less the reward of her great deeds than of **her love**... Now I wish to live solely by love."[3]

---

[3] St. Elizabeth of the Trinity, *The Praise of Glory*, 210.

# COUNSEL 7

## Unity: Disquiet about the Holy Father
(Addressed to a Prioress, October 27, 2020)
*Difficulty: Some can become disturbed by the actions of the Holy Father.*
*Counsel: To inculcate unity with the Holy Father while acknowledging human weakness.*

**Unity with the Holy Father is Central to our Faith**

First, let me tell you what a spiritual director told me when I myself was struggling with similar issues: "The measure of a priest is his unity with his bishop and the Holy Father." St. Catherine of Siena herself had to deal with the vacillating and weak Pope Gregory XI, and, though she was like his mother, she regarded him as her spiritual father, and called the pope "the sweet Christ on earth" (this example was used earlier). In her *Dialogue to Divine Providence*, she wrote: "Even if [the Pope were morally dissolute], we ought not to raise up our heads against him, but calmly lie down to rest on his bosom… He who rebels against our Father is condemned to death, for that which we do to him we do to Christ: we honor Christ if we honor the Pope; we dishonor Christ if we dishonor the Pope." St. Escrivá's unity of life in this regard is exemplary. Arriving in Rome after a tempestuous boat journey, facing Pope Pius XII's room, he was so moved that he prayed all night for him. His love for the pope is expressed in his saying: *Omnes cum Petro ad Jesum per Mariam* ("Everyone with Peter to Jesus through Mary"). This tender devotion was continued in A. del Portillo's warm friendship with, and support for, Paul VI, John Paul I, and John Paul II. He met with John Paul II personally and with groups about 48 times, supported him in difficult moments (e.g., after the assassination attempt, even flew back to Rome when he was sick on another occasion, saying that a son should be close to his father), and acted on his every wish for help for the Church.[1]

**Respecting Office and Person**

It might help to make a distinction between the person of the pope and his office. As Jesus taught, "The scribes and the Pharisees sit on Moses' seat; so practice and observe whatever they tell you, but not what they do; for they preach, but do not practice" (Mt 23:2-3). Thus, we must respect their office and, by extension, their person. I sense it is vital that we stay away from any blogs or writings that attack the Holy Father, as division is the work of Satan, while unity is the work of the Spirit. I find that, if I read just one polemical article about someone, I can't stop thinking negatively about him.

---

[1] John F. Coverdale, Saxum, 187-199.

## The Pope's Acting Personally vs. Ecclesially

There is a precedent in the Church's dogmatic theology history that can illuminate. Pope John XXII had erroneously held privately that we will enjoy the beatific vision only after the eschaton (which he retracted before his death). This occasioned Pope Benedict XII's promulgation of the papal bull, *Benedictus Deus*, issued in 1336, which settled the question once and for all. Whatever the pope teaches must conform to the deposit of faith (Scripture and Tradition, that is transmitted through the Magisterium) entrusted by Christ to the apostles and elaborated by the Spirit through the Church. No pope can go against this deposit, that is now guarded as a sacred trust by the Church, which can neither subtract from nor add to it.

## Rising above the Human to the Level of Faith

Where some at Vatican II were preoccupied with the conservative vs. liberal debate, Wojtyla rose above it. With a divine perspective, he simply viewed the Council as occasioned by the Holy Spirit and as His work. And as pope, he viewed his primary mission as simply to implement the Council's teaching. In contrast, when we stay at merely the human level, then every new piece of news about the Holy Father that comes out may disturb us.

## Simplicity vs. Multiplicity

Holiness is simplicity (being one). Our Lady, after she became pregnant, allowed God to take care of her divinely caused pregnancy and simply focused on doing God's will in each moment (A. von Speyr). The Holy Family were like pencils in the Spirit's hands and helped to save the world in doing so, while not being overly concerned about the Roman yoke or the failure of the priestly and Pharisee classes. Thus, your holiness lies in simplicity, "oneness," being focused on God's will and abandoned, such that He can work in you. The opposite is "multiplicity," being troubled by what others are doing and losing your peace, a sign of the evil spirit.

## Jesus in our Midst through Unity

Chiara Lubich, foundress of the Focolare movement, was taught by Jesus that, when two people try to love one another, to have unity, Jesus becomes present in their midst ("For where two or three are gathered," Mt 18:20), and light and joy enter; and that when we have disunity or unforgiveness, then we lose Christ's presence, along with light, peace, and joy. Saints love even their enemies: "True charity consists in doing good to those who do us evil, and in thus winning them over" (St. A. de Liguori).

Out of love for the Church, let us use all possible means so as not to damage, not even remotely, the unity of Christians: "you should always avoid complaining, criticizing, gossiping... avoid absolutely anything that could bring discord among brothers" [St. Escrivá, *Furrow* 918]. On the contrary, we should always foster everything that is an occasion for mutual understanding and concord. If on some occasion we are not able to praise, we should say nothing [idem, *The Way* 443]. In the words of the Liturgy: "May we overcome today all envy and dissension." (F. Fernandez, *In Conversation with God,* vol. 2, "Unity," 354)

## Seeing the Pope's Accomplishments with an Elevated Vision

It may help to consider Carrón's deeper vision. He points to the pope being known as "the pope of mercy": "His gaze is so irresistible that he attracts the people who are farthest away. The thing that happened in the Gospel [with Jesus] is being repeated" (*Where is God?*, 52). He sees continuity between Benedict XVI and Francis, and that the latter's vision corresponds to Communion and Liberation's intuitions and today's needs: "Pope Francis is a grace for the Church in the world today" (128). He was awarded the European Charlemagne Prize for exceptional service to European unity.

> We see today the same attitude in Pope Francis, who speaks with great realism about the situation we are experiencing, with a piecemeal Third World War, arms trafficking, violence, "throw-away" human beings, the phenomenon of migration, injustice, hunger, and corruption. Equally interested in the particular vicissitudes of individuals and global scenarios, he has become a world leader everyone acknowledges precisely because his gaze is full of the realism born of Christian hope. (Ibid, 3-4)

## General Remarks

A key sign of holiness is an openness to anything the Spirit brings, but which entails development with newness (Newman). The Fathers highlight the "newness" of Christ. As de Lubac taught, we cannot limit the Spirit, who blows where He wills. His gift of the Franciscan and Dominican Orders fuelled opposition from the secular clergy, and ecclesial charisms today endure resistance. When Christianity has lost the renewed encounter with Christ, it becomes staid, like a possession, a focusing on doctrines and moral precepts, but unable to touch hearts and galvanize evangelization. Carrón explains how the Church's history has always been a responding to the newness of the Spirit in each age. To be faithful to the core of faith received, there has to be "communication, transmission of the tradition, it must renew itself" (ibid, 119). One who is faithful to Christ is not merely "conservative" nor "liberal," but open to all the ways of the Spirit.

# COUNSEL 8

**Occult: Couple whose Son is Reading Occult Works**
*Counsel: We must take our eyes off our trials and keep our eyes on Jesus.*

[Email note from the couple to the priest from whom they sought help]
    *Good morning, Father*

    *Thank you for your advice last month. We have been praying the chaplet of the Precious Blood every evening along with the Rosary, St. Michaels, and calling on the intercession of St. Joseph, Terror of Demons. We've been placing our son on the altar at daily mass and blessing his room with holy water and holy oil.*

    *It seems that he is taking more interest in the occult, crystals, and seances. Yesterday, he challenged us on discussing the occult as a religion. We calmly answered his questions (while inwardly praying to the Holy Spirit to put the right words in our mouths). At one point, he said that he was very uncomfortable (somewhat agitated) and didn't know why. Could he have an evil spirit within him? There are many red flags that I would like to talk to someone about. We would like to speak with someone who is knowledgeable in the topic of deliverance and could guide us. We will continue in prayer but feel we also need hands on guidance. Could you refer us to the appropriate individual? Thank you again. In Christ, (Couple)*

[This priest addressed above then contacted the author for help, and the author communicated with the couple with the following two emails.]

Dear Mr. and Mrs. M,
I am sorry to hear about your son. What he is doing is not uncommon today, as the occult area is very accessible through the internet, and there are now apparently substantial sections devoted to it in large book retailers.

1. He likely has no serious infestation. An easy test for this is to add a bit of holy water to a dish you have cooked and see if he reacts. If he does not react strongly, he likely has no serious infestation.

2. The real problem is that he may be opening doors. If you want to know a little about this area, read the last chapter of my new book, *Mystical Incarnation: "You are my Son, the Beloved,"* available at Amazon.

3. But your main problem is what to do with and for your son. First, you must understand that, no matter what you say, he will likely not listen. During adolescent and teen years, the young are not prone to listen. This is where we look to divine power by turning to our Lady (and St. Joseph). As parents, you have the moral authority to entrust him to her, and then allow her to take care of the results (see quotation from *In Sinu Jesu* at the end of this note). To worry after entrusting him to our Lady is to manifest a lack trust and

confidence in her intercession (recall Divine Mercy image's words, "Jesus, I trust in you"). Do not obsess about the problem, keep your eyes on her. St. Peter started sinking in the water when he looked at the storm; as long as his eyes were on Jesus, He could walk on water and do miracles.

However, if he is willing to listen, the first step with possible infestation is for him to go to the sacrament of Confession. Fr. Gabriel Amorth, now deceased former exorcist of Rome, wrote that the evil spirits are more afraid of Confession than of exorcism. For the former effects sacramental or divine regeneration, the latter only expels demons.

-------------

*From the wife's distraught reply, it was very evident that they were still agitated and overwhelmed, obsessed about reading books on deliverance and trying to take authority of spirits. So a second and more substantial email was sent to them, copied below.*

Dear Mrs. M,

**Eyes on Jesus and not on the Storm**
May I make a suggestion? Avoid getting all wrapped up in reading about deliverance ministry and doing all kinds of deliverance prayers on your son. That is exactly what the devil wants. To reiterate, what I am recommending is that you stop reading about fighting the occult and taking authority over the devil and all of that— that becomes obsessive, which is not of the Holy Spirit. All you have to do is to entrust your son to our Lady (even only once) and then wait for her arranging of the outcome. Do not be concerned about his salvation, our Lady will take care of it. I once had to teach a new permanent deacon not to be thinking too spiritually, about the devil attacking him and God giving him a special word when he preaches. I told him to be like his devout parents who have their feet on the ground, and revealed to him that I seldom think of the devil, because I try to keep my eyes on Christ. The devil would love it if you focused on him and not on Christ. Above all, we want to avoid fascination with the dark side, and focus instead on the sublime mysteries, like the ineffable Mass or grace, and on Christ.

**"Think of my Interests, and I will Think of yours" (Jesus' words)**
In any case, our task is not even primarily about our own children, though we begin there. Our task is primarily to look after God's children in the world who are suffering grave trials. Jesus taught St. Margaret Mary Alacoque, "Think of my interests, and I will think of yours." When we are thinking of, and praying for, our own children all the time, what do we think Jesus thinks of us when his children are under corrupt or totalitarian governments, in war-torn areas and being raped, living in poverty, etc.?

Keep things simple. If you simply trust in Jesus through Mary, you don't even have to contact me further. When you are continually worrying about your son and thinking about him, then (i) it is about self-interest (not caring about God's suffering children) and (ii) it is a lack of trust in Jesus and Mary. Jesus told St. Faustina that what wounds Him the most is the lack of trust in Him, that we fail to trust that He will look after us.

### St. Monica Turned to God, Waiting for His Intervention
We might now consider the disposition of parents in the mould of St. Monica. She not only struggled with her husband, who was sometimes unfaithful and of violent temper (converted to Christianity a year before his death), a difficult mother-in-law who lived with them, and especially the erring Augustine. Jean d'Elbée noted that God refused Monica's prayer that he not go to Rome to give her a much greater gift of great conversion to become a doctor of the Church. She turned to divine means:

> When he [Augustine] was young, she enrolled him as a catechumen according to contemporary custom, but his irregular life caused so much suffering that she once refused to allow him to live in her house. But she soon relented; realizing (through a priest) that *the time for his conversion had not yet come, she gave up arguing with him* (or asking others to do so) *and turned instead to prayer, fasts, and vigils,* hoping that they would succeed where argument had failed.... He went on [from Rome] to Milan, but Monica followed him. She was highly esteemed by its bishop, Ambrose, who also helped Augustine towards a deep moral conversion besides acceptance of the Christian faith. This took place in 386. As a consequence Augustine renounced also his mother's plans for his marriage, deciding to remain celibate; with Monica and a few chosen friends, he went away for a period of preparation for Baptism.[1] (emphasis added)

### Intercede with Confidence, but allow God to Choose the Outcome
But God asks of us great trust and to allow Him to choose the outcome. (*In Sinu Jesu*, Wednesday, September 7, 2011, 182-183)

> When you intercede for another, do so with a boundless confidence in My love for that soul. At the same time, relinquish every desire to see the outcome of your intercession as you would imagine or desire it to be. Allow Me to receive your prayer and to respond to it in ways corresponding to My infinite wisdom, to My love, and to My perfect will for the person you bring before My Eucharistic Face.
> *Do not come to Me with solutions; come to Me only with your problems, and allow Me to provide the solutions.* I have no need of your solutions, but when you bring Me

---

[1] David Farmer, "Monica," *The Oxford Dictionary of Saints* (Fifth Edition, rev.) (Oxford: Oxford University Press, 2011), 312-313.

problems, sufferings, questions, and needs, I am glorified by your confidence in My merciful love.

Bring Me your questions, your problems, and your fears, and I will attend to them; for Me darkness itself is not dark and night shines as the day. There is no situation and no suffering so heavy that I cannot make it light to bear, and even, if such be My will, remove it altogether from those which are crushed beneath its weight.

Pray to Me with confidence and with abandonment, and not with a secret desire to force My hand and to obtain from Me only what you have in view. Ask and you shall receive. Only ask with a trusting faith, *believing that whatever I will give is best for you and most glorious for Me and for My Father*. Seek and you shall find. Yes, seek, but allow Me to guide you to the object of your seeking. Seek My Face, and all the rest will be given you besides.

There are souls *so attached to what they think I should give them* in answer to their prayers, that when I give them what is best for them, and most glorious for Me and for My Father, *they fail to see it. This is because they do not intercede or ask in the Holy Spirit*. Instead, they pray out of the obscurity, blindness, and narrowness of their *own perceptions, limiting what I can do for them, and using their prayer as an attempt to control My loving omnipotence*.

When you ask, do so with a *complete abandonment* to My wisdom, My love, and My perfect will. Pray in this way, and you will begin to see *wonders* surpassing all that you can imagine.

How unfortunate are those who come to Me proposing their own solutions, when all they need to do is to bring Me their problems, their needs, and their requests. When you intercede for one who is ailing, it is enough for you to say to Me: "Lord, the one whom Thou lovest is sick." Leave all the rest to My most loving Heart. If you ask for a cure or healing, do so with such confidence in My love that your faith is ready to embrace My response to your prayer in whatever form it takes.

If I am teaching you how to intercede before My Eucharistic Face, and how to present souls to My Eucharistic Heart, it is because **I want you to intercede much, to ask boldly, and to obtain great things** from My omnipotent love. If you are praying well, that is, praying as I teach you how to pray, then act boldly and confidently, for I am with you and I will not forsake you, and My blessing will rest upon all that you do with a pure heart for My glory and the glory of My Father. (emphasis added)

# COUNSEL 9

## Divine Joy: Christ's Three Dispositions during Trials

*Difficulty: A person who was burdened by troubles, as many are today, sought help.*
*Counsel: To reveal that we can rise above troubles through a divine (not merely human) joy, that was first lived by Christ in the midst of His life-long martyrdom.*

How can we live amidst our inevitable life troubles and yet find peace in serving God? Francis Fernandez's meditation, "The Joy of Advent, describes the heart-warming knowledge that Jesus' drawing closer brings the unspeakable joy we experience in Advent and Christmas, from which arises a longing, *maranatha*, "Come, Lord Jesus" (a hymn adds, "do not delay"). It is expressed deeply by the texts of Isaiah in the First Readings of Advent Masses. A foretaste of this joy is Jesus promised in His first words after His Resurrection (Jn 14:27)[1]: "Rejoice in the Lord always; again I will say, Rejoice" (Phil 4:4). We draw close to divine joy when we ascend the Mystical Mansions, but it depends on living Jesus' dispositions of divine joy: *divine filiation, flight towards heaven, and sacrifice.*

**1. Living Jesus' Sonship**

St. Thérèse summarized her teaching thus: "To let nothing disturb me." Her path of divine joy begins by seeing that the Father, who knows best, is allowing all life's events, while living holy indifference. It is to live the joy of divine filiation (sonship, daughtership) in serving God, as Blessed Alvaro del Portillo described:

> Authentic joy is based on this foundation: that we want to live for God and want to serve others because of God. Let us tell the Lord that we want nothing more than to serve him with joy. If we behave in this way we shall find that our inner peace, our joy, our good humour will attract many souls to God. Give witness to Christian joy. Show to those around you that this is our great secret. We are happy because we are children of God, because we deal with him, because we struggle to become better for him. And when we fail, we go right away to the Sacrament of joy [Confession] where we recover our sense of fraternity with all men and women. (Homily 12, Apr 1984, *In Conversation With God*, vol. 5, 155)

Remarkable was his cheerfulness and affability during trying times in Rome: much difficulty in obtaining Opus Dei canonical approval; a plot within a Vatican Congregation to remove the founder; over a dozen years in making ends meet to pay for costs of building Villa Tevere and other properties;

---

[1] Francis Fernandez, *In Conversation with God*, vol. 2, 111-117.

holding several key Opus Dei positions; handled opposition; appointed to three Vatican II commissions. Oppressed by heavy burdens and over-work, his divine filial trust in God left him with a higher joy (*Saxum*, Chs. 10-11).

## 2. Living in the Higher Part of our Souls, a Flight towards Heaven

Jean-Pierre de Caussade teaches that Jesus and Mary at Calvary felt as if their humanity was being destroyed, but kept their eyes on the Father and His holy will in the midst of the storm. We too, through our senses, can experience the heavy burdens of sickness, trials, and even inner turmoil, but can remain at peace if the depths of our soul are at peace. Our soul can experience periods of desolation or storms, but if it perseveres, then the sun will appear again. St. Thérèse offers a remarkable example in saying that, even in the Dark Night of the Soul, the spirit of her soul was already united with God: "I do not know what more I shall have in heaven. I shall see God, but as for being with Him, I am entirely with Him now" (*Last Conversations*, May 15; *Story of a Soul*, Ch. XII). Chiara Lubich experienced it (2004-2008) as if "God had disappeared," yet said, "My night has no darkness, but all things shine in the light." Such souls live only for God, and are continually united to Him in the silence and solitude of their soul.

## 3. United with Christ's Holy Spirit for Self-Gift (Expropriation)

Those who love Christ seek to be one with Him. But He is pure Gift, pure Sacrifice, pure Kenosis, and therefore on earth He identifies with us and descends to take upon Himself all our troubles (Phil 2:6). Those who truly love God seek to enter His eternal Act. To do this, they renounce happiness so as to become pure gift. But the joy comes precisely from the sacrifice: "… [Jesus] for the joy that was set before him endured the cross, despising the shame, and is seated at the right hand of the throne of God" (Heb 22:2). This path entails seeing spiritual life, not as about acquiring spiritual goods, but about "losing our life" for Christ. St. Francis de Sales taught Bishop Camus to expect ingratitude from his flock. St. John of the Cross moved his unique crucifix from his convent in Segovia to the Church so that it could be honoured not just by the friars but by everyone.

> After moving the crucifix, our Lord said to John: "Brother John, ask me for what you wish, and I will give it to you, for the service you have done me." And he said to Him in return: "Lord, what I wish you to give me are sufferings to be borne for your sake, and that I may be despised and regarded as worthless."[2]

---

[2] Stanncharlotte.org, accessed November 13, 2021, https://www.stanncharlotte.org/wp-content/uploads/2021/07/14th-Sunday-in-Ordinary-Time-2021-homily-Fr.-Reid.pdf.

# COUNSEL 10

## Sacrifice: Offering Christ with His Mysteries

*Difficulty: Christians often find their prayers before and intercession to God not efficacious. Counsel: Dina Bélanger teaches that the highest path of God is to offer these mysteries of His Son, which we can offer to fulfill five ends owed to God: love, adoration, thanksgiving, reparation, and intercession. A three-stage path is delineated here.*

As mentioned in the back cover of this book's description, Christians serving Christ are inclined to focus on prayers, mortifications, and acts of charity; yet they all seem so puny an offering to God. We look to Blessed Dina Bélanger, of whom one commentator wrote that she has gone a step beyond St. Thérèse, the one who helped form her. Let us examine this in three steps.

### 1. Offering Jesus' Mysteries to the Father

First, besides going through Mary as the indispensable mother and mediatrix, Blessed Dina Bélanger was taught by Jesus to offer His mysteries to God as the most perfect sacrifice. This is not new, as other saints have understood this secret. For example, we find this in St. Gertrude in a letter in the OOR of her feast day, when after repenting for failing to look to God in the first twenty-six years of her life, now offered Jesus as reparation:

> … until I was nearly twenty-six, I was always so blindly irresponsible. Looking back I see that but for your protecting hand I would have been quite without conscience in thought, word or deed….
> To make amends for the way I previously lived, I offer you, most loving Father, all the sufferings of your beloved Son, from that first infant cry as he lay on the hay in the manger, until that final moment when, bowing his head, with a mighty voice, Christ gave up his spirit. I think, as I make this offering, of all that he underwent, his needs as a baby, his dependence as a young child, the hardships of youth and the trials of early manhood.
> To atone for all my neglect I offer, most loving Father, all that your only-begotten Son did during his life, whether in thought, word or deed. That sacred life was, I know, utterly perfect in all respects, from the moment he descended from your heavenly throne and came into this world, until finally he presented the glory of his victorious human nature to you, his Father.

Within the Church we understand that Christ's mysteries have become our mysteries, and we have them at our disposal now to offer them back to God, these mysteries that are so pleasing to the Father. There is no greater offering than Jesus' acts (expressed by the Father's pleasure, "You are my Son, the Beloved") that ravishes and glorifies the Trinity.

### 2. Offering our Work and Selves in the Holy Mass

A second step is to offer everything through the Mass. The sacrifice of Christ on Calvary is His greatest mystery, and that has now become perpetuated in the holy Mass, so that we are mystically or sacramentally present at Calvary's sacrifice. We can offer our day's work at the Offertory, but, even more, ourselves, united to Christ's pleasing sacrifice to the Father in the Holy Spirit. St. Josemaría Escrivá taught his spiritual children to place their day's work on the paten, for which they must sanctify their work as a pleasing offering to be united with Christ's offering. Here we note a key action of Blessed Dina Bélanger. She did not seek to adore and thank God after Holy Communion, but allowed Mary to offer Jesus within her to thank and glorify God. Herein we see the degree of her allowing Christ to act.

### 3. "Substitution of Christ" with Eyes Fixed on Jesus (D. Bélanger)
A third step is found in Blessed Dina Bélanger. In the substitution of Christ that was revealed to her in a vision, Dina had been "annihilated" (perhaps during a Dark Night of the Soul) and Jesus had substituted Himself in her place, the transformation that allowed Him to act in her. After this transformation of substitution that was depicted in a mystical vision, all that was left for her to do was to keep her eyes on Jesus, which effectively allowed Jesus to act in her. She saw that "one sigh of Jesus in her was sufficient to save worlds," so powerful was Jesus' acting in her.

So powerful and efficacious was this fixing her eyes on Jesus that the devil strove to divert her. On one occasion, a "holy" thought came to her: "You are not generous or mortified enough." Being saintly, she immediately proceeded to examine and accuse herself on these two points. Perhaps through enlightenment by the Spirit, she asked herself, "Where did this thought come from?" She was given to understand that the devil had inserted the thought, and we see that his goal, his greatest goal, is that we should take our eyes from Jesus, and to look at ourselves and our spiritual condition. This is the trap into which many Christians unconsciously fall. We often are troubled by our sins, but Christian life is only 10% about avoiding sin and 90% about loving God and union with Him. A man always thinking of his weaknesses as a husband and father is not a good husband nor a good father, for his focus should be on his wife and his children.

So with offering (1) Jesus' mysteries and (2) our sacrifices in the Mass, the apex is (3) the substitution of Christ, which we foster and develop by keeping our eyes on Him (and not on the past, future, our spiritual condition, or troubles). Then we become, as it were, a "replica" of Him, and He is now able to act powerfully in us. We become His other self; Christ in a mystical incarnation has descended into our humanity.

# COUNSEL 11

## Chastity: Seminarian's Desire to Protect Celibate Vows

*Difficulty: A seminarian, disturbed by reports of a few priests having struggles with living celibate vows, asked for counsel to live total chastity (renunciation of all sexual activity).*

### Building Series of Castle Walls to Protect Chastity

The author suggested an image of a castle, like that found in J.R.R. Tolkien's *The Lord of the Rings: The Return of the King*. The capital of Gondor, *Minas Tirith*, during the war of the Ring, was besieged by the evil forces of Mordor. What offered protection were a few walls or ramparts. Even if the enemy broke through the first wall, there were still further walls. Until they broke through the last wall, they could not be assured of victory.

If one views the spiritual or Christian life as having concentric walls, even if the enemy breaks through the outer wall, the inner walls are sufficient to protect from defeat. During that spiritual direction meeting, the author came up with the following series of walls to protect chastity, the bottom of this list (wall 1) representing the innermost wall, moving upwards to the outermost wall (wall 7), with specific guidelines offered to protect chastity. If we keep most walls up, we do not lose God, who is at the center.

| | |
|---|---|
| Wall 7 | Specific guidelines for protecting chastity |
| Wall 6 | Plan of Life |
| Wall 5 | Obedience (Church, bishop, spiritual director) |
| Wall 4 | Priestly Fraternity |
| Wall 3 | Jesus in our midst through unity (C. Lubich) |
| Wall 2 | Spiritual Director |
| Wall 1 | Our Lady (St. Joseph, guardian angel) |

*Wall 1*: First and foremost, the greatest power for protection for any danger is *our Lady*. Consecration to her not only protects us but also helps us attain holiness. We should also consider entrusting ourselves to St. Joseph, the Lily of purity, who is also our spiritual father, St. John the beloved disciple, as well as our guardian angels, who have been our guardians since birth.

*Wall 2*: While our Lady represents help from above through God, we benefit greatly through the aid of *a spiritual director*. Chapter 3 of *New Christ: Priestly Configuration* has developed the vital role of the spiritual director in the Church's history, as well as how to benefit from this great gift from God. If a consecrated soul or a married lay person feels attraction to another, then he or she, by revealing it to God through one of his ministers (director or confessor), more easily defeats the enemy, who wants that person to hide the attraction. Bringing it out to the open, especially to a spiritual director, reduces the power that attraction has over a person, while affording valuable counsel to proceed forward, not to mention a certain peace and assurance.

*Wall 3*: Chiara Lubich speaks of the greatest power and protection as that coming from *being united in love, which brings Jesus into our midst*. She recalled at the beginning of Focolare when they were detached from their community and felt alone and their fragility: "we felt confused; our will was weak and unable to carry out what we planned. We could no longer see why we had left everything to follow Jesus. The light was missing. When we were united, on the other hand, we felt all the strength of Jesus among us. It was as if we were armed with the power and blessing of heaven." United, there was more than presence; it was Jesus Himself. (*Living City*, Feb. 2020, 21)

*Wall 4*: As human beings, we are created to find love within marriage. If God calls someone to a consecrated life as a priest or consecrated soul, then that desire for love, friendship, and communion has to be filled in some way, and that is where *priestly fraternity or religious communities* can help fill the void in our hearts. Augustine teaches, "Whenever a person is without a friend, not a single thing in the world appears friendly to him" (*Letter* 130:2.4). But our heart's greatest desire is for divine union, which will be fulfilled in eternity. That spousal love of Christ must be initiated and fostered (e.g., loving dialogue): "The unmarried man is anxious about the affairs of the Lord, how to please the Lord… the unmarried woman… how to be holy in body and spirit" (1 Cor 7:32-34).

*Wall 5*: *Obedience* is a fundamental virtue of Jesus and Mary, and is the foundation of all spiritual life. Jacques Philippe teaches that docility to the Spirit's inspirations becomes the norm in the Mystical Mansions, but that his first inspiration is to obedience (e.g., to bishop, superior, pastor, spiritual director, Church). This one wall protects against many things. St. Faustina said that the devil can feign humility, but not obedience (the *non serviam*, "I will not serve," is attributed to him).

*Wall 6*: *The plan of life* is probably the foundation for chastity, as it encompasses so many pillars that protect: fixed rising and retiring times; fixed prayer times; and possibly daily Mass, weekly Confession, and monthly spiritual direction; duties of my state of life; sanctifying work; living in the present moment, etc. Fidelity to the duties of state of life or horarium and ministry (religious or priest) already forms a wall by itself. Order deriving from a plan of life gives a stability and strength not otherwise found. If the devil wanted to undermine a religious community, a subversive way would be to compromise their horarium and discipline.

*Wall 7*: We still need specific guidelines for protection for chastity. A very helpful chapter is found in St. Escrivá's *The Way*, "Holy Purity," as well as the need for temperance and mortification (e.g., see *In Conversation with God*, vol. 3, 652-657). A vice that makes one more open to attacks by the devil is idleness (*acedia*). Perhaps another area that could protect is "minding our own business," St. Philip Neri himself taught that we should "stay within our own house." Special prayers (e.g., three Hail Marys) said before going to bed can help. Those who have attachments, being rooted to the Ascetical Mansions, may also be more easily tempted. St. Catherine of Siena teaches that "A full belly does not make for a chaste spirit" (*Dialogue,* 125). We can perhaps add two additional walls: zeal for souls, which weakens temptations (wall 8); and meditation on the Passion of Christ (wall 9). St. Thomas More teaches that meditation on Christ's passion enabled him to await his decapitation with serenity (*The Sadness of Christ*), and St. Escrivá was given a mystical experience of the power of finding refuge in Christ's wounds.

As noted, if we find we have attractions to another, we protect ourselves by taking precautions: not embracing, dancing, or having private meetings with, or looking out for, that person. Men are aroused through the eyes, and the saints know that we can let an angel or a devil in through this window of the soul (e.g., protect ourselves by not taking a second look). Today, the dominant source of temptation is internet pornography. If necessary, we must stop internet access (one priest left his cell phone each night on the altar). To protect our hearts, we can imitate a saintly friar who would acknowledge the beauty of one for whom he fell, but then add, "Lord, I give her up for you." Temptations are easily stopped at the beginning, keeping the tempter outside the walls or the snowball from getting large.

On the one hand, Archbishop Luis Martinez calls priests to victimhood and purity, to be Jesus: "We priests must be victims by reason of our loving sacrifice; we must be altars by reason of our purity. The soul that shares in the mystical priesthood of Jesus must necessarily be priest, victim, and altar, that is, that soul must be Jesus" (*Only Jesus*). Yet, as Dom Crenier noted, "Most of the saints experience this trial [temptations against purity] by fire" (*Autobiography of Dina Bélanger*, 23, footnote 2). We find this in St. Benedict, St. Francis, St. Bernard, St. Catherine of Siena, Dina Bélanger. These should remain at peace in God. Sr. Briege McKenna was taught by Jesus not to try to fix her tent when experiencing temptations but to allow Him to look after the tent (*Miracles Do Happen*). When struggling in this area, we must understand that holiness is primarily living humility and charity (90%), while trying to maintain purity (10%). The devil wants us to be all troubled about our struggles in chastity (make it 90%) if we but forget about Christ. When St. Augustine still struggled with chastity after his conversion ("Lord, give me chastity, but not yet"), his primary focus was not on preserving chastity but on loving the Lord. The primary focus of St. Paul, whose "thorn" St. Francis de Sales interpreted as temptations against chastity, was "[He] loved me and gave Himself for me" (Gal 2:20).

**The Dark Nights Bring Temptations**
St. Alphonsus' depiction of the temptations during the Dark Night of the Soul suggests that there are two levels. For example, regarding purity, the first or active level can be represented by St. Escrivá's chapter on "Holy Purity" in *The Way*, as in this pithy saying: "To defend his purity, Saint Francis of Assisi rolled in the snow, St. Benedict threw himself into a thorn bush, St. Bernard plunged into an icy pond… You…, what have you done?" (n. 143). This is a manly way of fighting, but at the "active" level.

Yet, there appears to be a higher passive abandonment that we find in the Unitive Stages that St. Alphonsus described: "the Lord sometimes permits a thousand other temptations to accompany this desolation of spirit, temptations to *impurity, anger, blasphemy, disbelief, and above all despair.*" St. Teresa of Jesus teaches a truth known to some: "It constantly happens that the Lord permits a soul to fall so that it may grow humbler." This level likely corresponds to "God living in them," inverting the priorities of "our living in God." We find that saintly and dedicated people, including consecrated souls, face temptations, resulting in doubts in their consciences.

Regarding purity, there are saintly people for whom temptations against chastity are recurrent: St. Paul's "thorn" and Dina Bélanger's "trials." Regarding prayer, we find St. Thérèse falling asleep during her meditations because of illness. Regarding patience, we find a saintly soul like Padre Pio able to read hearts, with divine instinct sternly berating someone for abusing the sacrament (who would usually return with remorse). Regarding those who preached "Christian joy," we find three souls rarely smiling: John Paul II because of Parkinson's disease, Mother Teresa in her spiritual darkness, Bishop Miklósházy with his multiple burdens (surgeries, unable to sleep at night). Regarding food, one bishop on his ad limina visit was "surprised" (scandalized?) that John Paul II really enjoyed his Polish meals.

De Caussade says that, at the second level, the primary focus on virtues and asceticism give way to abandonment and receptivity of what God allows, including irritability and temptations against purity. The saintly soul is in consternation because these trials seem at odds with sanctity. It is the depiction of the trials of the Dark Nights that can console and guide these privileged souls, and their primary task is abandonment in God's arms and accepting expropriation. But the test of their holiness are their "fruits."

## Addendum

As noted earlier, one exorcist focused on wounds or traumas from our earlier life causing very escalated reactions. Msgr. Rossetti focuses instead on spirits: "But there are times when people's emotions don't come from their psyche; they come from the bowels of hell. Or more likely, the person may feel a *little* of these negative emotions, and then Satan *exaggerates* them into an overwhelming crisis."[1]

Besides the spiritual level, we must become aware of our not addressing human emotions, the human level. Msgr. Rossetti, who is a psychologist and former President and Chief Executive Officer of St. Luke Institute in Maryland, delineated this dimension in his book on exorcism.

> As a psychologist, I typically endeavor to have people get in touch with their feelings and to "own" them. If they don't, they are liable to "stuff" their emotions, and then those emotions come out "sideways," in all sorts of dysfunctional ways, such as alcohol abuse, drugs, sex, porn, nasty behavior, and more. This is particularly true of what people call "negative" emotions, such as anger, hurt, resentment, and darker emotions such as despair. We humans need to learn to manage these more difficult emotions. (Ibid.)

People who struggle with chastity may be assisted by looking at these negative emotions of "anger, hurt, resentment, and darker emotions such as despair," since they can come out sideways, in "alcohol abuse, drugs, sex, porn, nasty behavior, and more." At a deeper level (not to play psychologist), our need for affection and affectivity may not be met. We need the intimacy with God in prayer, love of our family, friendship with others, as well as the fulfillment from giving ourselves in serving others. The author becomes concerned when he encounters isolation, self-absorption, a victim-complex, or any breach in the human foundation. Where the human virtues constitute a bulwark, we can withstand much.

There is a deeper issue spiritually as well. Falls against purity offend God, as do all sins. But as one retreat director noted, St. Thomas calls these sins of children. One supposes he means that they are smaller relative to the great sins of Satan, like pride, disobedience, division, schism, heresy, etc., that close hearts to God (e.g., Pharisees of Jesus' time), where God can allow temptations against purity to the saints (e.g., Dina Bélanger). It is a diversion to be focused primarily on the shameful guilty feelings from sins against purity. Our primary focus in the spiritual life should be on humility and self-gift (90%), and the secondary against impurity (10%).

---

[1] Stephen Rossetti, *Diary of an American Exorcist*, 271.

# COUNSEL 12

## Struggles: Overcoming all through Jesus in our Midst (Lubich)

*We Need to Walk on Two Legs: Risen Christ and Christ among us*
You might wonder why it is so necessary to put Jesus in our midst. It's because we *are* immersed in the world and the world belongs to the devil, who is the prince of this world. Besides this, the world itself is full of allurements, materialist values and secularism. You *can* manage to go ahead on your own— it is possible, but at a certain moment, you will collapse. Why is that? Because everything around you is much more powerful. You have to reinforce yourself, and as we know, two friends together, two people who are united with one another are like a fortified tower (Prov 18:19). You have to be as strong as that. That's why Mary invented this spirituality and the Holy Spirit gave it to us. It's a way of life in which it's necessary to live with the risen Lord within us and also among us. We need to have both of them; we cannot go ahead without them. Sooner or later, we will surrender to a merely human, if not evil, way of life. We will give into a merely human, if not evil, way of life. We will give in to human reasoning, to a human way of thinking.... So we need to journey with Jesus in our midst.... These two elements— the risen Jesus within us and the risen Jesus among us— are essential for us. They are necessary for our sanctification. We cannot become holy by ourselves. We have to become holy together. Ours is a collective way to holiness. (81)

*To See Others as if for the First Time, Giving Full Amnesty for all Failings*
We have to love everyone with the merciful love that was characteristic of our life in the early days of the Movement. In fact, we decided that when we woke up every morning, and throughout the day, we would see all the neighbors we met— in our families, at school, at work, everywhere— as new, totally new. We saw them like that, not remembering anything about their faults or failures, but rather covering over everything with love. To love just as the Word of Life this month suggests to us, "Forgive seventy times seven" (see Mt 18:22). To approach everyone with complete amnesty in our hearts, forgiving everyone and everything. (77)

*Jesus in our Midst Enlightens us, Guides us, He is the "Exegete"*
From the very beginning, it seems to us that his [Jesus'] presence was the reason we understood the Gospels and the Scriptures in a new way. Likewise, we feel that his presence also helped us to understand, in a deeper way than ever before, the teachings of the pope and the bishops. His presence among us also influenced our understanding of His Word. He was the one who was our master, teaching us how his words were to be understood. It was a kind of exegesis, not given by a doctor of theology, but by Christ himself.[1] (43)

---

[1] Chiara Lubich, *Jesus in our Midst*, 81, 77, 43.

# CONCLUSION

## 1. The Holy Spirit Renews the Church in All Ages
The Church and the world are in great need of renewal— of Christ. But it is the Spirit who has a master-plan and who takes charge, as was manifest in the Acts of the Apostles. As He had led the Catholic Reformation with new saints, so now He sends especially lay movements into the Church. But though these can influence many, they still constitute a small though key minority within the Church. What about the Church at large, the dioceses, parishioners, hierarchy, diocesan priests, etc.? There seem to be two overall paths of reform. (1) St. Bernard and St. Catherine of Siena were dominant figures who reformed the Church of their age. But this path is not open to all the faithful. Is the Church as a whole not to be reformed? What about Vatican II's universal call to holiness, especially to the laity?

(2) The more general path to reform the Church is represented by Mary and Joseph at Nazareth. They tower over all the saints; they, in fact, generate Christians as Mother in the order of grace and Spiritual Father of the Church respectively. They have a surpassing influence in all ages that is far more powerful and efficacious than St. Bernard's, yet also more hidden. The hidden path was lived by St. Charles de Foucauld or Pierre-Marie Delfieux (founder of the Jerusalem Monastic Community) in their desert charism. But the Holy Family's path is open to all, the path of universal holiness. The holiness path of Nazareth is outlined with clarity by Jean-Pierre de Caussade on abandonment— like Jesus, being led each moment through the Mystical Mansions to attain spiritual marriage with Christ and to become Christ. Though these abandoned souls remain hidden to the world and to themselves, they exert powerful influence, being like the biological heart that pumps blood to the rest of the body. Beyond Vatican II's primary image of the Church as the "People of God," it may be time to take up the ecclesial image of the Spirit as the "living heart of the Church."

The perennial norm for the Church is the Holy Spirit's masterful generalship in the early Church that created universal forms of sanctity: saintly bishops, martyrs, virgins, Church and Desert Fathers, and communities united in love. With the Spirit, the early Church evangelized the then-known world. The transformation began with the outpouring of the Spirit at Pentecost, a veritable flood. But it continues today in hearts open to the Spirit that experience an encounter with Christ. This book centers on the enchantment by this love, of this call to mystical union with Christ (and filiation to the Father), but all in the Spirit. The key is the Spirit, who renews the Church in all ages. John Paul II called for a "new pentecost" with a "new evangelization" in this "new millennium": "the new springtime of Christian life will be revealed by the Great Jubilee if Christians are docile to the action of the Holy Spirit" (*Tertio millennio adveniente*). As de Lubac long taught, "The Spirit can unite much more than we are accustomed to think."

## 2. The Holy Spirit's Template: Marian Principle

But the key to the Holy Spirit's program is not so much about obeying the Spirit's inspirations, but doing this through His form, Mary. He expresses Himself in myriad forms, like the many flowers in a garden. Those affiliated with a congregation (e.g., A. Miklósházy as a Jesuit) or a lay movement (e.g., a PIME priest to the Focolare) are blessed. But the vast majority have no specific affiliation, but can have influences, like John Paul II (John of the Cross) and Dr. J. Langan (French theologians). The Spirit typically works through mediation in Mother Church (Orders, ecclesial movements, saints). We follow de Lubac, who wrote of the *Splendor of the Church* and lived a "*sentire Ecclesiae*" (become a Church-person, "feel one with the Church").

And the one form that the Spirit has established today is the Marian Principle; not just devotion to Mary, but a living of her form in all dimensions of the Church. But Mary, before she became Jesus' Mother, was first His spouse: the heart of Mary is that she is spouse and disciple of Christ (Aug., *Discourse* 72A.7; LG); only then does she give birth spiritually to Christ and to others. We can point to this Marian form in Dina Bélanger. She is known for her spousal love for Christ, and which led to a "substitution of Christ." This substitution was a mystical incarnation: Christ had taken her humanity into Himself and lived again on earth in her and led her to His Father. Once this transformation into Christ has taken place, then Christ's mission or apostolate follows. We find the striking similarity in the overflow of fruitful apostolate in the spiritual children of diverse founders, like J. Escrivá, L. Giussani, and C. Lubich.

Thus, the key is the spousal union with Christ (R. H. Benson uses "friendship with Christ"). But it is the Holy Spirit who does all: (i) inspires this spousal love, (ii) accomplishes the substitution of Christ, (iii) continues Christ's mission through us, and (iv) who leads us to the Father. Through this, Christ Himself lives again in each soul and renews the Church in each age. With the key openness to the Spirit, a flowering takes place in ordinary souls (e.g., Kateri Tekakwitha), who have a deep attachment to Christ. It is the "Architect," the Spirit, who accomplishes the masterpiece of the new creation in souls, as in the hearts of Joseph and Mary at Nazareth. Through surrender to the Spirit to accomplish the Father's redemption, it lives in pure love that leads to the cross (expropriation). These souls are marked by the three great loves of Church ("*sentire cum Ecclesia*"), Eucharist, and Mary.

## 3. The Holy Spirit's Goal: Spousal Union with Christ

Thus, while our mission on earth is dominated by work and the cross, its heart is love, with its destiny of Trinitarian love. It is not the journey but the destination that must dominate in our hearts. The core is not the two present tasks of sanctification and apostolate; it is being wowed by Jesus' love of the Father and of us in the Father. St. Thérèse's spousal heart too was "won by the divine Eagle," and possession of His heart gave rise to her zeal for redemption. Giussani taught John Zucchi to be mesmerized by Christ's "Exceptional Presence," and then to allow apostolates to flow from that mystical encounter. Mother Teresa's core was a spousal love for Jesus, expressed itself in a vow never to refuse Him anything, telling a would-be biographer, "Tell them I do this for Jesus." St. Agnes made a vow of virginity to Christ and was martyred for it: "Christ made my soul beautiful with jewels of grace and virtue. I belong to him whom the angels serve."

Chiara Lubich explains this paradox as mirroring the Trinity in which the Spirit is "third," the fruit of the love between the Father and the Son, and yet was always there from the beginning. So too we have to first become Christ by living for the other (ascetical, what we do), and then experiencing the fruit, the gift of a moving experience of unity that comes from God (mystical). The joy-filled experience of the "exterior castle" of Jesus in our midst (like God's presence in the "interior castle") powers us (*Jesus in our Midst*, 93-94). The full itinerary is illustrated in the stages of Conchita's spiritual ascent. She lived the first two stages of overcoming sin and heroic virtue in an ascent to God from adolescence through adulthood. Then at the age of 32 and 35, she experienced spiritual betrothals and spiritual marriage respectively, and this then led nine years later to a mystical incarnation (*Conchita*, 156-157). This mystical marriage-incarnation explain the all-consuming zeal found in the apostles who fanned out and in the heart of John Paul II, who constantly promoted evangelization: "How many people there are still who have to be brought to the faith! How many have to be brought back to the faith they have lost!… The Church, however, aware of the great gift of the Incarnation of God, cannot pause, can never stop. She has to seek continually the way to Bethlehem for all men all times. The Epiphany is the feast of God's challenge" (e.g., Epiphany 1979).

Going more deeply, the two greatest human loves of the tender and unconditional love of parents and the spousal love of marriage find their archetype within the Trinity: in the paternal love of the Father for the Son and the "supra-sexual" spousal bond between them, for their infinite love contains all loves. The Spirit can be viewed as the "progeny" of the "spousal" love between the Father and the Son. Thus, the two great human loves find their origin and, more importantly, fulfillment in Trinitarian love.

**4. The Spirit's Plan: Restoration of Spousal Union to Heart of Church**

Thus, what is being proposed in this book is, as with Thérèse, a restoration of divine love (not apostolate) to the heart of the Church. As von Balthasar teaches, action and contemplation must be rooted in the deeper "love." This insertion of love at the heart of the Church aligns with John Paul II's setting the "Spirituality of Communion" as our primary task in the Third Millennium. Already in the Early Church, we see *koinonia* (communion) as the main image or identity of the Church, to mirror the Trinitarian communion of love. The apostles left all because of their attachment to Christ (not primarily because He was the Son of God), and especially after Pentecost, when they were ravished by the Living Flame of Love, and felt loved as they has never been loved before (Mother Nadine Brown). St. Margaret Magdalene, whom some saints have identified with the sinful woman at Simon's house, known for her personal love for Jesus, must have experienced the warmth of His affection and mercy. Similarly, Lazarus, Martha, and Mary must have been moved by Jesus' affection.

Many Christians have some general love of Jesus, but do not penetrate to the three inner Trinitarian unions. (1) St. D'Youville and St. Escrivá have introduced the first dimension of divine filiation of the Father (*Mystical Incarnation*). (2) But the vast majority do not allude to this book's focus, spousal union with Christ. For our hearts long for this union with Christ, anticipated in this life by human marriage. Such a deep longing for human marital union speaks of a much deeper longing for One who will be our "all in all," for no human spouse can fill this "infinite void" in our hearts. As one ascends the Unitive Mansions, spousal love increasingly dominates. It explains why the mystical John is known as the apostle of love, referred to six times as the "beloved disciple," the one who proclaims that "God is love" (1 Jn 4). (3) This book does not develop the union with the Spirit (e.g., Mary as "spouse of the Spirit," in whom He is "quasi-incarnate").

We find this yearning for Christ expressed in different ways in the saints. Among the contemporary saints, we find that yearning expressed in the desire of Mother Teresa to satiate the "I thirst" of Jesus on the cross. We find a similar desire in Chiara Lubich who seeks to console the abandoned Christ on the cross (this is the inner core of the Focolare, unity is its outer garment), and who lives this spousal love for Christ by expressing her desire to be willing to die for others out of love for Him.

We wish to draw upon two insights employed in *Mystical Incarnation* to illustrate its depth more fully. In the Song of Songs, that is a depiction of lover and Beloved, the Shulamite maiden has been wounded by the Beloved: "Let him kiss me with the kisses of his mouth" (1:2). She goes out to search for Him in the garden of contemplation, but assuages this thirst of love in the active life of serving others (justice):

> But light [gift of knowledge] engenders love and love enkindles desire, and desire is the spur that tortures and prods, that starts us to act, to work, to sacrifice, with the sweet restlessness and the strong desire of the lover. Urged on by this holy madness of desire, the soul comes out of itself and goes through the world like the spouse of the Song of Songs, asking everywhere if, perchance, the Beloved has passed by...[1]

*Mystics Offer Light on Spousal Marriage*
The greatest clarity and light on spousal union are perhaps found in the mystics' teachings. We find much light in the teaching of St. Teresa of Jesus and St. John of the Cross, who both depict a spousal marriage between Christ and each soul in the Seventh Mansions or the Third Stage respectively. Christ has wed Himself to some saints in mystical visions. For this book's cover art, we have chosen the "mystical marriage" of St. Catherine of Siena, in which Christ weds and gives her a ring that only she could see. Many too are the unions that Christ has arranged with saints. Conchita was taken through the Mansions to the highest union, accomplishing a "mystical incarnation." The call to this marriage is captured by the joy of the Solemnity of Epiphany, expressed in the antiphon of Morning Prayer: "Today the Bridegroom claims his bride, the Church, since Christ has washed her sins away in Jordan's waters; the Magi hasten with their gifts to the royal wedding; and the wedding guests rejoice, for Christ has changed water into wine, alleluia." This will be fulfilled in eternity.

Yet this spiritual marriage, as a priest taught Elizabeth of the Trinity, is not about suffering for Christ but allowing His free action in her, like our Lady's "Let it be done to me according to your will." Dina Bélanger, after experiencing a "substitution of Christ," set her goal as saying "yes" (abandonment, surrender) to her Spouse in many little ways.

## 5. The Spirit's Endgame: Fulfilling the Trinity's Desire for Union
And it is above all the Eucharist that now accomplishes unions to form Christ's Body and Bride. On the cross, the Bridegroom, the second Adam, gave rise to His Bride from His pierced side, the New Eve, the Church. And the Eucharist, which perpetuates or makes present the one sacrifice of Calvary, gives a foretaste of the mystical embrace of the Bridegroom with each soul in "Holy Communion." It fulfills the marital embrace by which the couple consummate their union ("two become one flesh"), with our becoming in this mystical embrace one with Christ through His sacrifice.

---

[1] Luis Martinez, *The Sanctifier*, 315ff., 318.

> There can be nothing of the Spirit in the Church that does not also coincide with Christ's reality, christologically, that does not let itself be translated into the language of the Eucharist— the surrender of Christ's own flesh and blood, the streaming outward from Christ's self up to the very point of his heart being pierced and his side flowing with water and blood.[2]

Spousal union with Christ completed in eternity will be the fulfillment of all loves and yearnings. And it is accomplished by the Spirit who is Personal Love within the Trinity. He who is the "Living Flame of Love" fuses two hearts (Christ's and ours), as St. John of the Cross' log is consumed and becomes one with the Flame. And the same Living Flame is the Spirit of sonship, after mystically incarnating Christ in us, makes us "sons in the one Son," divinized children of the Father. Charity poured into our hearts by the Holy Spirit enables this assimilation. And to *know* God through the Word, and to *love* God through the Spirit, is to attain the Father.

*God's Desire for our Love*
In heaven, there will be endless love, an endless wedding banquet. But we must not forget God's desire for our love, as expressed in the Sacred Heart apparitions and the oblation of St. Thérèse to make up for the love that Jesus did not receive. We reprint St. Bernard of Clairvaux's moving text:

> For when God loves, all he desires is to be loved in return; the sole purpose of his love is to be loved, in the knowledge that those who love him are made happy by their love of him. The Bridegroom's love, or rather the love which is the Bridegroom, asks in return nothing but faithful love. Let the beloved, then, love in return. Should not a bride love, and above all, Love's bride? Could it be that Love not be loved.... Possession of love is the first condition of the knowledge of God.[3]

The saintly soul arrives at this peak of selfless love. He becomes distressed that God is not loved, and seeks, like Mother Teresa and Adrienne von Speyr, to make the Bridegroom (Christ) and the Father loved, all in the Spirit. But God, in His unselfish love, like that of a good parent, seeks our divinization, that we become His Son's Bride and Body, the Spirit's Temple, and His beloved children, circumscribed and permeated with this infinite furnace of Trinitarian love, beauty, light, and joy for all eternity (Dan 7:13-14). Evangelization is simply the call to the joy of this love (we are created for eternal joy), the anticipation of which can draw hearts to Christ.

---

[2] Hans Urs von Balthasar, "Spirit and Institution," in *Spirit and Institution*, vol. 4, *Explorations in Theology* (San Francisco: Ignatius Press, 1995), 237-238.
[3] "St. Bernard of Clairvaux," Britannica, accessed August 20, 2020, https://www.britannica.com/biography/Saint-Bernard-of-Clairvaux.

We end with the key to this vast economy— Mary. The renewal by the Church in the Spirit goes through Mary and the Marian Principle. There are four dimensions (summarizing S. De Fiores). (i) *Trinitarian*: Mary is a creature formed by the Trinity. She is the beloved daughter of the Father, mother of the Son, and temple of the Spirit (LG 53). She is present before the creation of the world as the one the Father has chosen as Mother of this Son, as did the Son simultaneously choose her, entrusting her eternally to the Spirit (*Redemptoris mater* 8). She has become "tri-form," image and icon of the Trinity, of the merciful goodness of the Father, of the obedience of the Son, of the redemptive work of the Spirit. She is consecrated in the most perfect way (receptivity): a listening, believing, and offering virgin.

(ii) *Ecclesial*: Mary is prefigured as the "daughter Sion" (Israel), her personal "fiat" or yes was made on behalf of all humanity at the events of the Incarnation and redemption. Paul VI proclaimed on November 21, 1964, the title "Mother of the Church." Having conceived and raised Christ, she now cooperates also in the work of the Saviour to restore supernatural life to souls, for which she is called Mother in the order of grace (LG 61). (iii) *Anthropological*: She is humanity recreated by divine grace according to God's original plan. Mary is the first creature to live with this new heart: to have the same sentiments of Christ (divine love); to work for that which Jesus worked; with readiness to suffer as Jesus suffered (in obedience to the Father, innocent and redemptive suffering, death, resurrection); and to live as Jesus lived, celibate for the kingdom. (iv) *Historical*: The cooperation of Mary has an impulse to apostolic life and action. Her being led by the Spirit has a dynamism oriented outwards (e.g., Cana). Her presence becomes a stimulus to action. Her cooperation in the history of the Church and humanity translates into a profound movement to apostolate and mission on the part of Christians (J. Galot); she is the key to evangelization.

> Today people of all ages and conditions continue to fulfil to the letter the ancient prophecy the Blessed Virgin herself made one day: *All generations will call me blessed...* Poets, intellectuals, craftsmen, kings and warriors, mature men and women as well as children who have hardly learned to speak, all offer her their praise.... The Holy Spirit has taught countless generations of Christians throughout the ages that the truest path to the Heart of Jesus is through Mary. With this in mind we need to accustom ourselves to entrusting our needs with confidence to the Blessed Virgin, since she is "the shortcut to God" for us. "Our Lady is rest for those who work, consolation for those who mourn, and relief for those who are sick. She is a refuge for those caught in the storms of life, a foundation of compassion for sinners, a sweet relief for the sorrowful and a sure source of aid for those who pray." (F. Fernandez, *In Conversation with God*, vol. 7, 342-343, quotation from J. Damascene).

Manufactured by Amazon.ca
Bolton, ON